The
FIRES
of
SPRING

The

FIRES

of

SPRING

*A Post–Arab Spring Journey
Through the Turbulent New Middle East*

Shelly Culbertson

St. Martin's Press
New York

www.stmartins.com

Map by Jeffrey L. Ward

Library of Congress Cataloging-in-Publication Data

Names: Culbertson, Shelly, author.
Title: The fires of spring : a post–Arab Spring journey through the turbulent new Middle East / Shelly Culbertson.
Description: New York : St. Martin's Press, 2016.
Identifiers: LCCN 2015043186| ISBN 9781250067043 (hardcover) | ISBN 9781466874954 (e-book)
Subjects: LCSH: Arab Spring, 2010– | Arab countries—Politics and government—21st century. | BISAC: SOCIAL SCIENCE / Anthropology / Cultural. | TRAVEL / Middle East / General.
Classification: LCC JQ1850.A91 C85 2016 | DDC 909/.097492708312—dc23
LC record available at http://lccn.loc.gov/2015043186

Our books may be purchased in bulk for promotional, educational, or business use. Please contact your local bookseller or the Macmillan Corporate and Premium Sales Department at 1-800-221-7945, extension 5442, or by e-mail at MacmillanSpecialMarkets@macmillan.com.

First Edition: April 2016

10 9 8 7 6 5 4 3 2 1

To Iliano Cervesato, my husband
To Richard and Linda Culbertson, my parents
To Christopher Culbertson, my brother

CONTENTS

ACKNOWLEDGMENTS

I would like express gratitude to the people who supported the writing of this book.

I thank my editor at St. Martin's Press, Daniela Rapp, and my agent at Trident Media Group, Don Fehr.

I want to express especial appreciation to the RAND Corporation for giving me the flexibility to work on this book as a separate personal project while I continued to work at RAND. I deeply appreciate the support and encouragement from RAND colleagues, although the work herein is entirely my own.

The advice, ideas, reviews, comments, feedback, introductions, and challenging questions of a number of people greatly contributed: Ambassador James Dobbins, Andrew Parasiliti, Ambassador James Jeffrey, Houda Bouamor, Mustafa Oguz, Howard Shatz, Wirya Ahmed, Merissa Khurma, Bruce Nardulli, Silvia Pessoa, Carole Sargeant, Rebecca Drake, Jeff Hiday, Khorshied Samad, Emily Alp, and Alexandra Stergiopolou. Any errors are my own.

I thank Michelle Horner for her work on the references.

I thank my husband, Iliano Cervesato, for his support, patience, and good counsel throughout the long and intense process of writing this book, and also for sharing the journey with me through several of the countries. And I thank my father, Richard Culbertson, for sharing the journey with me on a trip to Egypt.

A NOTE ON THE TEXT

I traveled to Tunisia, Turkey, Iraq, Qatar, Jordan and Egypt for this book between June 2014 and April 2015. While the narrative is consecutive, my travel for research was not always. I traveled sometimes by myself and sometimes with others. For the sake of continuity of the narrative, I wrote the scenes in the book without my travel companions. Public figures interviewed are called by their full names. Interviewees who are private individuals are called by a single first name that is not their own, and in some instances, identifying characteristics were changed.

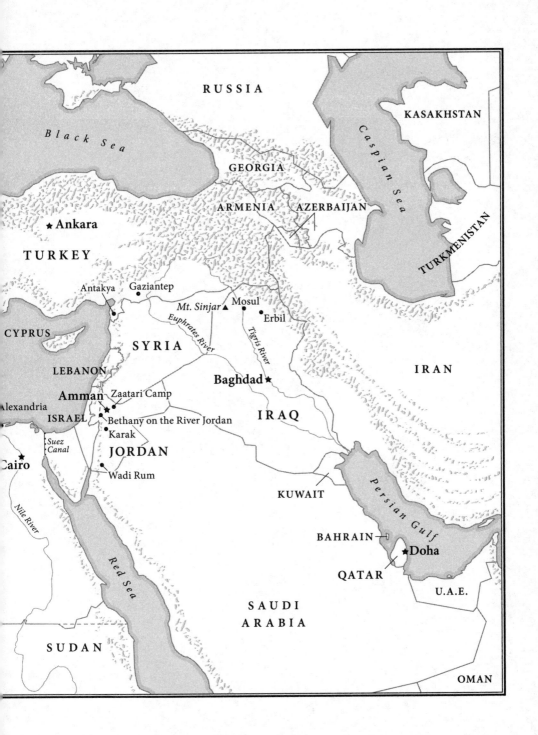

INTRODUCTION

In a small town in Tunisia, Mohammed Bouazizi, a young fruit seller, was angered and humiliated by a bureaucratic inspector who slapped his face and confiscated his apples. He poured paint thinner on his body and lit himself on fire. He died in January 2011. His story roused the sympathetic indignation of a generation of Tunisian youth. They saw themselves in him—lacking opportunities and doing their best to make do, subject to the petty whims of bureaucrats who could assault them and take away their livelihood with impunity.[1] And then that rage spread elsewhere around the Middle East, with citizens both demonstrating peacefully and violently overthrowing governments. The peoples of the region wanted something more than to eke out an existence amid stagnation and repression. A new generation revealed its frustration with the established order's corruption, patronage, authoritarianism, and failed governance.

These events were optimistically termed the "Arab Spring." The inspirational movements of the Arab Spring captured global imagination for what might be. Arab Spring movements demanded a better way of life and new models for societies that were not realizing their potential. But the aftermath has ranged from tentatively encouraging to halting processes for change to devastating civil wars that have resulted in challenges to the very borders of the Middle East and mass refugee crises.

What are we to make of the disparate and tumultuous events in this part of the world? What was the Arab Spring about? What was accomplished? What trends are shaping the Middle East after the Arab Spring?

I sought answers to these questions. And so I set out on a journey through six countries of the Middle East (not all of which are Arab countries) with varying roles in and experiences of the Arab Spring: Tunisia, Turkey, Iraq, Jordan, Qatar, and Egypt. This book is a narrative of that journey. I visited historical sites and delved into scholarship on the region. I conducted interviews with key figures in the protests and revolutions, government officials, media leaders, and people who lived through important events of the Arab Spring. To show multiple points of view, I spoke with people who vehemently disagreed with each other. It was a privilege to have had the opportunity to talk with people who played such roles, took great personal risks, and exhibited courage and creativity. I hope to capture some of that spirit in this book.

I chose the six countries in this book to illustrate the region's diversity and a variety of Arab Spring experiences. These experiences include government overthrows, peaceful protests and incremental change, interfering in other countries' Arab Springs, or being impacted by the Arab Spring. Among the six, there are stable countries, unstable countries, rich countries, poor countries, democracies, autocracies, and monarchies. The people in this book are of multiple ethnicities, including Arabs as well as Turks, Kurds, Berbers, and others. There are people who speak different languages and practice religion in different ways.

The journey of this book begins in Tunisia, the country where the Arab Spring revolutions started, and where there emerged a model of a positive, sustainable, and inclusive, albeit fragile, way forward. Next, although it isn't an Arab country, Turkey's protest movements challenged growing government autocracy, and the history of the fall of the Ottoman Empire provides historical context for understanding conflicts in the region today. I move then to neighboring Iraq. There, I traveled in the Kurdistan Region. While Iraq did not have a significant Arab Spring movement (although there were some protests), it was affected by the Arab Spring and was also an important part of the Arab Spring context. The Kurdistan Region underwent a "spring" of investment in development, after the American war in Iraq and before threats by the Islamic State,[2] itself a perverse outgrowth of Arab Spring desires for new forms of government. Qatar is next, a country of contradictory activities. While Qatar has made efforts domestically to build a cosmopolitan knowledge-based economy, it has been involved in other countries' Arab Springs through reporting by Al Jazeera, backing of Islamist political parties in other countries, and funding violent factions in Libya and Syria. The story continues with Jordan, a middle-income country that made strides in development despite its tough neighborhood. Jordan's Arab Spring protesters made demands for incremental economic and political reforms (not government overthrow), and the government responded with incremental change. Finally, Egypt is home to a quarter of the Arab world. Its dramatic 2011 revolution overthrew a man who had ruled for thirty years, followed by the democratic election of a Muslim Brotherhood politician, mass protests over his abuses of power, and finally his overthrow by the military. While Egypt's revolution is viewed as a disappointing failure that ushered in an even more repressive regime, the reality is more complex. Profound changes have begun in Egypt's social fabric. Finally, many of these countries have in some way been affected by the violent civil wars elsewhere in the region that were set off by the Arab Spring, whether through absorbing refugees, having their own stability threatened, or witnessing examples to avoid.

Writing this book has been an act of both love and frustration for me. It is written out of love for a region that delights with its friendships, aesthetics, heritage, adventures, and professional opportunities. It is written out of frustration with the destruction of people and places, mindsets that no longer serve the people there, and a squandering of human aspirations and ability through corrupt and inept governance.

I have lived, studied, worked, or traveled in the Middle East extensively, first as a student lured by the potential for adventure and by rich and ancient history. I have been coming back ever since. The region has been a formative part of my life and world outlook. For ten years, I worked at the RAND Corporation on the Middle East. This included living in Qatar for seven years advising on education and innovation policy, developing K–12 education plans for the Kurdistan Regional Government of Iraq five years, and analyzing public services for Syrian refugees in Jordan, Lebanon, and Turkey. I worked on the Turkey desk at the U.S. State Department, lived in Egypt to study Arabic, and studied in Morocco and Israel for short periods. And I have spent a considerable amount of time meandering through the bazaars, mosques, and museums housing great works of art and heritage of almost every other country in the region.

I have met with and briefed national leaders on a wide range of issues, from education to entrepreneurship, backpacked on a budget of ten dollars per night, smoked apple tobacco in a water pipe with friends over music, learned to belly dance, and been accused of being a CIA agent. It is from this perspective that this book looks at the changes under way in the Middle East.

The Middle East of today is in the news more often for its problems than its accomplishments. Societies that once contributed so much to the development of human civilization face myriad complex problems now, including economic stagnation, dysfunctional public services, and violent interethnic and religious conflict. However, there is much more to the Middle East than terror, violent upheavals, and disappointments. The nearly 500 million people who live there are rich with aspirations and accomplishments as well. A one-sided intake of information about problems in the Middle East obscures this complexity and handicaps us in our ability to understand the forces shaping the region and deal with its challenges. A one-sided understanding can lead to disastrous or inept policies. Here are six observations about the Middle East, explored in the journey for this book, that cast light on the future of a region undergoing transformation.

1. *The Middle East Is Not Monolithic*

What we call the Middle East spans three continents—Europe, Africa, and Asia—and contains the diversity that results. It is all called "the Middle East" or "the Arab world" as if it were one place, with one people, one culture, and one set of problems. Even this book is structured around that idea. Certainly there are commonalities, such as Islam, the Arabic language, and a shared regional history. But countries in the Middle East are distinct, the same way that Europe is vastly varied, as London differs from Kosovo, as the arid island of Sicily differs from the fjords of Sweden, and as the German economic powerhouse differs from the collapsed economy of Greece.

Consider economies. There is a Middle East of innovation and investment and a Middle East of stagnation, wasted opportunities, and squandered capabilities. Dubai has established itself as an international financial center. Jordan is a regional center of entrepreneurship. On the other hand, 12 to 16 million Egyptians live in slums.[3] Qataris now rank as the richest people in the world. Qatar's GDP per capita is $140,000, while in contrast Yemen has a GDP per capita of $4,000.[4]

Consider stability. There is the Middle East of turmoil and the Middle East of new beginnings. Some countries are mired in conflicts that likely won't be resolved for decades to come, splintering along ethnic and religious lines (Libya, Yemen, Iraq, and Syria) with mass displacements of people because of violence. People in other countries enjoy a more tranquil life. For example, Morocco has been ranked as having the best quality of life in Africa, even ahead of South Africa.[5] The United Arab Emirates and Qatar boast comfortable infrastructure, a cosmopolitan atmosphere, and professional opportunities.

Consider culture. Some countries are more culturally open, while others are very conservative. You can enjoy sophisticated nightlife, bars, and clubs in Beirut, while Saudi Arabia's strict interpretation of Islam mandates separation of genders in social life and prohibits women from driving.

Consider language. In theory, people in Arab countries speak Arabic. But nobody actually speaks Modern Standard Arabic as a native language. They speak different dialects descended from Arabic and mixed with other regional languages; some of the dialects are far enough apart as to be mutually incomprehensible. Many Arabs do not have a solid mastery of Modern Standard Arabic. The less educated may struggle to understand it, and Arab elites may be more confident in English or French. Minorities speak Kurdish (in Iraq, Turkey, Syria, and Iran), Amazigh (also called Berber, in parts of North Africa, including in Tunisia), and other languages. Although they are considered countries of the Middle East, Turkey's and Iran's national languages are Turkish and Farsi, not Arabic.

Consider identity. Middle Eastern countries contain Muslims, Christians, and Jews, and among Muslims, there are varying branches, the most noteworthy of which are Sunnis and Shiites. There are people of diverse ethnicities—Arabs, Kurds, Persians, Amazighs, Turks, Assyrians, Copts, Yazidis, and more. Therefore, there are multiple identities. For many people in the Middle East, "Arab" is not the primary identity.

2. The Fall of the Ottoman Empire Provides Insight into Today's Conflicts

A century ago, most of the Middle East was one political entity, the Ottoman Empire, ruled from Istanbul.[6] The Ottoman Empire was one of the largest, most powerful, and longest-lasting empires in history. At its height, it ruled territories that circle the east and south of the Mediterranean and beyond. Its former territory encompassed all or part of what are today more than fifty countries. It was also seat to the last Islamic caliphate and included the holy cities of Mecca, Medina, and Jerusalem.

The defeat of the Ottoman Empire after World War I (preceded by decades of weakness) precipitated the birth of the modern nation-states that splintered off in the Middle East, North Africa, and the Balkans. Allied victors carved up the once mighty but ailing empire into pieces, controlling or colonizing parts for themselves. The colonial period was characterized by European domination but also by support in establishing institutions. Among others, new countries born from the Ottoman death include Turkey, Iraq, Syria, Jordan, Lebanon, Israel, Libya, Egypt, Tunisia, Yemen, Qatar, and Saudi Arabia. The political structures that the people of the region had lived with for centuries vanished. From the 1940s to 1960s, the countries that had been under British or French colonial domination gained independence. Several became monarchies. Others followed similar patterns of military autocratic leadership that lasted until the Arab Spring; a first generation of strongman leaders worked as modernizers, while their successors remained autocratic but oversaw stagnation. The military autocracies echoed each other in style and substance, setting the stage for the Arab Spring protests.

At the end of World War I, Turkey abolished the Islamic caliphate. The psychological impact of this in the Middle East is similar to what abolishing the papacy in Rome would be to Europe. The end of the caliphate left the Sunni Arab world with a gap in identity and values. With this change, the past century has seen an ongoing raw, violent power struggle in societies over developing a new definition of the role of Islam in public life. Some want separation between religion and state, and others want a greater public role for Islam. Some have a historic longing for the greatness of being part of a powerful Islamic empire. As an extreme example of this, ISIS now tries to lay claim to the Ottoman Empire's vanished title of caliphate.

World War I was not only the end of the Ottoman Empire, but also the end of the empire as a predominant form of government in Europe and the Middle East. World War I spelled the end of four empires: Ottoman, Russian, German, and Austro-Hungarian. The demise of the British and French colonial empires followed not long afterward, in the decades following World War II.

The empire, a large, multiethnic political entity with a dominant center ruling far distant lands,[7] gave way to the nation-state, where the majority of people theoretically share a common culture and identity, where cultural boundaries are supposed to line up with political boundaries.[8] The countries of the Middle East struggled with the evolution toward becoming nation-states. This century's process of forging new nation-states from the ashes of the Ottoman Empire has been a troubled story of population swaps, ethnic cleansing, iron-fisted dictators, civil wars, and popular backlash due to the desire for something better.

The new borders combined ethnic and religious groups who vied for dominance within countries and separated other peoples who wanted to stay together. Other territories were contested. While the Ottomans had ruled a multiethnic empire with a number of (imperfect) mechanisms for enabling tolerance, the new borders, in combination with desire for self-rule, pitted ethnic group against ethnic group, leaving power vacuums and culminating in wars that have flared up over the past century into today. Whereas before peoples with differing identities had lived together for generations, now they were caught up in struggles to define new nation-states, over who would be ruling whom, and which values, traditions, and faiths would dominate the others.

Examples are many. Iraq, destabilized by dictatorship followed by war, is torn asunder in conflict between Sunnis, Shiites, and Kurds. The new post–World War I borders split the Kurdish people (whose numbers reach 30 million today) into four countries—Turkey, Iraq, Iran, and Syria. What had been the Ottoman territory of Palestine has been split into Israel, Palestinian territories, Jordan, Syria, and Lebanon, with Israelis and Palestinians left with competing claims on what is today Israel.

Power struggles led to instability, preventing development. Some governments, fearing the bubbling undercurrents of turmoil, quashed political life, innovation, and Islamic movements. For the past century, the countries of the Middle East drifted along, for the most part, languishing. The period was interspersed with territorial wars, conflict between ethnic and religious groups, and struggles between secularists and Islamist political parties. This combination of new states, power struggles, autocratic governments, ethnic conflict, and disagreement over the role of Islam in public life did not bode well for the people of the region. Educational levels are among the worst in the world. Illiteracy is high. Corruption is rampant. The region is notorious for its mistreatment of women. A brain drain of educated Arabs means the region has lost some of its most capable people. The world is still reeling from the repercussions of the disastrously managed disintegration of the Ottoman Empire.

The Arab Spring and its aftermath are about challenging the order that was set up upon the death of the Ottoman Empire. First, it is confronting the model of autocratic government that began then, calling for a new social contract, a changed relationship between governments and their people, and more pluralistic inclusion in governments. Second, in some cases, it is challenging the very borders of the countries established after World War I, plunging the region into chaos.

3. *Islam Is Undergoing an Identity Crisis*

There are several transformative debates about central issues in the Islamic faith, shaped by a diverse array of actors: scholars in universities, preachers in mosques, politicians blending policy with faith, voters at the ballot box, jihadist groups and militaries in violent conflict, and foreign policies of governments toward political Islam. Some argue that even with the current instability, Islam is undergoing something similar to the Renaissance, an era of struggle with ideas.

First, there is a schism about Islam's role in government and public life. Islam historically has been viewed as a communal pact between God and society, while Christianity today is viewed as a relation between God and individuals. This conceptual difference has profound influence on how people view the role of religion in government. In the West, norms of separation of religion and state evolved over time because of conflict over political power between the church and European monarchies. In the Middle East, separation of religion and state did not happen until forcibly imposed by colonial powers or secular autocracies in the twentieth century, after the abolition of the caliphate in Istanbul. While some people in the Middle East view religion as private matter, others do not view the separation of religion and state as legitimate. Furthermore, in some cases, there is tension between the identity of being part of the nation-states formed a century ago in the Middle East and the identity that comes from being part of the Islamic idea of *umma,* the wider community of Muslims, that existed under empire.

The second issue is the approach to interpretation of modernity versus the past. Khaled Abou el Fadl, a leading Islamic scholar at UCLA, writes that the Islamic world is polarized between two opposing sets of values and worldviews—what he calls "moderate" versus "puritanical" Islam.[9] He writes that while all Muslims agree on the central tenets of the faith (such as monotheism, accepting Mohammed as a prophet, and praying five times per day), there are areas of profound disagreement: understanding and applying Islamic law (shariah), approaches to modernity, and the legitimacy of holy war (jihad). For example, while most Muslim societies blend modernity and faith, a growing Salafist movement aims to imitate life at the time of the Prophet Mohammed, through either peaceful approaches (the quietist Salafists) or violence (the Salafist-Jihadists).

These differences over the role of religion in public life have played out in the post–Arab Spring world. Constitutions have been written with various prescribed roles for religion in the state. In Turkey and Tunisia, there is a delicate balance among democracy, Islam, and secularism, with Islamic parties participating in government. At the same time, ISIS is violently imposing its vision of an Islamic past on peoples today. The Muslim Brotherhood and its affiliates have taken government roles in Tunisia, Egypt, and Jordan, only to be democratically voted out, forced out by the military, or kept out through technicalities of electoral laws. Increased democracy in Middle Eastern countries has meant a rising role for Islamist parties (with differing approaches to democratic participation), and therefore greater tensions with secularists. Islamic political movements will be powerful for the foreseeable future; stability in the region will depend upon developing a consensus regarding the role and limits of religion in public life.

4. *The Status of Women Is Changing*

It is not hard to find stories or statistics about the challenges that women in the Middle East face in employment, legal systems, family rights, or social norms. The Arab world ranks last in the world on gender parity indices.[10] Women's employment is only a quarter of that of the men across the region.[11] Surveys have found that 95 percent of married women and 50 percent of schoolgirls in Egypt are circumcised.[12] Social norms limit women's autonomy and ability to interact with men in public life and in the workplace.

But Middle Eastern women are step-by-step defining their own version of modernity. The path they choose will be rooted in their own culture and values, different from the path that Western women have chosen. Several trends bode well for women in the region.

First, women played significant roles in some of the Arab Spring movements. They protested, blogged about human rights abuses and corruption, served as members of parliament, founded newspapers, created political parties, negotiated compromises, made forceful arguments shaping public debate in the media, and wrote constitutions. Women have served as political leaders in both secular and Islamist parties. Throughout my interviews for this book, women described how the Arab Spring movements had served as a platform for women's increasingly strong voices.

Next, across the Middle East, girls and women are outperforming boys and men in education.[13] In elementary and secondary education, girls score higher than boys in reading, math, and science on international tests. Women have higher university graduation rates than men in over half of the countries in the Middle East. This educational achievement may increase women's future employment, with more women having the additional choices and autonomy that earning one's own money brings. The data actually shed light on a different and counterintuitive problem— the region should be concerned about better educating boys and men.

Next, Middle Eastern women are demanding changes in rights, family law, and custom. While women in Turkey gained the right to vote in 1930, women in most Middle Eastern countries began to secure voting rights in the 1950s, with a few more countries joining each decade. In 2005, Kuwait straggled in as the latest country in the region to grant women suffrage, and Saudi Arabia committed to allow women to vote in munici-pal elections.[14] It takes time for voting rights to lead to tangible changes. Furthermore, in the past ten years, a number of countries (including Egypt, Bahrain, Jordan, Algeria, and Morocco) ratified improvements in family law affecting women, including equal divorce laws, right to travel without a guardian's approval, and protection against domestic abuse. New post–Arab Spring constitutions in Tunisia and Egypt proclaim that women and men are equal. Furthermore, there are movements of "Islamic feminism," in which women pursue additional rights, arguing that such rights are guaranteed to them in Islamic texts.[15]

It is efforts like these that will create changes, with women from the region pushing for advances that they want within the context of their own culture. Social norms change slowly, but over time they do evolve, in particular in the face of determination from a region's women.

5. *The Future Depends on Meeting the Needs of Youth*

The Middle East and North Africa (MENA) region has a "youth bulge," with one of the youngest populations in the world. From 1950 to 2010, the population of the region quadrupled, with social structures, economies, and opportunities not keeping pace.[16] Today, 70 percent of the region is under the age of thirty.[17]

Arab Spring movements started as youth movements. While motiva-tions are varied and complex, an oft-noted reason was the frustration of youth in the lack of opportunities they have to succeed on the basis of their own abilities, and their belief that changing their governments could improve those opportunities.

Youth in the Middle East and North Africa have the highest unem-ployment rate of any region in the world, with over a quarter unemployed.[18] As a region, the Middle East and North Africa ranks next to last in the world in educational achievements in primary and secondary education, just before sub-Saharan Africa.[19] Furthermore, Middle Eastern universities have not excelled in quality by international standards, with few making international rankings lists and many not providing youth with the skills they need to meet the needs of the labor market.[20]

The task of improving opportunities for youth certainly faces challenges.

These include poor education systems, stagnant economies, stifled private sectors, instability, government budget shortages, and a mismatch between skills provided by education systems and skills demanded by labor markets.

Yet media and technology have created powerful tools for youth to drive change. Youth have organized protests via Facebook, and individuals have communicated their dissent on blogs. Al Jazeera created public dialogue and showcased unprecedented criticism of governments in Arabic; other media stations followed. Citizens have access to open media from around the world and can clearly see that societies elsewhere function better. Governments are no longer able to control public discourse about politics. These factors have forever changed the Middle East and what youth are willing to accommodate. (Yet these new tools in media have also been used by extremist groups.) Now we will see how societies' leaders and youth will translate these new circumstances into tangible plans and actions for improvement.

6. *The Arab Spring Has Multiple Storylines*

When the Arab Spring uprisings dominoed across the Middle East, friends and family frantically called and emailed to ask about my safety. I looked out the window of my apartment in downtown Doha, overlooking a tranquil cove of sparkling sea. Along the coast was a green expanse of meticulously manicured lawn, a park with families picnicking, spandex-clad joggers, and strolling couples holding hands. Shiny skyscrapers designed by some of the world's biggest names in architecture glinted in the sun.

Things were different elsewhere. I looked at the Al Jazeera footage of crowds of protesters filling Cairo's Tahrir Square like a sea of people, with youth gathering in collective proud fury and demanding something better, the thrill and chaos of people uniting in hope, exasperation, and strength. During the first wave of protests, I was texting my Egyptian friends late at night: "We are all Egyptians." I felt like one of them, protesting for something better, and proud.

The Arab Spring was about renewed aspirations for positive change in society. But these shared aspirations have led to very different outcomes. In four countries (Tunisia, Egypt, Yemen, and Libya), stagnant leadership was overthrown. Two years after Tunisia ousted its president, the country adopted a new constitution, praised as one of the most balanced in the

Middle East. Yet Tunisia suffered a series of bloody terrorist attacks in 2015, killing sixty tourists; extremist groups aimed to destroy the economy and destabilize the country. In Egypt, protesters overthrew a repressive government; voters elected an Islamist government; protests demanded removal of the Islamist government; and the military violently overthrew the Islamist government—with Egypt thus arriving back where it started. Syria, Yemen, and Libya became embroiled in civil wars. The Islamic State stepped into the vacuums in Syria and Iraq, weakened by warfare; they killed or displaced millions of people, and destroyed ancient heritage sites. These wars have led to the worst refugee crisis since World War II, with refugees fleeing to neighboring countries and some seeking safety in Europe. Protests in Bahrain led to a forceful military crackdown. Iranians conducted protests in support of the Arab Spring in 2011; Iran's 2009 Green Movement protests that resulted in government violent suppression were viewed as a precursor to the Arab Spring. But protests in Jordan and Morocco led to incremental changes, including new or modified constitutions. In other countries, such as Qatar or the UAE, there were no significant protests, but continued investment in developing the economy and public services. While Turkey had protests during the same period, these were undertaken within the context of a struggling democracy, not demands to change the entire system of government.

Where is all this going? The unifying themes of the Arab Spring movements were aspirations for public accountability, dignity, a greater political voice, and more economic equality and opportunity for youth. The new directions countries are taking are divergent—some optimistic and others leading to turmoil and despair. Even with such dramatic contrasts, taken together as a whole, we are witnessing profound political and cultural changes that are reshaping the Middle East.

Starting the Journey

This is a pivotal period of history in the Middle East, with civilizational upheaval, redefinition of roles of governments and citizens, struggle over core societal values, and challenges to existing borders. Through the journey in this book, I would like to plant the seeds for reflection and paint a picture of issues that are shaping Middle Eastern society after the Arab Spring.

Tunisia

Avenue Bourguiba on Election Day

It was Election Day in Tunisia—December 21, 2014.

Concrete barriers, metal partitions, and hoops of razor wire divided the Parisian-style city blocks of Avenue Bourguiba in Tunis. Underneath tranquil hedge-cut ficus trees and ornamental iron lampposts, white police vans with metal bars on the windows were parked every few blocks. On the corners, policemen and soldiers in uniform stood guard with machine guns. Tanks in desert camouflage pointed guns into the street.

But there was a general sense of calm and order, a stillness in the streets. There were no banners, no election slogans, no rallies, no music, no chanting crowds of people, and no one was handing out flyers to promote candidates. It was quiet. People walked past me on the street with index fingers stained brown with ink, a mark that showed they had voted so that they could not vote again. Others chatted outdoors in the chilly December weather, sipping cappuccinos in prosperous cafés fronted by palm trees. A newscaster with a film crew quietly spoke into a microphone in front of a camera on a corner. I walked past the Art Nouveau Municipal Theater, a Mac makeup shop, Benetton, pizza parlors, and shawarma stands.

People were acting like it was normal, not a historic peaceful transfer of power based on elections and the rule of law as set out in a new constitution, after a major revolution that toppled a dictator and sparked other revolutions around the Middle East. With the bright blue sky and fluffy clouds, all in all, it was a peaceful day of democracy in beautiful Tunisia.

During the revolution in Tunisia, the first Arab Spring country to unseat a national leader, crowds surged through this street. "*Dégage. Dégage. Dégage,*" they chanted, French for "Get out, get out, get out." In January 2011, when protesters scaled the walls of the Ministry of Interior here on Avenue Bourguiba, President Zine el Abidine Ben Ali fled the country to Saudi Arabia, after nearly three decades in power.[1]

The *Economist* chose Tunisia as its 2015 country of the year because of its transition: "The idealism engendered by the Arab Spring has mostly sunk in bloodshed and extremism, with a shining exception: Tunisia. . . . Its economy is struggling and its polity is fragile; but Tunisia's pragmatism and moderation have nurtured hope in a wretched region and a troubled world. *Mabrouk*, Tunisia!"[2] And a group of Tunisian civil society organizations won the 2015 Nobel Peace Prize for their role in negotiations and building a pluralistic democracy during and after Tunisia's revolution.

Tunisia's elections were hailed as momentous, both for Tunisia and for the troubled Middle East. The 2011 upheaval had been followed by constructive negotiations within society about Tunisia's values, the ratification of a new constitution, peaceful elections, and a national truth and dignity commission to investigate past government abuses.[3] However, Tunisia's tenuously hopeful new direction was threatened by terrorist attacks that killed sixty people in 2014 and 2015.

Avenue Bourguiba is a place of deep symbolism for Tunisians. The street tells the story of Tunisia.[4] Avenue Bourguiba's architecture reflects the era of French colonialism that began in 1881 when the French took what was then the Ottoman province of Tunisia from the weakening Ottoman Empire. It is named after Habib Bourguiba, who led Tunisia's anticolonial struggle against the French, became Tunisia's first president, and modernized the country. But Bourguiba also created an autocratic government that his successor, Ben Ali, took to new levels. Protesters who toppled the dictatorship of Ben Ali assembled in Avenue Bourguiba's wide-open spaces, demanding that he leave because of his excesses. Avenue Bourguiba has been an avenue of tear gas, as well as of cafés, florists, and bookstores.

Under Ben Ali, suppression of dissent, torture, imprisonment for political views, and trumped-up charges against political challengers were common.[5] Indeed, as I sought out interviews with Tunisia's political and thought leaders, I found that a surprising number had been charged with crimes relating to their political views and communication. Some had been tried, imprisoned, beaten by police, tortured, or lived in exile.

Tunisia's economy under Ben Ali was a corrupt den of crony capitalism, with business policies set up to favor himself, his wife, his family, and friends.[6] The World Bank described Tunisia's economy as "asphyxiated by its own corruption."[7] Business regulations, according to the World Bank, were manipulated to such an extent that a fifth of private sector profits in the country accrued to Ben Ali's associates. When U.S. diplomatic cables released by Wikileaks described the extravagant lifestyles of Ben Ali's extended family, including lavish mansions and a pet tiger fed with prime steak, the public became enraged.[8]

Then, in the hardscrabble town of Sidi Bouzid, the young fruit-seller Mohammed Bouazizi set himself on fire in protest of the petty corruption of officials that prevented him from supporting his family by selling fruit at his fruit stand.[9] Something resonated with Tunisians all over the country. They wanted change. Protests spread through villages and towns along the coast, in the interior, and in the south.

The revolution started as youth protests. And then civil society came out in mass: the labor unions, the military, Islamists, secularists, and the political parties.[10] When the protests started, the military's decision to not intervene sent a signal of support to the protesters. Bloggers organized protests and narrated the events inside Tunisia to the outside world when journalists were prohibited. Western journalists dubbed it the Jasmine Revolution, after Tunisia's national flower, and in a nod to the wave of protests and government overthrows named after colors and flowers that swept countries of the former Soviet Union and Balkans in the early 2000s, such as the Orange Revolution in Ukraine and the Rose Revolution in Georgia.

The revolution in Tunisia took the world by surprise. From the outside, Tunisia looked moderate, prosperous, and stable. But underneath that façade of stability were layered decades of frustration. The Tunisian people had had enough of suppressed freedom of speech and conscience, corruption and nepotism, a stifled economy, and imprisonment and torture.

And then Ben Ali and his hated regime, suddenly, were gone.

Dégage. Dégage. Dégage, I repeated to myself as I walked along Avenue Bourguiba.

Revolution spread elsewhere in the Middle East. Tunisia's upheaval against its oppressive government made other Arab youth want the same for their countries. Al Jazeera broadcast images of the protests, captivating the world with a narrative of heroic youth demanding change. Al Jazeera's reporting created a common narrative, with shared assumptions that the governments were bad and revolutions were good.

Fraught with conflict and uncertainty, the years since then have not been smooth for Tunisia. After Ben Ali fled, elections were held for an interim government. While the revolution started as a youth movement, democracy favored Islamist groups, long repressed by Ben Ali's government and excluded from power, but the only significantly organized opposition to the regime. A plurality of votes for the interim government was for Tunisia's Islamist political party Ennahda. Ennahda, recognizing the need for power-sharing with parties that were not Islamist, joined with the next two largest political parties (both center-left) for a unity government called the troika. They were set with the task of drawing up a constitution in a year. But despite the jubilation and solidarity of the revolution, negotiations for the constitution that would define Tunisia's postrevolutionary order gridlocked. The Islamists and the secularists could not come to agreement on fundamental questions about the basis for society in the constitution.

While the constitution was being negotiated, both domestic and international events made Tunisians fearful of instability in their country. Two Tunisian opposition parliamentarians were assassinated by extremists.[11] An angry mob firebombed the U.S. embassy in Tunis and an American school.[12] More protests erupted in Tunisia against the assassinations and violent events. As many as three thousand Tunisians traveled to Iraq and Syria to join ISIS, making Tunisians the largest group of foreign fighters for ISIS.[13] Tunisia's Ministry of Interior announced that it had blocked an additional eight thousand Tunisians from going to fight. While Ennahda was not the perpetrator of those incidents, many criticized them for ineffectiveness in maintaining security, creating a permissive environment for extremist Islamist groups, incompetence in administration, and pushing the country in a more religious direction. Elsewhere in the region, after Arab Spring movements, Libya and Syria deteriorated into civil war. Events in Egypt provided a tale of caution. Like in Tunisia, after Arab Spring protests, Egyptians had also elected an Islamist-led government (the Muslim Brotherhood). After widespread civilian protests about the Muslim Brotherhood's abuses of power and poor performance in government, in 2013, Egypt's military overthrew them, with killings and mass imprisonments.

These events inside and outside of Tunisia provided an example of what Tunisians did *not* want—the disorder, violence, and chaos overtaking other countries in the region. In retrospect, these events served a purpose. They brought all sides together, incentivizing compromises. After negotiations, in a display of pragmatism, the Islamist Ennahda-led government agreed to step aside for a technocratic government, but remained a leader in the constitutional process. Negotiations for the constitution got back on track. In January 2014, Tunisia's newly drafted constitution was approved nearly unanimously by the Constituent Assembly.

After ratification of the constitution, a new political party called Nidaa Tunis formed as a coalition of essentially anybody but the Islamists. A figure from the Ben Ali regime, Beji Caid Essebsi, was at the new party's head. With a political career beginning in 1941, Essebsi had served as minister of interior, minister of defense, and minister of foreign affairs.[14] His appeal to experience, stability, and being non-Islamist attracted support from broad sectors of society.[15] The secular Nidaa party came out first in parliamentary elections, the Islamist Ennahda party second. And then, there were the presidential elections that very day as I walked around Tunis. Essebsi won.

With Essebsi elected, however, others worried that this could signal a return to the abuses of power of Ben Ali. The pendulum had swung back to the government of a member of the old regime—a democratically elected counterrevolution.

This would be the test for the provisions of Tunisia's new constitution that institutionalized more participation and placed limits on presidential power.

But even with all this, unlike the other Arab Spring countries, Tunisia weathered the Arab Spring aftershocks. Why was this? During my journey through Tunisia, I wanted to learn how Tunisia stayed stable when other

Arab Spring countries did not. How had Tunisia managed to balance the interests of its Islamists and secularists? What will prevent Tunisia from returning to dictatorship? What did Tunisia's revolution accomplish?

I think that the biggest factor to Tunisia's post–Arab Spring accomplishments was the commitment of Tunisia's strong civil society and leadership—both secular and Islamist—to working out differences at the negotiating table. Throughout my interviews in Tunisia, people repeatedly talked about tough compromises and persistent efforts at solutions. Over and over, people used a curious phrase: the need to respect "the other." Use of the phrase is a recognition of differences, our inherent tendency to dehumanize those who are not like us, and the explicit need to make conscious efforts to overcome that.

My Tunisian friend Adel summed it up: "Tunisia is a showcase, and it has got to succeed. We would like to be the lighthouse for everybody. We got rid of a dictatorship."

To learn more about the protests in Tunisia's revolution, I walked to a café along the Avenue Bourguiba to meet Lina Ben Mhenni, a blogger and protest leader.

Blogging the Arab Spring

When Mohammed Bouazizi set himself on fire in Sidi Bouzid, setting off the youth demonstrations that sparked Tunisia's revolution, blogger Lina Ben Mhenni rushed there to record what was happening and tell the world about it. While the censored Tunisian media was not covering the protests, Ben Mhenni took pictures of the demonstrations and police violence, and posted them on her blog, A Tunisian Girl.[16] She was the only blogger present in Sidi Bouzid and Kasserine when government forces killed fourteen protesters.[17] The international press was severely limited, and local journalists could not report freely in Tunisia. Her blog became one of the most influential sources of information during Tunisia's revolution.

"I went to the hospitals and saw the corpses. I met the families," she said. "What we were trying to do was break the media blackout to show what was going on in Tunisia and mobilize people," she explained, as we sat sipping café crème in a marble-floored aging grande dame of a hotel on Avenue Bourguiba.

Other people sent her videos that she posted on her blog; she helped other bloggers; and she organized protests. Ben Mhenni also did freelance reporting for news channels like Al Jazeera English, among others. She was widely reported to have been nominated for a Nobel Peace Prize in 2012 for her role in Tunisia's revolution.[18] Since Tunisia's revolution, she has served as a spokesperson for freedom of speech and human rights in Tunisia.

"Why did you start blogging?" I asked.

She started her blog in 2007, writing about a mix of personal and political issues, including her poetry, photos, and essays on human rights and social problems. The trouble started in 2010 under Ben Ali, she said, when she and two friends organized an antigovernment demonstration. Police arrested her two friends (both men) and raided her parents' house to take her computers, equipment, and cameras. The government blocked her blog inside Tunisia, and so only people outside Tunisia or people logging in through a proxy could access it. Her audience became the world outside. She wrote in English and French.

"When Tunisia's revolution happened in 2011, the rest of the world did not expect it. But something about it resonated and spread through the Middle East. What was Tunisia's revolution about?" I asked.

"They wanted a decent life," she said. "We were living under a dictatorship, with too much corruption, nepotism, and violence. It was a police state. There was injustice, and marginalization of the remote areas of the countryside. People were fed up with all of this. The slogan was 'employment, freedom, social justice, and dignity'—that summarizes it."

"Did the revolution accomplish what you and others hoped it would?" I asked.

She shook her head no. She was very disappointed. She argued in op-eds in *The Guardian* and on CNN that Tunisia's leaders have failed the "dignity revolution."[19]

"We can't say that a country is free and that we have democracy just because we had elections," she paused. "I don't think that people died to have elections."

She did not see progress in the four purposes of the revolution: employment, freedom, social justice, and dignity. "People are suffering with the same social problems and dignity problems. Until now, despite the fact that we had a new government, there was no real willingness to change things."

The revolution was hijacked by the political parties, she thought, and in particular by Ennahda. "Instead of dealing with the real problems of Tunisians, to find a solution and fulfill the directions of the revolution, they drove us into a useless debate about religion and identity and succeeded in dividing the county. Those who are with them are good Muslims, and those who are against them are viewed as nonbelievers."

Ben Mhenni was exasperated with the election of secularist Nidaa as well. "Now the revolution is confiscated again. The Nidaa party is infiltrated by people of the old regime. As a person who took part in the revolution, I am so sad to see people from the old regime."

She boycotted the elections because of this. "I chose not to vote because neither of the two candidates represented me," she explained. Essebsi, who had just been elected, was part of the old regime, and his opponent, Moncef Marzouki, was unofficially affiliated with the Islamists. But Ben Mhenni was widely criticized for that position, as both candidates had been chosen with significant democratic support among Tunisians; not voting seemed not constructive, as Tunisia needed a way forward based on pragmatic compromise, not a desire for an unattainable idealistic perfection that could lead to gridlock.

"But Tunisia is stable, while other Arab Spring countries are not," I noted. "Why is that? It is being held up as a model."

"We don't have bloodbaths," she said. "But it is not true that everything is okay. We have terrorism. The situation is not stable. When we do a revolution, it is to improve things, not to regress. Unfortunately everything is regressing in Tunisia."

But giving her optimism were the many young people who continue to play the role of watchdogs of democracy. "Freedom of speech is the only thing that we have from the revolution, and we have to preserve it," she said.

I wondered if freedom of speech was enough; Tunisia needed institutions, new initiatives, and security to lead them forward as a functioning, healthy state.

"Your blog in particular has been an important part of freedom of speech, and social media has been crucial as well. What do you think was the role of your blog, and the blogs of other people in the revolution?" I asked. For example, the blog *Nawaat* provided a platform for citizen dissidents and political debates and offered advice to other bloggers on circumventing government censorship. Other blogs had exposed corruption or government power abuses.

She pondered, and then said that blogging and social media had certainly been important to inform and mobilize people. But she objected to the portrayal of the revolution as being about technology and social media and stressed that it was really about people who were acting to make changes. "What was happening on the ground was much more important. Don't forget that we lost at least three hundred people, that young people faced tear gas and live ammunition, with bare chests, that they risked their lives."

Bloggers continue to face risks even now: arrest, threats, harassment, or removal of their right to travel outside the country. Ben Mhenni had been late for our meeting because she was attending the trial of another blogger to offer moral support. She did not know how many times she had been beaten by the police, but she estimated about ten; she had been beaten more times by the police after the revolution than before.

She added that her safety was further endangered lately because she wrote about the threat of Islamism on her blog, "I started to receive threats three months after the fall of Ben Ali." Sitting next to her was a man in his mid-twenties in jeans and a zipped-up windbreaker. At first, I assumed he was a friend coming along with her to our meeting. But he was her government-appointed bodyguard, one of a team that accompanied her day and night since the police had found her name on a hit list of Ansar al-Shariah, an Islamist terrorist group in Tunisia. The Minister of Interior insisted that she accept round-the-clock security. The guard sat silently with us while we talked. A small woman in her mid-twenties, Ben Mhenni wore a mid-thigh-length black sweater dress and tall black boots, with an eyebrow piercing, nose piercing, and tattoo of a star on her hand—she looked more like a kid going to a party than someone on a terrorist hit list.

"With these threats to your safety, do you want to leave Tunisia?" I asked, noting that it took a lot of courage for her to play the role of the conscience of the revolution.

"I'm staying here. I think that the fight has to happen here. If I have to die, I prefer to be assassinated here."

"And you still continue with all of this?"

"I think it is my duty. I choose that."

The Bullshit Revolution?

"I wasn't always a taxi driver," Seif said in excellent English, glancing over his shoulder at me as I sat in the backseat of his cab. "I had a different job before this bullshit revolution." His company had laid him off because of the economic problems after the revolution. "But it is better to work, even at a job like this, than to not work at all—you know what I mean?" he explained.

A bullshit revolution? Like buyer's remorse, this was a case of Arab Spring Remorse, a sentiment among people who lived through it of "Oh no, what have we done!"

On the drive through the tree-lined streets of Tunis, he told me his story. He had worked as a dispatcher for a gas company which had even sent him for training in Egypt and Finland. He bemoaned that since the revolution, both unemployment and prices had gone up. A lot of people wanted Ben Ali back, Seif said, since Ben Ali was good to the poor people. "There used to be three classes—high class, middle class, and the poor people," Seif said. "Now there are just two classes—rich and poor." He did not like the direction of the country and thought that Ennahda had done a poor job. "No plans," he said about their platform.

Clearly not all Tunisians thought that Tunisia was better off after the revolution than before the revolution. After the conversation with Seif, I made a point of asking every taxi driver: in your opinion, is life better or worse after the revolution? And tellingly, every driver really wanted to talk about the revolution and his opinions. The results of my informal taxi driver poll were not uniform. About two thirds said that life is better, while one third thought that it was worse. They agreed that security and the economy were better before the revolution, while there was more freedom of expression afterward. Whether they thought life was better or worse depended on how they weighed those factors.

Wassim, a taxi driver with a stubble beard and dark hair, also thought that things were better before the revolution. He pointed out the condition of the Bardo neighborhood, where we were driving. Before the revolution, it was clean. Fountains burbled water. There was upkeep of the plants in the parks. It used to be a beautiful district of the city, with the Bardo Museum and the National Assembly. But not now, he said, pointing to trash in the streets and waterless fountains. Later in March 2015, terrorists would kill twenty-one people at the Bardo Museum, and in July, they would kill another thirty-nine at a seaside resort in the town of Sousse. "The revolution removed one set of problems and put in another. It removed one set of corrupt people and put in another set of corrupt people," he said. "The new president is eighty-eight years old," he continued, referring to Essebsi. "What can he do? He will be in office for half an hour." He anticipated that Tunisia would suffer a political crisis once the aging president died.

But the optimists outnumbered the pessimists among the taxis.

When I asked Hamad, a fifty-ish taxi driver sporting a French beret, if life was better after the revolution, he responded with an emphatic, "Of course. Of course!" But he acknowledged, "Yes, prices have risen and things are more expensive. But now we can say whatever we want. We have the right to talk about politics. If we want to criticize the president, we can criticize him." I asked him what he thought about the economic problems and the higher prices. "What do you expect?" he asked. "Right now things are in transition. In the long run it is going to be better. France had several hundred years to develop its democracy. We have only had three years." He thought that Tunisia was doing better than the other Arab Spring countries because Tunisians were more gradual in their steps. "Rather than just breaking things, we thought ahead. The other countries just broke things and then figured it out. Tunisia was intentional." He also thought that Tunisia's high level of education (he himself spoke fluent French) kept Tunisia on the right track. While Habib Bourguiba had not been perfect, he said, one good thing he did was to promote education, which was serving Tunisia well now.

Among the other taxi drivers I asked if life was better after the revolution, a typical response started with, "Of course." They pointed to new freedoms. Ahmad acknowledged the economic problems, but said "it will get better little by little over time." Salim said, "Yes the economy is worse, but we are better psychologically. Things are going to get better." Skander said, "There was a lot of oppression under Ben Ali." But he acknowledged that public order had broken down. "Now there is a lot of garbage on the streets. There is no money to pay for services." Tunisia's public waste system had broken down after the revolution due to lack of money and a shortage of garbage dumps.[20] Throughout Tunisia, I noticed garbage on the sides of the roads, intertwined in the cactuses, on the beach, piled in bags around town, burning in metal garbage bins, strewn everywhere in the sand, in the palm fronds, in the bushes, and underfoot in the market.

Bilel said, "Before the revolution, if you criticized the president, they would jail you and beat you. It is better after the revolution, although the police cannot keep order. They are afraid to intervene when there are problems. But now there is liberty." He liked the constitution now, as it defines rules that everyone must abide by and limits on the government.

Karim, a driver in his twenties in jeans and a hoodie, said that things are a lot better after the revolution. Right after, tourism declined. But now, little by little things were getting better and tourists were coming back. "The world saw that we are not Islamists," he said, making a gesture like shooting a rifle with his hands, "Not *tak-tak-tak*," imitating the sound of bullets. "I am a Muslim," he said. "But if I want to go to a cabaret or to a mosque, that is my choice, between me and God, not for someone to tell me what to do." He said that he, his mother, and his wife had all been at the protests on Avenue Bourguiba. *"Dégage. Dégage. Dégage,"* he chanted, as he sped through a light transitioning from yellow to red. He was happy that Ennahda had not been reelected.

"Why?" I asked.

"Because the world is afraid of them," he said. Now that Tunisia has a secular government, it gives confidence to the world, and the French, Spanish, Italians, and Germans are all coming back, he said.

But Tunisia's secular Nidaa-led government was similarly struggling with security threats and concerns about whether they will bring back practices of the old regime, I observed. I went to meet with a Nidaa leader to understand the government perspective.

Nidaa—The "Call for Tunis" Party

"Tunisia is a very small country. If you split it in two, the 'Islamists' and the 'other,' or the North and the South, then it would be catastrophic," said Salma Elloumi, when I asked her how Tunisia weathered the storms of the Arab Spring and stayed stable.

Salma Elloumi was one of the eleven people who founded Nidaa

Tunis with Tunisia's newly elected president Essebsi. She was subsequently appointed minister of tourism. Before entering politics, Elloumi was CEO of Société Cofat Med, a family conglomeration of businesses that includes one of the world's biggest makers of wires, and of Stifen, an export agribusiness that she started and grew, selling frozen strawberries to Nestlé and Danone.[21] I met Elloumi at the Nidaa Tunis party headquarters, in an upscale quarter of Tunis called Les Berges du Lac, in a neighborhood of villas, offices, and cafes. Elloumi was in her late fifties and blond, wearing beige pants, a long orange suit jacket, and black stiletto boots. In her office, a photograph of Rodin's *The Thinker* hung on the wall next to a child's pink princess drawing, next to a portrait of Bourguiba and the Tunisian flag.

It was a few days after Essebsi had won the presidential elections.

Elloumi continued her explanation for why Tunisia is on a stable path. "We are against exclusion. We discuss and find the points where we can be together, not the points where we are against each other. We are small, not so rich, with a big history, and we have to protect our country." She added that Tunisia's history of a succession and mixing of civilizations (Carthaginian, Roman, Byzantine, Islamic, and French) kept Tunisians tolerant of other people and ideas.

She added that another factor underpinning Tunisia's stability was the involvement of many kinds of people in the government. The elections in parliament allowed many people to be represented—with eighty-five seats for Nidaa, sixty-nine for Ennahda, and the remaining sixty-three seats for other parties.[22]

Nidaa was working *with* Ennahda, she emphasized. "We are Tunisia. We are not enemies. When there is an election, we are in competition. And when there is no election, we have to think about the interests of our country, of Tunisia, on top of anything." She had hope. "Even with Ennahda, we can reach an agreement," she added.

While one could certainly challenge the sincerity of such statements of inclusion, it was telling that this was the party line. In later conversations in Egypt, for example, there was no such effort to set a tone of inclusiveness.

"How and why did Nidaa Tunis start?" I asked her.

She explained that in Tunisia's first election after the revolution in 2011, all the other parties were small and splintered, unable to serve as a counterweight to Ennahda. Elloumi and other founding members of Nidaa believed that democracy could not work when the political parties were so unbalanced.

"We must have real opposition to guarantee democracy, another party that is able to argue and discuss problems. If not, we will return to the former situation of one big party," she explained. There were also concerns that the Ennahda-led government lacked the experience to govern the country; its leadership had never worked in government, but had been in exile. "It was a government-in-training."

Nidaa's party base included four kinds of people, she explained: independents from civil society, the labor unions, people from the party of Ben Ali, and the center left. (I knew that they had come together with one issue in common: they were not Islamists and had campaigned on that basis.) "We can improve but not go backward, and not go back to the fourteenth century," she added, making reference to Salafist groups' desires to live according to norms and practices of earlier days in Islam.

Increasing conservative Islamic rhetoric had led her to enter politics for the first time. "I have daughters. I don't want my daughters or grandkids to have a life different from mine, or to return to a situation where women have a secondary role," said Elloumi. She did not want Tunisia to turn into a country like Iran.

"What is Nidaa trying to achieve now that it has the reins of government?" I asked.

The party had two main priorities, she explained: security and the economy. "Security is our first priority. We have to eradicate terrorism," Elloumi stated. "There is a link between these two problems. If you solve the problem of security, then the investors will trust the country, both Tunisian and foreign investors." Terrorist attacks on foreigners loomed as a challenge, as extremist groups viewed this as a direct route to undermining tourism, a key sector of the economy, with the aim of weakening the government. Extremist groups in Egypt were also using the same strategy of attacking tourist sites.

A big appeal of Nidaa to the Tunisian electorate was confidence that Nidaa could avoid the security problems that happened on Ennahda's watch. However, the terrorist attacks at the Bardo Museum and at the seaside resort town of Sousse had been on Nidaa's watch.

Unemployment was another big problem, she noted. Tunisia needed investment in new projects for jobs. There were 700,000 unemployed Tunisians, nearly 200,000 of whom had a university degree.[23] She described a short three-month program "to light the fire," followed by a five-year program, the length of the presidential term. The program would emphasize opportunities for youth and women, the groups with the highest unemployment rates.

However, I knew that the economic problems were about more than security. The World Bank's assessment of Tunisia's economy detailed a set of regulations and policies that had been effective in benefiting Ben Ali's cronies, but not in spurring the economy.[24] There were also many needed reforms in economic and business policies.

"There are a lot of people who are concerned that the election of Nidaa with Essebsi as president means that there is a risk of return to the problems and repressions of the old regime. Is that possible? What can protect Tunisia from that?" I asked.

She shook her head, emphatic. "No risk. Impossible." There were several checks on Nidaa's power, she said. The first was that Tunisians would not allow it: "What we won in this revolution is liberty of expression." Even so recently after the election, there was already open criticism of Essebsi, of a kind that would not have been permitted under Ben Ali, she pointed out. Second, Nidaa Tunis did not have a majority in parliament but a plurality; it controlled about 40 percent of the National Assembly. "It means that it is impossible for us to make decisions without the agreement of the parliament." Third were new constitutional constraints on the power of the president; I would learn more about those in later conversations with people who had drafted Tunisia's constitution.

But Tunisian democracy still had a way to go, she thought. "We are not in a democracy yet, but we are starting to learn. We have to start with our kids in school to explain democracy. We have to respect the 'other.'"

These seemed like solid checks on power—but were they enough to balance presidential power when the country faced down terrorism threats? In July 2015, Essebsi declared a "state of emergency" that gave police and the military renewed authority and restricted freedom of assembly.[25] Tunisia, Egypt, Jordan, and other countries had had on-again, off-again states of emergency for decades to deal with terrorist threats. They did not have a history of getting the balance right between addressing security problems and maintaining civil and human rights. Only time would tell if these checks on power were sufficient.

I asked Elloumi what the role of Tunisian women had been in the revolution. She was proud of the role of Tunisian women and thought that they had provided equilibrium. "When the country was in danger of going toward Islamism, women were present to say no—we are Muslim, but we don't agree to have a secondary role. Before the revolution, women were absent from politics. Now we are starting to work in politics. We are learning."

She thought that the prominent role of women had kept the revolution on a peaceful path. "Tunisian women are very strong, and the role played by Tunisian women was very important in these three years." As I stood up to leave, she shook my hand. "Tunisia was created by a woman," she said with a smile, referring to Dido's founding of Carthage.

Carthage: "To Retrace One's Steps to the Upper Air"

"A woman leads the way," wrote Virgil in the *Aeneid*.[26]

According to Carthaginian legend and Virgil's retelling of it, Carthage was founded by a colony of seafaring Phoenicians (from what is now Lebanon) led by Queen Dido.

After its founding around 800 BC, over the centuries, Carthage swelled into a mighty trade empire. It ruled most of North Africa, what is now southern Spain (Cartagena in Spain was originally a Carthaginian colonial trade city), and parts of Italy (Sardinia and Sicily). The Carthaginians were the first to establish an empire on both the African and European shores of the Mediterranean, laying the foundations of urban and agricultural development for the Roman Empire later. For six centuries, Carthage thrived as a maritime power, with manufacturing, agricultural exports, advanced engineering, navigation skills, and a great library.[27] But after competition with Rome over dominance in the Mediterranean, there ensued a succession of wars, called the Punic Wars, during which the great Carthaginian general Hannibal marched his troops and his elephants over the Alps to lay siege to Rome for fifteen years, threatening Rome's very existence.

"Carthago delenda est"—Carthage must be destroyed—Roman senator

Cato the Elder told the Roman senate, advocating the total destruction of the capital of mighty Carthage. In 146 BC, Carthage fell to Rome. The Roman army razed the city to the ground, burned what was left, killed untold civilians, and sold fifty thousand surviving Carthaginians into slavery. As legend has it, Rome sowed salt into the earth so that Carthage could not rise again. Carthage never again posed a threat to Rome, later becoming a wealthy province in the Roman Empire. But in the centuries that followed, Rome suffered war guilt for the total annihilation of its rival.

Carthage today is a wealthy suburb of white villas, west of Tunis. I took a taxi to Byrsa Hill, where lie the only excavated ruins of what was once the capital of a mighty empire. The Carthaginians had good taste. It was a stunningly beautiful spot, with leafy gardens of cyprus, pine, cactus, and eucalyptus, and an expansive view overlooking the sparkling waters of the strait of Sicily. Dominating this strait, only eighty miles between Carthage at the northern point of Africa and Sicily at the south of Europe, enabled Carthage to control sea traffic between the east Mediterranean and west Mediterranean. This gave them hegemony over trade routes among Western Europe, Asia, and Africa. It was a very strategic (and beautiful) location for the capital of an empire.

I wandered around ruins of what had been a Carthaginian street of jewelers and other artisans. There were brick homes, alleyways between them, and a cistern to collect water. The cleverly engineered cisterns provided citywide piped running water and indoor plumbing long before ancient Rome developed the same technologies. Remains of plaster covered brick walls. When the Romans destroyed Carthage, they filled this quarter with rubble and later built on top of it, which had the effect of preserving it for later generations of archaeologists. Lucky for us now, we can see in three dimensions what street life might have been like. More evocative than the actual ruins is the site itself, overlooking the sea with a bright sky and the chirping of birds in the background.

I walked down to the coast from Byrsa Hill, descending stone staircases, meandering cobblestone streets, and passing by sumptuous white villas with cobalt-blue doors surrounded by lush bushes, palm trees, and hot pink bougainvillea. Groups of junior high school kids walked by wearing school uniforms and carrying backpacks, on their way home from school.

I arrived at ancient Carthage's famous ports, a set of two interlocking marinas within a harbor that were a source of maritime dominance of the Carthaginian Empire. Carthage's port endures as one of antiquity's greatest engineering masterpieces. Today, the harbor built by the Carthaginians well over two thousand years ago still creates a sheltered space where the seawater is as smooth as glass, reflecting the palm trees. The port is surrounding by sloping stone walls. Now small pleasure boats line the shores, tied onto what had been old Carthage's port walls.

It was from this port that an international trading empire was built. The port was technologically superior to others in any city of the world at the time. It had a seventy-foot-wide entrance from the sea that could be closed with chains. The first marina had wharves where merchants could unload their goods, and the second marina could dock nearly two hundred warships.

I strolled along the circumference of the port and onto a promontory in the port's center. On the promontory path, I walked on sand and broken pieces of red pottery, through bushes and blocks of ancient stone. Nearby, men cast fishing lines into the sea. A toddler ran by me in a pink sweatshirt. On the promontory, one of Carthage's dry docks had been excavated, and I kneeled to inspect strips of ancient stone that did not look so different from where we would dock boats now.

Two hundred years after razing Carthage to the ground, the Romans came back and built a Roman provincial city on top of the destroyed city. Roman Carthage rose to become the third biggest city in the Roman Empire, after Rome and Alexandria.

Now, the ruins of Roman Carthage in North Africa are some of the richest troves of ancient mosaics in the world. Tourism plays a big role in Tunisia's economy, with the lure of Carthage, Rome, and Islamic North Africa, in combination with beautiful Mediterranean white-sand beaches. One in five of Tunisia's workers are employed in the tourism industry. The *Lonely Planet* guide listed Tunisia as one of the best value destinations of 2015.[28] But tourism dropped by a third the first year after the revolution and dropped further after the 2015 terrorist attacks.[29]

Tunisia is part of the West's heritage too, as Carthage laid the foundation for Rome's empire, which borrowed and built upon Carthage's achievements. The Romans imitated Carthaginian warship engineering and studied Carthaginian agricultural manuals. Ancient trade patterns apply today. Like Carthage, most of Tunisia's trade today is with Europe.

Over 80 percent of its exports are to and 70 percent of its imports are from Europe.[30] The Euro-Mediterranean Free Trade Area, a negotiated pact to enable trade between European countries and other countries on the Mediterranean, follows this heritage of trading in the Mediterranean.

As I left Carthage, I thought of lines from Virgil's *Aeneid:* "It is easy to go down into Hell; Night and day, the gates of dark Death stand wide; but to climb back again, to retrace one's steps to the upper air—There's the rub, the task." Similarly, now, Tunisia must build itself back up again after colonialism, dictatorship, and revolution.

Bizerte: Last Battle of Colonialism

"You cannot leave Carthage in the hands of the Barbarians,"[31] said the British foreign secretary to the French foreign minister in 1877, giving the French the go-ahead to invade Tunisia and take it from the weakened Ottoman Empire. Tunisia had been a province of the Ottoman Empire since the sixteenth century. The French invaded Tunisia in 1881 and ruled it for the next seventy-five years.

In the Tunisian Mediterranean town of Bizerte is Le Sport Nautique, a French restaurant built as a club for the French colonial military officers who held the last French colonial outpost in Tunisia. When Tunisians won independence from France in 1956, the French kept military control of the port of Bizerte until 1961 against the wishes of the Tunisians, arguing that it was important for France's role in NATO and their war in Algeria to have a port in the southern Mediterranean. Le Sport Nautique opened in 1956. No longer a French officers' club, now it is one of the finest restaurants in Tunisia.

My table at the restaurant overlooked another canal that the ancient Carthaginians had built. The French redug the canal, using it as a port for military and trade vessels. Then a new port had been built before Tunisia's Arab Spring revolution, with the aim of spurring Tunisia's economy by attracting yachts and cruise ships. Across the canal from the restaurant were palm and pine trees, interspersed among warehouses in need of maintenance. Nearby were cargo shops and tankers.

Today, the restaurant (now under Tunisian ownership) is still very French, with white tablecloths and a menu in French. Waiters wear white shirts, button-down vests, bow ties, and black pants, and speak perfect French with the mannerisms of a waiter in Paris. Tunisian elites dine here now as opposed to the French.

In addition to Tunisia, European colonists also took control of other parts of North Africa from the Ottomans. In the nineteenth and early twentieth centuries, France took Algeria and Tunisia, Britain took Egypt, Italy and France took parts of Libya, and France turned Morocco into a "protectorate." Morocco was the only part of North Africa that was never part of the Ottoman Empire. Faced with nationalist revolutionary movements across North Africa and its own weakened condition after World War II, France relinquished Libya in 1951 and Tunisia and Morocco in 1956.[32] This enabled France to keep her resources focused on quelling rebellion in Algeria, where French interests and the French colonial population were greatest.

Tunisia's struggle against colonialism began with the formation of a nationalist party that promoted a constitution, parliament, elected government, and equality among Tunisians and French. The struggle progressed from a political movement to armed resistance.

Habib Bourguiba led Tunisia's struggle against French colonialism. As Tunisia's first president after independence, Bourguiba's legacy included sweeping reforms of government and society.[33] He separated the state from religious traditions, abolishing the shariah courts. He aimed to modernize Tunisia, with investment in industry, tourism, and agriculture. He prioritized education, making it the largest expenditure in the state budget. He passed Tunisia's Code of Personal Status, the most liberal code of rights for women in the Arab world. His charisma held Tunisia together during the difficult transition from colonialism to independence. An obituary read, "Habib Bourguiba's time in office saw Tunisia take a mighty leap from the Middle Ages into the twentieth century."[34] But while he reformed and modernized Tunisia, he did so by quashing dissent. After three decades in power and becoming increasingly out of touch with the world at the age of ninety-four, Bourguiba was deposed in 1987 by Ben Ali (the prime minister at the time) in a bloodless coup.

After all Tunisia but Bizerte won independence from France in 1956, Tunisians did not want the French occupying any part of their country. Now president, Bourguiba attacked the French in Bizerte. In the battle that ensued, twenty-five French and one thousand Tunisians died. When the French went to the UN to seek support, the United States sided with Tunisia. The French withdrew, and finally the Tunisian government held complete sovereignty.

French colonialism had longlasting impacts on Tunisian language, identity, culture, society, economy, and institutions—negative and positive. The French in Tunisia set economic policies that favored French *colons*, or settlers, over Tunisians, leading gradually to a disproportionate ownership of agricultural land by the French, with disproportionate taxation on the Tunisians. They introduced French law, reducing the role of Ottoman and Islamic institutions. They built infrastructure, such as roads, ports, and railways, and advanced European education.

The impact of French colonialism on Tunisia was also deeply psychological, communicating a status of inferiority to the Tunisians, and superiority to the French.

Albert Memmi, a Tunisian Jew, wrote *The Colonizer and the Colonized*, one of the world's defining essays about the psychological impact of colonialism. Published with an introduction by Jean-Paul Sartre, the book was read by participants in rights movements around the world, ranging from the South African anti-apartheid movement to the civil rights movement in the United States. Memmi wrote, "No one can treat a man like a dog without first regarding him as a man. The impossible dehumanization of the oppressed, on the other side of the coin, becomes the alienation of the oppressor. . . . In short, he must dehumanize himself, as well."[35] Memmi described the internal emotional conflicts of the colonized—hating the oppressor on the one hand, while admiring him and wanting to be like him, on the other hand.

Tunisia had come a long way since then. The independence struggles of the 1950s transitioned into new sets of issues around creating a new independent country. The dehumanization of colonialism transitioned to the dehumanization of political opponents.

I left and walked around Bizerte's old historic port, with its buildings painted white with cobalt-blue doors and cobalt-blue filigree on windows. Inside a covered market with peeling paint, local vendors wearing the traditional white Islamic caps of North Africa sold fennel, radishes, carrots, lettuce, snails, freshly butchered meat, shoes, and plastic toys.

We Are Living in the Same House

"Common ground is the name of the game right now in Tunisia," observed Kamal al-Sammari. "I'm privileged to have the chance to contribute to it."

Al-Sammari spent the past thirty years as an activist and dissident, fighting for human rights in Tunisia. In the 1970s, he was a founder of a socialist opposition political party affiliated with trade unions (le Mouvement de l'Unité Populaire) and was editor in chief for *Unité* (a Tunisian opposition newspaper published in Paris). Later, he wrote for the BBC, held a number of senior positions at Amnesty International, including as Middle East spokesperson, and served as head of the London office of Al Jazeera.[36] He has been sentenced to prison twice. He was first tried and convicted in absentia in the 1970s under Bourguiba. In 1996, under Ben Ali, he was put in prison and released a week later, after international pressure and intervention from Amnesty International.

Now, al-Sammari consults with various programs in Tunisia to train journalists and advise media, and he also spends his time quietly, in the background, counseling the political parties on building consensus. He said that political parties after the revolution asked him to take a role in communication, but he declined. "What I am doing is fine. I can sleep at night. I don't have an agenda. I have principles. I give advice. Tunisia needs to be saved."

In particular, he tries to bring the Islamists and secularists together. "We are living in the same house," he explained.

We sat in an outdoor cafe near the tree-lined Place Pasteur in Tunis. In his early seventies, Kamal wore an orange and green scarf and a thoughtful look on his face.

Because of his stance in the center and his effort to bring people with differing points of view together, I wanted to seek his opinion and perspective as a neutral party.

"What happened while the Islamists were in government in Tunisia?" I asked. "They made a lot of mistakes and had to step aside because of those mistakes."

"The Islamists have the excuse of being new to government. The challenges were huge. We knew that whoever would take over would have problems. Their political mistake was that they thought that they could govern by fait accompli," he explained.

Al-Sammari described the challenges that the Islamists were up against—the legacy of a country run by one party, a history of having thousands of Islamists in prison (and therefore not having public management experience), and a lot of new problems that arose after the revolution. "That is a heavy legacy. Not to defend them, but to be fair. There was an expectation having justice *right now*. Their electoral victory made them think that they were on the top of the moon, and they could do whatever they wanted," he said. "They didn't make the right analysis that their electoral and political base was more radical and ignorant than they were," he explained, noting that there were significant differences among the Islamists in Tunisia. Some wanted Islamic values blended with democratic values, others wanted a strict Salafist interpretation of shariah law, and still others followed radical jihadist movements.

Under the Bourguiba and Ben Ali regimes, the Islamists (and all other political parties) were marginalized and so, as a group, they lacked both political and administrative experience. "They were not allowed to go to leadership. They were not allowed to work. As a result, they were ignorant of what administration means."

Another veteran journalist I spoke with, Rached Khechana, explained why even after these problems, Ennahda still had strong support: "The electorate sees that we have to have a balance between two poles. So in the first elections, they gave the chance to the Islamists, as they had been marginalized. But the Islamists failed in this role, so when the elections came after, they were punished. The Tunisian electorate wanted to conserve Islam as a part of the political scene, but not as a leader."

Al-Sammari thought that despite Tunisia's positive momentum, there were still risks to stability in Tunisia. Ideology made finding common ground a challenge among the parties. Most of the people who voted for Ennahda didn't want terrorism, but rather changes in their own lives. "They hadn't gained anything from this revolution," and so Ennahda might lose their support if it did not deliver economically. On the other hand, there were good relations between some factions of Ennahda and some factions in Libya. There were factions within Ennahda that were not happy with its moderate direction. ISIS and Al-Qaeda also presented threats. There were risks of terrorism and violence. There were economic challenges, among many others. Finally, there were risks of return to the oppression of the old regime.

"If the political classes are not up to the challenge of working together, they will not be able to address Tunisia's problems," he said.

"Why is Tunisia the only Arab Spring country that overthrew a government that avoided significant levels of violence? Why is Tunisia not like Libya, Yemen, or Egypt?" I asked.

Al-Sammari pointed to a number of reasons, "an accumulation of facts," as he put it.

First, Tunisia had a strong civil society (in particular the trade unions, lawyers associations, human rights activists, and business community, a group of whom won the 2015 Nobel Peace Prize), a unified population without major religious sects or minorities (most of Tunisia is Sunni Muslim), human rights activists serving as watchdogs on Facebook, a history of constitutions (Tunisia's first constitution was adopted in 1860), and 150 years of stability and administration experience. During the Ben Ali regime, members of civil society from different political backgrounds had worked together, for example, with secularist human rights activists and lawyers defending jailed Islamists in courts. "At different points in time, the Islamists and the democrats worked together, fighting a repressive regime together," he said.

Second, Tunisians (in particular Ennahda) saw what happened in Egypt: revolution, an elected Islamist government, and a counterrevolution. Egypt's military coup overthrew the Islamists, with many killed or jailed. "Egypt was important. It made the leadership of Ennahda realize that their turn was imminent. It made them realize that they better play it as consensual to save the day," he said. The past of many Ennahda leaders, with prison, torture, or exile under Ben Ali, also motivated them. "That is why they are defending their freedoms," he said. He thoughtfully observed that Ennahda understood that if it appeared to grab too much power, there could have been a coup like in Egypt, or mass confusion, or Tunisia could join Syria or Libya in chaos and violence.

Third, al-Sammari also thought that Tunisia's history of accepting changes and multiple cultures contributed. Tunisia had the Berbers, the Carthaginians, the Romans, the Arabs, the Ottoman Turks, and the French. That meant that Tunisians were open to blending ideas, even in government.

"You have spent your life as a dissident. What is your perspective on the historical changes in Tunisia? What do the elections mean?" I asked.

"It is a new page of history in Tunisia," he said. "It is a transitional period, which means that there will be confusion, temporary decisions, and temporary analysis." He emphasized that the way forward is to steer a middle ground, uniting disparate groups when possible. "What we are hoping to see is a president who will be wise enough to be the president of *all* Tunisia, to play the role to bring people together, which means mainly the Islamists and the others."

Al-Sammari was proud of how far Tunisia had come. "We have succeeded in a transitional period. We overcame the obstacles. We managed to have a free election. Yes, certainly with some excesses," he acknowledged, but Tunisia was coming from a situation of dictatorship. "This didn't stop the political leaders from agreeing on the need for a fair election. This happened. For a country that had been ruled by one political party for sixty years, this is a big achievement. This is an indicator that we are entering a new phase in history."

As we finished up, al-Sammari reflected on his life's work. "I am a lucky citizen of the world who believes in ideas and values," he said. "You fight for them and you pay for them."

Ennahda—the Islamic "Renaissance" Party

Tunisia's Islamist political party had played a polarizing role. However, Ennahda had also played, won, lost, and then kept participating by the rules of democracy, not violence. Their pragmatic course of action differed dramatically from other Islamist political parties in the Middle East. Their substantial levels of support indicated that the Islamists would be a force in Tunisian politics for the years to come. I wanted to learn about their perspective.

The Ennahda headquarters in central Tunis is a white multistory building, with a large Ennahda sign out front. As I entered, a guard bade me to sit in a waiting room and a television broadcast recitation from the Quran. A man in the next room announced the call to prayer.

I walked upstairs to the fourth floor to meet Sayed Ferjani. Ferjani, in his fifties with gray hair and a thick gray beard, serves as an international spokesperson for Ennahda as part of Ennahda's Central Bureau leadership, with additional responsibility for negotiating with other political parties. Once tortured with his spine broken under Ben Ali (describing the ordeal as hanging from a metal rod in the "roast chicken" position)[37] Ferjani now presents the calm, thoughtful demeanor of an elder statesman. His return to Tunisia in 2012 after decades of exile in the UK prompted a welcome by hundreds of Tunisians at the airport and a feature about him in *The New York Times,* about how his return (and the return of a few others) marked the reentry of moderate Islam in Tunisia after its revolution.[38] Ferjani's return coincided with that of of Rached Ghanouchi, an internationally recognized moderate Islamist thinker who founded Ennahda in 1981. After imprisonment, Ghanouchi similarly fled Tunisia to live in exile for the next two decades in the UK, which granted him political asylum.[39]

In Tunisia and elsewhere in North Africa in the 1980s and 1990s, the Islamist movement was the most powerful opposition movement to governments because of its ability to mobilize vast numbers of ordinary people.[40] After violent government repression with many Tunisian Islamists jailed and tortured, Tunisia's Islamist movement was crushed and dormant for decades. Ennahda's return to Tunisia led to many questions among wary secularists: How much support would Islamist movements receive? Would they try to impose shariah law? Would they roll back women's rights? Would there be terrorism and instability? What would this mean for relations with the West?

I asked Ferjani, "What does it mean to Ennahda to be an Islamist political party?"

I thought that the Associated Press (AP) had adopted a clear definition of Islamist: "An advocate or supporter of a political movement that favors reordering government and society in accordance with laws prescribed by Islam."[41] AP differentiated Islamists, a wide range of people who favor more Islam within government (including mainstream politicians), from Islamic militants and extremists, who commit violence in the name of Islam.

Ferjani said he did not like to apply the word "Islamist" to Ennahda because of the connotations of the word in the West. He preferred Muslim Democrat, like the Christian Democratic parties in Europe. "Islamism means 'related to Islam,'" he said, "but in the West, it means harsh, dogmatic, unpredictable, neither civic nor civil, and violent. We are trying to set the example of a model for the Muslim world, as well as for the *world*, when we are trying to reconcile Islam with democracy. Democracy is the product of the West. Islam is part of the culture and identity of the people in the East." He pointed out that Ennahda means "renaissance" in Arabic, with the word chosen because of its idea of renewal and revival.

After an early history in the 1970s and 1980s of violent attacks attributed to Ennahda or people affiliated with it (actual events are unclear), Ghanouchi made efforts to distance his Ennahda movement rhetorically from violence, endorsing liberal democracy and women's rights. Ghanouchi said that the closest comparison with his party is Erdogan's Justice and Development Party (AK Party) in Turkey, not the governments of Iran or Saudi Arabia.[42] *Time* described Ghanouchi as "once the enfant terrible of political Islam" and now a "voice of sanity."[43] Brookings scholar of Islam Shadi Hamid described Ennahda as being as moderate as you can get and still be an Islamist party.[44]

"There are many who talk about an 'Arab exceptionalism,' " I said. "They point out that Middle Eastern countries are among the least democratic in the world, and some view this as related to religion. Are Islam and democracy compatible?" I asked.

"We have demonstrated in our actions and deeds, while we were in power, as well as now, that Islam and democracy are very compatible," Ferjani said. "Muslims are trying to make it compatible." He thought that democracy and its principles of governance were very needed in Tunisia.

"There are many kinds of Islamist movements in the Middle East now—many of them violent. What is the difference between Ennahda and these others?" I asked.

Ferjani thought about it and gave three differences.

The first difference, he said, was Ennahda's emphasis on the civic dimensions of Islam, as opposed to violence. He thought that true Islam was different from its reputation; Al-Qaeda, Boko Haram, the Taliban, ISIS, and others were wrongly using the name of Islam for killing. "With all of these negative examples, we have to set an example which is different, which is full of citizenship and civility, not dogmatic." He added, "I do believe that we are an alternative and a model for the Islamic world, as against ISIS and its sister groups."

Second, he emphasized that Ennahda now had experience in government, serving as the largest political party in Tunisia's 2011 Constituent

Assembly and now as the second largest political party in the National Assembly. By way of contrast, Egypt's Muslim Brotherhood and other affiliated parties in the region had mainly served as opposition, without the pragmatic experience of administering a government for any length of time before being overthrown.

Third, he pointed to the blend of East and West that Ennahda promoted. "We stitch the two things. That makes us unique." In Sunni Islam, there are four main schools of Islamic jurisprudence (*madhhab*). Tunisia's *madhhab* was "Maliki." Ferjani explained that the Maliki *madhhab* was developed both in Tunisia and Spain (when much of Spain was Muslim from the eighth through the fifteenth centuries), in dialogue with European Christian traditions. He added that at the Zaytuna, Tunisia's thousand-year-old center of Islamic scholarship, the sheikhs had initiated their own school of thought about modernizing education and the emancipation of women, serving as a starting point for Bourguiba's reforms of the status of women. Furthermore, many Tunisians studied in the West, mixing Western ideas with Islamic faith.

"You have described differences in experience; what about values? What are the Islamic political values that Ennahda is trying to promote?" I asked.

"Islamic values are bringing peace and bringing benefits to the human being. That is the way to worship God. Also freedom, justice, and taking care of the poor. The Prophet Mohammed said that the best amongst you is the best in serving the people." Ferjani emphasized that he did not view Islamic values as imposing those values on others. "We believe that freedom is a precondition for faith. Theologically, how we read Islam, is that God created a human being and gave a human being freedom to worship him or to avoid worshipping him."

As he spoke, I reflected that while there were large parts of Ennahda who thought as Ferjani did, Ennahda was also struggling to bring multiple varieties of Islamism under a single umbrella. There were others who did not share such cosmopolitan and tolerant views. Others I spoke with in Tunisia were frustrated with the spread of the Salafist-Jihadist interpretations of Islam, both peaceful and violent, funded by Gulf countries like Saudi Arabia and Qatar. This tension over the interpretation of Islam and the role of Islam in public life would continue to play out in Tunisia.

"Within Ennahda's platform and goals, what is the role of shariah?" I asked.

Ferjani responded by describing some of the debate that had taken place during the drafting of Tunisia's constitution. There were two kinds of debates: first, within Ennahda and second, between Ennahda and the secularists.

Tunisia's new constitution protects both freedom of conscience and Muslim Arab identity, he noted. Ennahda thought that the role of Islam within Tunisia was important, and so Ennahda had insisted on describing Islam as the religion of the state. Many people within Ennahda wanted the constitution to say that Tunisia's law was based on shariah. However, after the debate within Ennahda party ranks, the leadership made the decision to not use the word "shariah," given the backlash from others in Tunisia about use of the word. "The word is vague. Which shariah?" he said, asking if this meant the shariah of the Taliban, Saudi Arabia, Iran, or Sudan. "We decided no. We have shown leadership, as well as that we have shown that we have to build a constitution for all, not for a specific group."

I next asked him about Ennahda's track record in government. A 2013 Zogby poll showed that only 28 percent of Tunisians still had confidence in Ennahda's leadership, the same level of support that Egypt's Muslim Brotherhood had in polls before the popularly supported military coup against them in July 2013.[45] Ennahda voluntarily stepped down in September 2013, installing a technocratic government, until a new round of elections could be held.

"Our main accomplishment is that we avoided for Tunisia the fate of the other countries in terms of turmoil and violence," he said. "We were willing to leave office when we had a workable guaranteed way to get a constitution and elections. That was the tradeoff and that was the deal," he said. Ferjani noted that Tunisia was in transition and required sacrifices.

"What was the thinking behind Ennahda's moves to make the compromises that it did?" I asked.

"We felt that we are in transition, and people don't like people who control everything. To control everything we would lose everything." He added, "Participation is a goal in itself." Under Bourguiba, Islamist groups did not participate, but were excluded and imprisoned. The Muslim Brotherhood in Egypt, with its leadership in exile or jail, had lost its ability to participate.

"Did the events in Egypt affect Ennahda's decision to voluntarily cede power?"

"Of course. Who doesn't read? The balance of power, nationally, regionally, internationally is important. You could take your country to the unknown."

To me, some of the smartest things that Ennahda did involved ceding and sharing power, not grabbing power when they could, and stepping away from controversial issues. With worldwide suspicion regarding whether or not Islamist political parties could participate in democratic systems, the best thing that Ennahda could do to build a lasting and stable place at the negotiating table for themselves was to show that they could participate according to democratic rules. This meant winning sometimes, losing sometimes, and being good losers when they lost. Ennahda's forbearance and shrewd political calculations gave them credibility for the next round. It now remained to be seen if their leadership, like Ghanouchi and Ferjani, using words of political participation and tolerance, could trump the more radical elements within the party.

"Given your past, what do you hope for the future of Tunisia?"

"I was tortured, and that was hurtful and painful," Ferjani said, not wanting to dwell further on that. "Our country is not developed. Why are we like this? Some people say because you are Muslims. Others say, like Bourguiba, get rid of everything and follow the West. I think development should be a mix, to absorb the best of your heritage and be open to what is good in the world." He continued, "We should not look at 'the other' in terms of what they have inflicted on us, but what we can do for our country so that such things never happen again. So we have to break the cycle of hatred and excluding others. Inclusiveness is the key word. Inclusiveness is to look at the best of the world, what is beautiful, and to look at the human being, whether he or she shares your faith or not. That is what could compensate for the suffering that we have been through."

The Fourth Holiest City in Islam

The drive from Tunis to Kairouan took me south along the Mediterranean coast through rolling green hills and olive groves. There was something special and luminous about the light of the sky. Then the road turned inland away from the coast toward Kairouan, the city where Islam first took hold in Africa. I had left the coastal land of urban, cosmopolitan, secular Nidaa supporters and entered the more conservative interior. I was heading there because I wanted to better understand Tunisia's historic Islamic heritage. The scenery turned to flat desert, as I traveled through neglected little villages, marred by ubiquitous garbage. I now understood what everyone meant by the differences between the prosperity of the coast and the poverty of the interior.

When I was nearly at Kairouan, a policeman in an olive green uniform motioned me to the side of the road to stop. He came to the window of my rental car and took my driver's license. My license in his hand, he told me that I owed him a fine of forty Tunisian dinars for not stopping at a stop sign. Then he changed his mind and told me that I actually owed him sixty dinars. I told him that I didn't see a stop sign and that no other cars were stopping. I asked him to show the stop sign to me, making a point to get out of the car to inspect. He showed me a knocked over stop sign behind a bush. Then he backed down, said no money was needed, returned my driver's license, and let me go.

He had just tried to shake me down. The policeman's behavior represented the pattern of police corruption that had angered so many people under the Ben Ali regime. Certain things had not yet changed in Tunisia.

Kairouan is the fourth holiest city in Islam, after Mecca, Medina, and Jerusalem. Its founding events bequeathed it its holiness. In the seventh century, Islam was a new religion, a few decades old, and it spread fast with Arab armies conquering North Africa. The story goes that in 670 AD the conquering Arab general Uqba ibn Naqfi was seeking a location for a new city. He accidentally kicked a cup on the ground and water sprang forth. According to tradition, this water was the same water as the holy Zamzam water in Mecca. The finding of holy water signaled to him that he was at the right place.

What is now Tunisia was a natural place for a new Islamic empire, as

it had been recognized by the Carthaginians and the Romans as a strategic location connecting Mediterranean sea trade with African overland
trade routes. Arab rulers based themselves in Kairouan, expanding ir-
rigation and trade routes and developing a flourishing economy and
luxurious court life.[46] What had been Christian, Jewish, and Berber
communities gradually converted culturally by the eleventh century into
mainly Muslim communities. Kairouan became the seat of an early Islamic
empire in North Africa, but lost status as a trade and military hub, as it
was bled by ongoing rebellion by the local Berbers against the conquering
Arabs. But Kairouan remained the leading center of North African Sunni
scholarship for centuries.

In Kairouan, I wandered through the old medina, with narrow alleys
of whitewashed homes with peeling paint, pastel pink and turquoise doors
and window grills, and stone archways. I meandered through beige brick
vaults of the markets and labyrinthine alleyways on cobblestone roads.
Market vendors sold date-filled pastries, jewelry, fruits and vegetables,
baskets, glazed pottery and unglazed amphorae, shoes, carpets and
kilims. For offer also were long brown wool capes that look like a Francis-
can monk's habit, leather handbags, everyday items like kitchenware and
clothing, and tourist trinkets. Renovations and repairs to walls were
ongoing. Men sat in domed blue-and-white tiled cafés smoking water
pipes. Women walked around draped in traditional white, doing their
shopping.

I arrived at the great mosque, known as the Uqba Mosque, named
after the city's founding general. The Uqba Mosque was the first mosque
in Africa, before other great mosques and centers of learning such as Al-
Azhar in Cairo or Fez in Morocco. The Uqba Mosque, also serving as a
university, was the preeminent center of learning in North Africa from
the ninth through eleventh centuries. Gradually, the university associated
with the Great Mosque Zaytuna in Tunis overtook the Uqba in importance. Here were developed law, grammar, history, mathematics, astronomy, and botany, as well as theology, with debates over theological topics
such as free will and predestination. The Maliki *madhhab*, or school of
Islamic jurisprudence mentioned by Ferjani, developed in part here.

I stood in front of the mosque to observe it, next to a man selling sweets
made of semolina and honey from a cart. The mosque was a massive and
beautiful structure of beige brick with nine gates. It looked like a fortress.

An important example of Islamic art and architecture in North Africa, it served as a model for subsequent mosques. I entered its wide-open courtyard, paved with stone. Arches and columns, many of which were transplanted here from Roman and Carthaginian ruins, surrounded the courtyard, symbolizing absorption of accomplishments of other civilizations into Islam. I sat down on steps under the arched colonnades to absorb its ambience of order, power, calm, and tranquility. I peeked into the mosque itself (forbidden to non-Muslims), observing its ancient wood carving on the *minbar* (pulpit) and columns from Roman Carthage. It was dim, and no one was inside.

Bourguiba ended the status of the Uqba and Zaytuna as great centers of Islamic thinking. In the process of bringing most aspects of life under the state, Bourguiba absorbed the Uqba and Zaytuna into Tunis University, dismantled their faculties, and put the mosques under state control. At the same time, he established the Personal Status Code and integrated the shariah courts into Tunisia's secular legal system.[47] Ben Ali similarly kept the mosques and Islamic colleges under tight control.

There never was a wide consensus within Islam that the Islamic empire and caliphate should give way to the secular nation-state as the legitimate basis for government. But in the wake of the sudden fall of the Ottoman Empire, followed by colonialism, new governments across the Middle East sought both to centralize state authority and achieve a fast conversion to modern ways (with the West as their model). They viewed political Islam as a threat. State leadership across the Arab world took control of mosques and centers of Islamic thought. While the question of separation of religion and state was fought out in multiple wars over several hundred years in the West, state control of religion was imposed suddenly in the span of a few decades in the Middle East. Like Mustafa Kemal Atatürk in Turkey and Gamal Abdel Nasser in Egypt, Bourguiba was part of these trends in Tunisia.

Perhaps because of the closure of these once great centers, North African Islamist movements developed earliest and strongest in Tunisia, rather than Morocco or Algeria. The rise of the Islamist movement in the 1970s can be directly attributed to the earlier takeover of the religious sphere by state authorities. First, cooption of the ulema (the body of religious scholars associated with great mosques) meant that they lost their traditional role as arbiters between the people and the government, and the Islamists stepped into this vacuum. Second, the state's secularizing reforms put it in the realm of family law, taking the place of religious structures, creating opposition. Third, economic and social problems fed the Islamist critique of the faults of the secular government.[48] Tunisia's Islamist movement started at the Zaytuna in Tunis, with religious scholars saying that they, rather than the state, represented true Islam.

What would it mean now to have independent schools of Islamic thought? Would they develop new syntheses of Islam with the modern world, or would they be powerful bastions of resistance to governments, providing grounds for the inciting of militants? When the state absorbed centers of Islamic scholarship was much of Islamic thinking frozen in time? Did the closure of the great centers of Islamic thought mean that the intellectual work and forging of ideas that needed to happen within Islam during the past century failed to happen, so that when people sought answers to problems of politics and daily lives, they found instead a gap between what their faith allowed and the modern world? Did the closure of these centers mean that some faithful Muslims now turn to direct imitation of life during the time of the Prophet Mohammed, not moderated by traditional interpretations, as the Salafists do?

Ennahda reversed some of the restrictions on Islamic institutions that had been imposed by Bourguiba and Ben Ali. They freed up the mosques, betting that freedom of speech would encourage Islamists to participate constructively. The Uqba, the Zaytuna, and other old schools of Islamic thought were given license to open once again.[49] This was a controversial decision, but there was hope that the old historic Islamic centers operating in open space would develop a tolerant and modern body of Islamic scholarship and a bulwark against violent extremism.[50] But after Ennahda's freeing up of the space for Islamist groups, jihadist-Salafist preachers took over one thousand out of Tunisia's five thousand mosques. When it became clear that these sudden changes threatened the stability of Tunisia, the Ennahda government rolled back the number of the Salafist-controlled mosques to about a hundred.[51]

In the fight for identity within Islam, where do these historic centers fit? Can they be a part of civil society and scholarship? Released from tight state control, will they encourage extremism or an embracing of the world? These are the questions that states and centers of Islamic scholarship alike are grappling with.

Complementary or Equal?

My friends Sarah and Adel pulled out their cellphones and showed me videos of thousands of people in a crowd, at night, with lights, music, and Tunisian flags waving. They were quiet Tunisian professionals in their fifties yet they went together to protest. What spurred them was draft language in the constitution about women. "They wanted to change the status of women. That women are complementary to men. No, for us, women are equal," Sarah emphasized.

The issue was that Ennahda had introduced language in the first 2012 draft of Tunisia's constitution describing women as "true partners to men in the building of the nation and as having a role complementary thereto within the family."[52]

The word "complementary" sparked a debate that shook Tunisia to its core. The implication was that women were not equal to men and that their roles were not as individuals but in relationship to men, as wives and mothers. The language also assumed that all women were married.

The process of developing the constitution turned into a national debate about the roles of women, with Tunisian women staunchly refusing restrictions on their rights, in theory or in practice. Many women viewed the draft language as a step backward or the beginning of a gradual erosion of rights. Between seven and thirty thousand women and men turned out in protest against this provision on the Avenue Bourguiba, in front of the National Assembly at the Bardo, and elsewhere in the country over the contentious word.[53]

Under both Bourguiba and Ben Ali, Tunisia had the most progressive laws toward women in the Middle East. Those laws over time led to significant roles for women in Tunisian society.

The 1956 Code of Personal Status (under Bourguiba) mandated the abolition of polygamy, ended men's privilege of unilateral divorce, enabled women to file for divorce, and enhanced women's rights to custody of their children.[54] State protection was provided for women through a national court system, rather than local religious structures. The code was updated in following years with the right to work, to open a bank account, to travel, and to establish a business—all without the permission of a husband. There were further reforms under Ben Ali, including raising the legal age of marriage to eighteen for both men and women. Later legislation removed requirements that a woman obey her husband and allowed a woman to pass her nationality to her children, where before nationality could only pass through a father. Domestic violence is penalized under the criminal code. Alone in the Middle East, Tunisian women have abortion rights.[55] (However, inheritance rights for men and women are not equal, as specifics about inheritance are proscribed in the Quran, making it difficult for the religious establishment to accept changes.[56]) All of these together were a radical set of changes that enabled a level of independence for women as well as a set of rights within the family.

These laws were one of most noted elements of Bourguiba's legacy. In the absence of a significant women's movement in Tunisia at the time, Bourguiba granted women these rights as a top-down decision. (He called the headscarf an "odious rag.") Taking his cue from Ataturk's reforms for women in Turkey, Bourguiba desired to present Tunisia to the world as a modern country, and he believed that the status of women was key to modernity.

Bourguiba believed that these changes were compatible with a liberal interpretation of Islam. He was also building on the tradition of Tahar Haddad, an Islamic scholar at the Zaytuna who had written the 1930 book *Our Women in the Shariah and Society*, arguing that incorrectly conservative interpretations of Islam inhibited both women and society.[57] Haddad wrote, "Islam is innocent of the oft-made accusations that it is an obstacle in the way of progress. Rather it is the religion of progress par excellence, an endless source of progress. Our decadence is the consequence of the chimera with which we have filled our minds and the scandalous, paralyzing customs within which we have locked ourselves."[58]

Bourguiba and Ben Ali's legal reforms set the stage for Tunisian women to make gains in education, employment, and leadership. A *Freedom House* report concluded: "Tunisian women enjoy the greatest degree of freedom in the MENA region."[59] In education, rates for primary and secondary school enrollment between the genders are about equal in Tunisia.[60] Tunisian women have higher rates of tertiary education than men (42 percent versus 27 percent), although women's employment participation is 26 percent in comparison with 71 percent for men. This is half the global labor force participation rate of women, which is 52 percent. Tunisian women also have high rates of political participation: 31 percent of Tunisia's 2015 National Assembly are women,[61] Tunisia's proportion of women parliamentarians was larger than the 2014 global average (22 percent), the proportion of women in the US Congress (19 percent), and the proportion of women in the UK Parliament (23 percent).[62]

Indeed, for my interviews for this book, Tunisia turned out to be the country where more often than in other countries, the right person to talk to about a particular issue was a woman.

For Tunisia's 2011 elections for the Constituent Assembly that would write the constitution, there was a quota to put women on political party lists: 42 out of the 49 women elected in the 217-member Constituent Assembly were from Ennahda. Eileen Byrne of *The Guardian* wrote, "When it was decided that 50 percent of parties' candidates should be women, many saw it as trying to wrong-foot An-Nahda [Ennahda]. If so, it failed spectacularly, and the Islamist party met the quota."[63]

However, these laws and changes to women's rights lacked legitimacy in some parts of Tunisian society. The profound changes that happened in the West relating to women's rights, roles, and responsibilities, happened gradually for the most part over the last century, at a time when the Islamic world was on the defensive, hunkering down and clinging to traditions as a way of resisting Western cultural dominance. Western-style women's rights came to be associated with authoritarian secular regimes, adhering too closely to Western values instead of Islamic values. Western encroachment and cultural hegemony could be resisted through the symbolism of women's rights and dress.[64]

What would happen to women when those authoritarian secular regimes left Tunisia? On the one hand, women had been empowered through education, employment, and family law, and on the other hand, those changes seemed to come partly from outside and partly from an authoritarian regime, not from organic Tunisian internal societal processes.[65]

After the protests and national dialogue about the roles of women, the language about complementarity was removed, and now Tunisia's constitution proclaims the equality of men and women: "All male and female citizens have the same rights and duties. They are equal before the law without discrimination."[66]

He Said, She Said: How to Write a Constitution

It took two years, three months, and three days to write, negotiate, and agree upon Tunisia's new constitution. The Constituent Assembly ratified the constitution in January 2014, with 200 out of 217 votes "yes." Photos of the event show a group of exultant men and women in the assembly, smiling, hugging, shaking hands, and talking with one another.[67]

Tunisia's revolution overthrew not only individuals, but also called for a new system. Indeed, Tunisia had a history of using a constitution to define the structure of government and society. Tunisia's 1860 constitution was the first constitution in the Arab world.[68]

Tunisia's new constitution has been hailed as a landmark in the Middle East for civil liberties, freedom of the press, freedom of conscience, due process, freedom of worship, and more.[69] It is groundbreaking because it balances democratic values and Islamic values. It sets an example of how an Arab country with Islamic heritage can create a democratic constitution, define the role of religion within the state, set out rights and responsibilities, and chart a path forward for elections.

The constitution was adopted despite significant cleavages between secular politicians and Islamist politicians and between moderate and conservative Islamist politicians.[70] The Constituent Assembly reached consensus even amid the turmoil in Tunisia and elsewhere in the Middle East that threatened to derail negotiations. To their great credit, Tunisian politicians stayed at the negotiating table until the job was done, bridging widely divergent initial positions.

How do you write a constitution? I met with two leaders of the Constituent Assembly to learn about the constitution's design, negotiations, and how the biggest points of contention were resolved.

Fadhel Moussa, a man with curly salt-and-pepper hair and a mustache, is dean of Tunisia's law school, the Faculté des Sciences Juridiques, Politiques et Sociales. I met him at the school, a white fin de siècle building, painted and repainted, surrounding a courtyard filled with mandarin orange trees and chatting law students.

During the drafting of the constitution, Moussa was the president of the judiciary committee. Moussa was the only committee president from an opposition party—the other five committee presidents were from

Ennahda. Moussa also served on the Joint Commission of Coordination that resolved disagreements among the six committees.

I asked him if he could describe the main points of debate in the constitution.

"The relationship between state and religion. The first and the most important," he summed up. "The problem of Ennahda is a problem of identity. They wanted to make a religious state. They understood finally that it was not possible to make it," he said.

"How did you come to consensus on all of the issues in the constitution, with such diverse political parties participating?" I asked.

All in all, he described a process of forging consensus between the Islamists and the secularists about what they had in common. Some agreements happened at the very end, even the day the constitution was signed. In the beginning, the secular opposition felt bulldozed by the majority Ennahda who were controlling committees and introducing religious language. When two opposition parliamentarians in the Constituent Assembly were assassinated by extremists, the fear of what could happen to Tunisia without agreement served as a powerful motivation for consensus.[71] "The pain and horror of the assassinations after a time brought everyone together, with a renewed understanding of the urgency to come to agreement to avoid the violent chaos that was troubling other Arab Spring countries. After that, we obtained the resolution of all the points of discord," Moussa said.

Sitting at his desk, Moussa opened up a paper booklet of the constitution and talked me through issues, point by point. He first placed his finger on Article 2, which reads: "Tunisia is a civil state that is based on citizenship, the will of the people, and the supremacy of law. This article cannot be amended."[72] He thought that this was the most important provision in the constitution.

"Why is that so important? What does it mean to be a civil state?" I asked.

"That means based on citizenship, the will of the people, not the will of God, and the supremacy of law, not the supremacy of shariah," he said. "It is not the state of the believers. It is the state of citizens," he described, emphasizing that this language allows many kinds of people with many kinds of beliefs to be Tunisians.

In referencing the will of the people, not the will of God, Moussa's comments recalled a debate within Islam about whether sovereignty of the people is acceptable. In particular, Islamist writers such as Pakistani Abul Ala Maududi and Egyptian Sayyid Qutb argued for sovereignty of God, with the state as regent, protecting God's will.[73] They argued that sovereignty of the people might lead to circumstances that were against God's will or lead to tyranny of some over others. Their writing has influenced both political Islamist groups like the Muslim Brotherhood and violent extremists.

The word "civil" was chosen rather than "secular," as "secular" has a negative connotation in much of the Middle East, where it is understood to mean being in opposition to religion. The result was that Tunisia is a "civil state" as opposed to an Islamic or secular state, and shariah law is not mentioned in the constitution as a source of legislation.

Moussa carefully emphasized, however, that this constitution does not separate religion and state. Balancing the civil state language is another statement saying that Islam is the religion of the people. "In our identity and culture, Islam is here." This was a long and difficult negotiating task with Ennahda, he explained. Tunisians defined their own version of the role of religion within the state with these provisions.

The language in the preamble about universal human rights was particularly contentious because of human rights ideas that may be counter to Islam, such as gay marriage. "This was great fighting here. They didn't accept the principle of universal human rights." Yet again, the solution was including language about the intersection of both Islam and other values. After negotiations, the preamble emphasized "the teachings of Islam" and "principles of universal human rights," side by side. It referred to multiple identities, both "our Islamic-Arab identity" and "our civilizational heritage accumulated over successive epochs of our history."

Moussa anticipated that now there would be some significant work in the courts, as cases are brought that require determining how these principles will be balanced against each other.

He next pointed to Article 6. "It guarantees freedom of conscience," he said with great pride, tapping the article on the paper with his finger several times. "There is not this mention in any other Islamic constitution in the world." He was contemplative. "We explain and interpret Islam with moderation and balance. The problem is the interpretation of

Islam. Jihadists and orthodox have their own ideas of Islam. In Tunisia, we have a soft interpretation—Islam Soft. Islam is universal. There is no difference between the ideas and values of Islam and the values of international accords."

I asked him how the constitution will prevent a return to the autocratic practices of the old regime.

"Executive power is reduced in all questions that are important in the fields of human rights and democracy," he said. He described multiple provisions designed to prevent a return to dictatorship: elections, a constitutional court with the power to impeach, and an independent judiciary. They created a set of independent constitutional bodies (an idea borrowed from South Africa) with responsibility for oversight of good governance, combatting corruption, reconciliation processes, and human rights.

Months later, however, the Truth and Dignity Commission responsible for ensuring accountability and reconciliation for the previous regime's human rights abuses and corruption was running into significant obstacles in its operations. The constitution also gives the presidency significant control over security and allows the president to take "any measures" in case of "imminent danger."[74] As I observed while meeting with Salma Elloumi, this provision risks enabling a tendency of Middle Eastern leaders to declare states of emergency for lengthy periods, using that as justification for arrests and intimidation of opposition.

With a sigh of relief, Moussa concluded, "It was very difficult to imagine that we would succeed in the beginning."

I congratulated him on the constitution, and he walked me out of the building, through the mandarin trees, and out to the street where I caught a taxi to Tunisia's National Assembly to meet Meherzia Labidi. Labidi was the vice president of the Constituent Assembly during the drafting of the constitution, and at the time held the highest elected office of any Arab woman. A member of Ennahda, she is also a coordinator of the Global Women of Faith Network and a co-president of Religions for Peace, a multi-religious forum in the United States with offices in the United Nations. She described herself as both an Islamist and a feminist, and she lived in France for twenty-five years before returning to Tunisia after the revolution.[75]

Tunisia's National Assembly is in the Bardo. Once the palace of the beys, the semi-independent rulers of Tunisia while Tunisia was part of the Ottoman Empire, it now hosts both Tunisia's National Assembly and Tunisia's national museum, with the parliament on one side and mosaics of Roman Carthage on the other (where several months after my visit, gunmen killed twenty people).

After passing through tall, swinging wrought-iron gates surrounded by razor wire and iron bars and guarded by men with guns, I entered the building. Marble floors and ceilings painted in green and red geometric and floral patterns spoke of Ottoman tastes. It was the elegance of a bygone era, made new and hopeful by new activities.

Labidi met me at the entrance, wearing a headscarf, long skirt, and suit jacket, a blend of Islamic dress and Western business attire. We wandered the halls together looking for an empty room in which to talk. As there were none, we finally sat and talked in the lobby. She lamented that while the building was beautiful, its lack of meeting rooms befitted a bey, or a dictator. It was not built for a democratic state where people need to have private meeting spaces.

"What were the main points of debate about the constitution?" I asked, as I had asked Moussa.

She brought up first the issue of women being complementary. When she herself had seen the original draft language, she had been puzzled. "When I read it, I thought it was useless. What does that mean? Also, it is dangerous because that may tell women that their role is to work at home with children." But she reflected that no one had expected that to be as controversial as it was. However, the controversy was useful. "It helped us women in general to insist that the rights and status acquired by Tunisian women are to be kept and advanced. This helped us to find consensus about mentioning parity." She pointed out with significant pride and emphasis that the constitution also commits the state to take measures to eradicate violence against women.

Labidi described debates not only with the opposition groups, but within Ennahda itself. In order to come to consensus with the secular groups, Ennahda had to have consensus on controversial issues within Islam.

"The second issue was the place of Islam in government and the place of universal human rights as a vision versus Islamic values." One of her roles as vice president of the assembly was to meet with civil society. Some civil society groups were adamant about the need to emphasize human rights, while others were adamant about the need to emphasize Islamic principles and shariah.

"When we started working on the constitution from scratch, the pressure was very, very high. The debate was very hard. There was big polarization in our society, the pro-Islamists against the pro-secularists. The development of the situation was a bit dangerous." She said that the intervention of Ennahda's leader Rached Ghanouchi was a "salvation," when as head of a movement promoting Islamic values, he made a leadership decision to remove the word "shariah," while keeping references to Islam and Arabic.

She explained that as a specialist, she knew that shariah meant a corpus of legal texts that had been used in Islamic societies. "But internationally this word has a lot of negative connotations," she said. "So it would divide our country into two groups around the constitution. We wanted the constitution to instead bring Tunisia together."

Not referencing shariah in the draft constitution, however, caused dissent among the Islamist groups. "Some parts of the grassroots said that this is a betrayal. But it was good because we led a process in Tunisia of explaining what we mean by belonging to Islam and the Arabic world. Is it a belonging that provides fences that prevent us from getting in touch with the world? Or is it flexible, with reconciliation and connection with our roots?"

These debates had implications for national dialogue in Tunisia: "All the country was drafting the constitution together at the same time. We had this opportunity to discuss the value of liberty, the meaning of dignity, of the meaning of rights. What does it mean to have freedom and liberty? What is common between us Tunisians? Is it belief? Yes or no? Officially we are mostly Muslims, but we have non-Muslims, and we have agnostics. The link between us is citizenship."

She explained how the committee charged with drafting the preamble to the constitution dealt with a debate about whether the concept of citizenship in a nation-state contradicts Islamic values, as many Muslims prefer to identify as part of the Islamic *umma,* the greater community of Muslims around the world. She recalled that one scholar on the committee reminded his colleagues that the first document of the Prophet Mohammed was the Charter of Medina, an accord between Mohammed and the tribes of Yathrib. Some scholars view the Charter of Medina as the first constitution in the Islamic world and possibly the entire world. It outlined rights and duties of citizens and described conflict resolution through law instead of tribal military action.[76]

"The document says that all citizens, Muslims, Jews, and Christians, belong to one *umma*, not based on religion but on citizenship. This discussion was an opportunity for all of us—secularists, Islamists, pan-Arabians, neutrals, half secularists, half Islamists—to create consensus," Labidi explained, making up categories of people to show the diversity and conflicts in people's views on these matters.

"I think that this process of discussion was very hard, contradictory, and conflicting. But it led all of us to a common ground," she said. "Agreement about the civil state came in next to last. It is a fruit of the maturity of our thought and discussion."

Similarly, Labidi described the debate about freedom of conscience. Ennahda had another internal party debate about that. She explained that Ghanouchi supported the freedom of conscience phrase, as belief is essentially a free act, and another colleague developed a paper describing freedom of conscience from a Quranic perspective. These internal debates created an intellectual basis for fusing Islam and human rights. These were big victories, she thought. "It is a battle that we won not only for Tunisia but for all Muslims."

Labidi noted that Tunisia has many kinds of people. There are those who pray and those who want freedom of expression to be artists. There are people who want religious symbols and those who fear them. "And all of us need to ban hatred from our speech and our behavior. It was difficult. We spent nights and nights. It is for me the emblem and the symbol of reconciliation. It reminds me of our fate to live together, to build Tunisia together, and to accept one another."

Her assistant, a man in his twenties, came up to her and whispered something. It must have been good news, because she grinned, slapped him high five, and they did a fist bump in the air.

I asked her one last question, "Is Islam having an identity crisis?"

She thought, and then said, "Islam is as diverse and conflict ridden as any other religion. What makes things more difficult for Muslims is that they are searching their way to get out of despotism and into democracy." She said that she had learned a lot from meeting Catholic women in Latin America as part of her interfaith groups, as these women had relied on their faith as a tool for liberation against oppressive dictatorships in the 1970s.

The state had used religion in dangerous ways in the Arab world, she thought. "If you look at the Arab world you can see states using Islam to either prevent people from speaking or to make people speak. The first led to despotism," she said, referring to the autocratic governments across the Middle East, "the second to chaos and violence," in reference to ISIS. "The task of me and people like my party, we said there is a third way. Let's try to reconcile Islam with democracy and human rights. Let's tell people that we are not doomed to despotism or to chaos. There is a third path that you can build and bridge with others."

"To set these bridges," Labidi continued, "we had to first set them in our head. Our process is reading Islam differently, in light of history and society, and finding the real Islamic values."

From Tunisia to Turkey

As I closed out my time in Tunisia to move on to Turkey, I understood that Tunisia had accomplished something difficult and important, both for Tunisians and as an example to other countries emerging from the Arab Spring. Despite the significant schisms within society, Tunisia stayed stable and crafted a new beginning as a country because of its commitment to pluralism and to accommodating multiple world outlooks. This commitment was not always because of shared values; at times pluralism was imposed on Tunisia because of fear. The chaos overtaking other countries was far worse than compromise. The result was negotiation, consensus building among people separated by chasms of differences, and pragmatic choices. Tunisia will face tough times ahead, however, as it struggles to ward off further violent terrorist attacks, while maintaining the civil liberties obtained with so much difficulty, and gaining accountability for past regime abuses.

My conversations and the journey through the country left me with a measured optimism that Tunisia will succeed. Its success will be fraught with conflict and frequently tenuous, but Tunisians are determined to make it work. I next headed to Turkey to understand how the nation-states in the Middle East were formed and how Turkey's protest movement fit into the Arab Spring.

Turkey

The View from Galata Bridge

The Galata Bridge spans the waters of the Golden Horn, an inlet of the Bosporus where it meets the Sea of Marmara. The bridge connects old Istanbul with the modern city. This sheltered harbor has protected ships since the days of the ancient Greeks. I stood on the bridge, a hand on the railing. Boats passed nearby, and I could hear the sounds of horns, gulls, and the clamor of the city. Rows of restaurants lined the shore, and buildings densely carpeted the hills of Istanbul around me, with ancient mosques and churches, multicolored apartments of pink and yellow grayed by pollution, red clay roofs, streets clogged with traffic, new highrises, and bustling bazaars. The face of President Recep Tayyip Erdoğan peered down from a giant billboard.

This city has been the seat of three great empires. This was the capital of the Roman Empire, then the Byzantine Empire, and then the Ottoman Empire. Istanbul ceased to be the capital of empires at the end of World War I, when the capital of the new Republic of Turkey moved to Ankara. Istanbul spans two continents, Europe and Asia, with its identity and heritage in both. Today, with 15 million people, it is the second largest city in Europe (after Moscow) and the second largest city in the Middle East (after Cairo).[1]

Turkey belongs to multiple worlds. Four cultural blocks meet and mingle here. It is the eastern edge of Europe, the western edge of the Middle East, the southwest edge of the range of the Turkic peoples who stretch from the Uyghurs in China through Central Asia to Turkey, and the northwestern edge of the home of the Kurdish people. It was once the capital of Christianity in the east, and the capital of Islam in the west. Its people speak Turkish and other minority languages, not Arabic. It is a member of NATO, and a member of the Organization of Islamic States.

It is here that the story of the modern Middle East begins.

And so the Galata Bridge is a good place to ponder the demise of empires and the formation of new countries, with great consequences for the world that still linger today, even after a century of transition.

I stood on the bridge and watched the passersby, Turks and tourists, by the sea.

Istanbul started its existence as Constantinople, founded by the Roman Emperor Constantine in 330 AD. The city of Rome was declining, and Constantine wanted a new imperial city. He didn't view himself as starting a new empire, but as moving the capital of the Roman Empire to a new location, at the time a Greek fishing village.[2] Constantine chose this site for his new capital in one of the world's most strategic locations. The water passageway through the Bosporus connects the Mediterranean with the Black Sea, connecting Europe and North Africa in a sea route with Russia.

From here by the Galata Bridge, I could see the seven hills of Istanbul. When Constantine chose the site for his new capital, these seven hills took on an almost mystical symbolism. The city of Rome had seven hills, and so the seven hills of this new location transferred a certain imperial legitimacy to it.

The Roman Empire had once commanded all of the lands around the Mediterranean, including Western Europe, North Africa, and today's Middle East. When it became too big to govern, Roman leaders split it in two administratively. Over time, the Western European part of the Roman Empire declined into the dark ages. The eastern part of the Roman Empire continued flourishing; today's historians view the empire that continued from Constantinople as capital of a new empire, the Byzantine Empire. But residents of Constantinople called their city Rome and viewed themselves as Romans. Constantinople was a Christian city, the capital of the Orthodox Church. The Byzantine Empire lasted a thousand years here.

In 1453, the Ottoman sultan Mehmet the Conqueror captured Constantinople. He viewed it as taking Rome and saw himself, the leader of the Muslim world, as successor to the caesars. He renamed the city Istanbul and declared it the new capital of the Ottoman Empire.

As I walked along the bridge, I contemplated monuments of great empires on Istanbul's seven hills. The Hagia Sophia, the Church of the Holy Wisdom, was the crowning artistic and religious monument of the Christian church in the east. The Süleymaniye Mosque perches on another hill. On another is Topkapı Palace, the seat of the Ottoman sultans' might and culture. Once the glory of empires, these buildings are now museums.

Today the skyline, with densely built buildings and thick tree growth, somewhat obscures the shapes of the seven hills.

The Ottoman Empire collapsed, but Turkey has rebounded. Other countries that were once part of the empire have not done as well. Nations that were born from the death of the Ottoman Empire continued on similar paths. After establishing themselves as separate countries, rather than provinces of the Ottoman Empire, many became colonies, "mandates," or "protectorates" of Britain or France. Independence from European colonial powers came in the 1940s to 1960s. Autocratic governments came to power in some Arab countries, initially as reformists pushing through difficult changes for their countries. But over time, leaders and their successors lost momentum, maintaining autocratic government but doing little to develop their societies, resulting in stagnation. The Arab Spring movements collectively challenged that old order and demanded a new order, a change in the relationship between governments and their people.

I exited the bridge, weaving through the crowds, leaving the Galata neighborhood and passing into Eminönü, as people have been doing for fifteen hundred years. Men stood at the railing of the bridge with fishing lines hanging into the sea. Tourists took pictures. A truck stopped, offloading goods meant for the line of cafes tucked under the bridge, with crates of eggs, lemon juice, tins of sunflower oil, a big vat of tomato paste, and boxes of chickpeas. Many things are the same here on Galata Bridge as they were during the peak of Ottoman might.

Hugging Trees in Gezi Park and Taksim Square

"To understand Turkey's protests, you have to go back to the Ottomans," said Korhan Gümüş.

Gümüş is sixty but looks to be in his late forties, with salt-and-pepper hair and dressed in a rumpled T-shirt and jeans. He is an architect, civil activist, and host of "Metropolitika," a radio show on civic and local participation in Istanbul. He has taught at universities, written for newspapers and architectural reviews, testified before the European Union Parliament, and served as a spokesperson for Turkey's protests to international newspapers.[3]

He is also one of the founders of the Taksim Platform. The civil disobedience of Gümüş and fifty or so others from the Taksim Platform in May 2013 and their subsequent violent eviction by the Turkish police set off wider protests throughout Turkey, involving 3.5 million people out of Turkey's population of 82 million.[4] What were they protesting? Gümüş and the others were protesting an urban development plan for Taksim Square—by hugging trees. The trees, in Taskim Square's Gezi Park, were about to be chopped down as part of that plan.

Turkey's 2013 protests happened after the 2011 wave of Arab Spring protests in other countries, and they did not result in the same levels of upheaval as elsewhere.

We sat in an elegant, Art Deco–style museum café, with a mirrored bar and marble floors. It was just off of Istiklal Street, a wide pedestrian thoroughfare packed with shops, restaurants, meandering people from all over the world, and vendors of mussels and roasted chestnuts—the heart of modern Istanbul. Istiklal Street flows through city blocks of the Beyoğlu neighborhood, emptying out into Taksim Square, the site of the beginning of Turkey's protests.

We shared a pot of rosehip tea, in a red velvet upholstered booth near a grand piano.

"So how do you go from the Ottomans to trees in Gezi Park?" I asked. I remembered watching the news about Turkey's protests from afar and feeling puzzled. While Arab Spring protesters in the other countries were justifying their protests on the basis of government repression and the need for new models of democracy, protesters in Turkey were talking about their public parks.

"This was not an environmental conflict. It was a sociopolitical struggle," he explained.

Gümüş sat back in his chair, and then he told me the history of Taksim Square. Taksim Square has been a site of political protests and challenges to the government for civic improvements since 1909, when clashes occurred between those backing the Ottoman sultan's power and those backing a system of constitutional monarchy with a parliament. In the decades before the Ottoman collapse, its citizens compared former Ottoman preeminence with growing Ottoman weakness and European cultural, trade, and military dominance. The conclusion among many was the need to modernize Ottoman institutions and introduce European-style constitutions and military. Thus ensued decades of power struggles between a weakened sultan and other forces, like youth movements (such as the Committee on Union and Progress, followed by the Young Turks), not so different from events today.

On multiple occasions since that time a century ago, Taksim Square has been a stage with potent symbolism where clashes of ideas over the course of Turkey's history and direction have taken place. The square has been host to a succession of protests and demonstrations. Taksim Square has gained a political identity of its own. Whoever rules Taksim Square rules Turkey.

"It is because of this that Erdoğan wanted to get rid of it and create a smaller public space for protests," he continued.

At issue was that the urban planning changes would reduce people's ability to congregate, removing an instrumental center for social change. Plans to redesign the square included additional buildings and a system of channel tunnels to redirect traffic. This would reduce pedestrian access to the square. In addition, plans would remove an opera house, replacing it with a mosque. Replacing the opera house with a mosque in Taksim symbolized whose values were ascendant in Turkey: those who want to identify with their European heritage or those who want to identify with their Islamic heritage. "There are two movements in Turkey, Islamist and secularist, and there is tension between those two," Gümüş said.

Indeed, for much of Turkey's recent history, this tension of identities

has defined it and defined its national struggles, ambitions, and problems.[5]

Following the fall of the Ottoman Empire after World War I, Mustafa Kemal Ataturk took the reins of Turkey to steer it out of defeat. Ataturk
gave Turks their pride back, fueled the economy, mandated education, and
implemented European cultural and legal reforms. Ataturk steered Turkey away from the Islamic world and toward Europe. He separated mosque
and state, abolished the sultanate and the caliphate, a revered Islamic institution that had existed for thirteen hundred years. He created a culture
of Kemalism, in which the military safeguarded secularism and progress
from a perceived backward and threatening Islam. Ataturk set the example for Arab leaders in the subsequent generation around the Middle
East.

Not all of Turkey loved this new direction. The last half century of
Turkey's history has been an identity tug-of-war between Kemalist secularists, pulling toward Europe, and traditionalists pulling toward Islam,
with the secularists having the upper hand until recently. Three times Turkey's
military conducted coups against elected governments that it perceived as
either too Islamic or incompetent. Over time, the Kemalist secularists
came to be viewed as repressive and undemocratic.[6]

In 2003, through a seemingly unlikely alliance between Islamists and
liberal democrats who wanted more participation and less repression for all
parts of Turkish society, Receep Tayyip Erdoğan became prime minister,
when his Justice and Development Party, an Islamist political party known
by their Turkish acronym as the AK Party, came to power in a decisive election. This model of "moderate Islamic government" succeeded for Turkey
as the AK Party focused on the economy, EU membership, improving
minority rights, and public services. But today a stark cultural divide has
grown once again in Turkey, between those who feel threatened by the
AK Party's direction (perceiving it both as authoritarian and too Islamic)
and those who like the stability, economic prosperity, and conservative values of the AK Party. And while the AK Party was elected with high hopes
that it would bring tolerance and participation to government, there is a
growing sense among many in Turkey that now the AK Party is ruling
with the same, or worse, authoritarian tendencies as the Kemalist secularists,
with comparisons made between Erdoğan and Vladimir Putin in Russia.

"I had wanted the Islamists to reform Turkey," Gümüş said, "but no."

In August 2014 presidential elections, Erdoğan was elected president (before he had held the position of prime minister) with 52 percent of the vote. Half the country supported him, while the other half felt alienated by the directions he was pursuing. Showing further signs of cracks in his support and longevity, his AK Party lost the majority in June 2015 parliamentary elections, but regained the majority in November 2015 elections.[7] Losing the majority would have meant that Erdoğan would not likely be able to follow through with his plans to change Turkey's constitution to further strengthen the power of the presidency.

Gümüş leaned forward. "But the protests were not about struggle between the secularists and Islamists." Rather, the protests were about how decisions about the use of public space were made in an authoritarian way, without a participatory process. And then when the police cracked down violently on the initial protests, the nationwide protests were about how the government treated the protesters.

To clarify, Gümüş narrated how the protests started. In May 2013, trees were cut down to build the mosque. Gümüş and fifty other people went to Gezi Park. In a show of passive resistance, they hugged trees to prevent more of them from being chopped down. The police came and evicted them with tear gas and clubs.

"You've seen the photo of the woman with the red dress?" he said, referring to a photo that became an iconic symbol of the struggle. A dark haired woman in a red dress stands still, while a policeman with a facemask sprays her with tear gas.[8] The photo looks disturbingly like the famous photo of Marilyn Monroe, coyly holding her white dress down while it is wafted by an air vent—only this woman's lovely red dress and hair are being blown by tear gas. "She's my friend. All she was doing was standing there and reading a book, and the police attacked her."

Gümüş said that he didn't resist the police when they came to cut down the trees. He didn't throw anything. He left. But other people were hit and sprayed with tear gas. After that, protesters wore helmets.

A new wave of protesters came out to support them, reacting both to calls for protecting the environment by saving Gezi Park's trees and against the government's behavior with the initial protesters.

"Everyone was side by side," Gümüş said, making a gesture of linking arms and walking together. "It was a confrontation with the political system." Protesters were from all walks of life. There were men and women, old and young, secular people and pious Muslims, and Istanbul's gay community. It had all started with a group of architects and urban planners defending a public space associated with their set of values, but then many other people joined.

Film footage from the protests sometimes looks like a giant street party, with twenty-somethings dancing in the streets and sleeping in tents. Erdoğan derided the youthful protesters as a few "looters," or *çapulcu* in Turkish, leading the protesters to reclaim the label of "chapulling" for themselves, to mean fighting for their rights.[9] A YouTube video of Turkish youth protesters dancing in the streets to the lyrics "every day I'm shufflin'" from LMFAO's "Party Rock Anthem" went viral; they called their parody "Every Day I'm Chapulling."

At other times, interactions between protesters and police were violent, with film footage looking like a war zone, with smoke and fire.[10] Over the course of the protests in May and June of 2013, an estimated eight thousand people were injured, with five deaths. There were nearly five thousand detentions. Police used water cannons, pepper spray, and tear gas.[11]

Turkey's 2013 protests came two years after the first round of 2011 Arab Spring protests, but during the same summer that Egypt had its second round of mass protests, leading to the military overthrow Egypt's democratically elected Muslim Brotherhood president, Mohammed Morsi.

In observing the regional protests associated with Arab Spring and government overthrows, the government of Turkey overreacted in its treatment of the tree huggers. It responded to Turkey's protests as an issue of national security rather than as part of a democratic process of freedom of assembly, further inflaming the situation.

Finally, under pressure, Erdoğan convened a group of protesters and met with them. Gümüş was invited to the meeting with Erdoğan, but he didn't go because at the time he was testifying to the European Parliament about what had been happening. He later met with the minister of justice, the mayor of Istanbul, and AK Party leaders about the protests.

"Observers debate whether Turkey's protests were part of the same movement as Arab Springs elsewhere," I said.[12] "Were Turkey's protests part of the Arab Spring?" I asked.

"Yes. Obviously," Gümüş said. "Before May 28, it was about trees. After, it became something else."

"What did the protests accomplish then?" I asked.

Gümüş shrugged and put his hands palm up in the air, in a questioning gesture that I interpreted as meaning "not much." He seemed resigned and disappointed. Taksim Square was left alone for the time being and not redeveloped. The trees are still there. But people were no longer allowed to gather and protest on Istiklal or Taksim.

Gümüş thought that the events had brought attention to the need for democratic rights, greater citizen participation, and rule of law in Turkey. "There are a lot of people who think we have problems with democracy," he said. "It reduced Erdoğan's legitimacy. He is afraid now. Now, with all of the media looking, he has lost legitimacy."

Many said that the protests led to greater solidarity in Turkey and a greater awareness of democratic possibilities.[13] The later 2015 parliamentary elections in which Erdogan's AK Party lost its majority demonstrated that, at least temporarily, Erdogan's autocratic behavior had weakened his appeal. Erdogan had been around a long time. Turkey's democracy was robust enough to express that disapproval through peaceful elections.

We finished our tea, stood up, shook hands, and said goodbye. Gümüş said in parting, "You can't transform society with such violence. This regime is not working. We need justice."

I walked from Istiklal Street to Taksim Square, a large, open, paved square. People crossed from side to side on their way from wherever to wherever. A woman in a black abaya was feeding about thirty pigeons. A girl walked by with a skirt and a midriff-baring shirt. I couldn't help being reminded what a mixing bowl Turkey is between East and West, an identity struggle played out visually in how women dress.

I exited the square to walk into Gezi Park, whose endangered trees had led to the skirmishes. I sat down at an outdoor cafe, on a tree-lined patio, with red awnings emblazoned with Coca-Cola signs. Waiters brought out trays of tea and sugar to the tables. On the grass around me, people took naps, sat, and contemplated the world. A woman with her back to a tree wrote in a journal. A few men sat on the grass with some suitcases, on a hill looking out over the buildings of the city. Across from me was a children's playground with bright red, yellow, green, and blue plastic slides. This was a nice place to sit in the breeze, under eucalyptus trees with peeling bark. Sitting here, I could see office buildings, a balloon seller, and a great historic mosque.

It was here that all the fuss started. But was this really part of the Arab

Spring? Well, for starters, Turkey is not Arab. The Turks are a separate ethnic group and speak Turkish, not Arabic. But they have the same cultural heritage, were part of the same empire until a century ago, and share a similar recent history of modernizing, secularizing, and Westernizing, enforced by authoritarianism.

It has a nice poetic ring, Tahrir Square to Taksim Square, with a similarity in names between Egypt's protest square and Turkey's protest square that leads to easy oversimplification. Perhaps because the names are so similar, people mistake them for one and the same, part of the same pattern and symptoms of the same problems. Perhaps it was because of this that Erdoğan's government overreacted and teargassed a group of urban planning activists, mistaking them for the youth movements that overthrew governments elsewhere. Each of the protest movements in the Middle East was unique, with its own, causes, patterns, and effects. In their uniqueness, they called for different kinds of responses from their governments and the rest of the world.

Turkey's protests have sometimes been compared with the Occupy Wall Street movement in the United States; that is not the most accurate comparison either. As I sat in Gezi Park and pondered Turkey's protests, the protests over police behavior in Ferguson, Missouri, were happening in my own country. There, people were out in the streets, violently smashing car and shop windows and looting. The police overreacted, coming out with military gear and arresting journalists; these police actions were later condemned. These are nation-wrenching events, but they are also part of democracy. In Ferguson, a disenfranchised group of people felt angry and took to the streets. In keeping the peace, the police overreacted and made serious mistakes, with levels of violence and treatment of the press that might be more expected in a country like Iran. Events led to a national discussion both about the issues of the protest (race relations) and the comportment of the police. And yet, the Ferguson and Occupy Wall Street protests were not about overthrowing the government, but about expressing collective rage and demanding change—within the current governmental system.

I went out and walked around Istiklal Street. As Istanbul's main nightlife thoroughfare and shopping district, it felt like a European pedestrian mall, with thousands of people out, walking, eating at restaurants, and window shopping. Street vendors sold children's remote-controlled flying airplanes. One vendor blew bubbles that floated through the air all around me. Massive posters of a politician hugging a baby hung from a building. Lights were strung along the street. The people were a mix—people in Western summer clothes, Syrian refugee beggars, and women in long Islamic dress. Shops sold ice cream, grilled meats, stewed vegetables, baklava, and the cheese-sweet *kunefe*. Along with Turkish designer clothes, there were brands I recognized, like Mango, Nike, and the Body Shop.

This used to be Istanbul's embassy district before the Ottoman Empire fell. It is filled with old embassies, now consulates, and Ottoman-era schools, some undergoing renovation. This street, with its European—rather than Ottoman—architecture, represented European cultural and political power that was pervading the city in the waning days of the Ottoman Empire. I wanted to go back to the height of Ottoman power to understand the empire at its greatest. I next went to Topkapı Palace.

Courtyards of Topkapı Palace

In May 1453, the nineteen-year-old Ottoman sultan known now as Mehmet the Conqueror rode triumphantly into Constantinople on a white horse.[14] He had conquered the city, after a militarily impressive campaign that involved building stone castles in record time, hauling ships overland on rollers, and building the world's biggest cannon. It was a turning point in history.

For much of its thousand-year history, Constantinople had been the wealthiest and most sophisticated city in Europe.[15] A complex society that drew from pagan, Christian, Greek, Roman, and medieval heritages, the Byzantine Empire had developed an imperial court with a diplomatic service and civilian bureaucracy, the female exercise of power, highly sophisticated military tactics, technology and engineering skills that built on Roman knowledge, a legal system with the rule of law, a secular education system, reliable trade routes, and a ubiquitous currency. Its imperial palace had been the largest in the Christian world, and its great church, the Hagia Sophia, was the largest church in Christendom for a millennium.

But in 1453, the Byzantine Empire was in turmoil. Weakened by Catholic crusaders from Venice who sacked the city in 1204 (Constantinople was Orthodox, a good excuse for sacking at the time), plundered its inestimable heritage and treasures, and made blood flow through the streets, Constantinople had never recovered. Into this power vacuum moved the Ottomans, nomadic Muslim Turkic tribes named after a tribal leader named Osman. Over a few generations, the Ottomans slowly conquered all of Anatolia and much of the Balkans. When Mehmet the Conqueror took Constantinople, it was no longer the majestic city it had once been. Its population had shrunk from its peak of 500,000 to 800,000 in 1000 AD to 40,000 by the fifteenth century.[16]

Mehmet looked over the ruins of the Byzantine imperial palace, with its statues looted and the lead on the roof already used to mint coins. With sadness over the rise and fall of empires before him, he recited lines from a Persian poet:

> The spider serves as gatekeeper in the halls of the Caesars.
> The owl calls the watches in the palace of Afrasyab.[17]

Painted portraits of Mehmet show a man with a short auburn beard, aquiline nose, intense eyes, a voluminous white turban, and flowing blue and brown robes—but with ringed fingers, holding a delicate flower to his nose and sniffing. The portrait gives the impression of both fierceness and refinement at the same time.

Conquering Constantinople had been a dream of Muslims since the founding of Islam. Constantinople represented imperial power and global success. There is even a hadith (a saying) attributed to the Prophet Mohammed: "Verily you shall conquer Constantinople. What a wonderful leader will her leader be, and what a wonderful army will that army be!"[18] Now, as events in Iraq and Syria unfold with ISIS filling a power vacuum and conquering territory with terror, ISIS made statements about (unrealistic) ambitions to take Rome, which meant Istanbul, echoing early Islamic leaders' desire to conquer Constantinople.[19]

Ottoman sultans who came after Mehmet the Conqueror kept up the expansion of the empire, moving further into Europe and North Africa and conquering the Holy Land, including Mecca, Medina, and Jerusalem. A later Ottoman sultan took title of caliph after conquering Mecca.

Mehmet wanted to rebuild a great capital; he built mosques, public baths, the Grand Bazaar, and many other buildings. Then he built Topkapı Palace, home to the Ottoman sultans for much of their five-hundred-year rule. It was a city of its own on more than 173 acres, with ten mosques, two hospitals, five schools, and twelve libraries. Its kitchens fed at least five thousand people per day and sometimes up to fifteen thousand. It had three courtyards and a harem. Moving from the outermost public courtyard to the innermost was getting closer to the center of power and to the person of the sultan himself. The palace represented the might of the empire.

The Ottoman Empire was a huge multinational, multilingual, multi-continental, multi-religious empire. It was an empire of contradictions. On the one hand, it conquered many peoples, but on the other hand, it was tolerant, allowing a variety of religious practices, including Christianity and Judaism, with much more tolerance than Europe allowed its minorities. It grew from its military might, but it was known for its just laws. As it conquered, it adopted the cultures of the vanquished.

I entered the gates and walked to the Divan, the meeting hall where the grand vizier (the sultan's chief minister) held meetings. In its two domed rooms, affairs of state were discussed. Debates took place under the first dome. Decisions were made in the second room. The rooms were small, built for intimate discussions. The dome represented the universe, and a hanging globe represented Ottoman dominance. Golden grills on the doors allowed in natural light that played on marble floors. Sofas lined the walls. Ceilings were painted in a floral pattern, and hand-painted Iznik tile of red, blue, and green adorned the walls.

Suleiman the Magnificent, viewed as the greatest Ottoman sultan, had built the Divan. He reigned over the empire for forty-six years at its peak. Inheriting the throne in 1520 at the age of twenty-six, he oversaw military expansion and conquest, a cultural and architectural renaissance, and the development of tax collection and a legal system based on precedent, case law, and Islam, and in compatibility with Christian tradition. With a powerful navy of two hundred ships, the Ottomans vied with Spain for control of the Mediterranean. Suleiman the Magnificent was the sultan who threatened the gates of Vienna. There is a popular Turkish soap opera, watched in the Balkans and the Middle East, about Suleiman, his harem, and the love of his life, Roxelana.

In the next courtyard was a school where the *devşirme* were educated. *Devşirme* were boys, typically from the Christian Balkan villages ruled by the Ottomans, taken in childhood from their families, converted to

Islam, and raised as soldiers. These boys became Janissaries, soldiers in Europe's first standing army. When the Ottomans first conscripted boys for the Janissaries, the boys were dragged off, to the grief of their families. But over time, the path of the *devşirme* became prestigious. Some rose to become high-ranking officials in the palace or administrators in their homelands. There was intense physical training and education in languages, administration, arts, law, and history. The idea was to educate an elite class of warriors with loyalty to the sultan and with the skills to become the leadership in the military and government of the Ottoman Empire. This meritocratic military enabled the Ottomans to conquer the lands around them.[20]

Meritocracy enabled the empire to thrive for centuries.

The Janissaries as an institution came to an abrupt end when Sultan Mahmud II had them all slaughtered in 1826, after the Janissaries had become too powerful, corrupt, and rebellious.

I passed out of the third courtyard and into the harem, where the sultan lived with his concubines, mother, and other female relatives. It was both a bastion of luxury and of human weirdness.

The harem is a maze of three hundred rooms with hand-painted blue tiles of flowers and geometric patterns, carved wooden cabinets inlaid with mother of pearl, painted walls and ceilings, fireplaces decorated with tile or carefully wrought metal, and marble floors. It is beautiful and luxurious, but also feels like a prison. There were often three to five hundred women in the harem, educated in music, dance, languages, and manners. Mothers of sultans became quite powerful, in particular when their young sons came to power and they could serve as regent. The harem was guarded by "black eunuchs," boys who had been taken as slaves from Africa, castrated, and raised in the palace to guard the women.

The Ottoman sultans preserved an unbroken line of succession for ten generations through a system of royal fratricide.[21] Upon taking the throne, a new sultan had his brothers put to death to forestall infighting about succession. While brutal, this system was stable and lasted for several centuries. The Ottoman Empire did not undergo the wars of succession that European kingdoms experienced.

After Sultan Mehmet III had nineteen half-siblings killed upon his succession, with coffins of dead royal babies coming in procession out of Topkapı Palace, society expressed outrage at the practice and it ended.

After that time, sons and brothers of sultans were raised and lived inside the palace, which was called the Golden Cage, so that they posed no threat to the Sultan. Isolated inside the harem while growing up, sultans from that time forward lacked the leadership skills of their predecessors. Some were mentally unstable.

Over time the empire decayed. There were a number of reasons. Raised in the Golden Cage, the Sultan stopped being a mighty warrior king. The Ottoman military declined when the Janissaries became corrupt over time and then were killed. The Ottomans failed to modernize military tactics and technology and started losing wars. The government administration also became corrupt and weak. Nationalist movements in the Balkans led to wars and the splintering off of what are now Bosnia, Kosovo, Macedonia, Greece, and Croatia. Britain took control of Egypt, and France took control of Tunisia and Algeria. The Ottomans failed to develop their economy. The building of the sultan's new Dolmabahçe Palace, with heights of extravagance such as a long staircase with a crystal balustrade, led to the government's declaring bankruptcy in 1876 and the financial control of the empire by European creditors. There were economic crises. There were political crises.

The Ottoman Empire became known as the Sick Man of Europe.

In World War I the Ottoman Empire was defeated and its territories carved up and partitioned into the collection of countries that today we know as the Middle East and the Balkans.

During World War I, from his office in London, Winston Churchill salivated over attacking the Ottoman Empire and conquering Istanbul. He said, "This is one of the great campaigns of history. Think what Constantinople is to the East. It is more than London, Paris, and Berlin rolled into one are to the West. Think how it has dominated the East. Think what its fall will mean."[22]

Its fall has meant a century of instability in the Balkans and Middle East. And Istanbul, the once mighty capital, decayed, but it is coming back.

A Neighborhood Walk through Beyoğlu

I walked through the streets of Beyoğlu, from Istiklal Street gradually down the hill toward the sea, following small winding streets wherever they took me and getting happily lost. The streets were filled with antique shops, cafés, and fruitsellers, as well as artsy boutiques, with modern interpretations of Ottoman furniture and cloth. I stopped at a fruit stand and bought figs and blackberries. Scents of dill filled my nose near a stand piled high with fresh vegetables. Dill is to the Turks as basil is to the Italians.

I passed a tall rickety wooden building with a window jutting out into the street, what had once been a typical Ottoman house. It looked like it was going to fall down. The sun was getting low.

Beyoğlu is Istanbul's district of art, entertainment, and nightlife. I was seeking the Beyoğlu of Orhan Pamuk, Turkey's Nobel Prize winner in literature. He grew up in this neighborhood. His book *Istanbul* is a meditation on the city and a meditation on his own life. He writes of *hüzün*, a melancholy of living amid the ruins of a great empire, of understanding that only a few generations ago his forebears lived with pride, dignity, achievements, and the beauty of a long civilization. His generation lived with the sadness of its remains, knowing what they did not have and living amid disrepair. He wrote, "We might call this confused, hazy state melancholy, or perhaps we should call it by its Turkish name, *hüzün*, which denotes a melancholy that is communal, rather than private."[23] He depicted a collective emotion that hung over the city, a city of defeat and decay. It was a tension that came from living in a time of transition from one civilization to the next.

As I walked, I sought this feeling of *hüzün*. But I didn't feel it.

Granted, the neighborhood was in need of a good paint job. Parts were dilapidated and some buildings were empty. Buildings that must have been splendid two hundred years ago were now coated with the grime of an ancient and massive city. Pamuk described old buildings that had once been gaily painted bright colors: "Poverty and neglect had ensured that these houses were never painted, and the combination of age, dirt, and humidity slowly darkened the wood . . . As a child, I would sometimes imagine painting all these houses."

Now instead of *hüzün*, I felt a vibrancy and creativity in the streets. I saw a people on the move. On Istiklal, thousands of people walked up and down the street, shopping, eating. There was bustling business at kebab restaurants, with families and friends enjoying the evening.

The cafés, shops, and restaurants in the old neighborhoods were all unique, set up lovingly by individuals. I passed a façade painted in a pink leopard pattern and a little café decorated in what must look like a Turkish grandma's style of lace and dark furniture. As I walked, I could see cobblestones underneath broken asphalt.

Here, I did not see sadness or defeat, but an up-and-coming middle-income city. There was an energy here, a rebirthing of an artsy, urban city center.

What has changed in Istanbul? Pamuk's memoir is about his youth of a few decades ago in the 1960s and 1970s, and perhaps then Istanbul was a sadder place. But now, the economy was booming. Construction was on the rise. Turkey was coming back to life, rebounding from being an empire in defeat to being an Anatolian Tiger. Soner Çağaptay, the director of the Turkish Research Program at the Washington Institute for Near East Policy, wrote, "Over the past decade, however, a new Turkey has awakened, built by unprecedented political stability, domestic growth and commercial and political clout overseas. This sea change has instilled a sense of global confidence in the Turkish people not seen since Suleiman the Magnificent ruled in Constantinople."[24]

I wandered down to the seaside, scavenging food as I went—a grilled mackerel in a brown paper bag, mussels stuffed with spiced rice from a vendor, and hazelnuts. I walked through multiple neighborhoods, some timeworn and some renovated, just a few blocks from each other. Then I crossed the bridge over the Golden Horn and walked along the waters in the Eminönü neighborhood, with boats and gulls and kids playing.

Even Orhan Pamuk acknowledged the beauty and joy by the sea. He wrote, "If the city speaks of defeat, destruction, deprivation, melancholy, and poverty, the Bosphorus sings of life, pleasure, and happiness." And Turkey's former wealth and power was growing again. Awakening, Turkey was shedding its *hüzün*. Other parts of the city attested to that.

17.2 Kilometers per Hour Up Sapphire Tower

I took the elevator up to the fifty-fourth floor of Sapphire Tower at 17.2 kilometers per hour, according to the computer screen in the elevator. At 890 feet, Istanbul's Sapphire Tower is the seventh tallest building in Europe. Where I exited the elevator, a sign greeted me with impressive statistics about how the building used 108,000 square meters of concrete, 168 km of pipes, 29,000 tons of iron, and other fun construction facts.

At the top of the building is an observation deck, an area with glass walls and no roof. I circumnavigated it, with a 360-degree perspective on Istanbul below. I could see bridges over the Bosporus, the strategic waterway cutting through rolling hills carpeted with apartment blocks, parks, highways, skyscrapers, and heritage, connecting the Mediterranean and Russia. Below me were tennis courts, cars moving along new highways like strings of ants, and housing developments, with ubiquitous red clay roofs. The Turkish flag waved on many a pole. Below was a construction site with the foundation being dug in a deep, water-filled mud pit.

Here in the Levent District, one of Istanbul's two main financial and business districts, were seventy-one skyscrapers and high rises.[25] Across a parade of highways was the competing business district, Maslak, also a cluster of skyscrapers.

It is easy to get lost in Turkey's past, wandering through heritage of mosques, old stone, and palaces. But here is modern Turkey. Its $800 billion economy makes it the seventeenth biggest economy in the world.[26] From 2010 to 2011, it was the fastest growing economy in Europe, with 9 percent GDP growth per year.[27] Per capita GDP rose from $5,000 in 2003 to $11,000 in 2013, putting Turkey in the upper ranks of middle-income countries.[28] Istanbul ranks fourth in the world in number of billionaires, coming after Moscow, New York, and London, and before Los Angeles.[29] During the last decade, its so-called economic miracle has been fueled by construction, manufacturing, agriculture, the financial sector, and tourism.

Such prosperity is recent. In 2001, Turkey's economy collapsed in crisis.[30] In a single year, the Turkish economy shrank 9.5 percent. Turkey's financial crisis was resolved both through an IMF bailout loan and an economic plan that involved public spending cuts, bringing inflation under control, introducing a floating exchange rate, and banking reforms.

Now, Turkey has become a strong, important economy. This is a major success that the AK Party, and Erdoğan, can take credit for. Turkey is no longer a financial charity case.

Perhaps Turkey's Spring was not about protests and government overthrow, but an emerging economy and a country growing in confidence in the past decade.

Despite these successes, there are significant risks to Turkey's economy.[31] In 2012, Turkey's economic growth slowed to 2 percent, having overheated in the preceding years. While Erdoğan makes optimistic statements about the future of the economy, other observers predict anything from a slowing down of the economy, to getting stuck in a low-growth middle-income trap, a coming decade of a boom-bust cycle, or a dramatically burst bubble with ramifications for the world economy.[32]

There are three main risks, some related to the social causes that led people to protest. The first risk was perception of growing authoritarianism and corruption. While Erdoğan's strong hand in public life was once thought to bring stability and growth, now it could be holding Turkey back.[33] Its censored and self-censoring media cannot pull its weight in bringing public issues, including economic issues, to the fore for discussion and solution.

The second risk affects youth and women—fundamental structural weaknesses in the economy. It is not clear that Turkey has what is needed in place for growth from value-added sectors, like technology. Its education system is among the weakest in Europe, although among the best in the Middle East.[34] Only about half of working age adults participate in the workforce, in comparison with the average of 68 percent in the Organization for Economic Cooperation and Development (OECD—an organization of mainly European and North American countries). One reason for this has been gender inequality: Turkey ranks 120 out of 136 countries in gender equality, according to a World Economic Forum Report, with women representing only 23 percent of the nonagricultural workforce.[35]

The third risk comes from Turkey's reliance on foreign investment and debt. This is cause for concern; for example, a reason for the 1997 Asian financial crisis was money flowing too quickly in and out of capital markets.

As I admired the view from the fifty-fourth floor of Sapphire Tower, I wondered whether Turkey was a sustainably emerging economic dynamo or a country headed for a slowing or even a fall if it continued in its autocratic direction. Can Turkey sustain this prosperity?

I got ready to leave Sapphire Tower, and took a final lap around the periphery. Against one glass wall, two women in headscarves and overcoats took pictures of each other with Istanbul's skyline in the background. One of them posed for a picture with her hands just so in the air, so that the photo would look like she was holding a mosque on the horizon in her manicured fingertips.

Hürriyet Daily News

Turkey has more journalists in prison than China or Iran.[36] Forty journalists are in prison in Turkish jails, most of them ethnic Kurds imprisoned under an antiterrorism law. Fifty-nine journalists were fired in the wake of coverage of the Gezi Park protests.[37] Freedom House, a U.S. organization that researches democracy and political freedom, reports that the government of Turkey uses a number of tactics to produce a docile media, including mass firings, buying off or forcing out media moguls, wiretapping of journalists, and imprisonment. Reporters Without Borders ranks Turkey 149 out of 180 countries in the world in its 2015 World Press Freedom Index, ranking right before the Democratic Republic of Congo.[38] Turkey's media has a reputation for being bullied and acquiescent to pressure from the government. During Turkey's protests, CNN Turk played a documentary about penguins, while CNN International covered the protests live from Taksim Square. That stunt was called out with ironic chiding for the cowardice of Turkey's media, and so penguins became a symbol on T-shirts of the protests in Turkey.

I had previously interviewed one Turkish journalist who didn't want to be named about pressure on the media. Frustrated, he said, "The quality of journalism is decreasing every day because of the political environment. The media is reflecting the government's points of view and statements. They publish excerpts from the president—they quote, quote, quote, quote without any context. It is not journalism. It is being a messenger. The media has lost its independence, when it should be part of organic political life." He thought that it had been better in the 1990s.

One example of media pressure is on Doğan Media, which founded *Hürriyet Daily News* in 1961 as Turkey's first English-language daily newspaper. It has a strong reputation both within and outside Turkey as analytic. When Doğan Media's 2008 coverage of Erdoğan's corruption scandal proved to be too critical, the government smacked a $2.5 billion tax liability on the media group, nearly as much as the value of the holding company.[39] This was widely viewed as a retaliatory attempt to silence it. After legal wrangling, they are still paying back the fines.[40]

Barçin Yinanç is the opinion editor at *Hürriyet Daily News*. I met her at the Doğan Media Holding building in Istanbul. She spent ten years as a diplomatic reporter for *Milliyet* newspaper, then shifted to broadcasting at CNN Turk, and then went back to print at *Hürriyet Daily News*. She is an elegant woman, with full curly black hair and multiple rings, necklaces, and bracelets. She wore a beige pencil skirt and sleeveless shirt that revealed toned biceps.

We passed through an open newsroom with gray floors and gray Formica furniture, with people writing on computers in an open seating plan. We entered an office decked out with minimalist gray furniture and plants. I explained my book and told her that I was trying to understand journalism, democracy, and the Arab Spring in Turkey.

I asked her about journalistic freedom and if she personally felt any pressure. She paused and chose her words carefully. "We live in a restricted environment," she said. "We are very careful in the coverage of the news. The structure in the media has changed. The majority of the media is in the hands of businesspeople who are very close to the government. I don't think we saw that in pre–AK Party Turkey." She said that the strategy of the AK Party was to choke the old mainstream media, to make them "shrink." But then she added, "Although we shrank, we are still influential."

Yinanç wanted to add perspective to criticisms of pressure on the media in Turkey. "But when you ask about pressure, I feel this is asking about physical violence. Let's differentiate. We are not talking about a Russia or a Burma situation where journalists are beaten or physically harassed. There is not such a situation here," she said. (Although later in 2015, riot police had to defend *Hürriyet*'s headquarters after an angry mob descended upon it and broke its windows, incited by denunciations by AK Party politicans.[41])

Yinanç paused again. "I still think that Turkey is a success story. We have setbacks. We are definitely at a setback. But we are the only country in the world, despite setbacks and shortcomings, that has blended Islam and democracy. We have the potential to be a model, an inspiration, and an example to show that the problem is not Islam. There is an orientalist attitude that says that wherever there is Islam, you can't have democracy. But Turkey has the potential to project stability to its environment, by spreading free market principles, circulation of goods and people, and universal values like democracy and human rights. We are on the way to implementing democracy, but we have run into troubles. We are stumbling, but we are on the right course."

When I had interviewed Matthew Bryza, a consultant living in Turkey who had served as U.S. ambassador to Azerbaijan as well as director for Europe and Eurasia at the National Security Council at the White House, he expressed a similar sentiment. "Turkey is the best democracy in the Middle East, although not entirely in line with European standards of democracy, and faces challenges," he said. "Fundamentally the rule of law works in Turkey—not like in the U.S. or Switzerland, but it works. I am optimistic about where Turkey ends up. Turkish voters do periodically correct democratic missteps."

Then I asked Yinanç if Turkey was part of the Arab Spring.

She paused thoughtfully. "Turkey's case is not the Arab Spring. No matter how we might have shortcomings, people have ways of expressing their views. The Arab Spring was a revolution against the system, decades and decades of dictatorship. The Arab Spring was questioning the legitimacy of the whole system. Gezi Park did not question the legitimacy of Erdoğan, but his style of ruling. It was saying to Erdoğan: you are ignoring us. In a way, it is more like demonstrations in Europe. They are not against the system—but about increasing the prices of the buses. It is a big difference in my eyes."

But to me, the demonstrations in Turkey seemed about bigger issues than European demonstrations against high bus fares. I wondered if they were something in between—not about overthrowing the system, but also not condoning its problems.

I took a taxi after the interview with Barcin Yinanç. Wide highways, well maintained, move through this massive, sprawling city of 15 million people. In the cab, I passed parks and pathways, and a cityscape of rolling hills jam-packed with rundown yet gaily painted apartment buildings and office buildings of glass and steel. There was not an inch of untouched land. Billboards of fashion models and smiling politicians mingle with the ancient stone walls of the city. Mosques with domes and minarets push their way through the modern sprawl. It was somehow odd seeing the Toyota dealership juxtaposed against the old buildings carpeting the hills. We passed through wide boulevards of grand old buildings of stone, gray with the patina of the city, and laundry drying out on the balconies. Erdoğan's face peered down in giant relief from the side of a tall building, overlooking barbers, butchers, sellers of Tupperware and brooms, cafes and restaurants, people sitting outside at little tables drinking tea, used book stores, fruit sellers displaying melons, cherries, nectarines, and figs, hairdressers, and a shop labeled "erotic shop."

To better understand the journey from the fall of the Ottomans to Ataturk to Erdoğan, I next went to one of Turkey's seminal World War I sites.

Gallipoli's Johnnies and Mehmets

The Gallipoli Peninsula stretches out, a slender finger, into the Aegean, forming a narrow strait called the Dardanelles, whose waters lead to the Bosporus, through Istanbul, and into the Black Sea to Russia.

I drove from Istanbul along a road straight south through the peninsula, at points so narrow that the sea was visible on both sides from the road. The water sparkled as the evening approached, and the roads were lined by windmills, fields of sunflowers and melons, fields yellowed in the sun after the harvest, pine trees, and spikey bushes. The sky was bright before dusk, and little islands dotted the water. I could not imagine a more serene view.

Yet this was the site of one of the bloodiest battles of World War I.[42] Half a million Allied forces fought half a million Ottoman forces in the Gallipoli campaign, from April 1915 through January 1916. While estimates vary, about 87,000 Ottoman forces died with 165,000 wounded, and 44,000 Allied troops died with 97,000 wounded.[43]

During World War I, the Ottoman Empire had sided with the Central Powers (a group that also included Germany, Austria-Hungary, and Bulgaria) against the Allied Powers (Britain, France, Russia, Italy, and later the United States). Because of a stalemate in Europe, the Allies were looking for other ways to weaken the Central Powers. The Ottoman position controlling the Dardanelles gave them the ability to lock Russian fleets in the Black Sea and out of the Mediterranean. If the Allies conquered the straits of the Dardanelles, they thought, it would take the Ottomans out of the war and also open up a sea route for Allied Russia to get its ships out to join the fight in support of Britain and the others. Winston Churchill led the strategizing for the Allies.

Through history, the Dardanelles have been the subject of wars and legend. In Greek mythology, Jason and the Argonauts sailed through the straits on their way to the Black Sea to steal the Golden Fleece. The ruins of Troy are nearby, leading to speculation that the mythic battles portrayed in *The Iliad* were less about the allure of lovely Helen and more about control of the entrance to this waterway and the lucrative trade routes beyond. Xerxes, the Persian conqueror, crossed this strait, as did Alexander the Great. Mehmet the Conqueror built castles along it as part of his strategy to conquer Constantinople. From Jason to Agamemnon to Xerxes to Alexander to Mehmet to Churchill, many have sought to conquer this waterway, one of the most militarily strategic points in the world.

In the end, the Gallipoli campaign was a failure for Great Britain and France (the main players) and for Churchill personally. The Allies did not manage to open up the Dardanelles, and there was massive loss of life. It was a Pyrrhic victory for the Ottomans, who won the battle but lost the war. After the Ottoman defeat, Mustafa Kemal Ataturk, the mastermind behind the Ottoman victory at Gallipoli, emerged as a leader.

The Allied strategy was first to sail up the Dardanelles straits and then proceed on to Istanbul. However, Ottoman mines blew up Allied ships, and Ottoman artillery on the coasts, positioned at a castle built by Mehmet the Conqueror, blocked them from proceeding farther. I couldn't help but note the irony of the mighty twentieth-century British military being defeated by a fifteenth-century stone castle firing artillery and anti-aircraft weapons.

When the Allies couldn't advance by sea, they developed a strategy to take the Gallipoli Peninsula by land. From the sea, they saw the highest peak visible, a hill called Achi Baba. Their land invasion plans were based on the overconfident assumption that they would take this hill on the first day of the fight. With control of this high peak, the Allies would then be in a position to take the coastal areas on the Dardanelles, so that no more artillery could be fired at them from there as they sailed their ships through the straits to Istanbul. The Allies never reached Achi Baba. At the end of the campaign, they were still two miles away.[44]

I drove inland from the coast to Achi Baba, through maritime pines, cypress trees, olive trees, scrubby bushes, and grass baked yellow by the sun. Limestone hills and rocks rose all around. From the top of Achi Baba I could see a panorama of the entire end of the peninsula, with commanding views of the straits. No wonder the Allies wanted this. All I heard now were the sounds of wind and cowbells. Before me were a flock of sheep and fields of sunflowers. In the distance, ships and tankers were entering the Dardanelles.

The Allied plan was to send two amphibious invasions—one from what they called V Beach (beaches were assigned identifying letters) at the very southern tip of the peninsula and one from Anzac Cove (so called because it was the invasion site of the Australian and New Zealand Army Corps, British supporting) on the western coast. The landing was disastrous for the Allies, with three hundred of the seven hundred men in the landing killed and many of the rest wounded. Eighty-five Turkish soldiers were killed.

I next drove to Anzac Cove. Standing on the beach, I looked at the red stone cliffs rising above. The Allies fought their way up the hill and then got stuck for months in a deadly trench battle. What fear they must have felt to land on that beach and have to run up the cliffs under fire from the opposing side.

A commemorative wall with pictures narrates the landing. What is interesting about the wall at Anzac Cove is that it presents the events neutrally. It could have demonized the attacking Allied forces. But it doesn't. Instead events are narrated as a tragedy that befell both sides. Words of Ataturk are carved into a stone plaque nearby: "Those heroes that shed their blood and lost their lives . . . You are now lying in the soil of a friendly country. Therefore rest in peace. There is no difference between the Johnnies and the Mehmets to us where they lie side by side here in this country of ours . . . You, the mothers, who sent their sons from faraway countries, wipe away your tears; your sons are now lying in our bosom and are in peace. After having lost their lives on this land, they have become our sons as well."

Next I drove up to the trenches, near a graveyard called Lone Pine, along a narrow road that was the no-man's-land in some of the heaviest fighting of the campaign. The Australian trenches were now filled with dirt. Fighting here would have been hell, with dead bodies lying around untended. Leaving a trench meant certain death as only that narrow strip of road divided one side from the other. Dysentery. Heat. Illness. A shortage of water. An infestation of flies on the dead bodies.

Now, it was peaceful and beautiful, a quiet day, with a faint breeze, sunshine, fluffy clouds, greenery all around, and shaded pine forests.

In November 1915, after much death and disease, the Allies realized they could not win. They took their men out at night, burned their goods, and made it out on boats, without the Ottomans realizing they had departed until the next morning. The exit under cover of night ended the Battle of Gallipoli. But this was still at the beginning of the war.

Defeated at Gallipoli, the Allies moved in to weaken the Ottoman Empire in other ways. To enlist help, the British and French opened up negotiation with Arab tribes within the Ottoman territories, promising Arabs independence from the Ottoman Empire in exchange for rising up in revolt. T. E. Lawrence, of *Lawrence of Arabia* fame, incited the Arab Revolt in what is now Jordan. The British did not keep their promises to the Arabs. At the end of the war, the Allied victors carved up the Ottoman Empire among themselves, ushering in an era of European domination of the Middle East and the creation of nation-states that exist today, followed by decades of autocratic government that revolutions around the region tried to throw off during the Arab Spring.

World War I saw the end of four European empires—the Ottoman Empire, the Austro-Hungarian Empire, the German Empire, and the Russian Empire. World War I was about a transition in world order, transforming it in a way paralleled at few points in history.[45] Princeton scholar John Ikenberry wrote, "At rare historical junctures, states grapple with the fundamental problem of international relations: how to create and maintain order in a world of sovereign states. These junctures come at dramatic moments of upheaval and change within the international system, when the old order has been destroyed by war and newly powerful states try to reestablish basic organizing rules and arrangements."

It was the end of the multiethnic empire as a dominant form of government, and the ascendance of nation-states. At the time, U.S. President Woodrow Wilson called World War I "the war to end all wars"; in retrospect, the postwar settlement has been called "a peace to end all peace."[46] The Treaty of Versailles spelled out the terms for the end of World War I in Europe, but its terms were viewed as harsh and not legitimate. This unstable situation eventually led to World War II. Ending the war with the Ottomans were the Treaties of Lausanne and Sèvres, signed in posh European hotels, creating the new countries of the modern Middle East.

Henry Kissinger described the resulting state of world imbalance: "Whether an international order is relatively stable, like the one that emerged from the Congress of Vienna, or highly volatile, like those that emerged from the Peace of Westphalia and the Treaty of Versailles, depends on the degree to which they reconcile what makes the constituent societies feel secure with what they consider just."

To this day, some of the borders of the new nation-states of the modern Middle East have lacked the legitimacy of feeling both just and secure. The idea of nation-states replacing a multiethnic empire led to mass migrations of people to accommodate that new idea: ethnic wars, population transfers, and refugees in the millions. Governments in the new countries resorted to autocracy and repression in trying to enforce the new states and to modernize their societies along the lines of their European conquerors.

I left Gallipoli and continued to Ayvalık, on Turkey's Aegean coast, to understand one of the first cases of mass migration of people, of Greeks and Turks, as borders were drawn and fought over at the end of the Ottoman Empire after World War I. The Ottoman Empire did not die quietly. And its successor wars in the Arab Spring are following similar patterns, with the worst refugee crises since the world wars, including the displacement of fully half of Syria's population.

Blood Is Red, Greek and Turk

Ayvalık is a tumbledown, grungy, shabby-chic, quaint little town on the seaside. It is known for a number of things: its vast olive groves and the quality of its olive oil (some of the finest in the Mediterranean), its charming old quarter, and its seafood. This coastal area holds an important place in ancient Greek history. Troy is nearby, as is Assos, where Aristotle set up an academy. The ruins of Pergamum, and the city of Ephesus (to whom St. Paul wrote his letters to the Ephesians) are to the east and south. I used to think that Ancient Greece was in Greece, but a lot of it was in

Turkey. In the more recent millennium, in what are now Greece, Turkey, and Cyprus, Christians and Muslims, Greek speakers and Turkish speakers, lived intermingled like fingers in clasped hands.

As the new borders were drawn from the Ottoman Empire, minorities caught on the wrong sides were sent out or fled to where they thought they would be safe. The Ottoman Empire, despite its faults, had been a multiethnic empire of Turks, Greeks, Armenians, Kurds, Arabs, and others. It encompassed Muslims, Christians, and Jews.[47] A 1906 census of the Ottoman Empire found that out of a population of twenty-one million people in Anatolia (roughly the area of modern-day Turkey), a quarter of the population was Christian (Greeks, Armenians, Bulgarians, Slavs), three quarters Muslim (Turks, Kurds, Arabs), and a tiny fraction was Jewish.

The nation-states that succeeded the Ottoman Empire were premised upon each people having their own state, with self-governance and self-determination, as spelled out in Woodrow Wilson's Fourteen Points. While this sounds like a just idea, it also rests on assumptions that clear borders can be drawn between peoples, that a state based on one national identity can be neatly fit into territorial boundaries. The problem comes when different peoples live together intermingled and any set of borders would not cut cleanly between them. The empire as a form of government had problems, but it was a system in which people who spoke varied languages, differed in appearance, or practiced diverse religions lived together, for the most part, with mutual tolerance. Its demise resulted in explosions in interethnic violence.

In contrast to the mix of religions a century ago, in modern day Turkey the population is only .2 percent Christian. 99.8 percent of the population of Turkey is Muslim. How did this happen? There are proportionately more Muslims and fewer Christians.

Several million Muslims from former Ottoman territories in the Balkans, the Crimea, and the Caucasus fled to Turkey.[48] Between 1 and 1.5 million ethnic Armenians were killed or displaced in what some countries have recognized as a genocide: the Ottomans viewed Russian backing of Armenians as an existential threat to the empire. Although not displaced in large numbers, another minority casualty has been the Kurds. Post–World War I borders divide today's thirty million Kurds among Turkey, Iraq, Iran, and Syria, resulting in decades of violence between them and the governments of the countries in which they reside. After the Greco-

Turkish War in World War I's aftermath, nearly 2 million people were forcibly swapped between Greece and Turkey, with 1.5 million Anatolian Greeks sent to Greece and about 400,000 Muslims from Greece sent to Turkey.[49] For decades following these events, Greece and Turkey had very strained relations.

Ayvalık experienced such population exchanges. Ayvalık's sixty thousand ethnic Greeks were forcibly deported to Greece, and forty-five hundred Muslim families were forcibly removed from their homes on various Greek islands and placed here in Ayvalık.[50] Arrangements were made to somehow, imperfectly, swap property ownership between peoples who were dealt out like playing cards by their governments.

Now, some of Ayvalık's old Greek stone houses have been charmingly restored. Some serve as bed and breakfasts. Others are dilapidated, but with people living in them. Some are locked up. Some have only doorframes standing, with the rubble of stone, plaster, and furniture all around. A hundred years after the population swaps, the town is still partly empty—abandoned by original inhabitants and not quite used by the population that moved in. The old stone houses in Ayvalık reflect a former level of prosperity that does not seem to have returned. I stayed in an old Greek stone house in the town's center, with wooden floors and stairs; this house would have been the home of a Greek family that was "swapped" to Greece.

I entered an old church that had been converted to a mosque. The pews had been removed to create an open space of carpet for Muslim prayer. Where the altar had been, now was a *minbar* (a kind of pulpit). A *mihrab* represented the direction of Mecca toward which all Muslims should pray.

I wanted to talk to someone whose family had been part of the Greek-Turkish population swaps. The next day, I went to a café to meet Mustafa, whose grandparents had come from Crete during the population swaps. He wore a silver chain on his sunburned neck and sported seafaring tattoos up his wrists and arms. We sat down over tea, and he smoked a cigarette as we spoke.

"Can you tell me about your family's experiences?" I asked. "How did it fit into the history of Greeks and Turks on the coast?" I explained that I viewed the civil wars in the Middle East after the Arab Spring as a remaking of the state system that was set up after World War I and a repeat of the kinds of mass ethnic refugee crises that happened during the world wars.

"History is bullshit" was his terse reply. He continued, "Our history isn't defined by 1914. We have thousands of years of relationships, since Alexander the Great." He took a drag on his cigarette. "The Ottomans were not only one nation—they were Turks, Greeks, Balkan people, Arabs, Kurds, and Persians too." He noted that all of those people had once lived together in relative peace. "I don't believe anyone is guilty. The population is not guilty. My opinion is that it is Britain's fault. Be angry at the British army instead," he said.

The history of the region in the past century has been a story of great power intervention in proxy wars that have played out and wreaked havoc on the civilians in these countries. The British had backed the Greeks in proxy war, as part of a strategy of weakening the Ottomans.

Mustafa took another puff on his cigarette. "Two nations have been hurting very much, the Greeks and Turks."

And then Mustafa told me about his family. He is part Greek and part Turk. In Crete, his grandfather was a Christian and his grandmother was a Muslim. Childhood friends, they fell in love when they grew up. After the war, with the population exchanges, his grandmother's Muslim family had to leave Crete and move to Ayvalık. His Christian grandfather came too.

They left everything in Crete—their olive trees (the source of their livelihood), their farm, their house. When they moved to Ayvalık, they had nothing but the clothes they wore. His grandparents started rebuilding their lives, and his grandfather found a farming job. Then, slowly, they achieved stability. "We have our life *here*. We made it." He brushed his hands past each other in the air. "Everything is past. Behind is behind. The important thing is the future."

Mustafa is Muslim, but he also reads the Bible. "The Quran and the Bible say the same thing," he said. "Don't steal. Don't lie," is his take on it. "Most Greek people want peace, and Turkish people the same. If you see a Greek and a Turk walking together, you can't tell who is who. It is the same face. Blood is red, Greek and Turk. Everything we have is the same."

He said that a reporter once asked him, "Do you feel Greek or Turkish?" He told me he responded angrily, with exasperation, "I feel that I am human, a person."

I wondered at the extent to which, then, as now, people's lives can be damaged by identity politics, when identity differences may not be important to them.

For many years after Mustafa grew up, he wanted to visit Crete to meet his grandfather's family. "A part of my heart is all the time with Crete," he said. Because of visa restrictions after the population exchanges and continued tense relations between Greece and Turkey, neither his grandparents nor his parents were able to return to Crete. It took Mustafa two years of persistantly applying for repeatedly stalled visa applications until he could finally make the journey.

"When I got down onto the harbor, I kissed the stone." He showed up unannounced in Crete and met his aunts and uncles. They all cried. One uncle had a small heart attack, ending up in the hospital, because he was so happy to see Mustafa.

Then, when Mustafa visited Athens, he was mugged by Albanians for his leather jacket and gold bracelets. They stabbed him in the leg six times. The Greek police officer in Athens who found him spoke Turkish to him, because the officer's grandparents were from Çeşme, a seaside town near Izmir in Turkey. "The police looked after me," he said. He was in the hospital for eighteen days.

While he was in the hospital, there was a Greek hospital employee, a lady of about seventy years old, who attended to him. "She looked in my face, and she was crying. Each day she brings me something. When I wake up and turn my pillow, I find chocolate or a sum of money. I ask her why. She opened her wallet, and showed me the picture of her son. He looked just like me—same size, same face." The woman's son had been killed in a motorcycle accident. Afterward, the Greek lady invited Mustafa to her house to recuperate, and he stayed there for four months. When it was time to go home, even though the lady and her husband did not want him to leave, they paid for his ticket back to Ayvalık.

I thanked him for telling me his story and walked back to the stone house where I was staying. Grapevines were strung between houses, shading the cobblestone streets. Families sat outside chatting in the heat, with little children running around.

The main street in front of the harbor is bustling with the sounds, clamor, and cacophony of daily life in Turkey. One street over is abandoned Ancient Greece, calm and quiet and shaded, and lost to Turkey, as the old empire was split into nation-states.

With societal upheaval, defeat in war, poverty, and mass migration, Turkey needed to heal. Ataturk, their national hero, led the way. I made my way to Ankara to visit his tomb.

Ataturk's Mausoleum

Ataturk looked out at me, with a penetrating gaze, from the glass wall of the bus stop. He sat cross-legged, gentlemanly and imperial-looking in a wicker chair, in a waistcoated suit and tie, a handkerchief in his pocket and a cigarette dangling from his fingers. He was intense and handsome, and photos of him were everywhere—in every hotel, nail salon, metro station, and office. Some people tattooed his signature on their wrist.

I walked up to Ataturk's mausoleum on the outskirts of Ankara along a pathway lined with pine trees, tidily cut lawns, clay pots of flowers, and flowerbeds. His mausoleum, a grand monument of massive ginger-colored stone blocks, sat on top of a hill surrounded by parks. It created an impression of tranquility and grandeur, stability and greatness. The Turkish flag rippled in the wind, high on its staff. All was quiet. Behind me was a bed of red flowers with a white crescent and star of flowers inside, planted to resemble the Turkish flag.

This monument was for Turkey's greatest modern leader and the founder of Turkey's republic, the George Washington of Turkey and model for a generation of Middle Eastern leaders. His accomplishments were extraordinary, and Turks have an almost religious reverence for him as the founder of the country and healer of the nation. Bill Clinton remarked, "Shakespeare wrote, Einstein thought, Ataturk built."[51] John F. Kennedy said, "The name of *Ataturk* brings to mind the historic accomplishments of one of the great men of this century . . . It is to the credit of Ataturk and the Turkish People that a free Turkey grew out of a collapsing empire."[52] Lloyd George, prime minister of the UK, said, "The centuries rarely produce a genius. Look at this bad luck of ours, that great genius of our era was granted to the Turkish nation."[53]

Mustafa Kemal Ataturk had a historically rare combination of charisma, capability, and vision that transformed his country. He navigated post–World War I politics, both internal and external, to create a Turkish state out of the rubble of the defeated Ottoman Empire. Through sheer force of will, he transformed his country into his vision for the future.[54] He created Turkey's parliament and abolished the weak Ottoman sultanate. He separated religion from state, ending the Islamic caliphate. He initiated giving Turkish women the right to vote eleven years before French women got the right to vote. He embarked on a mass education campaign to educate children and reduce Turkish illiteracy. He developed state enterprises.

This truly great man presented an alternative to the peoples of a defeated empire. His actions to reform and Europeanize the public and private sectors of Turkey provided an implied explanation for Turkish defeat, that they had not been modern enough, and showed a path forward out of that defeat.

I entered a vast stone and brick courtyard with the mausoleum at one end, passing goose-stepping soldiers in khaki. Their knees all rose together, followed by a kick out, with a straight leg lowered to the ground in time, in an audible march of slow dangerous rhythm. Stone reliefs on a wall were reminiscent of ancient Egyptian figures. A path was lined with stone lions that looked like the carvings of the ancient Assyrians.

There was a general hush and a sense of reverence.

This was a monumental mass of stone dedicated to one human being. It felt like a Roman square or maybe a Roman temple to a god. There was clearly a not-so-subtle attempt to tie the mausoleum of Turkey's greatest man of modern times to mythological gods and the greats of ancient civilizations—the Romans, the Assyrians, and the Egyptians. The message was that Ataturk stood with these greats. As he was among them, therefore the Turkish people were among them.

But here in this pantheon of history's great civilizations, there was something notably absent. There were no visual references to the Ottomans or to Islam. The architecture was all straight lines, stone, no nonsense, and grand. There were no Ottoman domes or calligraphy. There were no sensuous curves of Islamic aesthetics. There were no geometric patterns of stars or hexagons or other shapes. There were no blue tiled mosaics. It was missing something. The message was that there was a separation, a severance from the recent past. Ataturk was a descendant of the Romans, not of his recent Islamic forebears. I understood Turkey's urgent desire to modernize, to associate itself with Europe, the place of progress. But why this disavowal of Turkey's heritage? Some Turks assimilated that cultural shift; others wanted more from their Islamic heritage. The Ottomans had an ignominious fall, but they were a great civilization too, the descendants of the Roman and the Byzantine Empires, related to other Islamic empires, and a source of regional stability, of multiethnic tolerance, of great architecture, of beauty, of delicious food, of military might.

Inside the mausoleum itself, more recent heritage peeped out, in a more intimate way. The ceilings were gold mosaic reminiscent of the Byzantines, with patterned geometry imitating the woven kilims of Anatolia. Wrought-iron screens with geometric patterns invoked Islamic heritage, the only nod to it that I could see. A great block of mauve granite with veins of white encased Ataturk's body. It was simple, solid, unadorned, with no carving or ornamentation, just hard lines and smooth surfaces. This mass of solid stone represented the security that Ataturk brought his nation.

An alcoholic, Ataturk died of cirrhosis of the liver in 1938 at the age of fifty-eight. The nation went into mourning. Every year since, there is a moment of silence in Turkey at the time of Ataturk's death, 9:05 a.m., on November 10.

I wandered out to a gift shop that offered everything Ataturk. In addition to books, you could buy plates, wallets, hats, watches, coins, jigsaw puzzles, mugs, neckties, shirts, silver business-card holders, and key chains, all with Ataturk's face on them.

But Ataturk was not without his critics and detractors. Called a dictator, he faced an assassination attempt. He muzzled opposition and imposed single-party rule. Ataturk's vision of the future was a forceful turning away from the past; his successors in Turkey, as well as later Arab leaders who emulated him, relied on authoritarian methods to maintain that direction. He served as a model for other leaders of the Middle East in the coming decades, including Gamal Abdel-Nasser in Egypt and Habib Bourguiba in Tunisia, whose successors similarly relied on force to maintain modernizing and secularizing directions. The postwar and postcolonial generation called for rule by a strong leader, but that model, imitated for decades, produced dysfunction and excluded participation. The parts of Turkey that didn't feel European and wanted to be more Islamic felt alienated. The military inherited Ataturk's vision, performing multiple coups against democratically elected Islamic parties. They enforced secularism, turning it into something oppressive. They repressed minorities with the goal of creating a unified identity around Turkishness in the new country. This model of government, replicated around the region, set the Middle East up for the Arab Spring protests decades later.

Then, Erdoğan's Islamist AK Party was elected, and the pendulum swung other way. Instead of one half of the population feeling alienated, the other half of the population felt alienated.

I left the mausoleum and went back to the center of Ankara.

Founded by Ataturk as a new capital for a new Turkey, right in the middle of the country and far from the past of Istanbul, Ankara is a green city, with tall apartment buildings painted in pastel colors—towers of light pink, mauve, yellow, orange, pale green, some painted with geometric designs in brown, with cheerful purple flowerpots. Its wide streets are not too clogged with traffic. There is a feeling of affluence, order, cleanliness, and style. The streets feel very European, with European-style cars and European-style medium-height walk-up apartment buildings. There are glass-enclosed sheltered bus stops, tree-lined boulevards, and new blue-tiled tunnels decorated with motifs of geese. A few scattered glass skyscrapers dot the downtown, not densely packed. There are Turkish shops and a few familiar ones like Burger King, Shell gas station, and Caribou Coffee. They all have pictures of Ataturk.

From Ataturk to Erdoğan

I walked through Turkey's parliament building, the National Assembly. The assembly room had orange leather chairs, a wall of white marble with a quote from Ataturk that says, in Turkish, "Sovereignty unconditionally belongs to the nation," and sixteen chandeliers, each representing one of the Turkey's historic civilizations, from the Hittites to the Republic today. Parliament was on recess and repairs to the building were underway, with protective cloths draped over chairs. In the halls, I could feel the Art Deco era of Ataturk coming through, with leafy-shaped crystal chandeliers, brass doors with various motifs, marble mosaics on the floor, and a red carpet with a Turkish pattern that to me looked like red cross-eyed dots. And, of course, everywhere there were portraits and photos of the great Ataturk himself, looking dapper in a tuxedo or dashing in a formal uniform.

In the library, staff worked on laptops among tall shelves of books, including those that contained notes from all of the parliamentary meetings since the beginning of the Republic.

In the National Assembly, leadership of Turkey has moved from Ataturk's European secularism to Erdoğan's moderate Islamism.

Recep Tayyip Erdoğan defies easy categorization. He has been cast as many contradictory things.[55] Some say he is an autocrat; others say he has improved democracy. Some say he is the first leader in the Middle East to tie together liberal democracy and moderate Islamist politics; others say he a staunch Islamist who is pretending to say the right things while really entrenching crony Islamists throughout the government. Some say he is a defender of human rights, who has given minorities, in particular the Kurds, more cultural autonomy and stopped the practices of extrajudicial imprisonment and torture. Others say he is an autocrat, another Putin, imprisoning journalists, revamping the judicial system to serve his party, and opening up a war with the Kurds again to serve a political agenda of garnering support from nationalist Turks. Some say he is pro–European Union, making reforms to join the EU. Others say he is using those reforms to his own advantage to weaken his secular enemies. He is guided by noble ideals or he is driven by revenge. He is pro-women or he is anti-women.

Turkey has had significant accomplishments during Erdoğan's time in power. The economy was booming. The Kurdish minority inside Turkey enjoyed unprecedented cultural rights. The quality of education improved. The role of the military was reduced—a democracy cannot be a democracy at the point of a gun. On the other hand, Turkey's foreign policy was criticized as damaging and counterproductive during the Arab Spring, with support for the Muslim Brotherhood and Mohammed Morsi in Egypt, financing violent groups in Syria, allowing jihadist fighters access across Turkey's porous borders, and using the fight against ISIS as an excuse to attack Kurdish armed groups in Syria and Iraq, as Turkey worried about Kurdish success there leading to renewed unrest among its own Kurds. Relations with NATO have never been so low. And there are corruption charges and pressure on the media.

Turkey is polarized, riven in half by the man. The polarization may not be new—Turkey was similarly divided during the Kemalist days of dogmatic secularist nationalistic rule as well. Half was happy; the other half was not. Before the Islamists came to power, the more pious half of Turkey had felt like an underclass in comparison with Turkey's secular elite. Now the situation is reversed, with the secularists worrying about becoming an underclass. Turkey has one foot in Europe and one foot in the Middle East, and opinions about Erdoğan reflect this confused dual identity of Turkey.

One thing is certain: Erdoğan is the longest serving leader of Turkey since Ataturk. Turkey's history in the past century has been the journey from Ataturk to Erdoğan.

From 1994 to 1998, Erdoğan, a former semiprofessional soccer player and onetime candy salesman, served as mayor of Istanbul. When he was elected many feared that he would pursue an Islamist agenda. Instead, he focused on competent public governance, tackling a water shortage, air pollution, garbage management, public transportation, and the city's finances.[56] He combined Islamic leanings with competence in public administration. He could make the city run.

In 1997, Erdoğan read a poem at a speech. The poem was one taught in Turkish schools, written by Turkish nationalist poet Ziya Gökalp.[57] The particular lines and the particular context inflamed government leadership. The lines Erdoğan read included: "Our minarets are our bayonets, Our domes are our helmets, Our mosques are our barracks."

For reading that poem, he was thrown into jail for four months. During that time, so story goes, he did significant soul-searching and concluded that the solution was not a polarized country of secularists versus Islamists, but a system that accommodated the beliefs and practices of all.[58]

In 2001, he established the AK Party and ran for parliament in 2002. He had the image of an underdog, seeking a fair society in opposition to entrenched elites. The AK Party swept to victory, winning nearly two thirds of the seats, with a coalition of surprising bedfellows—Islamists who wanted more representation and Turkish liberals, who were tired of repressive leadership, even if the repression enforced secularism. This was one of the biggest victories ever for a Turkish politician.

Now, a decade and a half later, that initial excitement has worn off for the left. They seem to despise him. That initial idealistic union of people of faith and people of liberal values has disintegrated, and those on the left feel increasingly alienated. Erdoğan's behavior has become more and more autocratic. But the economy is still booming.

Soner Çağaptay of the Washington Institute speculates that Turkey's next leader will once again be a liberal. He argues that the ground has been laid for a post-Erdoğan Turkey with different leanings.[59] He writes, the AK Party "no longer represents the future of Turkey. True, Mr. Erdoğan has transformed the country economically—the Turks are not poor anymore—but he also rules with an iron grip, and Turks increasingly want a free society. Moving forward, Mr. Erdoğan's biggest challenger will be the amorphous liberal movement that led the Gezi Park protests. Today, Turkey's future has liberalism written all over it." Çağaptay argues that Turkey was ripe for an inspiring new leader to come forward and make that happen.

I finished my walk through the National Assembly. Ladies in uniform walked around with trays of Turkish coffee in tiny china cups and saucers printed with the Turkish flag. There was an air of tranquility in the halls, with their marble floors, wall-sized windows, and tall brass doors. The multiple pictures of Ataturk, combined with décor from his era, gave the impression that time only began with Ataturk and continued until now.

The Party of Erdoğan

The news was on television as I walked into Yasin Aktay's office. Aktay was vice-chairman of Erdoğan's AK Party, with responsibility for foreign affairs. He turned the television off and stood up to shake my hand. He had thick brown hair and a mustache and wore a brown jacket with an orange and white plaid tie and beige pants.

"I was watching the news," he said. "A Turkish journalist was just arrested while covering the Ferguson protests in the U.S. We're finding this ironic, because the U.S. criticized us for our treatment of journalists during the protests here." After the arrest, the American Civil Liberties Union supported the Turkish journalist in a lawsuit against the Ferguson police.[60]

Aktay was from a town in Turkey's east called Siirt and was of Arabic and Kurdish descent. He has a long and distinguished track record of serving as a professor at Selçuk University in Konya, earning a fellowship in Utah to study minority rights in the United States, teaching at the University of Maine at Farmington for a semester, writing as a columnist for

Turkey's *Yeni Şafak* newspaper, hosting two political commentary shows on television (*The Other Side* and *Perspective*) and serving as honorary chair of the Turkish think tank the Institute of Strategic Thinking. He has written multiple books about Turkey and the Middle East.

I met him at the AK Party headquarters, an ultramodern tower that projects simple lines, sophistication, and prosperity. I sat down on a white leather chair, surrounded by plants, the Turkish flag, and a rug made out of a patchwork of different leathers. Behind his desk was a map of the world and a portrait of Ataturk looking solemn.

I asked him what he thought the AK Party's biggest accomplishments were in the past ten years.

"Democratization in Turkey," he said, right away. "The AK Party brought people to power, to authority. We put an end to the elitism of Turkish society. It was a semi-democracy, and now it is a full democracy."

"And human rights increased in Turkey," he continued. "The concept of citizenship and nationality and national identity was changed to involve everyone—Turks, Kurds, Alevis, Sunnis."

"Concrete results," he ticked off. He described Turkey's accomplishments in growing the economy, health, and education.

The AK Party did have many of those accomplishments, I thought, but there were also multiple areas where the AK Party fell short, which I would explore by later speaking with a member of the opposition in parliament.

"As one of the leaders of an Islamist party, how do you think Islam and democracy fit together," I asked, as I had asked Sayed Ferjani of Ennahda in Tunisia, wanting to hear an additional perspective.

"Three principles in Islamic political theory are the necessary principles for democracy," Aktay said. He counted to three on his fingers: justice, *shura*, and accountability. Islam places great emphasis on justice, he explained. Islam also has the concept of *shura*, which means consultation, referring to a historic practice of Muslim tribal leaders conferring about decision making. And according to Islam, rulers should be accountable for their decisions.

He emphasized that he did not think that Islam has been the cause of the problems in Middle East peace and governance. Islamic civilizations had been multicultural and relatively stable until the past century. "In Turkey's history, you can see many cultures living together in peace. All the Middle East is the remainder of Ottoman society. If you visit any city, you can see in the downtown the mosque, the synagogue, and the church living together in tolerance," he said. He thought this demonstrated precedence within Islamic civilization for the values of democracy. "When we come to modern times, the question of whether democracy and Islam are compatible is artificial. When you compare this to European society, there are genocides and holocausts, which you don't see in Islamic history. In Europe in the Middle Ages, the wars were for homogenization of society," he said.

"But many of today's Middle Eastern wars are about homogenization of society: the Sunnis versus the Shiites, persecution of the Coptic Christians in Egypt, ethnic cleansing of the Yazidis in Iraq. How did the tolerant multiethnic Ottoman Empire society come to this?" I asked.

"It happened because of the Westernization of Turkey, not because of the Islamization of Turkey. Muslims were living with the principles of justice. Now, we have exiled non-Muslims and imported Muslims, in agreements with Greece and the Balkan countries," he said, noting Turkey's now 99 percent Muslim population. He pointed out that the Balkans, which had been both Christian and Muslim in the past, had been homogenized, to become more Christian with the Muslims leaving. I found the answer unsatisfactory. In multiple interviews and conversations with people in the Middle East, I found there is a tendency to blame the West for internal violence, an unwillingness to come to grips with it.

Aktay strongly felt that such homogenization was a loss for Middle East societies. "It is good to know people different than you," he said. "We should restore our region based on its history. Before that, we didn't know nationalist ideas, or homogenous societies. That was new to us. We are a mosaic society. Cosmopolitanism is part of the nature of Islamic society. When I was a child, I had Armenian and Kurdish neighbors. I know Kurdish, I sing their songs and speak their language. Human capacity should be enhanced by knowing each other. It is in the Quran." He paraphrased a verse from the Quran: we created you differently not to create superiority, but to know each other. "Every language and culture is a world in itself. God is the god of all worlds."

"So what happened with Turkey's protests?" I asked. "Was Turkey part of the Arab Spring?"

"Turkey is not part of the Arab Spring. Very different," he said. Now I had heard multiple different answers to this question.

He explained that with Turkey's history of coups d'état and the over-throw of other governments in the region, when the protests broke out, Turkey's government was suspicious. "In Turkey, we have elections. The decision maker is not the street in a democracy. It is the ballot boxes. We had an election, and Erdoğan won. His leadership was approved by people twice in two elections, on March 30 and then August 10. Fifty-two percent voted for him. If he were that bad, people would not vote for him."

It is a fine line, I thought. Some of the other Arab Spring protests turned into government overthrows that have not had happy endings. The importance of maintaining security in the wake of protests has been illustrated by the disastrous outcomes in other countries, but there is also the very important need to respect civil rights. What would have been the right way to respond to the protests, given the context?

"What do you think caused the Arab Spring protests elsewhere?" I asked.

"All of the Arab Spring countries were the remainder of the Ottoman society," he said. "Then there was colonialism, then dictatorship. They were led by leaders with fake elections or without elections. Countries were led by dictators for decades. Hosni Mubarak in Egypt for thirty years, Muammar Qaddafi in Libya for forty years, Saddam Hussein in Iraq for forty years, Hafez al-Assad and his son in Syria for fifty years. When you look at these regimes, there are common aspects of these societies. They had strong intelligence systems, to work against the enemies inside. They behaved as if their own people were their enemies."

"Turkey was the same," he continued. "Paranoia was an enemy of demo-cracy. Turkey's security system was based on the idea that all of society was an enemy of the state. Kurds were viewed as enemies. Islamists are restoring the monarchy and shariah, and they are your enemy. Then the Armenians, then the Christians, then the Alevis," he said ticking off how most of Turkey's minorities were marginalized, repressed, and held in suspicion by former governments. "That was most of the people. When you add all this, everyone is your enemy. You create an intelligence sys-tem against your people. You cannot be strong with this paranoia. You

can't be healthy like that. We changed that," he said, referring to the policies of the AK Party that reduced pressure on minorities. "We said we have
no inside enemies. All citizens are potentially friends, not enemies. That
is the beginning of the idea of democracy in Turkey. This is one of the
AK Party's accomplishments."

To hear the other side of the story as well, I went to speak with Aykan
Erdemir.

The Opposition

Aykan Erdemir, a member of the Republican People's Party (CHP), is one
of nine Turkish members of parliament under the age of forty. The party
of Ataturk, founded in 1923, the center-left CHP is the main opposition
party, heir to Turkey's secularist Kemalists. They represent much of
Turkey's other half, the half that feels alienated by the direction of the
AK Party. The CHP is often viewed as the party of the middle and upper
classes and of the educated elite. It is also criticized for being a weak
organization and not representing its youth base.

I entered Erdemir's office in a building in the Turkish National
Assembly complex. It was just a few days after the 2014 presidential election, won by Erdoğan. CHP candidate Ekmeleddin İhsanoğlu came in
second, with a solid showing at 38 percent.

With black hair, rimless glasses, a beige jacket, and a striped tie,
Erdemir looks like a cross between a brainy professor and a polished politician. He is both. With a Ph.D. in anthropology and Middle Eastern
studies from Harvard, he served as the deputy dean of graduate studies at
Ankara's Middle East Technical University before being elected to Turkey's
parliament from his hometown of Bursa.

Erdemir had just returned that morning from Istanbul, where his party
had been convening post-electoral meetings. "We are all doing a lot of soul
searching," he said about their electoral defeat, as he shook my hand.

The CHP was clearly disappointed. Some analysts argue that if the
CHP is ever to regain power, it must reconcile itself with Turkey's conservative religious base, a tack very different from its secular approach in past
decades.[61]

I wanted to get another opinion on my conundrum. "Was Turkey part of the Arab Spring? Or were the protests more like Occupy Wall Street or European labor strikes?" I asked.

He paused and then said, "Turkey's government, even in its darkest days, was never as authoritarian as those dictators. It would be unfair to think that Turkey's politics are similar to Egyptian, Tunisian, or Syrian politics. But at the same time, it is not as simple as French Metro workers. It is somewhere in between. This is about an imperfect democracy resisting the transition to authoritarianism. In Turkey, political competition has never been fair, but it has never been this unfair."

"So what happened with the presidential elections then? Why did CHP lose?"

Erdemir first acknowledged that Erdoğan had run the best campaign. But then he sat back in his chair behind his desk and went into professor-mode.

His view was that the presidential election was not only an election among candidates. It was an election among three different models of governance—the same models of governance that were playing out around the Middle East, through elections, Arab Spring revolutions, and gradual experimentation. First, there was the "strong man" model of government. Erdemir thought that Erdoğan represented a model of government common in the Middle East—a strong ruler who can push through initiatives and who makes people feel that someone powerful is in charge. Second, there was the institution model of government. The CHP coalition candidate, İhsanoğlu, represented the model of governing through institutions, according to Erdemir. (But it seemed to me that İhsanoğlu had become the CHP candidate largely because he was not as well known or as polarizing a figure as Erdoğan, but neither was he as accomplished. Wouldn't the "institution model" also require a skilled leader, although with limitations to power? I wondered.) Third, there was the increasing autonomy of the local governance model, represented by the People's Democratic Party (HDP) candidate, Selahattin Demirtaş, a Kurdish-Turkish politician, who favored devolution of power away from the central government and toward local government. Demirtaş garnered support from many liberals, who supported the inclusive values of his party.

"Turkey went for strong man leadership," Erdemir bemoaned. "As an institutionalist, I think we need new leadership, platforms, and a new generation of politicians to promise to Turkey a new model of governance, with strong institutions and good finances. Institutions should be socially inclusive, delivering quality services, accountable, and transparent."

Erdemir was very concerned that the AK Party was pushing through measures that would strip institutions of their capabilities. He said that despite being elected on the premise of righting the wrongs of the past, Erdoğan and the AK Party had "ended up strengthening state capacity, especially the coercive power of the state, the surveillance power of the state, the ruling power of the state, while weakening the institutions that really matter—the meritocratic bureaucracy, military morale and capability, services, and media. Turkey took a step in the wrong direction. It is clear suicide to dismantle and weaken institutions and attack the human capital of Turkish institutions. Erdoğan did this."

Erdemir saw connections between the tensions inherent in these three models with the mistakes of the protesters in the Arab Spring. "They thought, if we get rid of a strong leader, things will be better. What they didn't understand is that it is not about the strong leader but about building institutions. Once you get rid of the dictator, or the strong leader, you often also get rid of the thin institutional infrastructure that was there. Then people fall back on primordial identities—sect, kinship, religion, ethnicity. This is what the Arab geography is going through these days."

That observation reverberated with me. All of those hopeful protesters had thought that if they just got rid of the bad guy at the top that good governance would fall into place. Instead, the institutions were not there to transition to a better form of governance. What many Arab Spring protests did, in hindsight, was to invite chaos. Societies fractured along ethnic lines, making some countries vulnerable to proxy wars.

Erdemir acknowledged that the tension among Turkey's neighbors affected its own politics at home and the Turkish government's response to the protests. "We cannot build a successful social democratic state unless we spend our resources and build liberal democracy elsewhere in the Middle East. If Turkey was in between Norway, Sweden, and Finland, things could be different."

"What is Turkey's role with other countries in the Middle East? Can it play a constructive role?" I asked.

"I have always thought Turkey has a big role to play in shaping the Middle East. I thought it could be a beacon, or a role model, not necessarily for the states, but for the emerging middle class, and be a provider of the best examples and training in free markets, rights and freedoms, gender, media freedoms. Turkey is now doing the opposite. There is no Turkish model, from Turkey to Tunisia," he said. "Turkey could very easily be part of the solution. Now Turkey is increasingly becoming part of the problem."

Erdemir views himself as one of the reformists in the CHP. "I am trying to turn CHP toward developing a Westward-looking knowledge economy, a cutting edge, social democratic party, even ahead of our European counterparts," he explained. "These are big words and huge dreams, and I may not have the means of achieving them," he acknowledged.

Erdemir said that he had just tweeted that he had voted at the same ballot box that his father and grandfather had voted at. He hoped that his children would vote there as well, but he had his doubts about Turkey's future as a democracy, given the AK Party's centralizing authoritarian moves. His views were dark on the direction that Turkey was heading.

He seemed pessimistic, while I saw prosperity around me, although a prosperity tainted with corruption and pressure on journalists. "Is there hope?" I asked.

"Although Erdoğan has centralized power and destroyed quite a lot of nodes of power, he has not exhausted them. There is still life in Turkish democracy."

AK Party Women

I entered the office of Güldal Akşit, at AK Party Headquarters. Akşit is head of the women's branch of the AK Party. She has also served as the minister of culture and tourism and president of Turkey's Parliamentary Commission on Equal Opportunities for Men and Women. She was a woman in her fifties, wearing a dark green suit, and short puffed-out hair. Behind her desk in her large office was a picture of Ataturk lined up with a group of women, including his wife, dressed in 1920s Jazz Age fashion, with knee-length skirts and cloche hats. On the opposite wall hung a carpet woven into a picture of Akşit with Erdoğan.

As Erdoğan had just won the presidential election, it was the day that Turkey's new prime minister (Ahmet Davutoğlu) was supposed to be announced. I knew I only had a little of Akşit's time.

I was here to talk with her about women's rights in Turkey in general and within Erdoğan's Islamist party in particular. I wanted to know what Turkey's Islamist party said about women.

Many are suspicious about Erdoğan's views on women. "You cannot put women and men on an equal footing," he said in a speech in 2014. "It is against nature."[62] He controversially proposed to limit abortion, cesarean sections, and the morning after pill and was ridiculed for saying that he thought that all Turkish women should have "at least three children." In response, critics undertook a mocking campaign promoting "at least three beers," with the slogan painted as graffiti on walls and printed on T-shirts.[63] Erdoğan's wife wears the headscarf. Elif Shafak, a Turkish novelist whose novels have hit international bestseller lists, wrote in an op-ed in *The New York Times* that now there is pressure on Turkish women to wear headscarves to get jobs: "Just like their counterparts who were forced to discard their headscarves so many years ago, uncovered Turkish women are feeling uncomfortable and unwanted in their own country."

Where was the AK Party, an Islamist party, headed with its policies toward women?

I introduced my book and told her I was here to learn about women in the AK Party. "What are AK Party priorities and achievements for women?" I asked.

"One of our most important achievements is that women get positions with decision-making authorities," she said. Women need to be able to make decisions to ensure their rights. "Women have become more visible in both social and political arenas." She noted that in 2007, women represented only 9 percent of parliament (fifty women deputies, thirty of whom were AK Party). In 2011, 14 percent of Turkey's parliamentary spots were won by women, with seventy-eight women deputies, of whom forty-six were AK Party. With nearly 4 million registered members, the AK Party women's branch actively organizes to mobilize and represent women's interests.

By way of comparison, while this was a lower percentage than in Tunisia (31 percent) and the United States (19 percent) now, it is similar to the United States in 2000, when 9 percent of U.S. senators were women, and 13 percent of representatives in the House were women.[64]

Furthermore, in Turkey, although women are represented in professions (40 percent of teachers are women, 35 percent of engineers, 30 percent of doctors, 25 percent of professors, and 33 percent of lawyers), women have had little access to political power. In 2010, only two of the twenty-six ministers in Turkey's cabinet were women, and less than 4 percent of senior bureaucrats at the undersecretary and deputy undersecretary level were women.[65] However, women are better represented in private sector leadership. 12 percent of Turkey's CEOs are women; by way of comparison, in 2013, 15 percent of executive officers in the United States were women.[66] When I interviewed Barçin Yinanç at the *Hürriyet Daily News* and asked her about women in Turkey, she had noted regarding Turkey's private sector, "The top of the top are at international levels." When I had asked her about the biggest challenges facing women in Turkey, she said that they were in "providing the necessary conditions to have a successful blend of motherhood and professionalism," pointing to prohibitive costs of childcare, the lack of workplace conditions to support both, and a culture that doesn't encourage women to work. I found it interesting that some of the issues that women in Turkey face are the same issues that we are struggling with in the United States.

A secretary came in and said something to Akşit in Turkish. She excused herself. Erdoğan wanted to see her. Our meeting was over.

In parting, she gave me a brochure about measures and laws on women passed during the rule of the AK Party. It lists legal recognition of sexual harassment as a crime, establishing a hotline for victims of domestic violence, and adoption of "equal pay for equal work" as part of the Labor Law. The rate of women graduating from higher education increased from 5 percent in 2000 to 30 percent in 2011. The rate of the participation of women in urban areas in the workforce went from 17 percent in 2000 to 28 percent in 2011.

How much of that does the AK Party get to take credit for? Would these trends have happened anyway without the AK Party? Would the numbers be better without the AK Party? It's not clear.

I caught a flight to Gaziantep, a city on Turkey's border with Syria to explore yet another situation facing Turkey—a refugee crisis arising from the civil war in Syria, a consequence of the Arab Spring.

Anatolian Tigers, Refugee Havens

Gaziantep is a pretty town with square apartment buildings (some new, painted pastel colors with balconies and flowerpots) and shops that sell everything from wedding dresses to pastries to tires. Tall pine trees line the streets, next to little garden restaurants. The old Ottoman city center boasted a citadel and a market with crafts and jewelry, and caravanserai inns for travelers were under renovation to become boutique hotels. Pastry makers in Gaziantep were renowned for their pistachio baklava. In the downtown area were traffic jams and a few hotels—even a branch of the Holiday Inn. Groups of ragged-looking people, small children among them, walked along the road. Probably Syrian refugees.

One of the oldest continuously inhabited cities in the world, Gaziantep is known as one of Turkey's "Anatolian tigers." Gaziantep, along with several other mid-sized industrial cities, has played a significant role in boosting Turkey's economy, providing trade links to the Middle East and delivering political support to the AK Party.[67] With 1.7 million people, Gaziantep is one of Turkey's most important industrial and agricultural areas, with production of carpets, olives, and pistachios.[68] It is also thirty miles from the border with Syria, a mere sixty miles from the tragically destroyed Syrian city of Aleppo, and eighty miles from the Syrian border town Kobani, the site of fierce fighting between ISIS and Kurdish forces. Before Syria's civil war, Gaziantep attracted well-heeled Syrians from Aleppo with its new shopping mall, Sanko Park, one of the biggest in the region. Now it attracts destitute Syrian refugees.

Turkey also hosted one side of the Syrian opposition, which called itself the "Syrian interim government," in Gaziantep.[69] Headquartered here were the Free Syrian Army as well as an alternative Syrian Ministry of Defense and Ministry of Education. Rebel forces based in Gaziantep were viewed as "moderate." However, they produced limited success.

I hired a driver to take me from Gaziantep to Antakya, another of Turkey's "Anatolian tigers" on the coast and near the border with Syria. My driver took me out of the city on a route that parallels the Syrian border. We drove through rolling hills, scorched yellow grass, bushy green scrubs, and hills covered with white and gray rocks. The landscape was

dotted with villages, fields of tidy plants, and power lines. Turkey has incredible roads—wide, new, and well maintained. We passed some ravines,
areas where parts of the mountains are cut out for mining or quarrying.
We passed gaily painted houses of mauve and pale green, mosques, tennis
courts, and children's parks. Other cars on the road drove politely, obey-
ing the traffic customs. It was hard to believe that while it was so orderly
and peaceful here, a few miles away was violence and destruction.

Turkey's east shares a 510-mile border with Syria, a 220-mile border
with Iraq, a 310-mile border with Iran, a 170-mile border with Armenia,
and a 160-mile border with Georgia. These borders were set with the Treaty
of Lausanne in 1923 after World War I, separating the newly created
Republic of Turkey from lands that the Ottomans once controlled. During negotiations, the borders on the east almost ended up different from
what they are today.[70] Aleppo in Syria almost ended up in Turkey, as did
Mosul in Iraq. Syria still disputes Antakya belonging to Turkey, claiming
it for itself. The borders established then that defined Syria and Iraq are
now being challenged, as ISIS seeks to carve out a state for itself.

Turkey's eastern region is home to people of multiple ethnicities: Turks,
Kurds, Armenians, Arabs, and others. It has been host to successive conflicts over new post-Ottoman borders, such as the massacres of Armenians
during World War I.

Since 1984, Turkey's east experienced a succession of Kurdish uprisings, resulting in a civil war between the Turkish military and the
Kurdistan Worker's Party (PKK). The PKK viewed the struggle as being
about greater rights for the Kurdish people in the region. The Turkish
government saw the PKK as a terrorist organization that was threatening
to split up Turkey. Turkey in particular viewed the semiautonomous Kurdistan Region of Iraq (my next destination for this book) with trepidation,
as the Kurds there gained significant regional autonomy within Iraq;
Turkey feared that the Kurds in its own eastern regions would move to
unite with Iraq's Kurds. Kurdish civilians were the ones who suffered. In
recent years, under Erdoğan, the most egregious of the human rights
abuses by the Turkish police and military stopped. There have been gains
in Kurdish cultural rights, including Kurdish language classes in schools.
But tensions are rising once again, as Turkey fears the consequences of the
Kurds in Iraq and Syria achieving military success against ISIS.

The Syrian civil war is straining this region of Turkey. Syria's Arab Spring has not been an inspiring one. Arab Spring protests led to violent government crackdowns on protesters, leading to a revolution that devolved to civil war, threatening the stability of the region. A simplified version of the conflict is that Syria has splintered into a multiparty civil war among the regime of President Bashar al-Assad, Free Syrian Army rebels, the Kurds of northern Syria, Nusra Front (a coalition of Sunni Islamic groups affiliated with Al-Qaeda), and ISIS jihadists.[71] The complex version is that there is a tangled mess of groups operating in Syria: groups cross among these multiple sides, and it is hard to tell who is who. There are no good options. Assad has a brutal track record with chemical weapons and barrel bombs dropped on civilian areas in cities. ISIS brutalizes the population and destroys its heritage. The demoralized rebels based in Gaziantep do not have the capability to defeat anyone militarily.[72] Great powers in the region create further confusion with their own conflicting and overlapping interests, as the United States, Russia, and Turkey all view their security and the future of Syria depending on different parties to this war.

The United Nations High Commissioner for Refugees has called the Syrian crisis "the biggest humanitarian emergency of our era."[73] Not since World War II has there been a refugee crisis of this scale. Since 2011, more than 11 million people—half of Syria's population—have been displaced by Syria's civil war, both inside Syria and as refugees. Out of its population of 23 million, there are 7.2 million Syrians displaced inside Syria and 3.8 million registered refugees living outside Syria in neighboring countries.[74]

By 2015, over 2 million Syrian refugees seeking safety in Turkey had crossed the border that I was driving along.[75] Many of the refugees stay in the border areas. Some leave to other parts of Turkey, such as Istanbul or Ankara. Estimates are that 10 to 20 percent of Gaziantep and nearby towns are now comprised of refugees.[76] The refugees are changing the demographics of southern Turkey, leading to friction with local people, who see them as competing for low wage jobs, setting up shantytowns, driving up rents, and changing the ethnic composition of their towns.[77]

Turkey has been generous in keeping an open door policy for the refugees. Turkey's refugee camps are some of the best designed, constructed, and maintained in the world.[78] However, the camps accommodate only about 200,000, and the remainder of the 2 million refugees live in urban areas outside of the camps. They struggle to find and pay for shelter and food, in many cases cannot legally work to provide for their families, lack Turkish language skills that would enable them to better survive in this new country, and lack access to education and healthcare at the rates needed.

Turkey's border area is becoming ever more complex politically. While Turkey is backing the rebels with funding, logistics, and a home base in Gaziantep, Turkey has also been criticized for backing violent jihadist groups in Syria in efforts to unseat Bashar al-Assad. Turkey has supported the opposition, both moderates and the Nusra Front, allowing transfers of arms and people across its own borders.[79] For the first several years of the conflict, Turkey turned a blind eye to ISIS's activities on its borders. Things changed in July 2015, when ISIS carried out a suicide attack inside Turkey, leaving thirty-two dead at a town called Suruç. The attack roused Turkey: it began carrying out airstrikes on ISIS inside Syria, and gave the United States permission to attack ISIS from the U.S. base Injirlik inside Turkey.[80]

Turkey has been equally alarmed by how the Kurds have been emerging as powerful actors during the conflicts in Syria and Iraq.[81] Kurdish forces in northern Syria (People's Protection Units, or YPG) and in northern Iraq (peshmerga) were the only viable ground troops to fight ISIS and were backed up by U.S. and allied airstrikes. In some cases, Turkey's own Kurdish fighters, the PKK, crossed borders to fight with other Kurds. These events have raised questions about whether the Kurds in northern Syria will try to join the Kurdistan Region in Iraq. "The Middle East map is being unofficially redrawn as Kurdish forces control more of the north than ISIS," wrote Martin Chulov in the *Guardian*.

When ISIS laid siege to Kobani, which is a Syrian Kurdish city, the Turkish government did not intervene immediately, with Erdoğan claiming that the Kurdish fighters were as bad as ISIS. Protests about this inaction broke out in Turkey's Kurdish areas. Turkey has now been using the war on ISIS as justification for carrying out sorties against Kurdish targets. "Turkey enters the battle against ISIS, but its real target seems to be the Kurds," wrote Ian Bremmer in *Time*.[82]

I can't help but see parallels between what Syria is experiencing and what Turkey feared that it would experience in the decades after World War I. Turkey feared that in its weakened state, foreign countries would back the interests of ethnically related minorities inside Turkey to pull the country apart. They feared Greece backing the Greeks, Russia backing the Armenians, and the Kurds uniting with other Kurds. Now Syria has a parallel situation—with the United States and Turkey backing the moderate rebels, Russia and Iran backing Assad, Turkey targeting the Kurds, money from private individuals in the Arab Gulf countries backing various groups among the Islamic fighters, and fighters from around the world converging on Syria and Iraq to join various groups. It is not clear if Syria will be easily put back together again. The civilians are helpless with this civil war and great-power proxy war happening in their borders. Now, Turkey fears what this means for its own territories.

After driving parallel to the border from Gaziantep, I arrived in Antakya, in the middle of a traffic jam. This wasn't Ankara, and it wasn't Gaziantep. Antakya appeared crowded and messy, with crumbling sidewalks, mottled buildings in need of a good paint job, and weeds growing in the pavement. Laundry was strung outside apartment windows. Wires hung messily off buildings with peeling paint, satellite dishes dotted roofs, and air conditioners perched in windows. In the backdrop were jagged mountains, brown with rock and dried vegetation. A mosque with a shiny silver dome and a minaret were near a concrete-lined channel, dry and without water. I passed shops selling chandeliers, upholstery, boots, lawn equipment, and snacks. Dust-covered trees separated the opposite lanes of the road. A driver of a white truck piled high with watermelons took shade inside the cab, crates of cantaloupes sitting outside for sale.

Alarming the West, Turkey kept its borders here in Antakya particularly lax for the first several years of the conflict, and jihadists crossed the border here for rest and to see their families before returning Syria. Antakya had a large Arab minority.

Antakya, called Antioch in antiquity, was once one of the five great cities of the Roman Empire, similar to Carthage. It was a seat of the early church. It also had a central role in Christian heritage. St. Paul preached from here. I approached St. Peter's church through fields strewn with garbage and plastic bags, overlooking the city from a distance. But from this distance, the city was pretty, sloshing up the sides of the hill, with its multicolored houses, green and pink and orange. The church was closed.

I walked through the bazaar, the oldest section of town. Decrepit shops sold all sorts of goods—plastic toy trucks, traditional olive oil soap, a locally made string cheese, bread, clothes, pots and pans, dishes, honey, fruits and vegetables, jewelry, books. Occasionally something old popped through, a fountain, a wall, a few little alcoves under renovation. It looked like renovations were just beginning. It smelled of cheese, fresh air, and raw meat.

This decaying border city was sitting on ancient greatness, blending Turkish, Kurdish, and Arabic worlds, absorbing refugees, hosting fighters, and raising questions about the future map of the Middle East.

From Turkey to Iraq

The Ottoman Empire's fall set the stage for the creation of new nation-states in the Middle East. Turkey and the other new countries emerging from the Ottoman Empire struggle to this day with balancing among multiple ethnicities, defining the rights of all citizens (including minorities), and tensions between those who lean toward secularism and those who lean toward a greater role for Islam in public life.

Turkey's Ataturk set an example, for better or for worse (or both), emulated by Middle Eastern leaders in the past century. While strong leadership was crucial during the setup of the post-Ottoman world, the strongman form of government also precluded plurality and freedom of expression and led to autocracy, creating the conditions for the rage that exploded during the Arab Spring.

Now Turkey has a functioning democracy and is a state growing in confidence and influence, with a working (albeit tense) balance of power between Islamist and secular parties. Turkey's protests at the time of the Arab Spring could best be described as resisting the growing autocracy of the Erdoğan government within that system, as opposed to trying to create a new system.

I finished up my time in Turkey to head to Iraq. I entered the Kurdistan Region of Iraq to understand firsthand how the country boundaries established after World War I had created conditions for instability today and for ISIS, an ugly outgrowth of Arab Spring desires for new models for society in reaction to inept governments. I also went to the Kurdistan Region to better understand how its optimistic direction for development was threatened by the chaos just outside its regional borders.

Iraq

An Aspirational Airport

My plane arrived at Erbil International Airport. Every step resonated as I walked through cavernous new halls, with mottled gray granite floors. Spaces on the walls reserved for advertising held giant vacant frames. Designed by international architects, the airport building is aspirational, reflecting visions of a region with order, safety, security, and prosperity. It also feels empty.

In the baggage hall, vaulted ceilings of white steel and glass skylights opened up to the Iraqi sky. Guards walked around in neatly pressed uniforms of gray shirts, ties, and black pants. Tall banners hanging by multistory-high windows pronounced "Erbil International Airport—The Future Embracing the Heritage." Signs expectantly pointed to car rental offices that did not yet exist. There were only four billboards in the baggage claim area. An advertisement for a cellphone featured a stubble-bearded man in blue jeans running and jumping a hurdle while looking at his cellphone: "Be Unlimited with an Extra G from Korek." A Turkish bathroom fixture company advertised, "From Europe to your home," with a picture of an exultant-looking woman standing in a luxury bathroom with a gilded mirror, brass fixtures, and clawfoot bathtub.

I walked through the duty-free shop while waiting for my baggage. A wall of Marlboro cigarettes flaunted giant signs saying "smoking kills" and "smokers die younger" in English—a notable concern when death in Iraq comes from so many different causes. Apart from the cigarettes, the duty-free shop had a bare minimum of items. Shelves scantily offered up a handful of Dior and Lancôme perfumes, bottles of nail polish, imported wines and scotch, a few watches, sunglasses, and teddy bears.

The general message was that the Kurdistan Region of Iraq was open for business, whether anyone came or not.

This was my eighteenth trip to Erbil, the capital of the Kurdistan Region of Iraq. It was my first time coming back since ISIS advanced to within twenty miles of the city before being pushed back by the pesh-merga and newly engaged U.S. military assistance. The Kurdistan Regional Government's (KRG) own forces, the peshmerga, are now being relied upon as ground forces to fight ISIS in Iraq.

I had traveled back and forth to the Kurdistan Region for five years as part of a RAND team hired by the KRG to advise on socioeconomic and public sector development. My work was on developing a strategy for improving K–12 and vocational education.[1]

At the baggage claim, I looked around at the other passengers from my flight. There were many kinds of people. Iraqis came and went. International business professionals took advantage of business opportunities in what used to be a good-news spot of Iraq, with economic growth, a growing middle class, stability, an energy industry, and business opportunities in telecom and construction. International development and humanitarian professionals conducted projects. The Iraqi diaspora returned home through this airport, after having been flung far around the world in recent decades, leaving heritage and communities that were thousands of years old. There were American soldiers and contractors, Western oil executives, and laborers from South Asia meeting the needs of the construction boom in Erbil.

Since the airport opened in 2010, international airlines have flown from here directly to Frankfurt, Vienna, Abu Dhabi, Dubai, Doha, Cairo, Istanbul, and more. Airlines included Lufthansa, Qatar Airways, Etihad, Austrian Airlines, and Turkish Airlines.[2] Iraqi Airlines connected Erbil with other Iraqi cities. When ISIS came close to Erbil, some flights were cancelled or put on hold.

I collected my bag and walked out to the front of the airport. Egid, an armed driver for the KRG, waited there to pick me up in a white Toyota SUV.

Egid had been our driver for most of my trips. Today, he wore Kurdish traditional dress, a very dignified outfit of a gray wool long-sleeved shirt and billowy pants with a cummerbund around his waist. As a peshmerga in his youth, he had fought in guerrilla wars in the mountains against Saddam Hussein's forces. I handed him the English-language instructional CDs he had asked me, on a previous trip, to bring him. He wanted to improve his English. Egid, like many Kurds of his generation who had fought in the peshmerga, had not completed school. Now a father, he returned to night school to complete ninth grade to set an example for his two little boys.

We drove out of the airport, through vast green fields of tall grass swaying in the wind, surrounded by security fences. Black Humvees and guards in camouflage with machine guns guarded the perimeter. The road was lined with olive trees. The sky was bright and the weather was chilly.

U.S. military advisors were using the grounds of the airport now. On June 15, 2014, President Obama once again dispatched American forces to Iraq. The UK, Germany, France, Australia, and other countries supplied training and arms. By January 2015, on my trip there, there were nearly three thousand U.S. troops on the ground in Iraq providing training and advising to Iraqi forces. They set up five bases around Iraq for training of nine Iraqi army and three Kurdish peshmerga brigades.[3]

Most U.S. forces had been withdrawn from Iraq by 2011. One of President Obama's campaign promises was to bring American troops home.[4] "After nine years, America's war in Iraq will be over," he had said in 2011. But the drawdown happened at a time when the Iraqi military was still not capable of maintaining security within its borders, when the Arab Spring civil war in Syria had started and was about to spill over into Iraq, and when violent Islamist groups were mobilizing. The drawdown left Iraq exposed to the instability that has overtaken it in the years since, without the capability to manage security itself.

ISIS began expanding in northern Iraq in 2014. To the world's surprise, it captured Mosul, Iraq's second largest city, which was only 50 miles from Erbil, with the Iraqi Army fleeing and leaving its weapons behind. Iraq's minority Yazidi community fled up to Mount Sinjar. ISIS killed up to five thousand Yazidi men, sold five to seven thousand Yazidi women into

slavery or gave them as concubines to fighters, and left the rest of the
community to die on Mount Sinjar without food and water.[5] ISIS beheaded American, British, and Japanese journalists and aid workers. And
then in August, ISIS broke through the lines controlled by the KRG and
came within twenty miles of Erbil, with aims to take the city.

Many had thought that the Kurdish peshmerga was undefeatable. The
peshmerga were viewed as experienced, loyal, and dedicated to defending
the region, after having served as guerrilla warriors against Saddam. When
ISIS was still behind the borders controlled by the peshmerga, many con-
fidently thought that even if the Iraqi army had been defeated in nearby
Mosul, the peshmerga could keep ISIS out of the Kurdistan Region. But
while the peshmerga were motivated and fighting hard, they lacked equipment and training.

When ISIS broke through the KRG lines, I emailed my Iraqi friends
in Erbil to ask them how they were doing. They wrote back that they were
safe, but people in Erbil were starting to flee the city. I was supposed to
go to Erbil that month and then canceled my trip.

That was when the United States announced it would offer additional
help for Iraq against ISIS.[6] In early August, humanitarian airdrops to
the Yazidis on Mount Sinjar began. Air support was provided to the peshmerga to defend the KRG regional border from ISIS's advance and to
create a protective corridor to get the Yazidis down from the mountain.[7]

The Kurdistan Region is an important locus of stability in an uncertain Iraq. It is in a strategic location situated in between the rest of Iraq,
Syria, Turkey, and Iran. It is home to a fledgling democracy, and it was an
investment success story. It has contracts with major U.S. oil companies,
including Exxon and Chevron, and has the potential to be a major oil
exporter. With 1.3 million people in 2009 (now higher with 400,000
refugees), Erbil was the fourth largest city in Iraq after Baghdad, Basra,
and Mosul.[8] Thomas Friedman traveled to Kurdistan and called it "Iraq's
best hope" and "an island of decency in a still-roiling sea."[9] I was glad
that my country could help to protect it. I had the feeling that everyone
from the ministries to my driver was hopeful and depending on American
help, and they were taking steps to develop their region.

Beginning a new engagement in Iraq was a very difficult decision for
the United States. President Obama had been elected with a campaign
promise of ending U.S. involvement there, which had begun when U.S.

forces entered Iraq in 2003 to oust Saddam Hussein.[10] The war had cost many Iraqi and American lives. The Iraq Body Count Project estimates that 120,000 Iraqi civilians lost their lives to violence during the American occupation between 2003 and 2011.[11] Economists at Brown University estimated deaths of 8,000 U.S. uniformed troops and contractors, 300 allied security forces, and 11,000 Iraqi police and security forces.[12] Between 61,000 and 81,000 U.S. troops and contractors, 4,000 British forces, and 30,000 local security forces were wounded. The Brown study estimated the costs of war at $1.1 trillion, with the Department of Defense spending $760 billion in direct costs. The Congressional Budget Office in 2014 placed the costs at $815 billion.[13] A RAND study found that 26 percent of returning soldiers had mental health conditions.[14] The Iraqi people had been through a lot of trauma, and the American troops had been through a lot of trauma.

But arming and training the Kurdish peshmerga meant arming the military forces of a *region* of Iraq, not the Iraqi national government. U.S. policy was to support the territorial integrity of a united Iraq.[15] Would arming the peshmerga mean supporting creation of a de facto separate state within Iraq? Would doing so make Turkey even more nervous?

Egid and I passed out of airport security checkpoints and emerged into the wide new roads of the city. We passed by sites where the tall, prosperous-looking buildings of a city on the make were being constructed and saw the concrete and steel guts of partly built buildings.

As I entered Erbil, I wanted to explore Iraq's place in the Arab Spring. Iraq did not have Arab Spring protest movements on a large scale, although there were scattered protests in several cities. Some observers pointed to the Gorran (change) movement in the Kurdistan Region as the closest parallel to the Arab Spring protests in other countries. This included small-scale student protests against government corruption, government forces opening fire (killing one protester and wounding thirty), and growing success of Gorran as a political party in the Kurdistan Regional parliament. However, even though Iraq is not typically viewed as a country with a significant Arab Spring movement, Iraq is an important part of the Arab Spring context and is included in this book for a number of reasons.

First, Arab Spring movements involved removing a generation of autocrats, all with a similar model of leadership and who had held continuous power for decades—Mubarak in Egypt, the Assads in Syria, Ben Ali in

Tunisia, Qaddafi in Libya, Saleh in Yemen. Saddam Hussein was part of that generation, although his was a different ending and came well before the Arab Spring. But Iraq shared a common governance model with these countries before the war, combining the autocracy, repression, and stagnation that the Arab Spring rejected. Iraq now faced similar tests about whether it could create participatory, consensual, accountable government.

Second, ISIS is a cancerous outgrowth of Arab Spring momentum for new models of governance, in reaction to governments that did not meet the needs of their people. Capitalizing on disappointment in what the Arab Spring movement had failed to accomplish, ISIS had been enabled by state collapse in Syria (destroyed by the Arab Spring–ignited civil war) and Iraq (from war and decades of problems preceding it). ISIS now is a transnational phenomenon stretching out of Iraq and Syria, with affiliates in other countries, such as Libya, Tunisia, and Egypt. Because of it and the civil wars in which it is involved, by June 2015, 4 million Iraqis were internally displaced,[16] and there were 270,000 refugees from Syria in Iraq,[17] in comparison with Iraq's 2013 population of 33.5 million people. This meant that 10 percent of Iraqis were now displaced.

Third, the destructive chaos in Iraq and Syria, with unprecedented interethnic conflict, genocide, and mass displacement has served as caution to civil and government leaders in other countries, during Arab Spring movements and the government responses to them. Throughout my interviews in Tunisia, Egypt, and Jordan, people said that their protest movements and governments alike had exercised moderation after watching the post–Arab Spring violence that overtook Syria and Iraq.

Fourth, considering the Arab Spring as a range of movements pursuing changes in models of governance and society, including revolutions as well as longer-term economic and political development, the Kurdistan Region of Iraq is part of that development. But with ISIS on their doorstep, that was on pause now. Now Kurdistan was facing a security, economic, and humanitarian crisis.

Fifth, the growing autonomy of the Kurdistan Region, ISIS's control of large swaths of Iraq and Syria, and the mass displacement of people are calling into question the future of the borders of the Iraqi state, established a century ago when the Ottoman Empire split apart. The Arab Spring is challenging that created order of nation-states. Will Iraq stay together, with a three-way pull by the Kurds, the Sunnis, and the Shiites? How will the mass displacement of people set Iraq up for the future?

This would be a fast trip for me, and I supplemented it with phone interviews and insights from my previous trips. Because of security, I could not travel through Iraq as I could travel through the other countries, or as I had previously traveled through the Kurdistan Region before ISIS. On other visits, in addition to Erbil, I had taken road trips through rocky, pine-covered hills to the Kurdistan cities Sulimaniyah and Dohuk, and had conducted school visits in rural areas outside of Erbil. Not this time. Things were different now. I would get in and then get out.

Daily Life in Erbil

"We thought we would have a better future, a safe Kurdistan, with a bright new view, especially in Erbil. Everything was progressing. We were really hopeful and believed that everything good would happen. Now we don't look so far. We just hope that tomorrow will be better," said Shirin, a Kurdish woman in her late twenties with long brown hair living in Erbil. She wore a fashionable long skirt, tall boots, and a sweater. I had known her for a while. We greeted each other, and I asked her how she was doing, and how daily life had changed in Erbil.

"Everybody is nervous. People don't feel good," she said. At the same time, she added, "The city seems safe. We go out without any fear. We are not scared to stay out until late at night, to go to a picnic. But people are more careful," she said, with citizens reporting suspicious activity to the security forces.

"We believe in the peshmerga," she said, confident now that the peshmerga was backed with air support and training by the United States. "The only power that can stand in front of Daesh is peshmerga," she said. (Daesh is the Arabic version of the acronym ISIS.) "Even the Iraqi military couldn't do anything, and now they are asking for the peshmerga's help. Our safety, security, and self-confidence are all on the peshmerga."

To me, that seemed like a tall responsibility to place on a regional military entity when Iraq's national army was not even able to defend its borders.

Shirin was also proud of Kurdish fighters in Syria who had fended off

ISIS at Kobani, just over the border in Turkey. "If they were not in Kobani, it would be a bigger disaster," she said. "Even every single woman in Kobani fights. Even the children fight. They are very brave. They have a reputation these days." Kurdish women were becoming warriors by necessity. At Kobani, a Kurdish woman named Rehana gained international notice because of her skills as a sharpshooter against ISIS in an all-woman militia.

"How is your family?" I asked. "Is anyone fighting with the peshmerga?"

"Three of my cousins are fighting in Kirkuk," she said. "One has six children. The other has three. It is difficult but we are proud." She added with sadness, "Daily we are losing dads and brothers and sons. The government is bankrupt and can't help the martyrs' families. Peshmerga become handicapped, disabled, and need treatment outside of Kurdistan. Even those who were wounded in the war, there is no money to treat them. Wounds cannot wait. We just feel so sorry for that." She described how many of the wounded get support from the community. "Families announce on TV and radio that there is a peshmerga in need, and we send them money."

"How is the situation with the refugees and IDPs?" I asked. Refugees and IDPs (internally displaced persons) had led to a 28 percent growth in the Kurdistan Region's population, which had been 8.3 million in 2013, with an additional 2 million displaced people added to it since. Erbil itself had 400,000 refugees and IDPs.[18] There were pressures on services like water, education, housing, and health.

While it was difficult for the city to have so many additional people, Shirin was proud that Kurdistan was serving as a safe haven. "This is how Kurdistan is treating others," she said emphatically. "There are a lot in Erbil, in every area. They are staying in tents and unfinished buildings. Even on the main streets you can see them," she said. Refugees were sleeping in school buildings and half-finished shopping malls.[19] "They get supplies from the UN, NGOs, and our government, and some of them work." In Dohuk, a city in the Kurdistan Region near the border with Syria, schools for Kurdistan children were out of session because the displaced were living in the school buildings.

"Kurdistan is in the middle of an economic crisis, too," I said. "How are people coping?" I asked. The World Bank estimated in 2014 that Kurdistan needed $1.4 billion just to stabilize the economy because of the addition of the displaced people.[20] At the same time, oil prices had collapsed and ongoing standoffs between Erbil and Baghdad over how to share national oil revenues within Iraq led to delays in the Kurdistan Region getting its share of Iraq's national budget.[21] On top of that, oil prices were down 45 percent from last year.[22]

"The economic situation is making things hard on us. There have been no salaries for three months," she said, as the government had stopped paying the civil service workers. "Our banks are empty. But many families get things from shops now and pay later. They don't buy new things, but pay for food and electricity. The shopkeepers in the bazaar complain and say, 'We don't have anybody to buy things from us.'"

Shirin was disappointed. "People lost hope. They are angry, frustrated, and don't believe in government now. Every time they are on TV, our leaders make promises, but they never keep them," she said.

She was particularly sad as she was becoming convinced a Kurdish independent state would not happen anytime soon. "The people were so eager. The president said that we are going to have our freedom. Kurdistan would be free. Month by month, we see that it is talk. We have enemies. Turkey and Iran are against us. They didn't want a Kurdish country to be their neighbor."

While she was disappointed about the Kurdistan Region staying part of Iraq, this is a complicated issue. The Kurdistan Region is landlocked, surrounded by neighbors that resist its independence. It was not clear that it would make a viable state.

To Shirin, the future looked difficult. "It is heartbreaking. People are trying to travel, get citizenship from anywhere else. They don't want to live in Kurdistan. Whatever we do, we are not secure. Our children's future is not secure. I used to say that I would rather die in Kurdistan than live outside, but now I say I have to secure my children's future, so they are safe."

The Other Iraq, the Next Dubai

Egid and I drove through wide city streets of Erbil, newly built. We passed tall buildings that were raised with ambitions of hosting international hotels like the Marriott or the Kempinski. We drove past compounds called the English Village and the Italian Village, new constructions of beautiful houses that anybody around the world would be pleased to live in. We passed through older neighborhoods, with high concrete walls painted with street art surrounding schools. A wall painting with a colorful cubist rendition of village life caught my attention. Other city blocks were filled with concrete skeletons of houses and office buildings under construction. We passed parks with rosebushes and trees. Street signs advertised fun at the water park. Coffee shops, kebab restaurants, shops selling kitchen and bathroom supplies, car dealerships, vegetable stands, and pharmacies lined the roads. We passed my personal favorite, the Burger Queen, a Kurdish knockoff of the American Burger King chain.

The Kurdistan Region billed itself as "the other Iraq," and media outlets once quipped that Kurdistan was the next Dubai.[23] While that was an exaggeration, the point remained that there was a momentum and stability in Kurdistan that was not present in other parts of Iraq. In 2013, the Downtown Erbil project kicked off, a $3 billion investment effort by Dubai's Emaar Properties, the builders of the Burj Khalifa (the tallest building in the world). Their plan was to build five-star hotels, apartment towers, shopping malls, schools, and hospitals.[24] The KRG was investing in public infrastructure, and it got its electricity grid and water back online more extensively and reliably than in other parts of Iraq. And now the KRG was working on developing its education and healthcare systems and other public sector services. Plans were stated in an ambitious document, the Kurdistan Vision 2020.[25]

The advent of ISIS changed everything. In some ways, Erbil seemed much the same. But there was a new somberness, and I took additional levels of caution. Uniformed guards with guns stood on many street corners, a reminder of the need for security. While Erbil itself had largely remained stable, there had been several explosions—two in the center of Erbil and one in front of the U.S. consulate.[26]

A green traffic sign hung from a light post announcing directions to nearby cities. One arrow pointed in the direction of Mosul (a mere fifty miles away) and another pointed to Baghdad (250 miles away). While Erbil felt quiet, prosperous, and orderly, the signs gave perspective on where we were in the world.

At one traffic light, several small boys came up to the car window, trying to sell packs of tissues. Egid remarked that these were the refugees; Erbil rarely had children selling things on the streets before this time, but now it had become ubiquitous.

Over five years and eighteen trips, I had had the privilege of watching Erbil grow and develop. It developed from a sparsely populated city with older buildings and creaky infrastructure to something that looked like a giant construction site. There were new roads built, skyscrapers under construction, international hotels springing up, schools being built, large parks with beautiful landscaping and gardens, and renovation of the historic city center. There was a momentum, stability, and vision that seemed unexpected. I used to walk around parks, the historic city center, and the market. I bought carpets and mountain honey there. I ate kebab deep in the bazaar at the classic kebab shops that the Kurds preferred.

Now I felt grief at the threats facing Erbil.

The Oldest Inhabited Place in the World

In the center of Erbil, the yellow-ocher brick-walled Citadel rose up on a hill. Erbil is said to be the oldest continuously inhabited site in the world; the Citadel had been the site of a settlement for eight thousand years.[27] Egid and I walked up the hill from the base of the Citadel, past a line of carpet shops, and in through the gate. The gate was a large structure of yellow brick, a grand arch where people, cars, or bicycles could enter. As I walked through the arch, a red, white, and green Kurdistan Region flag whipped in the wind in front of me, surrounded by green trees.

The Citadel was under renovation as part of a UN project. Egid got permission from the renovation chief for me to walk around. Workers were shoring up the yellow brick walls with scaffolding, and I could hear the sounds of hammers and drills. It was a construction site, no longer a neighborhood. The inhabitants, 840 families, had been moved out of the historic living quarters in 2007, leaving only one family inside, so that that Erbil's Citadel could maintain an unbroken history of being the oldest continuously inhabited site in the world.

I walked through a labyrinth of muddy alleys and peered into what had been people's courtyard homes. Workers had chipped off old plaster, exposing brick frames. Many areas were roped off and strewn with blue tarps. Inside some of the brick houses were tiled bathrooms and bathtubs from the 1950s. There were over five hundred houses here within the Citadel's walls, in an area about a quarter mile in diameter. Rosebushes filled the open areas.

I entered the courtyard of an old Ottoman-era palace under renovation. Inside was a garden surrounded by living quarters, fronted with yellow brick and stone arches. The stone and blue-tiled fountain that once burbled with water in the garden was dry now. I entered through the stone arches to walk in the colonnade of the palace's courtyard. Its ceiling was painted with red, green, and blue geometry. Then I wandered the rooms. One of the rooms of the palace had been decorated with blue ornamentation on white plaster walls. There were beautiful features: plaster carved in geometric shapes, turquoise and gold tile, Arabic inscriptions, and the name of God carved in stone.

I left the palace and walked to the public bath. It was an octagon-shaped building with a large dome. The lintel to the door was carved stone, once decorated with turquoise tile that was now chipped off. Inside the public bath were plaster-covered vaults with carved eight-pointed stars. Light shone through a skylight. Geometric patterns exhibited a refinement of aesthetics and a desire to create beauty.

Nearby was a mosque. Its minaret was a tall structure of yellow brick decorated with turquoise and yellow tile, with loudspeakers at the top to broadcast the call to prayer.

As I walked the Citadel grounds, I could envision this as the center of charming nightlife with couples and families seated at outdoor restaurants, exhibits of local artists, some beautiful residences, and maybe a boutique hotel. Erbil had been named the 2014 Capital of Arab Tourism— chosen of course before ISIS came close to the city.[28] Places like the Citadel were meant to offer visitors a pleasant experience.

From up here, I looked over the streets of the city. Erbil's layout, concentric circles around the Citadel, was the same as it has been as far as time stretches back. I looked down over a grand public square with gardens and fountains of water that shot up into the air several stories high. There was one large, tall fountain and perhaps twenty smaller fountains and pools of blue water. Surrounding the square was a colonnaded brick market. Here was the center of city life. Across the way was a brand-new shopping mall that somehow tastefully blended in with the older styles of the city.

I used to be able to walk around the market that I peered over now.

My colleagues and I felt safe enough to go around by ourselves, strolling the market streets to buy antique brass pots, sample mulberries from a wooden cart, or choose among locally made tea cups. In one cluttered shop, an old man sold old black-and-white photos of Erbil of yesteryear.

Erbil's Citadel was a UNESCO World Heritage site. Erbil was an important Assyrian religious and trade city called Arbela from 2500 BC to the seventh century BC.[29] It was the site of a temple to the ancient Mesopotamian goddess of sex and war, Ishtar, the most powerful female deity in the Mesopotamian pantheon.[30]

Iraq was the cradle of civilization, the land between the two rivers, the Tigris and the Euphrates, where settled life and agriculture first started. It was home to important ancient civilizations, most notably Assyria (today's northern Iraq and parts of Syria and Turkey) and Babylon (southern Iraq). The Assyrians and the ancient Egyptians each independently developed written language around the same time. The Assyrians were the first to make beer by fermenting grain. They developed cities and political structures. Hammurabi's Code, one of the first written codes of law, was written in Babylon.

Later, Erbil was part of the empires of the Babylonians, Persians, Greeks, and Ottomans. Erbil had a sizable Jewish community, and then was an early center of Christianity. Islam came in the seventh century. Not too far away, Baghdad reigned as the splendid capital of the Abbasid Islamic empire and caliphate. The Islamic Golden Age, lasting from 750 to 1258, had two centers of gravity—Baghdad and Andalusian Spain. Baghdad was home to fertile agriculture, rich culture, fabled poets, and erudite scientists and thinkers. There were advances in the sciences and arts fostered by great libraries, building on the work of the Romans, Egyptians, Persians, Hebrews, and Greeks.[31] The Islamic Golden Age came to an end in 1258 when Iraq was invaded by Mongols, led by Hulagu Khan. They obliterated Baghdad, killing thousands and burning Baghdad's storied libraries. The city never quite recovered. The Mongols laid siege to Erbil for six months before conquering it also. In the sixteenth century, Iraq was absorbed by the Ottoman Empire, although there was intermittent rule by the Persians.

What is today Iraq was three Ottoman provinces, based in Baghdad, Basra, and Mosul. These cities were linked together, surrounded by natural barriers. Desert to the west separated them from the chain of cities that make up Syria today, and desert to the south separated them from Saudi Arabia. Mountains separated them from what are today Iran and Turkey.

In World War I, the British occupied Basra, Baghdad, and Mosul. At the end of the war, Iraq's current borders were set, combining these three Ottoman provinces into a country. The League of Nations granted Britain control of the Mandate for Iraq. Faisal bin Husain al-Hashemi was chosen to be king of Iraq; son of the grand sharif of Mecca, Faisal had headed the Arab Revolt against the Ottomans in Saudi Arabia, Jordan, and Syria, in collaboration with the British.[32] His brother Abdullah became king of Jordan. Iraq became independent in 1932 when the League of Nations ended the British Mandate. In 1958, a military coup d'état overthrew Iraq's monarchy, and Iraq became a republic. Brigadier Abd al-Karim Qasim became prime minister. In another coup d'état in 1963 by Baathists and Arab nationalists, Qasim was killed. A look at a timeline of Iraq's history shows a military coup d'état every few years, with six military coups d'état between 1936 and 1968.

In 1979, Saddam Hussein became president, ushering in a regime of torture, suppression of dissent, mass arrests, and warfare. He will go down in history as one of the world's most horrific despots. Saddam attacked Iran, hoping to take advantage of chaos in Iran after its revolution in order to gain the upper hand as the dominant country in the Gulf. During the Iran-Iraq War (1980–88), about half a million Iraqi and Iranian soldiers died. The war devastated Iraq's society and economy. In 1990, Iraq invaded Kuwait to access its oil resources, in part to try to recoup finances drained during the Iran-Iraq war. In 1991, U.S. forces liberated Kuwait in Desert Storm. (I recalled visiting in 2010 the "So We Don't Forget" Museum in Kuwait City, which had horrific photos of atrocities from Iraq's invasion and the stone head of the statue of Saddam Hussein that had been famously toppled in vivid drama in Baghdad, captured on film, after U.S. troops went in.)

In 2003, the United States invaded Iraq in Operation Iraqi Freedom, for which the Bush administration laid out multiple reasons, including that Iraq had an advanced nuclear weapons development program that was close to producing a nuclear weapon.[33] Such an advanced nuclear weapons capability never materialized. After a dramatic search, in December 2003, U.S. forces found Saddam Hussein in a hideaway hole in the ground near his hometown of Tikrit. Photos show him disoriented, with a long scruffy beard and unkempt hair. He was tried and hanged by Iraqis.

Iraq descended into sectarian violence. In late 2006, Iraqi tribal militias started a successful counterattack on the Salafist-Jihadist Sunni insurgency. In 2007, the United States sent a surge of 170,000 troops to preserve this fragile stability. The United States began to drawdown troops in 2007, with the troop draw down completed by the end of 2011—the year of the Arab Spring revolutions. Today, Iraq is a failing state, with ISIS taking over swaths of the country.

What went wrong? While much has been written about possible reasons, there were a few main causes. The United States did not have a plan to secure the population and maintain public services and security. The United States also expected to be viewed as liberators but were viewed by many as invaders. Up to fifty thousand Baathists in government and military positions were fired because they were associated with Saddam Hussein, but they were also the people who had skills and experience in running a government and undertaking military operations. Many former Baathist military leaders are now fighting with ISIS. Introducing democracy meant bringing increased influence to the Shiite majority, with Iraq's prime minister, Nouri al-Maliki, abusing his position to favor the Shiites. The United States left too soon, leaving security in the hands of Iraq's still inept government, which lacked the capability to maintain security and used heavy-handed military tactics that drove some Sunnis to side with ISIS. With leadership in Baghdad weakened from the turmoil, Iran's interference on behalf of Iraq's Shiites was further enabled. And then there was the regional context of violent Islamist movements in other countries.[34] Out of these troubles, ISIS emerged. ISIS succeeded where there was poor governance and societal fractures.

What happened in the Kurdistan Region of Iraq during this time? The new post-Ottoman borders split today's 30 million Kurdish people into four countries—Turkey, Iraq, Iran, and Syria. The Kurds are not Arabs, but rather speak an Indo-European language related to Farsi. Before the twentieth century, they lacked identity as a unified Kurdish entity. Rather, their identity was local and tribal; at a higher level, they identified as Muslims and Ottomans.[35] When state borders were being negotiated after World War I, the Kurds did not have a common position about a state at

the beginning. Some wanted a Kurdish state, and others wanted to be part
of the larger states around them. By the time a common position had co-
alesced, the Kurds had missed their chance.[36] Between 1918 and 1925,
argues David McDowell in *A Modern History of the Kurds,* the "Kurds lost
their one great opportunity for statehood."

Kurdish desires for self-governance led to a tragic civil war in Turkey
that peaked from 1984 through 1999, while lower levels of conflict continued since; some forty thousand people are estimated to have died.[37]
Conflict between the Iraqi state and the Kurds was ongoing from the end
of World War I through 2003, when U.S troops entered Iraq. Fighting
was most intensive from the 1960s through the 1990s, and the conflict
reached its apogee during the Anfal Campaign in the 1980s when Saddam Hussein's forces employed bombs, chemical attacks and firing squads.
All told, credible estimates are that 180,000 Iraqi Kurds were killed
and 3,000 to 4,000 villages destroyed, with at least a million Kurds displaced in northern Iraq. The Anfal campaign was recognized as genocide
against the Kurdish people by the UK and Sweden. "Al-Anfal" means the
spoils of war, the term perversely taken from a verse in the Quran.[38]

In 1991, the Americans, British, and French implemented the Northern No-Fly Zone to protect the Kurds, and the Southern No-Fly Zone to
protect the Shiites, prohibiting the Iraqi air force from flying there. This
was followed by civil war in the Kurdistan Region as rival political
parties—the Kurdish Democratic Party (KDP) and the Patriotic Union
of Kurdistan (PUK)—vied for dominance. The civil war was resolved with
the 1997 Washington Agreement.[39] The KDP and PUK remain the predominant political parties in the Kurdistan Region today. Protected by
the U.S. Northern No-Fly Zone, the Kurdistan Region developed au-
tonomously. Kurdistan Regional autonomy within Iraq inspires Kurds
in Syria as Syria is collapsing—spooking the Turkish government
because of fears about what this will mean for the map of the Middle
East and Turkey's own east.

The Smell of Rotten Apples

The largest chemical attack against a civilian population in history took
place in 1988 in Halabja in the Kurdistan Region of Iraq, during the

Anfal Campaign. An estimated five thousand people were killed, and seven to ten thousand people injured, when Iraqi central government forces dropped mustard gas and nerve agents on Halabja on March 16, 1988. Survivors fled to Iran.[40] Saddam Hussein and his cousin Ali Hassan al-Majid, known as Chemical Ali, were hanged in 2006 and 2010 for their culpability.

Rojen was a small boy living in Halabja when Chemical Ali attacked with chemical weapons. Today, he is a successful professional with a wife and small daughter and a penchant for well-tailored suits.

He described his family's experiences during that time to me.

"Halabja was one of the most attractive towns in Iraq," he said. "It is a mountainous area, very close to the Iranian border. In 1988, there were so many educated and talented people living in Halabja. We had our own hospitals in the town, which was rare in the 1980s, because Saddam tried to deprive Kurdish villages close to the borders of schools and hospitals. But Halabja had everything. My dad said we will never find another Halabja in our lives, because it was a beautiful city.

"On March 16, when Saddam attacked us with chemical weapons, I lost my elder sister in that bombardment. I was small, but I remember what happened. My dad lost his sight, but thank God, he recovered from that and now he can see. But the chemical weapon affected each one of us. We suffered a lot," he said.

The attack happened around noon. The outside air was pervaded with the scent of rotten apples, from the chemicals. "My dad said, 'Everyone move to the basement. Saddam is going to attack us, and we heard that some people died in the southeast of Halabja.' Everyone screamed, and we went to my uncle's basement. Other neighbors also came because they wanted protection. They said, 'We need help and we want to go to your basement. We are Muslim people, and we are very close to each other.' There were around two hundred people in the basement. Everybody was screaming. They put more than fifty blankets in water, to cover us. My uncle said, 'I smell rotten apples, so cover yourself.' My dad said, 'I can't see anything.' My mom was crying. And everyone in the basement was crying, saying 'this is going to be the end of my life.' People were saying, 'I love you.' My cousin said, 'I see dead bodies on the streets.' People were crazy that day. They had seen so many of their relatives and family members who had died.

"I lost my elder sister in the same day. It was a very tragic day. I was a kid. I can't feel the same pain that my mom went through, because it was her first daughter. So imagine what happened to her. Now I have a daughter, and I understand that feeling," he said.

After eight hours in the basement, Rojen's family decided to flee to the Iranian border, with the adults carrying the small children. Rojen chuckled as he remembered his uncle's annoyance at a detail of normal life in the midst of the traumatic journey: Rojen's little brother, a toddler, peed on his uncle while being carried over the mountains. His uncle blustered in irritation. To me, it is so striking how little details stand out as someone remembers a horrific childhood experience.

They arrived at the border around midnight, and the Iranian government provided food, clothing, and shelter in a tent.

"My dad and my uncle had been very rich, but they lost everything. There were no banks. All their cash and gold was in their house," Rojen said. Rojen's elder brother and cousin crossed the border from Iran back to Halabja to try to get their money from the house; as Rojen's dad had been temporarily blinded, he could not go. "They went home, and all of the money was gone. We were shocked. My mom was very sad, but she was clever because she kept some of her gold in her belt, under her clothes. My mom sold all her gold with a low price, and we stayed in Iran for two years."

Two years later, Rojen and his family returned to Iraq. The Iraqi government did not permit them to return to Halabja, and so they went to the city of Sulimaniyah. "We didn't know whether to go or not, but my dad was insistent—even if we are going to die, let's all die together." But in Sulimaniyah, conditions were difficult. "People treated us like we were traitors, because they were all Baath members. We couldn't even find a rental house. People asked, 'Where are you from? Halabaja? Oh, we won't give a house to people from Halabja.' My dad says he will never forget those days. He wished to die."

"I am strong to keep my family strong," he concluded. "I will never forget those days. I want to keep my family alive and support them and build a new life for my daughter."

Conditions for Rojen and his family improved in 1991 when coalition forces created the Northern No-Fly Zone, and the Kurds gained a level of autonomy. The Kurdistan Region developed and offered stability for a time. But once again, people in the region are facing devastating wars.

The Call for Help

On August 5, 2014, Vian Dakhil, a forty-four-year-old Yazidi parliamentarian and former university lecturer, gave a speech to Iraq's parliament. She pleaded for help for thirty thousand Yazidis who had fled from ISIS up to Mount Sinjar only to die without food or water.[41] In northern Iraq, Mount Sinjar is about seventy miles west of the border with the Kurdistan Region.

Video shows that as she began to speak, members of Iraq's parliament one by one stood up and walked to stand next to her in solidarity, until there was no more space to stand. The video shows the speaker of the parliament trying to control the situation, reprimanding the parliamentarians to stay in their places and repeatedly interrupting Dakhil to instruct her to stay with the agreed message. With determination and a voice cracking with horror, she continued speaking until she collapsed. "We are being slaughtered, annihilated," she said. "Our women are being taken captive and sold on the slave market . . . Please, brothers . . . Please, brothers . . . I speak in the name of humanity. Save us! . . . An entire religion is being wiped off the face of the Earth. Brothers, I am calling out to you in the name of humanity!"

The video of the speech spread on YouTube and was linked online in international newspapers, like *The New York Times* and *The Washington Post*. Dakhil's speech roused the Iraqi people and the international community. After the speech, Iraq's parliament voted for humanitarian airdrops to the Yazidis on Mount Sinjar, as well as strikes on ISIS in that area. Part of President Obama's decision to send U.S. troops again to Iraq was Dakhil's emotional, determined speech. Obama said, "Earlier this week, one Iraqi in the area cried to the world, 'There is no one coming to help.' Well today, America is coming to help."[42] Backed up by U.S. airstrikes and special forces, Kurdish peshmerga forces subsequently rescued most of the Yazidis on Mount Sinjar.

Who are the Yazidis? Monotheistic, the Yazidis fuse Zoroastrianism,

Islam, and Christianity.[43] Numbering about 500,000 today, they are an ancient people with a long history of persecution. ISIS views them as "devil worshippers," which ISIS claims gives them the right to kill Yazidis or take them as slaves.

Human Rights Watch released a report describing systematic rape and sexual violence against Yazidi women in northern Iraq.[44] ISIS fighters separated Yazidi girls and young women from their families and sold them into slavery, with 5,324 dead, missing, and abducted. From August 2014 to February 2015, there were an estimated 992,000 people displaced by ISIS from Iraq's Nineveh province, many of whom are Yazidis, according to the International Organization for Migration.[45]

I wanted to understand the circumstances of the Yazidis after the international interventions to help them and spoke to Dakhil by phone.

"We have two kinds of Yazidis," she said. "One group are the refugees who are settled in tents. We have about 420,000 Yazidi refugees in the Kurdistan refugee camps, approximately 16,000 in the Turkish camps, and around 8,000 in Syria. The situation is terrible. The temperature is 52 degrees centigrade (125 degrees Fahrenheit), and they are living in tents, not in houses, and it is very hot. There are no services at all, not even basic services like water. There is spreading disease. And the others are those who are under ISIS. They are having a terrible life, because even the children, Daesh is training and forcing to convert to Islam. They are trying to educate them to use weapons and fight for ISIS. They are raping our girls and using them in slavery, and they are torturing them. It is very important for us to bring back our girls and our daughters. We need now to urge the coalition forces to finish ISIS, seek support and aid from humanitarian organizations, and bring back our daughters."

Dakhil has used her position to tirelessly fight to bring back Yazidi women in slavery, direct attention to the plight of her people, and guide helping hands to their rescue.

"I am doing a hundred things every day," she said, describing her work in the parliament in Baghdad, speaking around the world to get help for the Yazidis, and undertaking other projects, such as helping Yazidis who had to flee without identification papers." She spends her days comforting traumatized people, trying to solve problems, and talking to the world. News reports show Dakhil counseling mothers whose teenage daughters have been taken, and talking to Yazidi girls taken by ISIS who have managed to conceal cell phones, strategizing about their escape. She has faced significant threats to her life and safety. Her leg was broken in a helicopter crash, when her helicopter was weighed down by Yazidi civilians latching on to it as it was taking off when the Yazidis were trapped on Mt. Sinjar. And Dakhil now ranks high on ISIS's hit list.[46]

"I am working very hard on bringing back our Yazidi girls from ISIS. It is my duty, and I consider my job as a holy activity. That is my priority. I am continuously in contact with humanitarian organizations and telling them these are the needs of these people, and there are shortages of tents, and other needed materials for the refugees. One of the most important and significant things that I am really proud of, sometimes when people are in need, they call me. I am speaking on a hundred calls daily," she said.

"Given all of this horrible trauma, how can Iraq heal from this?" I asked. I wondered how, when stability returns, the Yazidis will be able to move back to their homes and continue with a normal life.

"It is very important for the Iraqi people to live together, but that is something very hard. The reason why it is really hard is that the people who took our Yazidi girls, oppressed them, and raped them, were Arab neighbors. We have been living near them for centuries, and look what they did to us. How can we regain that trust and live with them again? I also hear from the humanitarian organizations that they are supporting us. But what kind of support are they giving? We were not expecting this very low-quality support from the humanitarian organizations. Throughout history, never have such things happened to human beings. The humanitarian community should have forced their countries to fight ISIS, bring back our girls, and protect our people."

Her remarks highlighted how hard it will be for the peoples of the region to return to normal lives in the future; memories of interethnic atrocities will make forging a cohesive state a formidable challenge. I wondered how Iraq as a country could peacefully house all of the different people who now had histories of violence toward each other.

Dakhil wanted law, not further warfare and destruction, to bring justice. "We have a proverb that violence cannot be solved by violence," she said. "We have to implement law, using law to punish people who contributed to such disasters."

Ideology of a Cancerous Quasi-State

I walked around the grounds of the Rotana, the hotel where I was staying, past high walls, gates, guards, and dogs. There were soldiers at the entrances and soldiers posted in buildings nearby. The KRG prioritized protection of the Rotana, where many foreign businesspeople, advisors, and aid workers stay.

Only a few days before I arrived, there had been a shootout not far from the hotel between the police and ISIS. Guests and hotel staff heard gunfire, and then the hotel was locked down by the military. What had happened was that the police tried to pull over a man who had stolen a car. The man got out of the car and shot at the police. The police took him down. The man had stolen the car for ISIS, with the intention of taking it across the KRG border.

While the KRG had fended off ISIS's approach toward the city in August 2014, the shootout near the hotel was a reminder of how close the fighting was. The Kurdistan Region of Iraq shares a 620-mile border with ISIS-controlled territory.[47]

ISIS is a dangerous quasi-state that governs territory. While ISIS evolved from Al-Qaeda in Iraq, it has surpassed being a terrorist group.[48] While Osama Bin Laden was trying to create change through terrorist cells, ISIS rules territory and has established some of the functions of a state. By 2015, ISIS had taken over swaths of Iraq and Syria, with control of an area larger than the UK, although much of that territory is desert.[49] Based in Raqqa, Syria, ISIS seized Mosul in 2014 and Ramadi in 2015, two of Iraq's biggest cities. ISIS now occupies territory that crosses the nation-state boundaries of Iraq and Syria.[50]

ISIS has a complex administrative structure, with provision of public services. It is ruled by an amir and supported by a structured civilian bureaucracy. It has a cabinet with ministers. It assumed control of electricity, water, gas supplies, factories, bakeries, the postal service, healthcare, vaccinations, and bus lines. While many under its rule do not like it, there is a level of acceptance of its governance at the local level, as it provides predictability, law (although brutal), and services. "It incorporates a practical model for social governance, one which has proven surprisingly effective within unstable environments," wrote Charles Lister at Brookings.[51]

ISIS has financial self-sufficiency, with about $2 billion in assets.[52] Howard Shatz, an economist and Iraq expert at the RAND Corporation, labeled ISIS as "the world's richest terrorist organization." Their funding comes from oil fields ($1 to $3 million per day), looting banks and antiquities, taxes on transportation routes, revenue from cotton and wheat, extortion, and ransom for hostages. There is little evidence that ISIS depends on foreign donations for money. But it is also a big spender, operating public services and paying salaries of fighters and allowances to their families if a fighter dies.[53]

It has a military. ISIS took over American tanks, artillery, and Humvees from the Iraqi army. Part of ISIS's leadership is a council of former Iraqi generals who held important posts under Saddam.[54] It operates training camps. It boasted thirty thousand fighters in 2014, with some fifteen thousand foreign fighters from European countries, the Middle East, and the Americas.[55] By 2015, fighter numbers may have doubled, because ISIS coopted smaller forces and conscripted young men from towns they took.[56] It exercises extreme brutality—beheadings, mass executions, crucifixion, and slavery.

ISIS uses the media. It publishes an English-language magazine called *Dabiq,* complete with advanced graphics. It uses Twitter accounts until they are shut down, then gets new accounts and pops back up.

It presents itself as a protector of the Sunnis. When Prime Minister al-Maliki pursued a pro-Shiite agenda, ISIS appealed to some Sunni tribes that found al-Maliki's actions threatening. It represented a rejection of Iraq's post–2003 political order of democratically elected leaders (who were largely Shiite because of the Shiite majority) instead of being selected from Sunni elites.[57] But while purporting to protect Sunnis, the Sunni areas controlled by ISIS are destroyed with wealth looted, cities nearly leveled, and heritage damaged. Since ISIS began conquering swaths of Iraq and Syria in 2014, 20 to 40 percent of Iraq's Sunni population has been displaced.[58] Sunnis will have a hard time recovering for at least the next generation.

ISIS attracts young men by giving them purpose and employment. Film footage shows young ISIS soldiers with long beards toting guns, waving the ISIS black flag, and driving captured U.S. military equipment, to a background of chanted Quranic verses.[59] It appeals to power, agency, sexual gratification for its fighters through enslavement of women, and conquest. It pays salaries to some of its fighters; people are so impoverished and desperate that this resonates.[60]

ISIS is dangerous because it is apocalyptic. ISIS wants to draw the United States into a fight, believing that it is heralding the imminent end of the world.[61] There is a belief that the armies of Rome will meet the armies of Islam in northern Syria (in particular in a town called Dabiq, after which ISIS has named its magazine) and that there will be a final showdown with Islam in Jerusalem. "Rome" could mean specifically Turkey (as Istanbul was called Rome during the time of the Prophet Mohammed) or any Western army. ISIS seeks to hasten the fight its fighters have been waiting for.

And it lays claim to being a caliphate.[62] Abu Bakr al-Baghdadi declared himself caliph, the first since Ataturk abolished the sultanate and caliphate in Turkey in 1924. By 2015, ISIS was operating in eleven countries, with groups declaring loyalty to al-Baghdadi as caliph. In the *Atlantic*, Shadi Hamid (Brookings scholar of Islam) described its appeal: "The caliphate, something that hasn't existed since 1924, is a reminder of how one of the world's great civilizations endured one of the more precipitous declines in human history. The gap between what Muslims once were and where they now find themselves is at the center of the anger and humiliation that drive political violence in the Middle East. But there is also a sense of loss and longing for an organic legal and political order that succeeded for centuries before its slow but decisive dismantling. Ever since, Muslims, and particularly Arab Muslims, have been struggling to define the contours of an appropriate post-caliphate political model."[63] In seeking to establish a pan-Islamic caliphate, ISIS was fighting to destroy the Iraqi and Syrian nation-states.

The Arab Spring was about seeking new models for governance and society. ISIS is a tumor that grew out of that. Charles Lister at Brookings wrote that this "occasionally meant that ISIS has appeared, at least in the immediate term, as a viable alternative to what are perceived as repressive, sectarian, and foreign-influenced governments and incapable, moderate oppositions."[64]

So how is ISIS related to Islam? It calls itself the Islamic State. Are its adherents Muslims following Islamic doctrine? Are they psychopaths whose actions are not rooted in Islam, a religion that provides spiritual solace for a large part of humanity? These questions are under heavy debate because they herald schism and clash of civilizations.[65] Graeme Wood, in a well-publicized feature in the *Atlantic*, concluded, "The reality is that the Islamic State is Islamic. *Very* Islamic."[66] Really? Where do its ideas come from?

ISIS follows a line of Islamic thinking called Jihadist-Salafism. Salafism is the idea that Muslims can understand the Quran by reading it and following the example of the Prophet Mohammed—they need not rely on the fourteen hundred years of interpretation of their forebears. Salafists differ from other Muslims in two areas, argues UCLA Islamic scholar Khaled Abou el Fadl: whether religious text should regulate most areas of life and whether human beings have an innate capability to judge what is good. Salafists emphasize the importance of the texts, and de-emphasize the capability of human reason.[67] In the Quran, as in the Bible, there are verses about war and verses about peace. Traditional institutions of Islamic thinking that had in the past mediated and interpreted circumstances for both have lost their influence. Many Salafists are not jihadists. Among the Salafists are "quietist Salafists" who focus on personal purification and view sowing discord and chaos as disrupting to lives of piety. Some Salafists have begun participating in electoral politics (for example, the Nour Party in Egypt).

Violent Salafist-Jihadist groups like ISIS draw from a strain of theology descended from thirteenth-century theologian Ibn Taymiyyah, who influenced Wahhabism, Salafism, and Jihadism.[68] In a Brookings paper, Cole Bunzel described the movement as predicated on "an extremist and minoritarian reading of Islamic scripture that is also textually rigorous, deeply rooted in a premodern theological tradition."

ISIS draws selectively from Islamic texts to support its violent actions. Indeed, while conquest and warfare are part of the history of Islamic civilizations (as they are part of Western history), ISIS is not supported by mainstream Islamic theology which has enabled a long history of multiethnic societies. ISIS has grown out of a vacuum of ineffective government and social strife in combination with an extreme reading of Islamic texts.

Islamic leaders around the world have condemned its violence. Al-Azhar's grand mufti Shawqi Allam (the highest official of religious law among Sunni Muslims in Egypt) announced that "everything ISIS does is far away from Islam. What it is doing is a crime by all means."[69]

Indeed, a group of 120 prominent Muslim leaders wrote in a long let-ter that ISIS's actions are not Islamic, refuting them with Islamic scripture and tradition. The letter argues that shariah does not allow the killing of innocents.[70] The list of signatories is impressive, including the grand mufti of Al-Azhar, current or former national muftis or religious ministers in Turkey, Bulgaria, Malaysia, Uzbekistan, and Sudan, and directors of Islamic universities and foundations in the Middle East, Africa, Asia, Europe, and North America.

In its magazine *Dabiq*, ISIS justified taking Yazidi women as slaves. "Their women could be enslaved," it wrote about the Yazidis. What fol-lows is bizarre: several pages of quotations from Islamic texts and inter-pretations by ISIS's scholars justifying the practice, concluding: "enslaving the families of the kuffār [infidels] and taking their women as concubines is a firmly established aspect of the Shariah that if one were to deny or mock, he would be denying or mocking the verses of the Quran and the narrations of the Prophet."[71] The letter from the 120 Muslim scholars specifically refuted these arguments, called these actions "abominable crimes," and proclaimed such actions as being against shariah.

ISIS will pose a serious threat to the region's stability for years. Some analysts believe that ISIS will eventually burn itself out on its own brutality. Its ideology is likely to be its own undoing.[72] Others argue that ISIS could entrench itself over time as a state. Stephen Walt at Harvard described ISIS as "a revolutionary state-building organization" that could ultimately keep the territory that it has conquered and gradually turn into a country, making a comparison with the early days of the Soviet Union, during which millions died.[73]

Will ISIS be defeated by Iraqi forces backed up by American air support? Will ISIS be defeated by Syrian government forces backed up by Russia? Will a coalition of outraged nations undertake a ground inva-sion? Will people inside ISIS territory eventually rise up against ISIS? Will ISIS evolve into a real state? Regardless of the path the future takes, it will be bloody, with difficult battles and significant displacement of civil-ians. How can ISIS be stopped? Ideas abound: kill their leadership, send in ground troops, support the Iraqi army and the peshmerga in defeating them, combat violent ideologies, shut down their oil smuggling and other sources of finance, conduct information campaigns so that Iraqis and Syrians understand what ISIS stands for, and build the capacity of stable governments with legitimacy in Iraq and Syria.[74] But ISIS became as strong and violent as it is because of state and societal failure, the same failures that led to Arab Spring movements in other countries.

"The Arab Spring taught that nonviolence doesn't work and violence does," said Shadi Hamid, when I asked him how ISIS fit into the Arab Spring. "That is the opposite of what it was supposed to be," he said, describing how the takeaway for some was not that the overthrown mainstream Islamist parties were too brutal or oppressive, but that they demonstrated weakness. "They can argue that working within the system, participating in the democratic process, doesn't work in the Arab Spring era."

Fighting ISIS

When ISIS advanced on Mosul in 2014 and Ramadi in 2015, multiple Iraqi army divisions collapsed, abandoning posts and leaving behind their weapons, vehicles, and uniforms.[75] The Iraqi army "was not driven out of Ramadi," reproached chairman of the Joint Chiefs of Staff General Martin Dempsey. "They drove out of Ramadi." U.S. Defense Secretary Ashton Carter claimed that the Iraqis lack the "will to fight."[76] *Foreign Policy* published an article titled "Why Are the Islamic State's Commanders So Much Better than the Iraqi Army?" The Iraqi state was not able to defend itself.

What happened? There were a number of reasons. Iraq's army suffers from many of the same ailments as the Iraqi state in general—splintering ethnic divisions, lack of human capacity, weak institutional infrastructure, and lack of leadership from Baghdad.[77] Prime Minister al-Maliki purged experienced Sunnis from the armed forces, replacing them with politically connected, inexperienced Shiites. Many skilled Baathist military leaders under Saddam were now fighting with ISIS, bringing ISIS a new level of experience, training, and planning. The Iraqi army had poor training and lacked strong leadership; it also was inexperienced, being put together essentially from scratch starting in 2004, after the United States disbanded the Saddam-era military.

After a set of failures fighting ISIS, in 2015, Iraqi's new prime minister, Haider al-Abbadi, nominated General Anwar Hamad Amin, the commander of Iraq's air force, to be the new army chief of staff (the appointment at time of writing still required parliamentary approval). General Amin was tasked with restructuring Iraq's failing army to fight ISIS, and I spoke with him just after his nomination about plans for how Iraq's army could support rebuilding the Iraqi state.

"Why did the Iraqi army have problems defeating ISIS in Mosul and Ramadi?" I asked.

"Training and chain of command. These two factors. Training was not enough. And the chain of command was not clear," General Amin said. "What happened was not the fault of the soldiers." He also thought that the lack of salaries, inadequate medical treatment, and poor housing for the soldiers were getting in the way. Other weaknesses in General Amin's view were logistics, corruption, and lack of modern headquarters.

Then he described the challenges of training Iraq's army. While the United States had invested in training, it had not lasted. "We returned back to the old military practices. Still now we are working with the old military technology because our officers, maybe 80 to 90 percent, can't use computers. For command and control, our commanders are depending on the mobile phone. You can imagine, this is our army. The prime minister wants to change this. But it is difficult."

With all of these weaknesses, I wondered how the army would be able to turn around the battle against ISIS, regain the territory that had been lost from the Iraqi state, and stabilize a fractured country once again. "What is your strategy to defeat ISIS?" I asked.

"You must work not only on the military side, but also on the political and economic side, and with the people," he said. General Amin described multiple elements to the strategy, including military activities, defending Iraq's borders, social and economic programs, and efforts to strengthen Iraqi national identity. Defeating ISIS depended upon well-trained regiments, smart weapons, good intelligence, special training, and technology, he said. Investment in Iraq's cities was also key.

He emphasized how important Iraqi national identity was for the strength of the army in defeating ISIS. (While General Amin was Kurdish, he never mentioned this during our conversation, emphasizing Iraqi identity.) "Units must be working under the central government, for Iraq. All the Iraqi peoples, all ethnic groups, Kurdish, Arabs, Sunnis, Shiites, Christians, and Turkman, must all share in fighting Daesh."

Such unified identity was important to underpin putting Iraq back together again, I thought. But that was a challenging goal when sectarian violence had destroyed trust between ethnic groups. How do you create a common identity within the army so that they work together as a force for Iraq, rather than as a force for different parts of Iraq?" I asked.

"We have a constitution, and our people voted for this constitution," he said. Iraq's constitution was drafted from 2003 to 2005 by the Iraqi Governing Council, with facilitation by the United States and the Coalition. The constitution was approved by Iraqis in a 2005 referendum. "In Article 9, the constitution says that the army is a mix of all ethnic groups.[78] This is very important. We must educate our officers and soldiers that this is for one Iraq."

"There is a proposed effort in parliament to create an Iraqi National Guard to solve some of the problems of ethnicity in the army and militias," I said. Military forces called Popular Mobilization Units (PMUs) had been successful in deterring ISIS in some areas; however, these local militias were mostly Shiite, and some viewed them as a harbinger of additional sectarian problems. The proposed initiative would create local National Guards, under command of the Iraqi central government. It was intended to harness Iraq's local loyalties for the sake of a unified Iraq. This would legitimize the PMUs. But it was not clear if the law would pass, as the Shiites feared that if Sunnis created armed Sunni National Guard forces, they would turn against the state one day. "What are your thoughts about how that initiative can solve the problems of weak Iraqi national identity that led to the army leaving Mosul and Ramadi?"[79]

"If they approve it, we can put them inside this umbrella. The problem now is how to change the Iraqi fighter and officer. You are in a job, you are in an office, you must think only for Iraq. When you return back to your house, you can be Arab, Sunni, Shiite, Kurdish, or other. But if you allow people in their jobs to say, I am from this ethnic group or that ethnic group, it will be difficult for Iraq in the future."

"What bodes well for defeating ISIS?" I asked.

"We are fighting Daesh together. The Iraqi side, the KRG, and the Coalition. We are working like one team. We are working together day and night. Our government has the best equipment in the world from the United States. The Coalition is supporting us from the air. But airstrikes are not enough. We must have forces on the ground fighting Daesh. It will take time, but we haven't any choice. We must defeat Daesh. If we can't, it will be dangerous for Iraq and the region in the future."

"What have been your successes so far?" I asked.

He was proud of the training of Iraqi's air force, which he commanded. "Their capability is good. It is not up to U.S. or NATO standards, but it is approaching," he said.

Along with the Kurdish YPG forces in Syria, the KRG peshmerga have been effective in holding back ISIS, especially after receiving U.S. air support. "What is the role of the peshmerga in defending Iraq?" I asked.

"It is a big role. They are also fighting Daesh. The Coalition backed the peshmerga. Now the peshmerga know how to fight Daesh. Peshmerga is part of our national security of Iraq." I made the mental analogy that depending on the peshmerga to defend Iraq would be like depending on the United States National Guard for security in a war.

General Amin and others were working hard to create a stable Iraq, but this was an array of daunting challenges, with a country that was pulling apart at the seems by ethnicity, a lack of capacity, and a confusion of political vision over Iraq's future. I asked my final question, what General Amin hoped to achieve in the next few years.

"My goal is for a federal Iraq," he said, expressing goals different from what Shirin and many other Kurds espoused in desiring a carved-up Iraq, for example, with an independent Kurdish state. A federal Iraq would mean a country that kept its territorial integrity and borders, but with greater levels of regional autonomy, much as the states in the United States have significant levels of autonomy. "My goal is to defeat Daesh. My dream is to build a strong army with good equipment, with very high technology, like NATO and U.S. army standards, with a good air force. My dream for my country is that we start building our country again, and we stay one united Iraq, all people living together, Arab, Kurdish, Turkman, Christian, and others. This is my dream."

A Three-Way Pull on the Iraqi State

"The Iraqi identity is splitting in three different ways," said Ali Allawi, describing Shiite, Kurdish, and Sunni identities within Iraq. "In Iraq it is nearly over, the myth of a unified state. It collapsed. There will be a re-definition of what the Iraqi state will be." This was yet another assessment of Iraq's identity and future.

Allawi served as the minister of trade and minister of defense in the Interim Iraq Governing Council from 2003 to 2004, after the American invasion, and later as minister of finance in 2005–2006. Born in Baghdad in a prominent Shiite family, he was part of the Iraqi exile community in London during Saddam's regime. He is the author of several award-winning books including *Crisis of Islamic Civilization*,[80] and *The Occupation of Iraq: Winning the War, Losing the Peace*.[81] He is also the author of a thoughtful essay on the Arab Spring.[82] He has had fellowships at Oxford University, Princeton University, Harvard University, and the National University of Singapore.[83]

"If the Iraqi identity is pulling in three ways, what will this mean for the future unity of the Iraqi state?" I asked.

"The first order is disengagement of the Kurds. Kurdish nationalism is the last of the nineteenth-century nationalisms. I see a kind of confederation," he said, similar to what General Amin had envisioned for a unified but federal Iraq.

"On the other side, stability in Iraq can only be engineered if the majority Shiites define the Arab state. The Shiites in Iraq are on the verge of identifying themselves as a nation. They see themselves culturally and politically as a group that shares a common background, history, and common concerns. In the past, we thought of ourselves as Iraqis who happen to be Shiites. Now the identity is different," he said. "The majority of Shiites are now saying, 'This is our country, people have to play by our rules'," he said. "This requires acknowledgment or collaboration with the Sunni minority. Whether this can take place in this context is something else."

"The opposite of that is happening in the Sunni world, where they feel dispossessed. They feel susceptible to revolutionary Islam, which is a transnational phenomenon. The Sunni Islamists hardly see themselves as restricted to the nation-state that they are in," he said, referring to ISIS and other movements that sought to unite Sunni Arabs across current nation-state lines. "A significant element of the Sunni Arab population of Iraq has been unable to acknowledge, accept, and collaborate with a state that appears to fall under Shiite groups." He added, "On the Shiite side, the attempt to create institutions that are an extension of Shiite power is hypocritical, because it assumes that others are not going to see it, like what al-Maliki was trying to do."

In other words, the Kurds want their own state, the Shiites are becoming aware of being a nation within Iraq, and the Sunnis are feeling a transnational loyalty across nation-state boundaries to other Sunnis. But as Kamal al-Sammari had observed about people in Tunisia, aren't the Iraqis trapped together in the same house? Even if Iraqis wanted to split, there are not clear lines to easily separate people of different identities, and small, fractured, landlocked new states would not be very viable, I thought.

Allawi reflected about how Iraq's experiences linked to Arab Spring movements, noting that while Iraq did not have significant Arab Spring protests, it was part of the Arab Spring landscape. "The main lesson I would draw from the experience of Iraq and the Arab Spring is the rootedness of the old system," he said, "In particular, the ancien regime was far more rooted than people thought, not easily brushed aside, leading to counterrevolutions. In Iraq it was expressed not in a counterrevolution, but more in the form of rootedness of the former system, the privileges of the Baath community, the ascendency of the Sunni Arab community, and the interconnectedness of the intelligence services and the military. Although they appeared to be smashed by the American invasion, they reformed themselves in ways that appeared to be potent," he said referring to many of the former regime elements who joined ISIS.

"Do you think that the way that Iraq was set up after World War I and the fall of the Ottoman Empire is responsible for the lack of unity in Iraq today?" I asked.

"If you take a snapshot of us in 1926 and a snapshot now, you could draw this conclusion," he said. "But in the intervening periods, there were points in time, episodes where the centrifugal forces that pulled Iraq apart were weaker than the centripetal forces that pulled to the center," he said, describing the beginnings of institutions and a non-sectarian Iraqi identity from the 1950s to the 1970s. "It is not a linear narrative."

That was an interesting idea. Could such a nonsectarian identity once again be formed, even after recent violent conflict? How could that be constructed? Were identities evolving constructs that changed over history? Could identities in Iraq evolve into something healthier and more unified?

"How will Iraq look when things settle down?" I asked.

"The form of the state, the boundaries, may not change, but the contents of it will change. The only stable outcomes that I see are two. One is a national reconciliation that presupposes a high degree of political maturity to transcend the conflicts in common liberal citizenship," he said. "I think that this is a pipedream."

"Or some natural predominance would prevail," he continued. I wondered what that predominance would be: the Iraqi army or ISIS? "The Kurds forming a crypto state would be more stable internally than some kind of forced reintegration into the Iraqi state."

"Do you think that Iraq's borders will change?" I asked. Turkey certainly feared a redrawing of the Middle East map to favor the newly ascendant Kurds, and ISIS was fighting to create new borders.

Allawi paused and thought. "It is not inconceivable, given the choice, that the Sunni Arabs might form an associated state with Syria, Jordan, or Saudi Arabia. If this is the way that this transpires, you might see changes in borders. Turkey might feel the pull of Mosul again," noting that in his book on King Faisal I of Iraq, he had described how Mosul almost became part of Turkey.[84]

But then he went on. "Is splitting the state the best outcome that would create the stability and security for the people of the region? I don't think so. The only way to achieve region-wide concord and harmony is to create some kind of confederation of the entire Middle East with strong supranational institutions that would guide the process," he said, expressing a vision of something like European Union structures for the Middle East. "I don't believe in the politics of nationalism. The world is moving beyond that. It is becoming the politics of localities and particularism. In the Middle East, we don't have significant common structures like regional trade, common transport policies, or legal systems. There is nothing common about it. This would come about with either a world war or a massive external force imposing its will on the area. The United States had its chance and blew it," he said, expressing a dim opinion of how the United States had managed the peace in Iraq after the fall of Saddam Hussein.

He added, "I don't see how the Iraqi state could withstand these stresses for any further length of time. You can't condemn the population to a chimerical search for a unified country where the basis doesn't exist."

A Bold Restructuring

"You cannot just redraw the map," said Fanar Haddad, when I asked him if he thought Iraq would stay together as a country. Haddad is an Iraqi-British scholar of sectarianism in Iraq at the Middle East Institute at Singapore University.[85] He is the author of *Sectarianism in Iraq: Antagonistic Visions of Unity.*[86]

"There is no other option. There really are a lot of hurdles facing any attempts to redraw the borders in a formal internationally recognized way," he said, explaining why he thought that the Kurds, the Shiites, and the Sunnis would need to find a way to make Iraq work. He noted that neither Turkey nor Iran would countenance Kurdish independence. "Anyway, the Kurds have been all but independent since 1991," he said, referring to their autonomous status as a region of Iraq. "Despite the intense division, we have yet to see any alternative to the Iraqi nation-state, with or without the Kurds. The only serious movement has been ISIS. But they aim for something outside the international system of nation-states. They are more an aberration than anything else."

I hoped that too. But given ISIS administrative structures, they seemed entrenched, unless there were to be a massive ground force invasion.

But Haddad thought that crucial issues defining the future of the Iraqi nation-state had to be worked out to keep Iraq together. "What sort of framework will emerge to regulate relations between Erbil and Baghdad? Will the ISIS areas remain indefinitely beyond Baghdad's control, and will Baghdad give up on these areas, rendering them like Pakistan's frontier, a perpetually unstable zone of conflict?" he pondered.

"Some people argue that Iraq has had the decades of problems that it has because of the way that the state was set up upon the end of the Ottoman Empire after World War I, and that Iraq is an artificial state with borders that never made sense in the first place. Do you think that Iraq is structurally doomed to failure?" I asked.

"When you look at history from the United States to the postcolonial world, any sort of state breakdown or implosion or carve up of an empire is seldom pretty. State birth is a traumatic event. I agree that the breakup of the Ottoman Empire did not go very well, but it was not likely to go well. I do not think the breakup of the Ottoman Empire or Sykes-Picot are still problems today," he said, referring to the secret 1916 Sykes-Picot Agreement between Britain and France, in which they agreed to divvy up parts of the Middle East between them upon the fall of the Ottoman Empire, drawing borders that suited Britain's and France's interests rather than the peoples' of the region. "You see other situations where state breakup has not contributed to instability a hundred years later. The concept of Iraq is old enough. It has been there since the Prophet's time. There was a loosely defined area called Iraq. What the early twentieth century saw was the *redefinition* of Iraq rather than the *invention* of Iraq. What the twentieth century brought in was the idea of Iraq as a nation-state. Like most nation-states, Iraq is built on preexisting pre-national concepts that resonated with people."

His comments echoed those of Sara Pursley at Princeton University, who argued in *Jadiliyya* against the "artificial state" narrative for Iraq. "It may be that no modern nation-state has been called 'artificial' more times than Iraq. . . . The story invariably begins with the post–World War I peace settlements, during which the borders of Iraq . . . were purportedly created, more or less out of thin air, by Europeans." ISIS even buys into this assumption: they released a video of the removal of border checkpoints entitled the *The End of Sykes-Picot*.[87] Pursley points out that the territory that ISIS now claims is closer to Sykes-Picot borders than are Iraq's current borders and that Iraq and the other new countries had local antecedents that did not materialize out of thin air. No borders could be drawn cleanly to make homogenous states, she argues.[88] Furthermore, most countries in the world are not homogenous, having minorities. The artificial state narrative, she posits, denies local conditions. The British played a role in shaping the country, but so did the Iraqis.

"In *The Washington Post*, you argued that the Iraqi state needs a bold restructuring," I said to Haddad, as he had argued for working toward Kurdish independence, formulating a new, more legitimate constitution with decentralization of power, and restarting Iraq's state-building process.[89] "What kind of bold restructuring do you think Iraq needs in order to create a stable, healthy, and prosperous society?"

"It would have to start with changing the constitution," Haddad said, describing Iraq's constitution as having too much room for ambiguity and structural problems relating to the framework of governance, especially between the powers of Baghdad and the provinces, such as the Kurdistan

Region. "One positive step would be far-reaching decentralization," he said. His decentralization comment sounded similar to the comments about a federal Iraq made by General Amin and Ali Allawi. "But political leaders in Baghdad are intensely resistant to that." Other needed steps were long-awaited overhauls of the judiciary, the elections law, and a hydrocarbon law for revenue sharing among the different parts of Iraq. He said that while he thought Iraq needed a restructuring, it was not likely under current circumstances.

"How did Iraq fit into in the Arab Spring movements that were about seeking new forms of government and society?" I asked.

"There were protests in Iraq in early 2012. They were not, however, revolutionary protests," he said, echoing comments I had heard in Turkey about Turkey's protests. "They were about better services, government performance, corruption, and reforming the system. I think what's missing in Iraq is the desire for a fundamental reworking of state-society relations. It was a step beneath that. And it was a fleeting moment. One thing that sets Iraq apart was that they had their regime change in 2003, which altered how Iraq was going to react to the Arab Spring. That is why the protests were not about bringing the regime down. They had already made the change from old school authoritarianism."

That argument made sense to me for the Shiite population of Iraq—they lived under a functioning, albeit imperfect, constitutional electoral democracy. But ISIS in Iraq survived not only by conquest, but also by discontent among Iraqis, with at least some tacit support among Sunni tribes and former Sunni members of Saddam's regime. ISIS's violent conquests and imposition of an extreme version of shariah were also in some way seeking a fundamental reworking of state-society relations.

"How did identity politics and sectarianism fit into the Arab Spring and the instability in Iraq now?" I asked.

"In many countries, take Bahrain, Syria, and Iraq, it is not easy to escape sect coding. It is not because people are divided. It is not ancient hatreds. It is because it is difficult to mobilize without revealing sectarian affiliation. Through the twentieth century, if a political threat emerged from a quarter that is sect coded, despite the nature of the political threat, for convenience, you highlight the identity of the protagonist. It is easy to code this or that as Sunni or Shiite. These strategies have a receptive audience, because they feed on and inflate preexisting prejudices. That is a crucial element in Iraq that you don't have in the other countries," Haddad said. "When the Arab Spring arrived, Iraq was already in a state of war. So much else was happening. It is easy to stifle movement by raising fears of conflict. The powers that be played on that quite well."

"What were the factors that led to ISIS? Were they based on Sunni nationalism or sect coding?" I asked.

"Above all, state collapse. ISIS's ideas are not new—setting up a caliphate, or this extreme ugly brand of Islam. State collapse gave space to turn fantasy into reality. And there is no denying that the sectarian element is strong. ISIS is a movement championing Sunnis, standing against non-Sunni forces, Iran and Baghdad."

"How do you think that Iraq will emerge from its problems in the future?" I asked.

"ISIS has highlighted how divided Iraqis are. If this threat couldn't unite them, then what will?" he said. "Now Middle Eastern societies and governments are being renegotiated. What will emerge when it dies down? In Iraq, my question is how sustainable is the current setup? What will emerge? It is bleak."

Defending the Nation-State

"I think that Iraq will stay together—even under pressure. The international community does not want to contemplate what happens if states melt down, or if a regional hegemon is swept away. It would be death to the international system. That's why there is the rallying of sixty-plus nations to support Iraq in the latest fight," said James Jeffrey.[90] A career diplomat who served in the military early in his career, Jeffrey was U.S. ambassador to Iraq from 2010 to 2012, during the Arab Spring, and U.S. ambassador to Turkey before that. Known for his blunt, blustery, colorful turns of phrase, he is a tall man with white hair and a thick Boston accent.

While most of the voices in this book are from the region itself, the story of Iraq in past decades is partly American, given the long U.S. intervention in Iraq. For that reason, I sought out an American perspective.

Jeffrey and a group of other foreign policy heavyweights now at the Washington Institute for Middle East Policy think tank had recently published *Key Elements of a Strategy for the United States in the Middle*

East. "In that proposed strategy, you wrote, 'The entire architecture of the Middle East state system is at risk.' Why and from what? Warfare? The Arab Spring?"[91] I asked.

"In terms of the source of legitimacy, the nation-state has weak roots of its own, and it has competition," he said, a viewpoint different from that expressed by both Ali Allawi and Fanar Haddad. "Part of that competition is violent. The nation-state is unable to provide security from neighbors or from internal uprisings. So it's just a mess. What we said is that our first step is to rescue the nation-states to the extent possible— Iraq, Syria, Lebanon, Jordan, and Egypt," he said.

"What is wrong with these countries as nation-states?" I asked.

"There is a general feeling that their leaders do not deliver law, prosperity, or peace. This feeling is pervasive among the countries that were theaters of the Arab Spring. In many countries, it was a crisis of legitimacy because of the frailty of the nation-state ideal in the Middle East. It was populations reacting against authoritarian forms of government. These are also artificial states, formed out of the Ottoman Empire, the Raj, and various colonial regimes," he said, disagreeing with Haddad and Sara Pursley, who argued against the "artificial state" narrative. Legitimacy of the nation-states, he thought, was being challenged at different levels— by the primacy of local identities as well as by the allure of identities greater than that of the nation-state. "The pan-Islamic movements are out to undo the nation-states," he said, echoing the comments of Ali Allawi, referring to pan-Islamic ideals of a unified Islamic *umma* that transcends national boundaries, as existed when the Arab world had been under the Ottoman Empire.

"What are the factors that will keep Iraq together as a nation-state or pull it apart? ISIS? Kurdish drives for independence?" I asked.

"ISIS is going to be a self-correcting phenomenon," he said, expressing yet another view on ISIS's future. "But it is one manifestation of a deeper phenomenon—the entire vulnerability of the nation-state in the Middle East to radical movements, millennial movements, or the Islamic *umma*. Kurdish independence is not going to happen because they are landlocked and surrounded by countries that will not countenance it. The international system looks askance at states falling apart."

"How did Iraq fit into the Arab Spring?"

"The Arab Spring was the reflection of totally illegitimate governments. They were not religious regimes, not hereditary royalty or constitutional. They were perverted versions of Ataturk's model for the Middle East, but they weren't even populist. They did not fare well when the population had no loyalty. Iraq didn't fit that model. We had public protests in Baghdad, Mosul, and much of the south, but they were put down with a nominal amount of violence. Therefore, I would have to say that the Arab Spring didn't have the same impact in Iraq as elsewhere. There are people who say that what the United States did in Iraq precipitated the Arab Spring. I don't think so. This is because Iraq was on a different track," he said, noting why he thought that countries like Iraq, Turkey, Lebanon, Pakistan, and Jordan had a different experience during the Arab Spring. "These were democratic systems—with some flaws. Those countries had some kind of constitutional system in process, and they were in a different world."

"You have argued for the need to support the nation-states of the Middle East, and U.S. policy has been to support keeping Iraq together. How can Iraq be supported as a nation-state? What is a good basis for Iraq's stability over time?" I asked.

"A good basis would be four things. A more aggressive implementation of the regional federal system like the Kurds have. The Iranians would have to be told that they can't control everything in Iraq, or they will get another collapsed country, and they can't expect America to come in and bail them out. Then the Kurds have to be told by everyone, we love you, we love your federal status, but we are not going to support your independence, and you are going to have to act like you are part of Iraq. And the Sunni Arab states and Turkey are going to have to be told to stop playing footsy with Sunni tribes with irredentist, breakoff, or extremist tendencies. The Sunnis will have to be told that their role is to be a minority, but one that is respected."

"But what happens if Iraq does not stay together?" I asked.

"We don't have an alternative to the nation-state system. The alternative to the nation-state is not an empire, but a Middle East that looks like Syria. There is no alternative model, not an EU of the Middle East. The alternative is total chaos and mass massacre of millions of people. We can't give up on the nation-state or say it was Sykes and Picot who drew these borders. I have never seen a border that makes sense. It is a problem if we are looking for alternatives to the nation-state system. The whole international system is based on America standing up for the nation-state system."

But Americans are tired of using military force, their blood and treasure, to hold together other nation-states.

Open for Business

"In 2015, Iraq is significantly harder and a less desirable destination for investment than it was a few years ago. Nevertheless, it is currently impoverished, but could lift itself fairly quickly into a middle-income or even a rich country. That is why investors invest," said Zaab Sethna, a principal at Northern Gulf Partners, a leading investment firm in Iraq that completed $200 million of debt and equity transactions in energy and oilfield services, financial services, telecom, equipment leasing, and real estate in Iraq. Based in Baghdad, Sethna has been working with global investors seeking opportunities in Iraq since 2003.[92]

"While Iraq has big oil reserves, Iraq seems like a country of both big opportunity and big risk, as its economy has had wild swings. How would you describe both the opportunities and challenges for business in recent years in Iraq?" I asked Sethna. Iraq has the fifth largest oil reserves in the world.[93] In 2012, Iraq had the sixth largest growth rate of GDP per capita in the world, with 9.8 percent growth. But in 2014, it swung the other way, with negative 8.8 percent.[94]

Sethna related a number of reasons to invest in Iraq, as well as challenges. "Between 2005 and 2013, things were going fairly well in Iraq from a political and security standpoint and from a business and investment standpoint," he said. "Iraq is sitting on vast hydrocarbon resources, mostly undeveloped, and it is a country that has incredible needs in every sector. It also has incredible human resources, smart people, young people with startup ideas and entrepreneurial skills, strong family businesses, and a diaspora," he said. While numbers are hard to come by, Iraqis have been leaving Iraq for decades due to ongoing conflict, as emigrants, exiles, or refugees, likely with over 4 to 5 million Iraqis living outside Iraq.[95] "They are very successful in many cases in other countries. That is a great untapped resource for Iraq. Those are the reasons to invest in Iraq," he said.

He added that Iraq has growing consumer spending power. GDP per capita grew from \$1,373 in 2004 to \$6,862 in 2015, a multiple of five in a decade.[96] "People are getting money in their pockets and spending. In emerging markets, when people get money in their pockets, they spend on health, finance, education, telecom, etcetera. All of those are growth areas to do business. All of those have suffered as result of the security and financial crises."

Despite Iraq's problems, Sethna noted some strengths in its government that had in the past made Iraq attractive for investment. "Iraq has a functioning constitutional system where elections are held. Since 2005, Iraq has had five nationwide elections. There are still elements of checks and balances in place despite all of the problems. Media in Iraq is pretty wide-open and free. Civil society organizations are allowed to exist," he said, making observations that were similar to those expressed by Fanar Haddad about the parts of Iraq that were functioning. "I am not saying everything is good in Iraq—public services are terrible, the economy is not growing fast enough, twelve years after the invasion there is no electricity in some places. But it is a functional constitutional system. People have the right and the means to express themselves. It gives them some dignity and self-respect, which is what is lacking in those other states," he said, referring to the states that experienced Arab Spring revolutions.

"What are the challenges for doing business in Iraq and for Iraq's economic growth?" I asked.

"Three factors made Iraq an increasingly difficult place to do business. One, Prime Minister al-Maliki began a systematic move toward autocracy. In business, he was consolidating power to himself in a Mubarak mode," Sethna said, referring to Egypt's president, who was ousted in the 2011 Arab Spring protests. Sethna described how al-Maliki installed political loyalists in Iraq's Supreme Court, National Security Council, the Human Rights Commission, the Central Bank, and the Trade Bank of Iraq. "That effort served to increase corruption, decrease competence within the government, and decrease levels of confidence from foreign investors," he said. "Corruption, bureaucracy, and regulatory uncertainty are a huge bottleneck.

"The second factor was the deterioration of security. Security increases your costs, because you have to take steps to mitigate risks. From a security standpoint, the security crisis of the last year has not affected the energy sector in any significant way, as oil is concentrated in the extreme south and north, while the problem is in the center. No oil company personnel have been harmed. You would imagine attacking foreign oil companies would be a good strategy for ISIS, because attacking foreigners could cut off the Iraqi state's source of revenue. It is an indication that those areas are well protected.

"Then the third was the decrease in the price of oil," he said. Oil dropped from $114 per barrel in June 2014 to $52 per barrel in July 2015 because of weaker world demand and high production from the United States, Iran, and OPEC.[97]

The business climate also demonstrated the Kurdistan Region's increasing autonomy within Iraq. "From a business perspective, Kurdistan is already a different place to do business," he said. "Separate legal jurisdiction, different regulatory structure, different government officials to deal with."

"What are the upcoming factors to watch?" I asked. "Are there reasons for optimism for Iraq's future from a business perspective?

He answered right away. "Young people in Iraq and technology and communications." Internet penetration in Iraq in 2013 was 9.2 percent, while in 2010, it was 2.5 percent—multiplying severalfold in just a few years.[98] Young people online would become a force for positive change like elsewhere in the region, he thought. "An Iraqi I know started a fast food chain called Burger Joint. His outlets are full of young people. I asked him how he advertises. The only advertising he does is on Facebook. He hired a young woman in Kirkuk, never met her, and her job is to be the social media person. Kirkuk is cut off and unstable, but there is a young woman staying at home using the Internet. Things like that give me optimism," he said. "Iraq is an important place. The people of Iraq have suffered from every bad idea mankind came up with in the twentieth century. I would like to see them live up to their potential."

Iraq's Finest Hotel

I stood in the lobby of the Erbil Rotana, named Iraq's leading hotel for five consecutive years (2011–2015) by the World Travel Awards.[99] Staff in suits served entering guests dates and Arabic coffee. The lobby had multistory high ceilings, stone floors, and a grand glass entryway with steel latticework. Arrangements of fresh hothouse flowers were situated on granite check-in desks. To my right was a cafe with slate tables and wide chocolate brown sofas near a fountain burbling over pebbles. A pianist played classical music on a black grand piano. I walked outside through the landscaped grounds, which also featured a pool, pavilions, fountains, and a Lebanese restaurant with trellises shaded by grapevines. It never ceased to amaze me that this hotel could exist in Iraq.

Outside the hotel was stiff security, with a guardhouse, barricades, and a setback from the road. Cars could not enter, except for official government cars. The hotel was under the full protection of KRG security forces.

I met with the hotel manager, Ghassan Dalal. He made me espresso in his office.

"Why did the Rotana set up a hotel in Erbil?" I asked. "Many people would be surprised to learn about a prominent hotel chain investing in Iraq." Rotana is a luxury hotel chain based in the United Arab Emirates, with a portfolio of over one hundred properties throughout the Middle East, Africa, South Asia, and Eastern Europe.

He related how the 2006 KRG Investment Law, intended to facilitate and enhance foreign investment, had created attractive opportunities for investors. "The Rotana saw that the opportunity to build a five-star hotel was feasible," he said. Construction took thirty-six months, which he thought in Kurdistan "must be some kind of a record." The Rotana was the first branded five-star hotel in Erbil.

"What do you think that the Rotana is contributing to the economy in Erbil?" I asked. A hotel like the Rotana supports the economic development of the Kurdistan Region as it enables international business and development travel. Travelers would be hesitant to come without a comfortable and safe place to stay. It also creates local employment. For my RAND colleagues and me on our research trips, it had felt like a comfortable and safe haven that enabled us to do our jobs there.

He related that half of the Rotana's staff is local, with the other half spread across twenty-five nationalities. "It's true that our staff do lack experience in this field, but they have exhibited strong capabilities and willingness to learn and adapt to the five-star environment. I think we are among the few companies with foreign investment that has managed to recruit and maintain a large number of locals," he said.

I had come to know the staff over time. On one trip, I had ordered a single boiled egg at the egg station in the breakfast room. The egg cook, a man from Mosul, somehow remembered that and, without me asking, served me a single boiled egg every day on every trip for the next few years. (While I ceased to really want the single boiled egg, I so appreciated the gesture.) In the lounge, a man from Kosovo served me drinks and a woman from Morocco sewed a button for me. I celebrated when a waiter from Syria found that his missing sister and parents had arrived safely in Turkey after fleeing from their home.

"There must have been many challenges in establishing and operating a hotel in Iraq. What were they? How did you overcome these challenges?" I asked.

"Managing a hotel in Erbil is not an easy task," he said, relating how the Rotana had to hire 380 staff members, train them, find all the items needed for the hotel, locate the food items that were missing from the city and even from the country, and then arrange the logistics of transporting these items by both flight and ground.

"A few years ago, things were more stable. There are a lot of security problems now with the war on ISIS so close. How do you view future business prospects in Erbil?" I asked.

"I think that the demand will continue to exceed supply. We have made market studies, which show that demand for top-end hotel rooms will continue to remain high, and increase year-by-year because Erbil is on the right investment track. This is the only area in the region that shows security and stability and, with the government's support of invest-ment, Erbil will grow. This will bring with it demand in terms of hotel rooms," he said.

I left his office and went to have a tea in the tranquil, elegant lobby with Dina, an Egyptian woman on the hotel staff, whom I had known for several years.

"How was it here at the Rotana when ISIS was advancing on Erbil?" I asked.

"It was one week," she said, describing fear after ISIS broke through the KRG-controlled lines. "You could feel the panic. The guests were scared. The staff was scared," she said. She explained that hotel staff who lived outside the hotel moved back inside the hotel, to be safer. There was one day with shooting nearby. A bullet hit the hotel, but not the glass windows. People were running everywhere. But the hotel staff made efforts to calm the guests. "Security did their procedures."

She was wistful for the way Erbil had been before ISIS. "We used to see people getting married in the park, enjoying themselves." But the week that ISIS approached Erbil was tense, with people trying to flee but airlines stopping services. "Tickets were sold out and prices were very high. I could not get a ticket out. I was stuck here."

But through it all, Dina and others reassured themselves. "America will not let Erbil fall," she told herself. "This region has struggled a lot, and America struggled to get it where it is," she explained; it was these thoughts that kept her going. "The world came and started to say, 'No. We have to take action.' ISIS got Mosul, and it was okay. But once they started to come close to Erbil, the world said no. But why was action not taken from the beginning?" she asked, with an indignant tone of protest.

"Once the Americans made the airstrike, Kurdish people celebrated," she said. "Then life was normal again, with people going to work. But what will happen the next day?" she asked rhetorically. She was still living in anxiety. "People go day by day. We keep our things with us. I started to sleep with my passport under my pillow and clothes nearby. But there was no comfort in sleep. You have to be ready."

"With all of this instability, why did you come to Erbil? Why have you stayed?" I asked.

She came because she thought that Erbil was peaceful, with opportunities for career advancement and a good income. "I loved it in Kurdistan. I enjoyed my freedom and my work. It was the perfect match for me. Erbil is my comfort zone," she said.

We finished talking, and I went to stand by the window on an upper floor to look across the street at a multi-acre public park and garden that to me invoked the gardens of Persian poetry. On business trips, I used to meander its tree-lined gravel trails for hours with colleagues after a day of meetings, feeling safe. It was a beautiful place to stroll and unwind. There were rose gardens, children's playgrounds, a manmade lake with paddle boats, a public library (still largely empty), a red tarmac running path winding through groves of trees, past benches and statues. A lot of thought had been put into selecting the plants, creating a little haven of intentional beauty in a world of turmoil and ugliness.

From Iraq to Jordan

Iraq was an important part of the Arab Spring context, and Iraq's future is being formed by the fallout from Arab Spring events and desires for new forms of government. As a country formed from three Ottoman provinces after World War I, Iraq was a confusing mix of identities and problems. And now nationalism, sectarianism, religion, and violence were challenging the very existence of Iraq as a nation-state.

How did Iraq come to this? There are many reasons. Its borders included peoples of different identities, and state collapse had brought about conflict among them. Nationalist movements and religious movements were pulling apart the major ethnic groups. Shiite Iraq seemed to be grappling with relatively recent consensual constitutional democratic government. The Kurdistan Region has been investing in public services and the economy, with electoral democracy. But Saddam's repression followed by the American-led invasion and early drawdown had so destabilized other parts of Iraq that ISIS was able to move into the vacuum. While grotesque, ISIS also represented a search for a new form of government as an alternative to the failed states that came before it and capitalized on the Syrian Arab Spring civil war. The levels of refugees and displaced persons in Iraq and Syria now are reminiscent of the displacement and refugees that came after World War I and World War II.

Iraq was in need of a dramatically different solution, a new structure of government that would enable the people who live within its borders to coexist, with unity of country, autonomy at the local level, and equal rights for citizens regardless of identity.

I next traveled to Jordan, to understand yet another form that the Arab Spring took—of protest movements followed by moderate change, tempered by the experiences of its neighbors.

Jordan

The View from Amman's Citadel

I stood beside the Citadel's stone walls and gazed over the hills of Amman. Most buildings are of creamy white limestone, making the view over the hills a uniformly pretty cityscape, interspersed with cars snaking through messy asphalt and green pine trees. Many of the neighborhoods on view from up here did not exist until the past few decades. Old black and white photos of Amman show a sparse, rocky landscape with a handful of buildings clustered in the valleys between the hills. The buildings today are a result of Amman's rapid rise as a densely populated city of importance in the past half century and of inflows of refugees.

I wandered and explored the ruins inside the walls of the Citadel, a veritable tour of Amman's past—stone pillars from the Roman temple of Hercules, a Byzantine basilica, and an Islamic Ummayad-era palace.

Under the Roman Empire, Amman was the city of Philadelphia, prominent in antiquity as a strategic spot on trade routes, a natural meeting point for caravan trails between the Arab peninsula, the Mediterranean, and Africa. But the city lost its importance after the Romans. During Ottoman times, it was a sparsely populated Bedouin village. While Amman's heritage is ancient, Jordan is a new country with a newly distinct identity and recent borders that define it, created about a century ago.

What are now Jordan, Israel, the West Bank, and Gaza were part of Ottoman Palestine from 1517 until the end of World War I. After the Ottoman Empire fell in 1921, the area became part of the bigger British Mandate for Palestine until independence in 1948.

On a map, Jordan resembles a pistol pointing south. The long border with Israel and the West Bank forms the top of the pistol, shaped in part by the biblical River Jordan and the Dead Sea. The mouth of the pistol aims south toward the Red Sea, and the pistol's handle juts north and east into the desert to border Saudi Arabia, Iraq, and Syria. Jordan is in a tough neighborhood. Jordan's King Abdullah II once joked to Jon Stewart on the *Daily Show* that Jordan is stuck between Iraq and a hard place.[1] Winston Churchill liked to boast that he invented Jordan with the stroke of a pen one Sunday afternoon, as borders for new countries were being formed out of the Ottoman Empire.[2]

When Jordan was created (called Transjordan then), it was largely barren desert, with few resources and a sparse population. It was meant to serve as a buffer zone between more populated centers of civilization—the Arabian Peninsula, Syria, Iraq, and Palestine. But what was created as a buffer zone has become a lynchpin of stability in the region. Jordan has ended up absorbing refugees from the conflicts of the countries that it was supposed to buffer. The country has grown from 1.1 million people in 1945 to 7.5 million people in 2015, a sevenfold increase in population in sixty years stemming from both immigration and natural population growth.[3] A desert country scarce in water and arable land, Jordan was not supposed to accommodate as many people as it has today.

Being Jordanian was an identity that had to be formed among the people inside this strange shape drawn upon a map. The main identities in Jordan are tribal East Bank Jordanians, Palestinians, Christians, Circassians, and Syrians. While the government did not collect ethnic data in the 2010 census, East Bank Jordanians (people whose ancestors lived east of the River Jordan before conflicts with Israel) are believed to make up 30 to 50 percent. Palestinian refugees who fled homes in Israel during the 1948 and 1967 wars with Israel (and their descendants) are believed to be about 30 to 50 percent of the population. There are now between 650,000 and 1.4 million Syrian refugees who have entered Jordan since the beginning of Syria's civil war. Circassians, descendants of Muslim refugees from former Ottoman territories that now are part of Russia, number about 125,000.[4] The remainder are Christians.[5] Politics of ethnicity shape Jordan's politics: Who is a Jordanian? As Jordan developed the institutions of a state, its forays over time into democracy meant balancing among delicate societal divisions.

The man who became the first king of the Hashemite Kingdom of Jordan, King Abdullah I (the brother of King Faisal I of Iraq), was a shrewd political actor who navigated the post–World War I period so that Jordan ended up a country, with himself as a king of Transjordan.[6] Jordan's rulers are from the Hashemite tribe, descended from the Prophet Mohammed. King Abdullah I's grandson, King Hussein, was a revered leader in both Jordan and the wider the Middle East, guiding Jordan through the next few rocky decades. When King Abdullah II acceded to the throne in 1999 after the death of his father, King Hussein, he was widely seen as a liberal reformer. He and his wife, the glamorous Queen Rania, promoted educational reform and invested in technology entrepreneurship. Jordan is now a Middle Eastern tech and entrepreneurship hub. Jordan enjoys a growing knowledge economy, an improving education system, strong trade relations, and a relatively robust business climate. Jordan is an upper middle-income country, with a higher standard of living than many of its neighbors in the Middle East.

However, Jordan struggles with significant economic problems that include low economic growth and unsustainable government subsidies for staples.[7] The unemployment rate is 12.6 percent, with youth unemployment estimated to be double that.[8] Many Jordanians were disappointed that reform and development efforts in recent decades delivered less than what was desired. Other issues include weak political parties, social tensions, and youth wanting greater opportunities.

When Arab Spring events erupted in other countries, protests spread to Jordan. Protesters' goals were mainly economic, although they also included a desire for greater political representation within the government system, not wholesale change in government. Scattered calls for the king to cede power to an elected government were not widespread.

Jordan's Arab Spring was sparked by East Bank Jordanians who were not happy. The Palestinians for the most part sat it out, not wanting to rock the boat. Protest movements fizzled out when Jordanians saw the chaos ignited by the Arab Spring in neighboring countries. Even with the problems in Jordan, the alternatives were worse.[9] Jordanians did not want to imitate what they saw in Iraq, Syria, or Egypt.

King Abdullah II weathered the storm largely by avoiding violence and making concessions and incremental reform steps.[10] Protests turned into moderate reform, not revolution. Jordan's Arab Spring is a story of taking the middle road, in contrast to other Arab Spring countries where governments were overthrown or wars resulted. Furthermore, before the Arab Spring, while Jordan faced challenges, it did not undergo the same levels of repression and stagnation as other countries of the Middle East. There was robust rule of law. Its royal family enjoyed high levels of respect and legitimacy. Its economy was not as dire as others'. Its government made consistent investment in development over time. Intellectuals, government leaders, entrepreneurs, and media personalities all pushed the boundaries.

Jordan remained stable, though just over the borders is chaos. But Jordan's stability should not be taken for granted. It is a delicate balance, with economic woes, demographic tensions, ISIS on the border, the Arab-Israeli conflict, and greater pressures for democracy. Furthermore, the problems that birthed Arab Spring protests in Jordan are not solved. David Rohde, in the *Atlantic*, described Jordan's Arab Spring as not over, but on pause.[11]

I wanted to understand what Jordan's Arab Spring protests were about, how Jordan stayed stable, what Jordan has done right, and what pressures remain.

I walked down winding ribbons of streets from the Citadel to the center of Amman. The walk took me past antique shops, with disorganized piles of old metal teapots that looked like genie lamps, coffee boilers, metal elephants, old phones, bent cutlery, bronze candlesticks, and strings of scuffed-up prayer beads. I passed small grocery and produce shops. A group of ten-year-old boys smoked cigarettes under a tree. I passed ruins of Amman's ancient Roman amphitheater, white blocks of stone nestled into the side of a hill with pine trees overhanging it. I passed a tea seller in a little kiosk, with old men sitting, chatting, and smoking nearby on white stone benches under eucalyptus and palm trees. They were enjoying a pleasant, sunny afternoon.

Reform, Not Regime Change, Not Revolution

Amman lacks a central public space that could serve as a focal point for protests like Avenue Bourguiba in Tunis, Tahrir Square in Cairo, or Taksim Square in Istanbul. However, many protests took place at a traffic roundabout in front of the Ministry of Interior, also notable because it is the site of the Jordanian stock market and international hotels. The site itself is nondescript and unremarkable, not even close to the size of the other Arab Spring gathering points. Roads feed into the circle and an overpass covers some grass. I walked around the circle and observed the traffic.

Here was the location of the March 25, 2011, confrontation, the apex of protests in Jordan. Youth gathered on the grass, chanted slogans, and set up camp, waving the green, red, black, and white Jordanian flag. Protesters called for the sacking of the prime minister, a reduced role for intelligence operatives, less corruption, and a new election law. Many of the protesters were university students or unemployed university graduates who had met on Facebook.[12]

And then antireformist, nationalist counterprotesters showed up. Rock throwing ensued. It is not clear exactly what happened, but it stoked fears that what happened in Egypt, where the government paid thugs (*baltagiya*) to beat protesters, would happen here.[13]

Police cracked down with water cannons and riot gear. Eyewitnesses reported that police surrounded hospitals, preventing the treatment of the injured.[14] There was one death and about 120 injuries, about equal in number between civilians and police. But March 25, along with other protests, spurred political and economic steps by the government of King Abdullah II, including sacking the prime minister, prosecution of high-profile corruption cases, constitutional amendments, government salary increases, the creation of additional government jobs, and early parliamentary elections. Saudi Arabia injected capital into Jordan's economy to help address some of the economic problems.

I wanted to hear the point of view of someone involved in protests in Jordan, and so I took a taxi to Abdoun, Amman's upscale district of white stone villas and shopping malls, to meet Ahmed at Blue Fig, Jordan's answer to Starbucks. Ahmed was a tall, wiry, and thoughtful Jordanian man in his late twenties wearing a light blue button-down Oxford shirt and jeans.

Ahmed was an intellectual activist during Jordan's Arab Spring. Not an organizer of protests, Ahmed instead was a leader of organized debates—the discussions that happened between and after protests, as youth were coming together trying to make sense of events and to determine what they wanted for their societies.

"How were you involved in Jordan's Arab Spring? What was it like?" I asked.

"It was an exciting time," he said. When protests started in Tunisia and Egypt, Ahmed and his friends were riveted. They started a Facebook page, where they posted articles and analysis about the events shaping the Middle East. Because of growing interest and discussions with others on their Facebook site, they began hosting live sessions, inviting politicians, academics, and intellectuals for discussions. They aimed to provide a neutral platform, in which people of many points of view could come together for dialogue about ideas, inclusive of everyone from ardent government loyalists to reformists to people in the Hirak, Jordan's youth movement. (While Ahmed wanted the platform to be a neutral space for all, he acknowledged that many viewed him as having a reform bias.)

In my travels in other countries for this book, I found that the kind of neutral platform for dialogue among youth with different perspectives set up by Ahmed and his friend seemed to be lacking. Open dialogue is crucial for a healthy civil society. This was also one of multiple examples of "middle road" approaches taken by actors in Jordan.

Ahmed attended some of the protests. At the beginning, multiple disparate groups were out together, the leftists, the Muslim Brotherhood, the Hirak, and independent activists. Later, polarized by events in Syria, solidarity in Jordan fractured, with different groups attending separate protests.

"I would chant on the slogans that I agreed with and not chant slogans that I didn't agree with. But I agreed with the whole act of expressing yourself in the public sphere, even if not all of the slogans reflected my views," he said.

"What was the Arab Spring in Jordan about? What were people trying to achieve with the protests?" I asked him.

"The protesters didn't ask for the fall of the regime like other countries," he said. "They asked for constitutional changes."

"What in particular?"

"Different people wanted different things," he said. "People didn't like the status quo, but they didn't like it for different reasons. Even if they agreed on the reasons, they didn't agree on the same process." Reasons for protests included lack of jobs and economic opportunities. People felt that the benefits from growth in Jordan's economy from 2000 to 2008 were not distributed in a way that was perceived as fair. "Inequality increased," he said. Ahmed described a desire for political reforms, with a list of very specific changes that various protest groups wanted, including changes to the electoral laws to enable more accurate representation by demographics in the House of Representatives, election rather than appointment to the Senate, establishment of a constitutional court, and prosecution of corruption. Some of the protest demands were met by the government, but not fully.

I observed that it seemed like there was a lot of disagreement about the way forward among the protesters; in other countries, there had also been a lack of consensus about next steps after the protests. Ahmed wanted to correct what he thought was a misimpression that the protesters lacked concrete goals. "It was not just a force for change that didn't know what it wanted."

"The king seems well-respected, and most protests were not aiming for the removal of the king. How did the protesters view the role of the king? What kinds of changes did they want in relation to the monarchy?" I asked.

Ahmed confirmed my impression. "People see virtue in him staying in power," he said. "They look at Syria. They correlate the Hashemite regime with the stability of Jordan. I would like to see a stable, more inclusive Jordan with a weaker Hashemite monarchy, but it is not possible because the main institutions are established around the crown—public bureaucracy, the intelligence, the army."

"What did you personally want to achieve?" I asked.

"I started thinking that political reform was the most important. Then I thought no, economic growth, reform, and equality has to precede political reform, so that people will be more knowledgeable to vote. Now I think that it is both at the same time. It is too complicated to say there is one path." He added, "A more representative parliament would better represent peoples' rights in a more important way."

"There were changes to Jordan's constitution after the Arab Spring," I said, noting that these included reinforced separation of powers, improved civil rights, prohibition of torture, reduced censorship, limits on the government's ability to use temporary laws, increased independence of the judiciary, introduction of a constitutional court to monitor constitutionality of laws, and creation of an independent commission to oversee elections.[15] This was the first set of major amendments to Jordan's constitution since it was adopted in 1952. Key changes were *not made* in the basic power structure. The king kept significant powers, and the prime minister and senators are still chosen by the king. Therefore, there are only weak incentives for political parties to develop. "I understand that reactions to the constitutional changes were polarized, with some viewing the changes as merely cosmetic and others viewing them as a leap forward in institution building. What are your thoughts about the changes in the constitution and powers for the government?" I asked.

He described many of the constitutional changes as "silly and meaningless," noting additional "draconian" laws enacted for counterterrorism and telecommunications.

"What do you think the Arab Spring in Jordan achieved then?" I asked.

"There were positive things but there are also negative things," he said. "A big change is in the mentality of people. People felt more courage in expressing their views, in adopting their positions, and their style of life. It is too complicated to label it in one sweeping word. I hope that in the movement that was created, it transforms the medium term to more representation, more public responsibility, less inequality, all these things that people demanded," he said. "On the other side there is more radicalization of the youth in terms of Salafists and jihadis." Then he added, "Hopefully the ideological and philosophical shift that happened in the region will not go away, the more progressive shift, even when we don't see it."

Ahmed also observed that during Jordan's Arab Spring, the power of the state weakened, in both constructive and destructive ways. He ticked off a few examples of how public services became worse: traffic wardens did not regulate traffic as well; illegal kiosks selling goods popped up all over; there were more thugs in the street. "You have to weaken the force of the state to create the political space for freedom of expression," he said, but this also unfortunately weakened the state's important regulatory forces. "Maybe it is a necessary thing. I don't see how you can divide them. Maybe the regime is too rigid to separate that into two spheres." He gave the new situation mixed reviews.

"Was it worth it then?" I asked.

"For me as an individual it was worth it. I would like to think that I was part of it. I didn't suffer. I benefited a lot. I became more interested in public affairs, and my values changed." He read a lot about the historical development of constitutions in the UK, United States, and elsewhere, whereas before he had taken little interest in matters of governance. He made lasting friendships. "Even if it is only Tunisia, that is still good," he said, but added, "If I were a Syrian refugee, I don't know if it is worth it."

The conversations among the youth were also an important process in and of themselves, he thought, helping them to think through what they wanted for their society. "One of our most emotional sessions was about March 25, a year after the events." He and others organized a session to have open discussion among all sides. "It was important for everyone to know what actually happened that day. We didn't establish a solution, but facts," he said. He described a heated discussion that eventually led to the splitting of the group into loyalists and reformists, even their unity of discussion splintered over the events of March 25.

Ahmed remained a member of both groups. He wanted to keep his neutral position in the middle. "Because I never knew who was right, and still don't know," he said.

Democracy, Jordanian-Style

Jordan's House of Representatives sits in a compound of large white stone buildings in the center of Amman. I stood in the hall where the parliament meets. The hall had Islamic green carpets, Islamic green tapestries, and green malachite stone. Desks with audio equipment and seats for the parliamentary deputies surrounded a central circle. Minimalist lights hung from the domed geometric-patterned white ceiling. A presentation screen hung on the wall, next to a portrait of King Abdullah II and the Jordanian flag.

What is democracy Jordanian-style? I went to meet Rula al-Hroub to talk about democracy and political reform after the Arab Spring. Al-Hroub gained national prominence in Jordan as a political talk show host on the Josat television network that she co-owns with her husband. She started a political party called Stronger Jordan and was elected as a member of the House of Representatives, where she chairs its human rights committee. She has a Ph.D. in educational psychology. Fifteen of the seats in Jordan's House of Representatives are reserved for women; al-Hroub won a seat in the open competition, not one of the reserved seats.

I waited for her in her office in the House of Representatives, and she entered, blond and in her late forties, carrying a large designer handbag. She gave hurried instructions to staff about a few issues before sitting down with me.

"I asked a Jordanian friend to list the most important women leaders in Jordan, and your name came up first. And then on the way here, my taxi driver said that you are one of the two most influential members of parliament," I said, remarking on her street credibility.

"I was able to do things that men did not dare to do," she said. She was proud of the image she developed on her television talk show for being tough. "It helped create the image in peoples' mind that this is a strong woman. Sometimes they call me Margaret Thatcher, the Iron Woman," she said with a smile.

"Across the Middle East, people are demanding more public discussion and public accountability. What are you trying to accomplish with your television show? What are the priorities and successes in the laws that you are proposing in parliament?" I asked her.

"My show is the most courageous show on TV," she said. "Before we started, no one dared to have debates on the TV channels in Jordan. No one dared to host the other point of view." As she described the controversial issues discussed on her show, she repeatedly used words like "brave," "courageous," and "daring," indicating her values. She continued, "In parliament, you cannot talk about *successes* for a person. You can talk about *stances* for a person. It is not like America, with two parties that achieve things. We have blocs, but they are weak and inconsistent." She viewed her role as asking hard questions of the government. She also noted her record of proposing the largest numbers of draft laws and modifications to laws.

Indeed, the structure of Jordan's government is such that parliament is relatively weak, with much of the power residing with the monarchy and the cabinet appointed by the monarchy. Some of the Arab Spring protest demands were for a more representative parliament that could chan-nel the voices of citizens and was powerful enough to govern.

"From your perspective as a talk show host and parliamentarian, what was the Arab Spring about in Jordan?" I asked.

"Most Jordanians were angry inside themselves," she said. "They know that there are violations of human rights, no justice, no equal opportu-nity for Jordanians, tribal thinking, *wasta*," she said, using a common Ara-bic word for nepotism. "If you belong to this family, you get the job, if not, no job." She described wages that were not high enough to live on, a lack of fulfillment of basic needs, low standards of living, poor quality of education, and police violations of human rights.

But the specific goals of the movement across the region were still un-clear, she thought, although they were forming. "We are in a stage where Arab societies are still discovering themselves. They are fighting for things that are not really clear in their minds."

I thought that this was an important observation. Protests across the region had been about demanding specific changes, sometimes described in terms of political structures, desire for changes in leadership, or more, but at heart, they seemed about something larger and more foundational, about the ideas and modes of government that could better support dignity and a desirable way of life. But ideals seemed to not yet have translated into goals. Her comments reminded me of the process that Ahmed had described among the protesters, undertaking deliberative debates to test ideas and determine aims.

"Given the lack of clear goals, after all of the protests, government negotiations, and more, what will the Arab Spring have accomplished in Jordan?" I asked.

"It is hard to predict right now. We are at a stage in which the Arab Spring is firing back," al-Hroub said, referring to the counterrevolutions sweeping the region. But she took the long-term view, comparing the Arab Spring to other revolutions, noting that the French Revolution led to a backlash that brought in Napoleon, and then a back and forth in France between empire and republic.

"In my view," she added, "the Arab Spring helped give women a great push. Before the Arab Spring in Jordan, we rarely saw women with free opinions and independent voices. In Jordan and elsewhere in the Middle

East, one of the Arab Spring advantages is that women's voices are heard louder than before. It is not just classic women, in authority, in compliance with authority policies," she said, meaning women related to or supportive of those who held government power. "Now we are seeing women in *opposition,* in Egypt, Iraq, Yemen, Jordan, and Syria." Specifically, she noted a more visible presence of women on television and within political parties.

I found this particularly thought-provoking, as indeed, in Jordan, only 15 percent of women participate in the labor force, the fifth lowest in the world, coming just before Syria, Iraq, Algeria, and the West Bank and Gaza.[16]

"After the protests, there were reforms in Jordan, and Jordan stayed on a middle path, unlike many of the other countries, with gradual changes. What do you think of the changes in government that were made?" I asked, referring to the constitutional changes, job stimulus, corruption trials, and more, as I had asked Ahmed.

She shook her head sadly. "Most reforms were formal, not substantive," she said, describing them as "toothless." Her views were similar to Ahmed's. "Except for the constitutional court," she added. The constitutional court had created a new check on political power, and this was a good step. She pointed to an amendment to Jordan's constitution that stipulated that legislation should not affect rights and liberties stated in the constitution.[17] "This addition is very important," she emphasized. For example, when security forces entered homes without warrants, a lawsuit was filed on the basis of a constitutional provision that protected people's privacy in their own homes. "With this article in place, it helped us to go to the constitutional court and say, this law is not constitutional."

"But Jordan is stable. Even if the changes in response to protests were not as much as desired, they have been effective from that perspective. How has Jordan stayed stable through all of this, while other countries have not?" I asked.

"We looked around, we looked at Syria, the bloodshed, and we didn't want this to happen in Jordan," she said. "Okay, we have problems, and we need reforms, but it is not to the extent that we would sacrifice what we have already to create an ideal society. We gave up some of our reform demands. We put them on halt. Most people thought like me." In other words, the Jordanian people had made a collective decision to not descend into revolution like their neighbors.

"This helped to put on the brakes, like a car," she said. "But for how long will this brake pedal still be there? If there is no real change, no real reform that is convincing to the public, we will move the leg and go to the other pedal."

"What are some of Jordan's biggest challenges in terms of seeking political reform and increased democracy in governance?" I asked. Jordan had an on again, off again relationship with democracy, impacted by regional Middle East politics. Martial law had been declared and parliament disbanded after both the 1967 war with Israel and Jordan's 1994 peace agreement with Israel. Many East Bank Jordanians feared that additional democracy would weaken their influence, because of the large proportion of Palestinians. And political parties are weak, centered around tribe and family.[18] Most parliamentarians are independents. A handful of political parties have two or three members in parliament. For example, Rula al-Hroub's party has only two members in parliament, which still makes it one of the most represented parties. The Islamic Action Front (the political party affiliated with Jordan's moderate Muslim Brotherhood) boycotted the 2013 elections, although it has significant support.

She thought that the biggest barrier to democracy in Jordan was political Islam. "Jordan has a big problem with the Muslim Brotherhood. It is an obstacle hindering our political reform. The state fears the Muslim Brotherhood and its growing popularity. They fear that if there were free elections that the Muslim Brotherhood would control the parliament. But there are no real figures." She described how Muslim Brotherhood popularity was fluctuating with the events in the region. When Morsi was overthrown in Egypt, their popularity in Jordan went down. But when Israel was bombarding Gaza, their popularity went up. With ISIS, Muslim Brotherhood popularity was deteriorating.

"What do you think that the Muslim Brotherhood would do if they came to power?" I asked. "What would their legislative priorities be?"

"Nothing," she said with exasperation, throwing up her hands. "They don't have a program. They are social reformers, not economic or political reformers."

She thought that the government had made mistakes in addressing the Islamist movement. First, the state allowed the Muslim Brotherhood to provide aid in poor areas, give students scholarships and teach on television and at mosques, schools, and universities. Second, the government handled Muslim Brotherhood popularity poorly. "The regime started demonizing them. What they did was stupid, giving them more sympathy. It raised their popularity. When the government puts them in jail, this helps them. With the authority oppressing them, they appear as heroes."

"What is a better approach? What do you think is the best way of interacting with them?" I asked.

"Give them spaces to work and express opinions and strengthen their opponents," she said. "The government should invest in the opposition, like us, who defend the civil state." She wanted to put hard questions to the Muslim Brotherhood about energy, education, healthcare, and other societal issues. "Do debates so that the people realize that they have nothing," she said, adding, "Come show me what you have. How are you going to solve our energy crisis and education? Everything they advocate for is only Islam. The prophet said so and so and so, so you should do so and so. They want to implement fourteen-hundred-year-old solutions to today's problems, which is ridiculous. But no one can challenge that, because there is no opportunity to challenge that.

"They have to be debated by someone capable," she continued. "The state has to stop playing the role of the bad guy in front of them, give them space, and don't oppress them. It gives them legitimacy." But she added that that was difficult, as political parties in Jordan did not have the right to have public debates or to host debates even at universities. "We need to be given spaces to counter their spaces."

It seemed that in Jordan, as in Tunisia and Turkey, politics was polarized between the secularists and Islamists. A healthy system needs to find ways to accommodate both.

The Case for Pluralism

"Those who are quick to pass judgment about the success or failure of the Arab Spring are way too early," said Marwan Muasher. Muasher served as Jordan's deputy prime minister, foreign minister, and first ambassador to Israel. He currently serves as vice-president of the Carnegie Endowment overseeing Middle East research.[19] He is the author of two books, *The Second Arab Awakening: And the Battle for Pluralism* and *The Arab Center: The Promise of Moderation*.[20]

"The Arab world needs a new social contract," he said, as his prescription for meeting the goals of the Arab Spring. "It does not need to be bleak. There is still time to do the right thing," he said, although he was frustrated with status quo forces that blocked change. "But I worry that the young generation is getting the impression that peaceful change is not possible."

He compared the Arab Spring to the 1848 revolutions that swept Europe. Called the Spring of Nations, the European revolutions grew from people's desire for greater political and economic rights, similar to the Arab Spring. Viewed as a failure in the immediate aftermath as reactionary forces soon took back control, the European 1848 revolutions planted the seed for individual rights and the end of the feudal system. "It took another thirty to forty years before they were translated into organized political forces. That is what we are facing. We are at the beginning of a very long process," Muasher said.

"What is the new social contract that you are proposing, and how can it be accomplished?" I asked.

He thought that there were three elements needed in a new social contract.

"First, you need as a start for all the different parts of the population—political, economic, and otherwise—to come together and agree on the rules of the game, with a constitution or bill of rights that defines the relationship between the state and the people. One in which everyone is assured a place in the system, a blueprint that is not a product of a particular government, but of society. That happened in Tunisia, in a system that upheld the rights for all to be part of the culture and the country, regardless of the very stark differences between secularism and Islam. It is a battle for everyone to be recognized as part of the mosaic. Once that is done and people are assured that their rights are guaranteed, they can fight, as long as there is peaceful rotation of power through the ballot box at a set time. That new social contract, other than in Tunisia, has not been attempted in other parts of the Arab world.

"In my view, pluralism is a must," he said, defining pluralism as the rights of all people to participate as citizens, regardless of identity, gender, or religious point of view. "The Arab world has a lot of non-Arabs who need to be recognized, whether they are Kurds, Amazighs, or Armenians."

"Why have identities proven so central now? The Ottoman Empire was multiethnic and multi-identity. Why do you think that wars based on identity have come to the fore now?" I asked.

"Identity under the Ottomans was cultural and religious, but never political," he said, noting that Ottoman citizens could identify as Muslims, Christians, and Jews, but that ethnic and linguistic identities (Arab, Turkish, Kurdish) were not at the forefront. "Given the times, there was tolerance there. In the modern area, the Middle East suffers from identity crises. Whether in Iraq or Syria, there was never a national Iraqi, Syrian, or other identity. As a result we see turmoil."

"The second item," he continued, "is a serious revision of the education system to focus on critical thinking, tolerance, recognizing other points of view, and regarding truths as relative and not absolute.

"Third, the diversification of the economy," he said. "Oil killed productivity and political representation, particularly in the Gulf. When money grows on the ground, people do not need to work for it. Where there is no taxation, there is no representation." He added that the incentive structure is particularly problematic. "The Arab citizen does not feel that he or she can have a bright future through their own merit, their own work. There is a feeling that unless you have *wasta*, you are never going to make it," he said, referring to the same *wasta* problem that Rula al-Hroub mentioned. "I cannot overstate the frustration that the young generation has in feeling that they cannot hope for a better future based on their own work."

These changes might take fifty years, he thought. "But people need to be convinced that there is a political will to put the countries involved on a track to achieve this. Right now, in my view, with the exception of Tunisia, no society is convinced that their government is doing that." The rest are trying to deal with the problem with a reactive short-term approach. "The Gulf tries to pour money on the problem. Other countries, Jordan and Morocco, are involved in what I call ad hoc reforms."

To me, Jordan's and Morocco's ad hoc reforms were wiser than the alternatives elsewhere—revolutions that threw out stability in favor of instant change.

"In the long term, my view is that the countries in the Arab world that will make it are those that will adopt inclusionist policies, as the Tunisians have done, and those that can deal with economies moving to a more productive system. And those that will be able to promote a sense of national identity as opposed to the sub-identities that exist in the Arab world, in Lebanon, Syria, Iraq, and elsewhere and that have led to the turmoil and wars that we have seen." He added, "So, this is my prescription. The battle has to be won for pluralism, not between Islamists and secularists. Not much has been done to promote a sense of national identity to trump all other identities."

A Revolution in Entrepreneurship

"Instability doesn't stop anyone from building businesses," said Fadi Ghandour. Ghandour had founded Aramex (the FedEx or UPS of the Middle East) in an unstable environment. "Instability is a constant, and I will never use instability in the region as an excuse for not building business. Governments are a bigger hindrance. It makes life easier for everyone when you don't have to spend months and days and years moving bureaucracies. People will build businesses, but you will not have a mass movement of people in that space unless they ease things for people."

Fadi Ghandour is probably the best-known entrepreneur in the Middle East. He is a role model and mentor for a generation of young tech entrepreneurs. Ghandour founded Aramex in 1982 when he was twenty-two and fresh out of college. Thirty years later, Aramex has transformed business in the Middle East. Today, Aramex employs 13,900 people in over 350 locations across 60 countries.[21] In 2014, the company's revenues topped $1 billion.

In *Startup Rising: The Entrepreneurial Revolution Remaking the Middle East*, Chris Schroeder argues that while the political changes from the Arab Spring have been disappointing, a quiet revolution is happening through entrepreneurship, as entrepreneurs in the Middle East persist in launching creative businesses and developing workarounds to circumvent the incompetence and autocracy of their governments.[22] He argues that technology is enabling connectivity and access to capital and ideas even when the political system is not supportive; global capital has become more comfortable operating in environments of risk like the Middle East; there is a large untapped market in the Middle East; and mentors like Ghandour are promoting and enabling an environment of entrepreneurship.

I wanted to learn from Ghandour about his experiences developing businesses, even in the instability of the Middle East, and how entrepreneurship in the Middle East fits into the new directions of the Arab Spring.

"What did Aramex contribute to business in the Middle East?" I asked.

"It made the Arab world borderless," he said, describing how before Aramex, it was very difficult for goods to cross borders in the Middle East. There were no multinational logistics companies operating across countries, and there were plenty of bureaucratic obstacles. "We were able to operate in the region, and it took a decade and a half to maneuver the geography. Once we were able to achieve that we became a big global company covering a major part of the world, and we were able to compete and operate against major players in the world."

When Aramex became the first company based in the Arab world to trade on the NASDAQ stock exchange in 1997, it set an example, thought Ghandour. "We became a role model for many people who saw that you could build a business and go public based out of Amman, Jordan."

Ghandour is now working to help other entrepreneurs through MENA Venture. After thirty years at Aramex's helm, he stepped away from direct management of Aramex to turn his attention to helping other entrepreneurs and startups through venture capital and providing advice.[23] "We are the largest seed stage investment firm in the region. We are the hatchery of businesses at the very early stage, which is very risky, and someone needs to do it." He continued, "We are entrepreneurs helping entrepreneurs build their businesses. The entrepreneurship ecosystem in the Arab world is in need of several things: access to capital, access to knowledge, access to networks, access to mentors, and access to markets."

"Many of the Arab Spring demands were about better economic opportunities for youth. There are strong links between Arab Spring aspirations for more political pluralism and aspirations for economic opportunities," I observed. "What were Arab Spring youth protesters trying to achieve?" I asked.

"The core of it was financial inclusion and the ability to have a decent life," he said. "People went to the streets because they did not feel that they had equal opportunity, specifically from the economic benefits that the region was going through."

"But now the Arab Spring does not appear to have improved economic opportunities. The Middle East still has many economic challenges, in particular for youth," I said. The Middle East has the highest youth unemployment rate in the world, with a quarter of youth unemployed. The 2011 Arab Development Challenges Report noted that there was about a 20 percent poverty rate in the region, 60 percent higher than in Latin America.[24] The region has the weakest GDP per capita growth in the world, except for Sub-Saharan Africa.[25] Only 1 percent of online Internet content is in Arabic, although Arabic is the fifth most spoken language in the world, and Arabic speakers are about 7 percent of the world.[26]

"There is stagnation," he acknowledged. "There are economic challenges across the region. We have yet to see the economic benefits," he said, but he thought that seeing actual results would take time. He didn't want to be overly optimistic or pessimistic. "You can break a system very quickly, but you cannot rebuild it in two or three years."

Improving economies and the entrepreneurship ecosystem required a societal effort from both the government and the business elite, Ghandour thought. It required legislation, infrastructure, correcting the education system, helping people build skills that enable participation in the market, having an open economy that allows for investment, and helping startups establish businesses quickly to meet needs.

"If the economic elites and rulers do not appreciate that their success requires proper delivery of services," Ghandour added, "then all the regimes that changed will not be successful going forward. People will go back to the streets, or the next generation will, if there are no economic benefits or feelings of fairness in the system."

He was concerned about more and more youth entering the job market lacking the skills they needed, facing an economy that could not absorb them. Historically, governments in the Middle East had been the employer of choice for youth, as they provided stable employment for many people and private sectors were weak. "But these are bigger countries now, bigger populations, bigger challenges," he said. While government's role has been shifting away from being the mass employer of choice, the business environment in the Middle East was not conducive to the growth that was needed to employ these youth, Ghandour thought.

"You will not be able to address the challenges of the region in terms of economic empowerment and job creation if you don't have a regional common market. That is the job of governments," he added. "The region is fragmented into twenty-two markets, each with its own rules and regulations." Governments needed to create conditions for a common market: reduced bureaucracy, reduced protectionism, faster business registration, easier access to capital, policies to incentivize banks to invest their portfolios in small and medium enterprises, and bankruptcy laws. His comments about needed economic structures reminded me of Ali Allawi's call for regional political structures as key to future stability and growth.

"Jordan has been getting a lot of attention as an entrepreneurship hub and has taken some of the steps you mentioned as necessary for improving the business climate," I said. Jordan has only 2 percent of the Arabic-speaking world's population, but produces three quarters of Arabic online content.[27] But Jordan still comes in fairly low (112 out of 189 countries) on the World Bank's ease of doing business rankings. I asked, "What is happening in Jordan that influenced this? Why Jordan?"

Ghandour described a deliberate Jordanian government effort to build a tech entrepreneurship scene, through private and public sector collaboration, with support from the king. This involved improving labor and business laws, creating independent regulation for the telecom industry, and introducing mandatory English and computer studies in elementary schools and universities. Jordan opened up investment in multiple sectors. Jordan met World Trade Organization entry standards in six months, one of the quickest countries to join at that time. Jordan has a solid education system, improved by an initiative called Education Reform for a Knowledge Economy.

"Everything that needed to be done was done. They brought in a minister of ICT from the private sector who understood that vision and who went to implement that with a vengeance with the private sector. It took ten years. We are just seeing the results in the past three to five years. It takes time," he explained.

Examples of Jordanians who had succeeded in business on the world stage also motivated people, Ghandour thought. In 2000, he and two others founded Maktoob, the first Arabic e-mail service, which was sold in 2009 for $175 million to Yahoo! "It is a Jordanian story of success par excellence. That story was impactful and got a lot of young guys to say that they wanted to be in the tech businesses." He described how Maktoob employees then left to form their own businesses. "All of these things make

Jordan unique." But other countries in the Middle East are catching up, he noted.

"How do you see the impact of the Arab Spring in changing some of the business climate and youth issues that you have described?" I asked.

"The Arab Spring has gotten governments to appreciate and understand the importance of addressing the challenges of the youth. There is a lot of talk and stuff happening. Some countries are faster than others. The most important thing is the realization that if you don't address the challenges of the youth, no matter how rich you are, you are in trouble."

"The Old Men Came Out Again and Took Our Victory"

> *I loved you, so I drew these tides of men into my hands*
> *and wrote my will across the sky in stars*
> *To gain you Freedom, the seven-pillared worthy house. . . .*[28]

T. E. Lawrence wrote those lines in the dedication to his book *Seven Pillars of Wisdom*, his memoir about the British collaboration in the Arab Revolt against the Ottomans during World War I.

When Great Britain failed in its campaign to defeat the Ottoman Empire at Gallipoli, it turned its attention to the Arab parts of the Ottoman Empire. If the Allies could not beat the Central Powers in Europe, they would take the battle elsewhere. British leaders plotted to incite rebellion among the Arabs to weaken the Ottomans—what today we would call a proxy war. Some Arabs were eager for revolt. The nationalism that was sweeping other parts of the world likewise found fertile ground among both Turks and Arabs.[29] With rising Turkish nationalism and increasing Turkification of the empire led by Istanbul, Arabs began to feel less like Ottoman citizens and more like Arab subjects of Turks. In 1916, the sharif of Mecca, Hussein bin Ali (father of Faisal and Abdullah, who later became the Hashemite kings of Iraq and Jordan), proclaimed the Great Arab Revolt against the Ottomans, seeking an independent pan-Arab state. The British reasoned that if they supported the revolt, they would be taking aim at the soft underbelly of the Ottoman Empire.

Wadi Rum, a barren stretch of red-gold desert surrounded by high canyon walls, was the site of some of these seminal historical events.

I stepped up onto the bumper and into the open back of a beat-up Toyota pickup truck and sat on a makeshift bench covered in cushions and faded flowered cloth. Ibrahim, a young Bedouin man wearing a funny combination of a traditional white *thobe* and a Charlie Chaplin esque black bowler hat, drove me in his pickup into the wadi. He made his living from tours here. The truck rattled over hard-packed rocky red sand, with valley walls rising high above on both sides. The sky looked like an immense dome overhead. Indeed, vast, empty, and striking in its desolate beauty, it makes a human feel tiny and insignificant in comparison with the infinite universe.

Wadi Rum was a transportation corridor of antiquity from the Arabian deserts to the Red Sea, a valley sliced into sandstone and granite. Its stone walls reveal inscriptions from the Romans, Nabataeans, Arabs, and Europeans. Shaded by the steep walls of the wadi, travelers on caravans journeyed from spring to spring over the wide flat ground. Wadi Rum was a natural highway for trading Bedouin with their camels and goats. Now it is taken over by pickup trucks.

T. E. Lawrence, a young British military officer, traveled to the desert to make common cause with Sharif Hussein's son Faisal and collaborate on British-Arab military action. Lawrence described Wadi Rum as "vast, echoing and God-like," and a "processional way greater than imagination."

Wadi Rum served as a base for guerrilla attacks on the Ottomans at the nearby port of Aqaba and for destruction of Ottoman transportation routes and supply lines. In particular, the British and the Arab tribes wanted to sabotage the Hejaz railway, still under construction and intended to connect the far reaches of the Ottoman Empire, from Istanbul all the way to Mecca. Destroying the railway would cripple Ottoman military logistics. For two years, British forces conducted a systematic demolition campaign against the railway, blowing up key strategic linkages.[30] By his own count, Lawrence personally blew up seventy-nine bridges of the railway. Sadly, the railway was never rebuilt in Jordan, except for a short stretch out of Amman. It would have been useful for Jordan's transportation infrastructure today.

Lawrence became immortalized in the West as Lawrence of Arabia, when American journalist Lowell Thomas sought him out in Wadi Rum and covered the events as they unfolded to a rapt American audience. In addition to Lawrence's memoir *Seven Pillars of Wisdom,* his story has been told in three movies and seventy biographies.[31] David Lean's 1962 film *Lawrence of Arabia* has been hailed as a classic, with Lawrence as a tragic hero, helping another people with their aspirations for independence, and with loyalties torn between his own country and the Arabs. But the situation was not as simple as that, a battle of good guys seeking freedom from bad guys.

With gridlock in Europe against the Central powers, the British sought allies in the Middle East. The British made duplicitous and conflicting promises to three separate entities in the Levant: the Arabs, the Jews, and the French. In the McMahon-Hussein correspondence (a letter between the British high commissioner in Egypt and Hussein bin Ali, sharif of Mecca), they promised a pan-Arab state to the Arabs."[32] The 1917 Balfour Declaration (a letter from the British foreign secretary to a leader of the Jewish community) promised a Jewish homeland in Palestine. And in the secretive Sykes-Picot Agreement (also described in the Iraq chapter), Britain and France divided up the Ottoman Middle East between them, with Greater Syria for France (because of cultural and commercial ties), Palestine becoming an international zone under British control, and Iraq under British rule (because of British interest in its ports, railways, and oil).

British promises to the Arabs were broken. At the end of the war, instead of creating a single pan-Arab country, the Arab parts of the Ottoman Empire were cut into pieces, creating multiple new countries. Independence was only achieved from Britain and France from the 1940s to 1960s. Part of the land that the Arabs hoped for during their revolt became Israel, and the Palestinians were displaced.

Ibrahim stopped the pickup truck at the ruins of a Nabatean temple, a foundation of old rocks backed up by dramatic red-gold cliffs. He showed me around the temple. With a dry sense of humor, he joked that this old temple was his house. He said that he wanted to marry a European girl and asked me if I knew any Europeans looking for a Bedouin husband. They could live here at the temple.

Next Ibrahim dropped me off for a short hike up to a stream. I walked along a sand and stone path that became increasingly green and freshly scented, with yellow and blue wildflowers. At the top was a spring, a gentle trickle of water coming out of the side of a cliff, forming a pool lined with ferns, with a few trees nearby. Hoof prints of animals in the mud near little puddles of water indicated where they came to drink.

I asked Ibrahim if we could go to a Bedouin camp and meet some
people. Ibrahim drove me to a set of tents in the desert. We got out of the
pickup truck and had tea with his cousin Abdullah, a blue-eyed Bedouin
in dusty robes with a dark, lined face. Abdullah lived here with his two
wives and ten children. This was one of the few families still living in the
desert. In the past the tribe had all lived in the desert in tents like this,
but now most of them had moved into a nearby village. The family tribe
and had been here for four hundred years, descended from a man who
had migrated from Saudi Arabia.

The tribes of Jordan also stretched up through Saudi Arabia and Syria.
Their way of life stayed largely unchanged for millennia. During the time
of the Ottoman Empire, the Jordanian desert was considered the wasteland of the empire, and no Ottoman army bothered exerting much
control over the tribes. Tribal lifestyle changed rapidly in the past century
with the onset of modernization and the lure of settled life. One Jordanian tribe member wrote about "acute consciousness and pride—all but
invisible to outsiders and foreigners because now covered under a layer of
nationalism and Jordanian patriotism—that every tribesman, Settled,
Semi-Nomadic or Nomadic, has in the back of his mind of belonging to
his tribe, of the history and particularity of his tribe, and of the tribe
being the last thing, 'if push comes to shove,' that will defend him."[33]

Abdullah's home was a set of tents made out of multiple materials: goat
hair fabric, ripped linoleum, UN refugee tents, chicken wire, corrugated
tin, sticks, woven mats, and wool carpets. Goats, sheep, and quail were
held in pens of bent wire.

A wife brought out an old kettle and boiled tea, and then we drank it
sweet in little glasses.

"So which way of life is better?" I asked. "The old or the new? In the
desert or the town?"

"It is easier now. It was harder then," said Ibrahim. "The men were very
strong then."

Abdullah preferred his traditional life. They lived on goats and milk.
Their parents, in addition to nomadic life here, took camels to Gaza to trade
for flour for their bread. Living in the village was intimidating, thought
Abdullah. "Life is hard, technology, electrics," he said.

The kids were dressed in a mismatched assortment of hand-me-down
clothes that looked like they might have been donations. Every day, a jeep

came to collect the children to take them to a village school. Abdullah and his wife pointed to their son—they wanted him to become a policeman. They pointed to their daughter—they wanted her to become a doctor.

We finished our tea, and then Ibrahim dropped me off at the camp where I would stay for the night. He joked that he had to go home so his girlfriend could make him dinner. Then he clarified that he wasn't allowed to have a girlfriend. His mom would cook. And then he drove off in his pickup truck.

I walked barefoot to a nearby sand dune with soft red sand in my toes. A haze obscured the setting sun.

At the camp were an Italian family and a Tunisian family, along with two Bedouin men who made the fire and cooked the food. The food was a bit disappointing, taken out of cans and put on plates for us, served with more sugary tea. I slept in a traditional black goat-hair canvas tent, on a cot, with blankets.

The next morning, I woke up to rain on the top of the tent, which smelled of goats from the wet goat-hair fabric. A gentle mist of water came through the tent. Light peeked in from the tiny holes between the warp and weft of the tent weave. The morning was cool and hushed, as the world was not awake just yet. I went outside, and the colors were waking up on the sides of the red-gold cliffs. In this light, the mottled erosion looked like hieroglyphics. Breakfast was sweet tea, boiled eggs, bread, cheese, fava bean stew, and hummus.

Ibrahim came back with the Toyota and drove me to meet his grandmother in the village, a cement compound of cinder-block huts and rusty gates where the tribe had moved upon leaving nomadic life. Children ran around playing with farm animals.

Ibrahim's grandmother was inside a little semi-open shelter of corrugated tin with a roof. She lay on a mat on the sandy ground, wrapped in a blanket. Ibrahim explained that she preferred being here instead of inside their concrete house; she refused to live inside. He said that she was very old, 115 years old. (But somehow that number seemed to be the kind of estimate that people make when a society cannot quite count the years.) His grandmother had over sixty grandchildren. She wore a purple velveteen nightgown with sequins on the top, and her head was wrapped in a black headscarf, a few hairs sticking out. She smiled and spoke, revealing two teeth. Her eyes were clouded over with cataracts. Along her chin and cheeks and forehead was a faded green tattoo. Ibrahim knelt next to her on the earth and gave her a kiss on the cheek.

He leaned toward her, cupped his hand over her ear, and shouted, "*Jedda!*" Grandmother.

"Eh?" Her cloudy eyes looked toward him.

And then he told her that he was here and that a foreign lady wanted to greet her and talk to her. She nodded. He then pulled out a cigarette, put it in his mouth, lit it and inhaled to get it going, then took it out of his mouth and put it in hers. She puffed on it.

"She likes to smoke," he explained.

Unprompted, the old woman began speaking. There was a rhythm to the words, a poetry, a rhyming cadence that sounded like proverbs or something ancient and wise. I felt that if I could somehow understand, I would understand the inherited wisdom of this woman and her people, and how they had lived hardy lives, taming the forces of nature in the desert. She finished her poetry, and then I looked to Abdullah to translate.

He looked at me and thought hard. "She say . . . she say it is important that people like you. Behave in a good way. Be good to other people."

Hmmm. . . . That was disappointing. Somehow, something was lost in translation.

Her other grandchildren, some small, some adults, gathered around. I asked a few questions.

Each time, Ibrahim leaned over, cupped his hand over her ear, and shouted "*Jedda,*" followed by "Eh?" followed by the question. And she recited something, with a rhythm and artistry, and he translated with a few brief words, without the poetry that I heard her speak. I felt like I was consulting a sage, the Oracle at Delphi, but that the words were falling on sand.

"That was Lawrence's girlfriend," he joked about his grandmother. He chuckled as he asked her his own question. "*Jedda!* Do you remember Lawrence?" She said no, but she remembered British soldiers from when she was a child.

Her grandchildren were giggling, and I could tell that she was viewed as quite a character in her family. She finished her cigarette and Ibrahim started another cigarette for her. As we departed, he left her three more cigarettes.

At the end of her life, the world was changing around her.

We drove out through the village, where the villagers were capitalizing on the fame of Lawrence with a certain entrepreneurial humorous cynicism. There was a Lawrence grocery store, a Lawrence tea shop, and a Lawrence tourist souvenir shop. He was not famous in Arab history, as he was but one British collaborator out of many during the revolt, but we in the West have written it as if Lawrence were the sum of the story, rather than a means to an end.

T. E. Lawrence had spent the war here, and as we drove off, I recalled his disappointment that after the battles that he had fought in as part of the Great Arab Revolt, the Arabs did not get their new world as had been promised, but instead colonial domination, conflict, and a refugee crisis. He wrote, "The morning freshness of the world-to-be intoxicated us. We were wrought up with ideas inexpressible and vaporous, but to be fought for. We lived many lives in those whirling campaigns, never sparing ourselves: yet when we achieved and the new world dawned, the old men came out again and took our victory to remake in the likeness of the former world they knew. Youth could win, but had not learned to keep, and was pitiably weak against age. We stammered that we had worked for a new heaven and a new earth, and they thanked us kindly and made their peace."

It reminded me of the Arab youth who have also yet to achieve their new world after their scorched-earth Arab Spring.

Online and Different from Our Parents

"The transformation in the Arab World is in its beginning. There have never been so many young people who are wired, connected, and different from their parents. I don't think that the Arab Spring is over, not by any stretch of the imagination," avowed Nadia Oweidat, a Jordanian fellow at the New America Foundation.

"This was round one. Round two will happen." Change required more than removing the heads of the state, she thought; it required first understanding, as a society, what dreams it had for itself. Round One was about revolution. Round Two was about figuring out what would come next.

Oweidat, in her mid-thirties with long dark hair and chunky tribal silver jewelry, views herself as part of a generation of change in the Arab world. From the Beni Hassan tribe (one of the biggest tribes in Jordan), she attended an Islamic school as a child. She later went on to finish a Ph.D. at Oxford University in Islamic Thought. Her thesis dealt with the basis for separation between religion and state in the Arab world. Given her journey from Islamic school to Western-educated public intellectual, I wanted to understand her views on the desires of youth in the Arab Spring, the basis for separation between religion and state in the Arab world, and why Jordan has stayed stable.

"How are people in the Arab world figuring out what will come next, in 'round two,' as you just put it?" I asked.

She thought that the Arab world had become polarized in two ways over the question of what people want for their societies: between the old ways and new ways and between divergent views of the proper role of Islam in public life. How this polarization is resolved will determine the future.

"How are the old and new ways different?" I asked.

"My parents' generation is comfortable trading safety for no agency. For my generation, it is not like this." And her generation, people under the age of forty, make up 80 percent of the Middle East.

"So you have two opposing systems trying to assert themselves. One has all the weapons, all the political infrastructure, and societal and religious institutions, and one only has the end goal of establishing different kinds of systems. I believe the future is not on the side of authoritarianism, given the creativity that I am in touch with that is intent on making changes."

The Arab youth online community was driving this change, she thought. She pointed to debates about politics and religion on Facebook, with kids making films, crafting poetry, and writing insightful reviews of books and ideas. "I see kids in Yemen, Sudan, Egypt, doing *amazing* things, teaching each other online, protesting, and creating a new set of ways. There is a generational gap. There are parallel worlds."

Change created by computers, the Internet, and social media was unstoppable, empowering youth who wanted something different. "When you are alone in front of your computer, you can let your imagination and your curiosity run wild. There is nobody standing there telling you 'Stop right there, you can't question.'"

"The implications are huge," Oweidat added, "because our elders are learning, very difficultly, slowly struggling, that the old days are really over for good. We're never going to go back to obedience and no agency. This is gone forever," she said.

These changes in Middle Eastern society, mentality, communication, and goals were big to her, akin to the Renaissance in Europe. "The Arab Renaissance is taking place. Social media is already creating a different kind of citizen. It's too late. We are in the middle of forming a new social contract." A "new social contract" was also the term that Marwan Muasher had used.

Later, I reflected that while social media enables youth to break free of traditional shackles, social media, radio, and religious TV have also enabled extremist groups like ISIS to recruit and organize. These tools are a double-edged sword for the region.

"And what about the second divide that you mentioned, religious versus secular?" I asked.

"The separation between mosque and state is really taking place right now," Oweidat said. It was happening in government policy, through thinkers at universities, and through youth use of social media. It was also happening as people saw violent events in war-torn countries and were appalled by them.

"There is not anyone in the Middle East who didn't grow up learning about the caliphate and Islamic civilization," she said. People in the Middle East longed for a better world, of Arab power, dignity, and civilization, without borders and without corruption, she added. Collective memory of a great past with an Islamic empire, refined civilization, and Ottoman caliphate gave them a vision of what this could be like. "Now, there is a delusion that by waging war and jihad that you come up with civilization. Many people adhere to this narrative and keep on thinking that the way to move forward is to go back, that the only way we can go back to being in power militarily and scientifically is by going back to the seventh century and doing what they did," she said, referring to the Salafist-Jihadist movement. "Having gone to Islamic schools, it paints a picture of what never occurred, of an Islamic past where everything was perfect because of Islam."

This longing for a better future based on the past led to misplaced emphasis on return to a stricter practice of religion. "The Islamic parties in all shades adhere to the very simplistic but very powerful idea that 'Islam is the solution.' But that doesn't tell you how to build schools, how to build a curriculum, how to enable freedom of expression. It just tells you to have Islam."

Oweidat observed that the narrative of an Islamic caliphate being the solution to problems in the Arab world is called into question by the brutality of ISIS, which has proclaimed a caliphate. "You get your caliphate. It is in front of you," she said, pointing to violence and failures of governance. "Where is the civilization? This narrative is going to its natural conclusion, where it is leading many to question it. But the most important thing is that the challenges are coming from within because of social media."

Furthermore, there are tensions about what Islam stands for. As is true of the Bible, many different messages can be found in the Quran, she noted. She thought that each end of the spectrum, both Salafist-Jihadists and secular liberals, manipulated the text to emphasize certain verses. "Extremists take texts from the Quran and they make it Islam. Like: 'Kill them wherever you find them.' And the liberals do the opposite. They take verses like: 'There is no coercion in religion,' and they make that Islam. So it is verse versus verse."

"How does this relate to an Arab Renaissance?" I asked.

She observed that contrary to this desire to imitate the past, a Renaissance depends upon freedom of thought and expression. "This is completely in direct contradiction and in conflict with the Islamic model," she said.

Her own personal experience as a child illustrated this point.

"I went to Islamic schools," she said. "*Imagine*," she emphasized. "We internalized that you are not allowed to voice any critique." Islamic teachings relied heavily on tradition. "In school you are not allowed to say something new, because the best has been said already." She spoke even more passionately. "And therein lies the problem."

She acknowledged that for a long time she felt alienated from her society about these issues. But then she realized, "I am not even allowed to participate in the debate if I am not speaking from within. This is what made me pursue a Ph.D. in Islamic Thought. I am now part of the conversation that determines my fate and the fate of my sisters and brothers in the struggle for freedom and equality. With a Ph.D. in Islamic Thought and my background, I am much harder to dismiss in my community."

Adhering to an Islam from another era, and associating Islam and violence, was not appealing to the majority of Arab youth, she thought. "What goes viral on the Arabic Internet tells me a different story. That despite the funding and narrative for terrorism, it is not the most attractive ideology for a critical mass."

Crusaders and Jihadis

There were many Crusader castles—more than fifty—scattered across the Mediterranean Middle East, in Cyprus, Israel, Jordan, Lebanon, Syria, and Turkey. Karak Castle is one of the biggest. It is a massive complex of beige stone, commanding the top of a hill, surrounded by cliffs. Standing inside its walls, I felt like I was touching the sky. It is the stuff of fairy tales. Or maybe nightmares. I walked up and down stone stairs, holding on to iron rails. From this perch at the top of the castle, I could see the extensive territories around me, a sweeping scenery of rocks and villages, a gold-brown patchwork of divided land, and trees, hill after hill, into the distance.

Begun by French Crusaders in the 1140s, the castle took twenty years to build and was in Crusader hands for forty-six years. It was used by Europeans as a base to attack Arab caravans on the way to Mecca, until armies led by Saladin (a Kurdish soldier who climbed the ranks until he became ruler of Egypt) attacked, took the castle, and stopped the European assaults on the caravans.[34]

Karak is architecturally magnificent. I walked through room after room aboveground, in caverns belowground, through stone arches, under defensive structures, and inside the barracks for the soldiers. Now an anodyne tourist site, this castle once represented something very different. This was a battle of civilizations for the Holy Land.

In the West, we often think of the Crusades as romantic, a period of adventure during which knights in shining armor went to the Holy Land in search of God, glory, and conquest, to retake Jerusalem and the Holy Land back from the Muslims. The Crusades were indeed a time of Western cultural expansion and adventure. They resulted in growth for the West, with new trade in luxury goods, cross-pollination of ideas with the Arab world, and an expansion of European power. They opened up trade in the Mediterranean, and inaugurated an era of poetry and chivalry in the West.

The Crusades are remembered very differently in the Arab world. It was a time of bloodshed and conquest in the name of religion. The battles of the Crusades raged for two hundred years, starting in 1095, with six major episodes and a number of minor ones as well. The Crusades were not a clean record for the West. They included atrocities of Christians against Muslims, Jews, and other Christians. In 1099, there was the slaughter of an estimated ten to thirty thousand Muslims and Jews in Jerusalem.[35] While these numbers are not verifiable today, such atrocities are remembered in Arab history vividly as a bloodbath by Christian Europeans against Muslims and as part of a history of Western aggression.

One Crusader account wrote of exultation in the destruction and death of Muslim residents of Jerusalem: "Now that our men had possession of the walls and towers, we saw some wonderful sights. Some of our men— actually the more merciful ones—cut off the heads of their enemies. Others shot them with arrows, so that they fell from the towers. Others tortured them longer by casting them into the flames. Piles of heads, hands, and feet were to be seen in the streets of the city. One had to pick one's way over the bodies of men and horses."[36]

This is what the Crusades mean in the Middle East.[37] This is not just romantic history for the Arab world, but living, painful history. Like Islam, Christianity has a word for violence in the name of religion. The way that the word "jihad" sounds to Western ears is the way "crusade" sounds to the Arab ears. Western leadership has made blundering statements using that word, for example, when George W. Bush said, "This crusade, this war on terrorism is going to take a while."[38] That did not sound like a passionate, adventurous battle of self-defense to Arabs. It sounded like a threat to conquer the Arab world, as Europeans had tried to do during the Crusades, a thousand years ago.

ISIS, in its propaganda magazine *Dabiq*, routinely refers to fighting the Crusaders and infidels, a historical reference that resonates in the Middle East in ways that it does not resonate in the West. *Dabiq* described Barack Obama and John McCain as "crusaders," who would "bring about the complete collapse of the American Empire."[39] ISIS released a statement condemning the "criminal Crusader coalition air-craft."[40] In 1998, Osama Bin Laden declared a fatwa of war against the West in his "Declaration of the World Islamic Front for Jihad against the Jews and the Crusaders."

Some have argued that ISIS wants the West to enter into another crusade against the Islamic world, as ISIS's leadership believes that they can use it to rally the Muslim world to their side.[41]

With two thousand Jordanian citizens fighting for ISIS,[42] Jordan's challenge will be to stop the flow of jihadist youth, disenfranchised by a sense of helplessness and lack of economic opportunity.

The Bible and the Border

The River Jordan is a divider of worlds. East is Jordan. West are Israel and the Palestinian West Bank and Gaza.

Much of the land around the River Jordan is now a militarized zone, separating peoples on both sides of the water. One place to stand on the riverbank and look across the water to the other side is Bethany on the River Jordan, the site where Jesus was baptized by John the Baptist.

The drive from Amman to the Jordan Valley and to Bethany took me through barren hills overlooking the river valley. The road edged a cliff, passing pretty pink flowers and various shrubs and plants. Far below the road, reeds grew in the dry riverbed of a tributary. A biker drenched in sweat biked up the long hills from the Dead Sea, in the opposite direction to which I drove. The road descended in elevation, transitioning ecosystems, from hills of pine, olive and white rocks down to a tributary with lush greenery, fig, pomegranate, and eucalyptus trees, farms, greenhouses, huts, and sellers of plants. The waters were a trickle; the riverbed of the tributary was about ten feet wide. While the tributary was muddy, it still gave off soothing sounds of running water when I stopped to walk on the bank. Continuing along, I passed banana fields, wondering at the diversity of microclimates. An hour's drive took me from olives to bananas.

I arrived at Bethany, the site of Jesus' baptism. The location has been

identified through passages in the Bible, traveler descriptions, and archae-
ological finds.

A shuttle drove me and other tourists down to the holy sites, past military checkpoints, with soldiers in camouflage and trucks. We walked
along a path shaded with plywood, through bougainvillea and green
plants. The site that has been identified as the likely place where Jesus was
baptized by John the Baptist was a long set of stone steps and piers. But
there is no longer any water at that spot. It is dry and dusty.

Where once the river was 150 yards across, now it is 6 yards. While
once the River Jordan was mighty with a billion cubic meters of water
passing by this site per day, now only twenty to thirty million cubic meters flow by. Seventy to 90 percent of the river's water has been diverted
for human use in Israel, Jordan, and Syria.[43] All three countries dump
raw sewage into it, and the river has evolved into a dirty polluted trickle
of sludge. Environmental groups have raised alarms about the demise of
the river, its continued capability to provide for human life, and the dan-
gers to its ecosystem.

I arrived at the bank of the river itself. A few yards away was the other
bank, in Israel, with Israeli flags. Everywhere was barbed wire. A family
from India waded into the water on our side. Their teenage son held his
smartphone in the water to take a selfie. Arabs on the Israeli side waded
into the water. Israeli soldiers on the other side lounged in the shade.

On the bank near me, there was a chipped stone basin of filtered water
from the river. This water looked cleaner than the polluted river water. I
dipped my hand in it and sprinkled it on my neck. The breeze dried it
and cooled me.

How did the Holy Land come to be a militarized zone with soldiers
and barbed wire? The land between the Jordan River and the Mediterranean, what is today Israel and the West Bank and Gaza, inhabited by the
Israelis and Palestinians, has two peoples making both past and present
claims to it, with their own narratives and their own existential quest
for survival based on that land.

Backing up in time to World War I and the Ottomans once again, the
story continues after Wadi Rum, Lawrence of Arabia and the Arab Revolt, and Britain's conflicting promises of land to the Arabs, the Jews, and
the French. In exchange for support during the Arab Revolt against the

Ottomans, the British led Sharif Hussein of Mecca to consider Palestine as part of his deal, as part of an independent pan-Arab state. This conflicted with the Balfour Declaration's promises of support for a land for the Jews in Palestine, as well as with Britain's and France's own colonial ambitions spelled out in the Sykes-Picot Agreement.

To Jews, the land of Israel was the biblically promised homeland of the Jewish people. In several waves, in wars from 700 BC to the first century AD, the Jews were either expelled from Israel or left voluntarily and settled around the world in diaspora communities. For millennia, there were significant Jewish communities in Europe, the Middle East, and North Africa. Over the centuries, the Jewish diaspora maintained a religious vision of returning to Jerusalem, the promised land of the scriptures.

In 1896, in response to anti-Semitism in Europe and pogroms in Eastern Europe and Russia, Theodor Hertzl, a Jew from Vienna, published *The Jewish State*. He concluded that Jews were not safe in Europe; they needed their own sovereign state. His book launched the Zionist movement and the emigration of the Jewish people from Europe to Palestine. In response to persecution in Europe and financed by wealthy Jews around the world, significant Jewish emigration to Palestine began in the 1880s.

After World War I, from 1920 to 1947, Arabs and Jews jockeyed for control within the British Mandate for Palestine, formerly the Ottoman territory of Palestine. The 1920 League of Nations' *Interim Report on the Civil Administration of Palestine* estimated the population of Palestine at 700,000 people.[44] It estimated that about 80 percent were Muslim Arabs, with 77,000 Christian Arabs and 76,000 Jews (about 11 percent of the population each). In a different estimate, in 1890, there were 43,000 Jews out of a population of 532,000 people in Palestine.[45] Because of continued persecution in Europe, culminating in the Holocaust, Jewish immigration continued. By 1948, Palestine was home to approximately 1.9 million people, two-thirds Arabs and a third Jews.[46]

After World War II, a weakened Britain wearied of occupying Palestine, granted independence to the region, and left. The United Nations provided a partition plan that would divide the land into a Jewish state, an Arab state, and a Special International Regime for the City of Jerusalem, but it was not enacted. When the British left, the Jews declared Israel a state in 1948. That same year, Arab states attacked the new Jewish state. Egypt, Jordan, Iraq, Lebanon, Syria, Saudi Arabia, and Yemen all sent troops. They were defeated by the new state of Israel. In the 1949 armistice to the Arab-Israeli war, the West Bank (majority ethnically Arab and later occupied by Israel) was declared part of Transjordan's territory.

Israel was now a country.

In 1948, according to the United Nations estimates, 711,000 of the 900,000 Palestinians living in the new state of Israel were displaced by Israeli soldiers or fled to Gaza, the West Bank, Jordan, Lebanon, and Syria.[47] The next wave of 285,000 to 325,000 Palestinian refugees fled Israel and the occupied territories during the 1967 Six-Day War.[48] Among other places, they sought refuge in Gaza, Lebanon, Jordan, and Syria, where their descendants continue to live. Israel took control of the West Bank and East Jerusalem from Jordan during that war. They also occupied Gaza. People in the West Bank and Gaza do not have citizenship rights in Israel, and these areas remain under occupation by Israel. In 1988, Palestinians declared independence of the state of Palestine (including the West Bank, Gaza, and part of Jerusalem); in 2012, the United Nations granted non-member observer status to Palestine.

The Middle East once had thriving Jewish communities in many cities dating from the eighth century BC, because of waves of Jews exiled after wars in ancient Israel. Jewish and Islamic heritage developed hand in hand over centuries, with Jews contributing to commerce, government, and scholarship in the Middle East cities in which they resided. With backlash against Jewish populations around the Middle East after the 1948 and 1967 wars, these historic Jewish communities fled Arab countries. In 1944, Tunisia had 105,000 Jews, Morocco had 265,000 Jews, Iran 100,000, Syria 30,000, and Lebanon 6,000. Before fleeing in 1967, Libya's Jewish community numbered 67,000. Now, the Jewish populations in the Arab countries have all but ceased to exist as Jews have left for Israel, the United States, and Europe.[49] By 2004, Tunisia 1,500, Morocco had 5,000, Iran 20,000, with only tiny numbers remaining in Syria, Lebanon, and Libya.[50]

Transfers of populations after World Wars I and II and the reshaping of boundaries in the past century have been extraordinary. Jews, Christians, and Muslims around the Middle East have fled their historic homes. All told, Jewish refugees from Arab countries (including Algeria, Egypt, Iraq, Libya, Morocco, Syria, Tunisia, and Yemen/Aden) to Israel numbered 851,000.[51] Palestinian refugees fleeing their homes in what is now Israel numbered about 750,000 between 1946 and 1967. Descendants of Palestinian refugees, many of whom still live in refugee camps in the West Bank, Gaza, Jordan, Lebanon, and Syria, now exceed five million.[52]

Many Israelis celebrated when the number of Jews in Israel passed six million, a historically symbolic number, as that was the number of Jews killed in the Holocaust during World War II.[53]

Sharing borders with Israel, Egypt and Jordan broke ranks with the other Arab countries and signed individual peace agreements with Israel in 1979 (Egypt) and 1994 (Jordan).

The status of the occupied territories and the Palestinians has been the subject of anguish, diplomacy, violence, and stalemate ever since. Palestinians in Gaza and the West Bank have lived under Israeli rule without citizenship rights for decades. Arab countries have kept many of the Palestinian refugees in a long-term status of limbo, with partial rights, hoping that the Palestinians will return to Israel. Both sides resist cutting a deal, thinking that time, justice, dignity, violence, and demographics are on their side. There is, on the one hand, the Jewish right to a national homeland after persecution and genocide in Europe, and they already have a state with control of territory. On the other hand, there is the Palestinians' right to their historic homeland, their right to confiscated property, and their right to return. There is a long and painful history of competing claims and violence on both sides.

Between the River Jordan and the Mediterranean (in Israel, the West Bank, and Gaza), today about half of the twelve million people are Jews and about half are Arabs. Israel's 2015 population was estimated at about eight million.[54] About 75 percent of the people in Israel are Jews, and a quarter are Arabs.[55] The West Bank and Gaza total about 4.2 million people. The West Bank is no longer a clearly Arab area; there are more than 350,000 Israelis living in settlements in the West Bank described as illegal by the UN.[56] Therefore, the two population—Jews and Arabs—are becoming ever more entangled, half and half, on a shared land.

What is the way forward? Options suggested by different parties in recent decades lie in several categories: a two-state solution (Israel and Palestine), a one-state solution (Jews and Arabs in one country), Jordan absorbing the West Bank, a confederation of Israel, Palestine, and Jordan with local self-governance, or an unresolved status quo. Decades of negotiations have not resolved this issue.

In addition to the direct impacts on the Palestinians, Israelis, and the Arab states like Jordan that have absorbed the Palestinian refugees, the conflict has had a wide impact on all Arab states. The collective anger of the Arab people was used as an excuse by autocratic Arab governments for why democratization and greater public participation in government could destabilize the region. Indeed, both Jordan and Lebanon had civil wars related to the status of the Palestinians in their country. The conflict has loomed so large over the Arab psyche that it has served as a distraction from dysfunctional Middle East governments' failure to improve public services or enable circumstances for economic growth for their own people. Jordan even disbanded parliament from the 1967 war to 1989 because of concern that democratic elections would be destabilizing. A state of emergency was declared in Egypt after the 1967 war; the state of emergency lasted, with only an eighteen-month break, until the Arab Spring. Egypt's state of emergency extended police powers and allowed indefinite detention without trial. A key demand of Egyptian protesters in Tahrir Square was abandoning this state of emergency that allowed violations of citizens' rights.

I walked back from the militarized east bank of the sludgy trickle of the River Jordan and left Bethany. The road to Mount Nebo—a winding asphalt road up barren reddish hills—passed herds of camels and Bedouin compounds of rough tents, with chickens scampering, rusty kettle drums, and water trucks, all very dusty and primitive-looking. The road snaked through the valley between barren rocky hills with bright blue sky above. It was stark but beautiful. I passed a few checkpoints manned by Jordanian police in military camouflage. They were polite. They merely checked my passport and said the one English phrase they seemed to know, "Thank you. Welcome in Jordan." Then the road led up through hills, up to the top of Mount Nebo, from where, according to the Bible, God showed Moses the view of the Holy Land of Israel before him. But Moses would never visit this promised land.

According to the Bible, Moses died on Mount Nebo, and his burial place is somewhere near here in one of several disputed sites. I stood on Mount Nebo and looked over the spectacular view across Israel and the West Bank, much as Moses had done. I saw before me undulating dry brown hills. It was a bit hazy. A cloud of dust sat over the valley, with patches of green trees in the view. A sign by the cliff where I stood identified significant sites in the distance with arrows. They pointed to Jerusalem, Jericho, and Bethlehem. Down below, visible through the haze, was the land of milk and honey, flat lush agricultural land, much easier to survive in than these harsh mountains. Turn in any other direction, and it is barren mountains, *not* the land of milk and honey. Ironically, like Moses, many Palestinians must have also stood at this point, forbidden from entering the land of their ancestors.

I entered a little museum chapel and lit a candle for people of all faiths who lay claim to the land.

Still in the Camps

Motasem opened the door of the car for me, and I got in the backseat.

"Mornin', ma'am," he said, with a surprisingly Southern-sounding drawl. I had hired him to drive me around Amman for a few days. A Palestinian who had grown up in Jordan, he had gone to university in South Carolina on a government scholarship to study to be an interpreter. But driving for this company was more lucrative, so he did that instead. We had hit it off right away, as he had even visited Pittsburgh, my hometown.

His speech was littered with "y'alls" and drawn out "ma'ams."

"Can you take me to Al-Wahdat?" I asked him. Al-Wahdat was a Palestinian refugee camp in the heart of Amman, established for the 1967 Palestinian refugees.[57] Fifty-one thousand people still live in Al-Wahdat, which means "the units" in Arabic, after the units of living quarters for the refugees. It was surprising to me that there were still Palestinian refugee camps at all, as the refugees had arrived in 1948 and 1967, a long time ago. Today, there are fifty-eight UN refugee camps for the Palestinians in Gaza, West Bank, Jordan, Lebanon, and Syria; about a third of the five million Palestinian refugees and their descendants live in the camps.[58] Jordan hosts the largest number of Palestinian refugees.

Many still live in the ten refugee camps set up for them in Jordan, while other Palestinians have integrated into the urban fabric of the country.[59]

"Al-Wahdat?" asked Motasem, with a puzzled tone. "Why do you want to go there?" he asked, genuinely perplexed at my interest. "I grew up in Al-Wahdat."

I was surprised. South Carolina charmer Motasem had grown up in a refugee camp?

I explained that I was working on a book about the Middle East, and I wanted to see what Al-Wahdat looked like.

Motasem, who had been particularly loquacious during our days driving together, fell silent.

We began the drive to Al-Wahdat, and Motasem turned on the radio, which was playing an eighties love song. "Brings back memories," he said. He had learned to slow dance to that song. When he had first arrived in South Carolina, he had been shy. But then a girl asked him to dance, and he said no because he had never slow danced before. With a smile on his face that I could see in the rearview mirror, he related how she wouldn't take no for an answer. "If you don't do it now, you'll never be ready," she had told him. "I don't want to step on your feet," he had replied. To that, she rejoined, "You'll step on my feet once, and then never do it again." Motasem chuckled as he saw she was right. He stepped on her feet once, and then never did it again. "I learned quick," he said, and next he was going out dancing on a regular basis.

We arrived at the camp and drove in. It is no longer a set of tents or prefabricated buildings. It looks like a poor, ramshackle urban area. Buildings were constructed out of concrete blocks and garbage littered the streets. Some of the houses had doorsteps decorated with potted plants and little corner stores sold beverages and snacks. Old beat-up cars were parked along the street. Plants hung out of the windows. "Palestinians like green," Motasem explained. "It is desert in Jordan, but it was green in Palestine."

He was thoughtful as we drove slowly through narrow, winding streets of the neighborhood. "I haven't been back here in years." He drove me around for about two hours.

"Here is where I played as a boy," he said, pointing to a little alleyway between rows of concrete houses. "That was the house I grew up in," pointing to a nondescript concrete dwelling, like the others around it, that had housed his parents and his ten brothers and sisters. His parents had come from Bethlehem in 1967.

He drove me by the UN-run school he had attended. It is astounding to me that a school that was set up as a temporary response in 1967 has turned into a permanent institution. UN schools in Jordan for Palestinian children were known for quality results, in particular considering the context; they scored above the world average on international tests, for the most part performing better than other Jordanian schools. About 500,000 Palestinian refugee children in several countries are educated in the UN schools, the largest nongovernmental school system in the Middle East.[60]

Motasem stopped the car and pointed. "When we went to school and didn't have our homework and gave excuses like 'There wasn't any electricity' or 'I didn't have a pen,' the teachers said, 'You don't have any excuses. All you have is your education, so make sure that you don't lose it.' That was a powerful motivator."

"What was it like growing up in Al-Wahdat?" I asked. I didn't know what to say. What had started out as me asking for a ride to a neighborhood had become me accompanying someone through his childhood memories, which were intertwined with an internationally intractable conflict.

"I was a kid. It was all that I knew," he said. "It was fun being here as a kid."

"Fun? Why?" I asked, incredulous. He was a refugee, growing up in a crowded slum.

"It's just fun being a kid. You have your imagination," he said. "People adapt, you know? You get used to it. When you grow up in tents, it doesn't get much worse. You can deal with anything after that."

We stopped at one corner store to get bottles of water. There was a pile of concrete blocks on the side of the road. Motasem walked over to the concrete blocks and motioned for me to follow. He put his hand on a block. The blocks looked roughly made. He explained that people made these blocks in Al-Wahdat to construct their homes. They first put up metal rods as a frame. Then they put the blocks surrounding the rods and filled the space between the blocks with additional cement. When the walls are finished, they cover them with a smooth coating of concrete to make them more attractive. At first the Palestinians weren't allowed to build, as their presence in Jordan was supposed to be temporary; they were refugees who, it was expected, would go back to their homeland soon. At first there were tents. Then they were provided corrugated tin shelters. When gradually the UN removed restrictions on building, the Palestinians built their own lodgings out of concrete blocks. Over time they were allowed to build one-story homes, and then they were allowed more rooms and additional stories. They couldn't own the houses, but there was some sort of implied right to them.

After that detailed explanation, I guessed that Motasem had done some building himself. "Did you build your house with your dad?" I asked.

He put his hands in his pocket, looked up at the sky, and then back at me. "Yes, ma'am," he said, with thoughtful pride.

"Arabs have been worse to the Palestinians than the Israelis," he said. He described how he had felt like an outsider in Jordan all of his life, and how the Palestinians have not been accepted in the countries they live in. "You don't feel fully human when you feel like an outsider. There is a lot of discrimination."

But Jordan had given citizenship to some Palestinians—the 1948 group, although the 1967 group did not have citizenship. Many had integrated in Jordanian society, while others were still in the camps, either for reasons of their own or because of outside circumstances.

"Motasem, you left, but why do other people stay? What keeps people here, living in the same neighborhood of refugees for decades?" I asked.

"Many Palestinians don't want to leave al-Wahdat," he said, with a shrug. "It would be like losing their identity or giving up hope or something." Many of the families still kept the keys to family homes that they had left in what is now Israel.

"To tell you the truth, Palestine isn't coming back," he said, acknowledging a hard reality. "There are five million Palestinians. We can't all fit there."

"What are your dreams for your children, then?"

"To emigrate. I want them to live in another country," he said, like the United States or somewhere in Europe. He did not have savings as he had put all of his earnings toward private schools for his children so that they could have the possibility of being able to leave some day. Nor did he want to go back to where he was born, Bethlehem, or for his kids to go there. "I could get a visa. But I don't really want to. I don't want to get a visa, permission, from people who took my land."

A van drove by and Motasem pointed out that it was a Palestine Liberation Organization van. The PLO were still active here. Hosting Palestinian refugees had also been a challenge for Jordan's stability.[61] In 1970, in the aftermath of the 1967 war and the Arab defeat, Jordan had erupted in civil war. The East Bank Jordanians had more political authority than Palestinian refugees who wanted additional control over government. The East Bankers feared that this would lead to further conflict with Israel. The civil war ended in PLO defeat. Palestinian fighters were driven out, regrouping in southern Lebanon. The PLO used southern Lebanon as a base for its military efforts, until they were once again driven out and relocated in Tunisia. The PLO, which had become recognized as the representative of the Palestinian people by a hundred countries, formally recognized Israel's right to exist in the 1993 Oslo Accords, which created areas in the West Bank and Gaza that would be administered by a newly created Palestinian Authority. The Palestinian refugee crisis turned into a domino effect of instability that spread from Israel/Palestine to Jordan to Lebanon and on.

We got back in the car. After driving through the marketplace, the ground covered with trash and the sides of the road lined with vegetable stands, we left and Motasem drove me back to my hotel. I thanked him for the afternoon and for sharing his childhood with me.

And then, he thanked me for asking him to go there. "Arabs are sentimental," he said.

I think of this history as I consider the Syrians and their displacement. The Middle East, in particular Jordan, is turning into a region of displaced people whose lives have been defined by exile and violence. What seem at first like temporary crises have turned into generational population shifts.

At the Intersection of Fifth Avenue and the Champs-Élysées

Hands shot up to be called on.

"A doctor," said a girl in a flowered headscarf.

"An engineer so that I can rebuild Syria," said another girl, with a serious and determined look on her small face.

"An archaeologist."

"A lawyer so that I can defend Syria."

"I want to work in the media."

"A teacher."

These were the answers given by a crowded classroom of Syrian refugee girls, sitting three girls in desks meant for two, at a girls' school at the Zaatari refugee camp.

This was the second question I posed to the girls. The first question was about the problems that they faced in education in the camp. To that question, not a single girl raised her hand. Silence. It was when I asked about their hopes and dreams, what they wanted from their lives, that hands around the room shot up. They didn't want to dwell on the negative. They wanted to look forward.

Yet a large proportion of these girls will enter into early marriage before finishing secondary school. Rates of child marriage have increased among refugees, as a negative coping mechanism, when families lack the basic means to provide food for everyone. Refugee families have exhausted their savings. Boys and girls are entering into child labor to survive when parents are missing, disabled, can't find work (as Syrian refugees are prohibited from working in most cases), or can't earn enough while working on the black market.[62]

Outside the classroom, the school grounds were surrounded by fences topped by hoops of razor wire. Security is high at the school to protect the children and prevent theft.

The girls' shift ended and they left the school grounds. The boys entered the school for their shift. They had been outside playing a game of soccer, on the hard-packed sand and rocks. One hit the ball with his head, scoring a goal. Other boys ran around, wrestling each other, letting off energy as boys do. They looked like normal kids, not refugees. Kids are resilient.

Jordan's Zaatari refugee camp is about an hour and a half drive from Amman, through desert and rolling hills. (In Arabic, za'atar is the name of a spice mixture with thyme, sesame, sumac, and salt.) Zaatari was part of Jordan's response to the tide of refugees flowing in from the Syrian civil war, opening up in 2012. At its height, in 2013, Zaatari housed 130,000 people, making it the fourth largest city in Jordan.[63] But most Syrians did not want to live in refugee camps. One Syrian man described Zaatari to me as "not fit for humans," as people lived in exposed tents on desert sand and crime was high. Some Syrians left for urban areas in Jordan. Zaatari's population had dwindled to 85,000 by 2015—still making this refugee camp Jordan's sixth largest city.[64]

In addition to many other impacts, the refugee crisis means that a generation of Syrian children is growing up without stable access to quality education. Only about 60 percent of Syrian refugee children in Jordan are attending school.[65] Some have been out of school for several years as the Syrian civil war has been intensifying since 2011.

Jordan, like Syria's other neighbors, has been remarkably generous in hosting the refugees. Jordan and Lebanon now have the highest per capita ratio of refugees in the world.[66] Before the crisis in 2011, Jordan's population was 6.2 million; the arrival of 620,000 registered refugees means that now, at least 10 percent of the population of Jordan are Syrian refugees.[67]

The number of refugees is straining Jordan's ability to cope. The vast majority (over 84 percent) of Syrian refugees in Jordan are living outside of the camps in communities; only a minority remain in the camps.[68] This means that refugees rely on national and municipal public services that are stretched to the limit. Government budgets and infrastructure (like schools, hospitals, and sanitation) are increasingly burdened. In addition, the presence of so many refugees is causing tensions with the Jordanian host communities, which experience rising rents and unemployment, dropping wages, and overstretched public services.[69]

Jordanians also remember absorbing Palestinian refugees. What was supposed to be temporary became permanent. With the Syrians, Jordanians fear hosting another protracted refugee crisis. In other such refugee crises around the world, the average time until refugees can return to their home country has been seventeen years.[70] The Syrian civil war does not have an end in sight. Even after the war ends, it may be decades before many refugees will be able to return because of the vastness of the destruction of infrastructure, tensions among people, and the devastated economy.[71]

As I visited Zaatari, I wondered if this too would become a permanent city. Set up as a temporary camp, it now has roads, districts, schools, hospitals, and plumbing. Zaatari seemed on its way to repeating the experience of Al-Wahdat, morphing from a refugee camp into a long-term urban slum, with UN involvement in managing and paying for it into the future.

Jordan, which was supposed to be the buffer country, is now absorbing human damages from yet another Middle East conflict, this one ignited by the Arab Spring.

My driver took me around the ring road that surrounds the camp-transitioning-to-a-city. A map of the refugee camp shows that it is so large, with a five mile circumference, that it is divided into districts with main streets intersecting it.

Zaatari residents have dealt with their hardship with a sense of humor. The main street of Zaatari has been named the Champs-Élysées, after the boulevard in Paris. It intersects what the refugees have named Fifth Avenue, after New York's famous avenue. These are dusty streets where the refugees have set up vegetable stands, a barber, a hair salon, a computer game shop, a cell phone shop, and a convenience and dry goods store. Haggard-looking people walked around outside. Tents and pre-fabricated caravans have been rearranged by the refugees to make little communities, with water tanks, laundry lines, and small gardens separated by barbed wire.

We drove out of the camp, through the UN "base camp," where there are UN offices, bathrooms, and a small cafeteria, and out the well-guarded entrance. A gray camouflage tank guarded the gate to the camp. Soldiers stood by with uniforms and guns.

This is how the post–Arab Spring generation of Syrian children will grow up.

From Jordan to Qatar

Much of Jordan's population is comprised of refugees or their descendants, and Jordan is in a difficult geographic neighborhood, bounded by warring Syria and Iraq and by neighboring Israel. While Jordan stayed stable after the Arab Spring because of moderate and specific demands by protesters, careful incremental steps in response by the government, and measured balancing of the different peoples within its borders, its stability is not assured. How Jordan will manage the pressures of absorbing ongoing waves of Syrian refugees poses a particular challenge. But Jordan's steps to meet societal demand for more representation, its support for entrepreneurship, and the moderate course of the government give good reason for confidence.

I next traveled to Qatar, moving from Jordan's threadbare stability to Gulf luxury and a "spring" of investment in building a knowledge-based economy, but accompanied by interference in other countries' Arab Springs.

Qatar

Skyscrapers Near the Corniche

The moon glistened on the sea. Ships were visible out at sea. The lights of the skyscrapers illuminated the night. I set out walking on the Corniche, Doha's four-and-a-half mile, palm-tree-fringed promenade along the sea that starts in Doha's downtown West Bay district. The Corniche comes alive at night, when the darkness softens the heat of the day. Spandex-clad joggers ran past me, enjoying a night run. Children played on a nearby jungle gym and a little girl sped by me on a tricycle. A woman in a black abaya speed-walked by me, carrying a smartphone and wearing white tennis shoes. A group of men prayed alongside the promenade in an area designated for Muslim prayer. A few families sat on blankets and ate picnic dinners. Couples walked by, holding hands. As I walked, I passed stations of fitness equipment for sit-ups or chin-ups and a line of bikes to rent and share. Other people walking by were a mix of ethnicities—Qataris, other Arabs, Filipinos, South Asians, and Westerners.

Doha is a desert city on the east coast of Qatar in the Persian Gulf, with searing heat and sun so bright it tires the eyes. Skyscrapers grow like stalks of wheat, covering land that had once been yellow sand and crystal blue saltwater.

Two decades ago, Qatar was barely on the map. It was a small, obscure country, a city-state, and not politically, economically, or culturally important like Egypt, Saudi Arabia, or Syria. Qatar was sand, with a tiny population, and without much of a distinct history.

But Qatar has the third largest gas reserves in the world, after Russia and Iran.[1] Qatar invested in developing technology to liquefy natural gas, enabling it to move gas to world markets by tankers instead of in pipelines through unpredictable neighbors' lands. And so its gas sales transitioned Qatar from sandy desert life to overwhelming wealth quickly. According to the IMF, Qatar has the highest GDP per capita in the world, about $140,000.[2]

If we consider the Arab Spring broadly to include replacing ineffective governments with optimistic investments for the future, even outside of the 2011 to 2013 years of protests, then the Arab Spring in Qatar might have started twenty years ago, in 1995, when Sheikh Hamad bin Khalifa al-Thani, father of the current amir, Sheikh Tamim bin Hamad al-Thani, overthrew his father in a bloodless coup. Sheikh Hamad ushered in nearly two decades of investment in education, health, research, and infrastructure. He and his wife, Sheikha Moza bint Nasser (the second of three wives, with the most public role), pursued the goal of transforming Qatar into a Middle Eastern center of higher education, research, media, sports, and culture by partnering with international universities (primarily American) to establish campuses in Qatar and by investing heavily in research. The amir funded the founding of Al Jazeera, which has grown into a solid, albeit controversial, international news media company that now operates a news channel in the United States. Qatar is rapidly building architecturally innovative new museums to showcase Islamic heritage. Qatar won the right to host the 2022 FIFA World Cup, although the process has been marred by accusations of corruption. In 2014, Qatar contracted $30 billion in infrastructure contracts, for a metro, bridges, and better roads, and an estimated $60 billion in infrastructure projects are planned in support of the 2022 World Cup.[3]

Growth has been fast and dramatic. In 2006, there were 750,000 people in Qatar. By 2015, there were 2.2 million.[4] People from all over the world flood into Doha to work for a few years and then return to their home countries. Since there are not enough Qataris with the needed skill sets to do the work, growth has depended on expatriate labor, both highly paid skilled professionals and low-paid unskilled workers. (Furthermore, because of the country's broadly distributed energy wealth, there are many jobs that Qataris are unwilling to do.) Working conditions of the unskilled workers in Qatar have led to accusations of human rights abuses. Only 13 percent of Qatar's population are Qatari nationals; 87 percent of the people in Qatar are expatriates, who make up 94 percent of the workforce.[5] Qataris have become a minority in their own country.

Qatar is the beneficiary of a brain drain in the Middle East, with some of the best and brightest from other Arab countries often going to Qatar, lured by outsize salaries (and stability) in a place that shares Arabic culture. For example, many Iraqis, Lebanese, and Egyptians find work there. Qatar blends traditional Arab culture with modern aspirations and investments. Thomas Friedman wrote in the *New York Times* that Dubai's prosperity and way of life was the real cause of the Arab Spring; Arabs could see an Arab country that offered opportunity and a comfortable way of life.[6] He described it as "a place where young Arabs from across the region can come to realize their full potential in arts, business, media, education and technology startups—with world-class companies—and in their own culture, their own language, their own religious milieu, their own food preferences, music and clothing." That argument could similarly apply to neighboring Doha, although to a lesser extent, as Doha is smaller and less culturally open than Dubai.

Doha is a mixing bowl of peoples from the world over—adventurers, builders, scholars, and schemers. It is a place of income inequality, with wealthy locals and expatriates in air-conditioning and laborers toiling on construction sites in the heat. Qatar has flashy new shopping malls with Louis Vuitton handbags as well as crowded Pakistani minimarts selling grimy unwashed eggs, mangos, and grape lollipops.

Evolving from the slow way of life among Bedouin tribes with an economy based on dates, pearl diving, camels, and tents, Qatar now hosts peoples of numerous cultures and traditions. It is a place where people wear distinct clothing—abayas, *thobes,* suits, and saris—like uniforms that represent identities. These are not subtle identities based on a preference for style, but rather the expression of norms: morality, culture, values, and history.

But this juxtaposition and rapid transition has led to uneasy changes and tensions between modernity and tradition, between peoples of different cultures and values. Few places or societies have changed as much and as quickly as Qatar, enabled by energy wealth.

Some Qataris say that the changes are happening too fast. This is a place transitioning from a traditional way of life that had not changed much over a thousand years to a multinational city-state in the span of a few decades.

The Arab Spring movement shook many other countries and over-threw governments in the Middle East, but the streets of Doha were quiet. There were no large demonstrations. There were no loud public calls for a new government. There was no imprisonment or exile of rulers.

But while the Arab Spring in Qatar was quiet, it was still there. The government response was conciliation—throwing money at it. In 2011, all Qatari national government employees (the vast majority of employed Qataris) were given a 60 percent raise, and the military and police received 120 percent raises.[7] Among Qataris there was worry about having their culture marginalized by the massive influx of foreigners who had come to pursue their ambitions in the country. The government rolled back its unpopular policy of teaching certain classes in English in public schools and at Qatar University (meant to enable Qataris to participate in the English-language dominated labor market in Qatar), and Arabic was reinstated. And then liquor licenses of restaurants were revoked at the Pearl, a popular offshore development and center of lively expatriate nightlife. Qataris were feeling shut out of the nightlife there; Islam forbids drinking alcohol and many Qataris do not want to be around other people drinking it. Even though this was a trivial matter, it was symbolic of the Qataris wanting to take their country back culturally. In December 2011, after Arab Spring protests that shook other countries in the Middle East and toppled entrenched rulers, the government of Qatar . . . announced a ban on serving alcoholic beverages at the Pearl.[8]

In Qatar, this was Arab Spring Light. It was about small changes being made in response to popular sentiments.

But Qatar was very involved with other countries' Arab Springs. The *Washington Post* had an insightful opinion piece that divided the Middle East into countries that meddle and countries that get meddled with.[9] Qatar is one of the meddlers, along with Iran, Saudi Arabia, Turkey, and Israel. Countries that are meddled with are Egypt, Syria, Lebanon, and the Palestinian territories. I would add the UAE to the meddlers and Libya, Yemen, and Bahrain to those that get meddled with.

I kept walking along the Corniche, the sea on my left and the city on my right, and arrived in front of the Diwan, Qatar's White House, the office of the amir. It sits perched on a hill of green grass, a stately building of white stone, arches, and fountains, but with a tacky Disney-Aladdin-like addition with turquoise paint on the side. Across the road are docks for fishing boats and nearby are Souq Waqif (Doha's traditional outdoor market) and the iconic Museum of Islamic Art, an elegant stone building designed by I. M. Pei. The sound of gulls harmonizes with the sounds of the cars driving by. Qatar's flag ripples from a tall post on the building. It is here that the business of the government is conducted, with controversial decisions of late in Qatar's foreign policy.

Like Jordan, Qatar is a small state in a tough neighborhood. It has maintained its independence by balancing the interests of competing powerful players in the region, playing all sides against the middle. It is a major U.S. ally, hosting both the biggest U.S. military base in the Middle East and branch campuses of U.S. universities.[10] Qatar shares its gas fields, the North Fields, with Iran. It borders Saudi Arabia. As journalist Hugh Miles put it, "Lying between Iran and Saudi Arabia, like a mouse sharing a cage with two rattlesnakes, the little Emirate has had to learn to live on its wits."[11]

During the Arab Spring, Qatar became interventionist, interfering in other countries' Arab Springs through the reporting of Al Jazeera, diplomacy, and financial support to both Islamist political parties and violent factions. Critics accuse Al Jazeera of instigating upheaval in the Middle East by first airing the grievances of protesters against autocratic governments and later providing coverage biased in favor of Islamist groups. In Libya, Qatar provided military support to the NATO alliance, but then there have since been allegations of the state's supporting hard-line, violent Islamist groups in Libya and funding the Nusra Front in Syria.[12] Qatar has pumped more money into the Syrian civil war than any other government (up to $3 billion from 2011 to 2013), including arming rebels and Salafist-Jihadists, getting refugee packages to defectors, and providing humanitarian aid.[13] While some money may come from Qatar's government, much of it is private donations by Qatari individuals. Critics say that its funding has splintered the opposition and weakened institutions in Syria. In Egypt, Qatar supported Mohammed Morsi and the Muslim Brotherhood. After Morsi fell, it hosted the Muslim Brotherhood in Doha, until the UAE, Saudi Arabia, and Egypt pulled their ambassadors from Qatar, complaining to such an extent that the Muslim Brotherhood was forced to leave.[14] Qatar has also provided funding to Hamas.

The undersecretary for terrorism and financial intelligence at the U.S. Department of the Treasury, David Cohen, noted that "Qatar has become such a permissive terrorist financing environment, that several major Qatar-based fundraisers act as local representatives for larger terrorist fundraising networks."[15] In the wake of criticism by the U.S. secretary of treasury about funds to terrorists, Qatar implemented a new law regulating funding to charities.[16]

Elizabeth Dickinson argued in *Foreign Policy* that Qatar has "played a major role in destabilizing nearly every trouble spot in the region and in accelerating the growth of radical and jihadi factions. The results have ranged from bad to catastrophic in the countries that are the beneficiaries of Qatari aid: Libya is mired in a war between proxy-funded militias, Syria's opposition has been overwhelmed by infighting and overtaken by extremists, and Hamas' intransigence has arguably helped prolong the Gaza Strip's humanitarian plight."[17]

Through its Arab Spring foreign policy activity, Qatar is increasingly losing the good reputation and careful branding that it built from its investments in education, research, culture, and sports.[18] These interventions have led to backlash against Qatar in the region, where it is viewed as overreaching. During my interviews for this book, people in Tunisia, Egypt, and Iraq expressed resentment over the perceived interference of Qatar in their internal affairs, in the form of support to Islamist political parties, funding of violent factions, networking with Salafist preachers, and the seeming bias of Al Jazeera.

Why is Qatar interfering, particularly when doing so is in such dramatic contrast to the cosmopolitanism of the country? To me, it seemed as though there were two Qatars: the Qatar that sought to create a glittering, tolerant city of the world in its capital Doha and the Qatar in the news for its discordant foreign policy. It could be that there was a mismatch between their ambitions and their institutional capabilities as a small country to manage what they had started.[19] Its own internal pressures of Islamism could have led to pressures to back groups that they mistakenly hoped had the potential for competent, just governance. It could be that they backed the wrong horse with the Muslim Brotherhood in Egypt, Tunisia, and elsewhere. It could be that Qatar is trying to prove a counterweight to both Saudi Arabia and Iran, with whom it has tried to compete diplomatically. It could be that Sheikh Tamim, who took over from his father at the relatively young age of thirty-two, lacks the experience and capabilities of his father in navigating Middle East diplomacy. (When the former amir, Sheikh Hamad, stepped aside in 2013, passing the role to his son, it raised questions about how the move was related to impressions that Qatar's foreign policy was overreaching.)

In Qatar, I wanted to explore how the old world is transitioning to the new, innovative investments in development, and its interventions elsewhere. I continued my walk on the Corniche, looking around at all of the new buildings and the people and wondering what the future holds for Qatar. To understand the future, we must understand where Qatar has come from.

Robots and Camel Racing

Drive away from the glass and steel skyscrapers of West Bay, through the stop-and-go traffic of the city—flanked by kebab restaurants, car repair shops, sports arenas, and compounds of villas—and emerge onto the new, open multilane highway toward the western oil fields. After twenty miles of power stations, the desolation of flat sand and scrub-grass, and a few red-bordered triangle camel-crossing signs, you arrive at the camel racetracks. To me, this drive from skyscrapers to desert is emblematic of the transformation happening in Qatar and other Arab Gulf countries. A new way of life juxtaposed upon the old.

I parked my car and got out next to the tracks.

A small train of dusty golden camels ambled along, sporting ragged tribal-looking cloths of red, blue, and yellow on their humps. Two men were training baby camels to run. A trainer sat on top of one of the camels; he was skinny and wore a sand-colored robe. Under the harsh sun, I was grateful for my sunglasses.

Near them stood a Qatari man. His short beard was red with henna. He introduced himself as Rashed.

Rashed wore the standard white Qatari *thobe*, but I could tell that his was special. The fabric had a soft, subtle sheen. He wore tan ostrich-leather sandals, the kind specialty stores in Doha sell for about six hundred dollars. There were diamond cufflinks on his wrists. Long white Qatari *thobes* look sort of like a Western man's dress shirt with collars, cuffs, and pockets, but they extend to the ground. A piece of white cloth called a *gutra* flows from their heads, secured with a black rope that circles the top of the head twice. When I first arrived in Qatar, the dress startled me. It looked medieval, not of our century. I had an early moment of culture shock when I saw men in white *thobes* and *gutras* sipping lattes at Starbucks. But then I got used to this, and it now looks elegant and distinguished to me. The cloth is fine, white, always very neatly pressed, and sometimes silky. White *thobes* are perfect for hot weather, strong winds, and the glaring sun of the desert—or a day in an air-conditioned office.

Qatari men all wear the same Qatari uniform, a *thobe* and *gutra* (although they often put on Western clothes when they leave Qatar). In a way, it's nice: wearing the same thing fits with Islam's ideals of equality, so that any man on the street looks equally important, all people the same before God. But there are loopholes; the money is in the details. It's all in the sandals, watches, and cufflinks.

"You want to buy my camel?" Rashed asked.

I offered him fifty dollars.

"Fifty dollars?" he snorted. "I paid three hundred thousand dollars for her." The camel was named Sultana, and he planned for her to win races in Dubai.

"Do you have a lot of camels?" I asked.

He estimated that he had thirty or forty. Surely they were not all worth as much as this one, but that was a lot of money in camels. There was going to be a race in an hour. He invited me to join him and then drove off in his Toyota Land Cruiser.

The Toyota Land Cruiser is the national car of Qatar. It is a sign of status and belonging as a Qatari. Why the Land Cruiser? Driving in the desert requires four-wheel drive and the best-performing of these is the Land Cruiser. A Land Cruiser can drive on the hard-packed rocky sand in the north of Qatar, the soft mountain-high sand dunes in the south, and the roads of Doha. The wealthier Qataris show off by getting a Porsche Cayenne or a Cadillac Esplanade, but the true car queen of Qatar is the Land Cruiser.

In the past, caravans of Bedouins and camels ambled across the sand between settlements that were barely towns. Camels carried people, did not drink much water when humans needed it more, and were important for trade. Now, camels are for aesthetics, to remember society's roots. To experience nature in the traditional way, Qatari families drive Land Cruisers into the dunes of the desert and pitch tents, just like the old days. A Qatari colleague of mine had a camp of five air-conditioned tents in the middle of the desert, with satellite television and carpets.

Qatar's history is both ancient and yet not so ancient. Islam started on the Arabian Peninsula in what is now neighboring Saudi Arabia. There were no country borders at the time, and the Arabian Peninsula shared a history—Islam, Bedouin tribes, oases, pearl diving, camels, fishing, tent camps, and trade. The Arabian Peninsula was a cultural block, with overland trade and sea trade, as well as nomadic tribal life and town life. Qatar is a small peninsula off the larger peninsula, shaped like a little thumb sticking out of the side of Saudi Arabia into the Persian Gulf, which Qataris prefer to call the Arabian Gulf.

From 1872 until 1913, Qatar and the much of the Arabian Peninsula was ruled by the Ottoman Empire. After World War I and the fall of the Ottoman Empire, the eastern part of the Arabian Peninsula was split among local tribal leaders, called amirs or emirs—an emirate in Qatar, the seven emirates in the United Arab Emirates, Bahrain, Yemen, and Oman. Qatar negotiated joining the UAE initially, but the deal fell apart and it remained separate, but still a protectorate of Britain. Qatar declared independence from Britain in 1971. The al-Thani family that ruled then still rules today.

And then everything changed. Oil was found, and then natural gas. The economy morphed from dates, camels, pearl diving, and small trade to an energy economy. Life is different now.

An hour later, I met Rashed at the starting point of the race.

The eager camels lined up at the beginning of the track, restrained by ropes held by their trainers.

Rashed pointed to small robots on top of the camels. The robots serve as jockeys. As recently as a few years ago, small boys rode as the jockeys.

The boys were purchased from Africa or Asia, often from Sudan. They could be injured, lacked education, and lived in risky situations among older male trainers, without parents to guard their safety. After an international human rights outcry, the Gulf countries got rid of the boy jockeys. This diminished camel racing for a few years.[20]

Then someone figured out how to race a camel with a robot.

I asked to see one. Rashed pulled a robot out of his Land Cruiser's trunk. It was small, about eight pounds, and the size of my forearm. It used a drill motor, with a small whip attached, which was operated by remote control. When Rashed pressed a button on the remote control, the robot whipped the camel. He talked into the remote so the camel could hear him through a speaker on the robot.

Rashed invited me into his Land Cruiser. (While it was culturally acceptable for a Western woman to sit in a car with a Qatari man, it would never be acceptable for a Western man to sit in a car with a Qatari woman.) We would drive next to Sultana during the race. Rashed cleared ropes, camel hair brushes, and a box of robot spare parts off the backseat of the Land Cruiser, removed folded red and blue wool blankets, and brushed camel hairs from the upholstery so I could sit. He jumped in the front and drove the Land Cruiser up to the starting line with the other Land Cruisers.

About fifteen black, white, or tan Land Cruisers lined up on three lanes of road next to the starting point of the race. All fifteen weren't going to fit in those three lanes, I thought. And then I was worried. Qatar has one of the highest death rates in the world from road accidents.[21]

I envisioned swarms of Land Cruisers all pushing to be in the same spot, violent accidents, flips in the air, and imminent death. "Are there accidents with this?" I asked.

Rashed gave a mischievous grin. "No problem. This race is for babies," he said. "For babies."

"There she is!" He pointed to his baby camel. "Ready?" The camel's trainer stood next to her, petting her and holding her rope.

Rashed rolled his window down. He gripped the steering wheel with his right hand and the remote-control for the camel-robot with his left hand.

I held my breath. And then. . . .

"*Yallah!*" someone yelled. A lead camel with a man (not a robot) riding her ran out in front of the other camels to get them moving. The trainers all started shouting at once and smacked the haunches of the camels to make them run.

They were off!

Rashed leaned forward, clicked the button on the remote control that operated the whip on the robot, and shouted into the remote's microphone, *"Yallah, yallah, la illah illallah! Yallah, Yallah!"* Let's go, let's go, there's no God but God! Let's go!

We launched. My heart leapt. A swarm of bees, the Land Cruisers revved up, kicked up dust, and sped off, crowding in next to the track. All the men shouted like Rashed, and the trilled *l*'s from their chant, the dust, and the car engines surrounded us with adrenaline.

The Land Cruisers wove in and out among each other. We had a spot right next to the rail separating the track from the desert. Land Cruisers were in front of us, in back of us, and to the right of us. We were besieged by clouds of dust, and shouting, trilling men. I shut my eyes as another Land Cruiser nearly shaved off our headlights. One impatient driver drove off the lanes and into the desert so he could pass all the other drivers and get in front.

We weren't going that fast, but we were swerving. I coughed on dust coming in through the open windows. Rashed was focused on his driving, his chanting, and his remote-control clicking.

But while the Land Cruisers united in dusty, chanting, swerving frenzy, the camels themselves were anticlimactically slow. They clopped along, awkward babies. Their legs did not look designed for graceful fast running. They kicked and flailed and got in each other's way. They did not match the insanity of the Land Cruisers. The robots looked like mini-pillars on top of their humps. The circular engines were whirring the whips in continuous circles, spanking the camels by remote control.

Rashed shouted into the remote. "Hurry!" His camel was not in the lead. Three camels were in front of her, while the rest of the pack was a few feet behind.

We approached the finish line, two poles on either side of the track with colorful rags dangling from them in the windless air. We reached the end of the track and then slowed to a stop. Just for dramatic effect, Rashed hit the brakes hard after slowing, a baby-sized screech to a halt.

And then, the race was over. Rashed's camel came in fourth.

"*W'allah,* that camel, she will win someday. Just wait until she is older," Rashed said. "Let's do another?" He beamed, excited.

We spent the rest of the afternoon doing baby-camel races. After each race, Rashed turned around to ask. "Another?" And I said, "Yes!"

At the end of the races, Rashed drove me back to my nice, safe Volvo with multiple airbags. As he drove, he said, "I want to explain something. You see, God gave us, the Arabs in the desert, this oil and natural gas, because of the virtue of our people and for following the principles of Islam. God is rewarding us for our religion. Other people around the world contribute things to history, to science, to technology, to medicine. But we here, we have contributed something much more important—religion. And for this, we get the greatest blessings from God."

Who was I to argue?

The camel is like so much in Qatari society. The old, dusty traditional parts are being replaced by new shiny technology. The old mud-brick villages are gone and have given way to glass and steel high rises and complexes of American universities. The old souks where traders met to parley their wares are gone, and now there are shopping malls with Armani stores. Foreigners, with our strange ways, have flooded the country. I wondered if this felt like a "spring" to the Qataris—or if it was just disorienting. Rashed gave a last wave and drove his Land Cruiser off in a cloud of dust.

Another Golden Age of Science in the Middle East?

Not far from the camel racetracks, Education City not long ago was a vast stretch of desolate, hard, hot sand. Yet now, it is a complex of six branch campuses of American universities, a French university, a British university, a Qatari university, a science park, research centers, a convention center, a research hospital, and an equestrian park—all in opulent architecturally innovative buildings. Pink stone pyramids surrounded the branch campus of Texas A&M, and branch campuses of Carnegie Mellon University and Georgetown University are of burnt orange and beige stone. Weill Cornell Medical College looks like a giant white space station. The Qatar National Convention Center was fronted with a multistory-high sculpture of giant silver branches of the Sidra tree, a tree that thrives in harsh desert environments and, in the Arab world, symbolizes perseverance. The amir's Arabian horses live in a 980,000 square meter, horseshoe shaped equestrian center of glass and steel. Big yellow metal letters spelling out "Think," each letter bigger than a person, were placed on the lawn. Qatar University, the national university, had a separate campus.

As I walked around now, I recalled the first university graduation night that I had attended in Education City. The ceremonial court was magnificent under the stars, with pools of water, a raised stage, and walkways with walls of lattice in abstract shapes reminiscent of Islamic geometric design. There were fountains and strips of grass freshly laid on the desert sand in preparation for the ceremonies. Students from around the world—Qatar, other Arab countries, India, and Pakistan, were dressed in ceremonial robes. As each student's name was read, he or she walked to the stage to accept a diploma. While all graduations are proud moments, this was an especially proud one. This was the first class of students to graduate from newly established branch campuses of American universities there. The amir, Sheikh Hamad, and his wife, Sheikha Moza, were present, sitting in the front row and clapping for each student, with a standing ovation for a student in a wheelchair. As the driving force behind Education City, Sheikha Moza came to the stage to give a speech, dressed in an elegantly designed abaya and stiletto heels. To celebrate, they flew in pop-opera singer Andrea Bocelli to sing after the ceremony, along with Kathem al-Saher, an Iraqi pop star.

The concept of American-style higher education in the Middle East was not new. The American University in Cairo and the American University in Beirut had educated many of the Middle East's elite for generations. But these universities have lost some of their stature because of instability in Egypt and Lebanon. The American University in Cairo and the American University in Beirut are also autonomous, not campuses managed by universities in the United States.

Education City was therefore a new model of international higher education in which American universities exported campuses abroad for students in those countries, each university offering the majors for which it is best known. For Qatar, in addition, hosting the U.S. universities is also a way of signaling ties with the United States.

Using its energy wealth, Qatar has been investing toward goals of creating a knowledge-based economy, with a regional center of higher education and research. Education City's American branch campuses represent a significant investment in quality higher education in the Middle East. The complex was founded by the Qatar Foundation (for many years chaired by Sheikha Moza), which invested some of Qatar's energy wealth in education, research, and community projects. There have been improvements in Qatar University as well. Dr. Sheikha al-Misnad, the first woman president of Qatar University and an abaya-clad, no-nonsense woman skilled in the rough-and-tumble of university politics, improved quality, set a strategy, restructured administration, and introduced research.[22]

Qatar sought to re-create the Arab world's history of educational and scientific excellence during the Islamic Golden Age, from the eighth through the thirteenth centuries, when pan-Islamic culture stretched from Spain to China, and which ended when Hulagu Khan sacked Baghdad, made blood flow in the streets, and burned its libraries. The effort recalls the Arab world's past at the forefront of progress in science, philosophy, medicine, and education, an era that was characterized by the Arabic language, the Islamic faith, movement of people and goods, and a common cultural reference.

In recent times, Middle Eastern universities have not excelled in quality by international standards. The Shanghai Academic Ranking of World Universities, an accepted world ranking system, does not place any Middle Eastern universities in its top 150 list, except for four in Israel, and *U.S. News & World Report* lists no Middle Eastern university in its top 100 list.[23] There are only a handful of universities in Saudi Arabia in the Shanghai Academic Ranking's top 500 list.

As Qatar was beginning to establish high-quality universities, it was clear that to be able to attract and retain research faculty from around the world, it had to offer research funding and opportunities. Qatar needed a funding agency, something like the U.S. National Science Foundation.[24] Qatar Foundation, with advising from the RAND Corporation (one of the endeavors that I worked on during my time in Qatar), established the Qatar National Research Fund (QNRF) for this purpose. QNRF funds merit-based research in Qatar, in partnership with researchers in other countries, to build research capacity in Qatar and connect it with the international research community.

Based on this model, as of 2015, QNRF had awarded over $800 million in research grants. This funding enabled the U.S. branch campuses, Qatar University, and other research entities in Qatar to grow. It also improved the quality of research in Qatar, with Qatar's "mean normalized citation score"—a statistical method of analyzing quality of research papers—rising from below world average to slightly above the world average in just a few years. Qatar-based research projects addressed a range of questions across academic fields: breast cancer trends among Middle Eastern women, robotics, cross-cultural differences in learning styles, DNA sequencing for date palms, computer security, and more.

I asked Abdul-Sattar al-Taie, the director of the QNRF, what this investment in education, science, and research meant for the Middle East.

"In support of its drive for becoming a regional hub in research and development and creating a knowledge-based economy, Qatar has put in place the right ingredients for a recipe of success," he said, describing multiple initiatives, including establishing Education City, the Qatar National Research Fund, and the Qatar Science and Technology Park. The Qatar National Vision 2020 outlined plans to achieve visions of innovation. "In so doing, Qatar has sparked 'an Arab Spring in research and development,' which will spur renaissance in the Arab world," he said.

Another initiative in Education City was the Doha Debates, held from 2004 until 2012. The Doha Debates were a forum for open, televised discussion of some of the Middle East's most controversial issues, at a time when leadership of many countries of the Middle East shied away from public discussion of sensitive social issues. Debate topics have included women's issues ("Arab women should have full equality with men"), relations between religion and extremism ("the war on terror has become a war on Islam," and "Muslims are failing to combat extremism"), the role of oil money in societies ("oil has been more of a curse than a blessing for the Middle East" and "Gulf Arabs value profit over people"), and Arab Spring government issues ("progress toward democracy has halted in the Arab world," and "Arab revolutions will just produce different dictators").

But a question often raised about the Education City endeavor is whether it is benefiting multiple parts of Qatari society or only a narrow elite. While there are no public figures on Education City's budget, it is a substantial investment for Qatar. While there are similarly no public figures for the total number Education City students across the university, there are estimated to be up to fifteen hundred students, with half or less of them Qatari nationals. To attend an Education City university, a student must be fully proficient in English and meet the exacting standards of the universities. It is difficult for Arabic-speaking students coming from Qatar's public schools to meet these criteria, and faculty report that many Qatari students are underprepared when they start as freshmen. Many Qatari families feel that Education City was set up in a way that makes it inaccessible to them and their children, and that Qatar University as the national university remains under-resourced in comparison.

There are also tensions between American-style education and traditional Qatari values. University education in the Gulf has traditionally been gender segregated. For example, Qatar University has a men's campus and a women's campus, while Education City mixes men and women. Change in Qatar has come so quickly that illiteracy is not many generations away; some of the students' grandparents can't read or write.

Despite these growing pains, students graduate with recognized degrees from American universities. Through Education City, Qatar is offering higher education, paralleled in few other places in the Middle East, within a Middle Eastern cultural context.

Education City is part of an emerging trend in the region as Arab Gulf countries invest in science, innovation, and education. Qatar has Education City. Nearby, the United Arab Emirates created the Business Park at Dubai World Central (meant to be a creative hub for startups and large companies alike) and partnered with MIT to establish the Masdar Institute of Science and Technology, which conducts research and offers graduate study in sustainable energy.[25] And Saudi Arabia established the King Abdullah University of Science and Technology, a sprawling architectural gem just outside of Jeddah, with an estimated endowment of $10 billion.[26]

But Qatar and other Gulf countries face human capital shortages— their big ambitions confront limits of tiny populations, and their educational pipeline is struggling to produce qualified scientists. They therefore rely on large numbers of expatriates—both Arab and Western, a reality that is itself accelerating the pace of change in the region and forcing sometimes overwhelmed citizens to adapt. Only a handful of the faculty of the universities are Qataris; most faculty members are Western or Arab expatriates. Qatar has made special efforts to re-attract the Middle East's brain drain to the West, Arabs who left their countries because of few academic and research opportunities.

These investments in research and higher education also have the potential to influence the gender landscape of the Middle East. In most of the countries of the Middle East, women are beginning to outpace men in educational achievement; more than half of university graduates in the region are women. In Qatar, for example, women make up over 60 percent of university graduates.[27] For women, education is viewed as a road to independence. On the other hand, in the Middle East and North Africa, women now have higher educational achievement than men but have double the rate of unemployment; this is called the MENA Paradox.[28] Education has not been fully translated into employment and professional opportunities for women. These numbers also point to looming challenges in marriage and family life, as traditional expectations that husbands have more education and thus greater earning power than their wives may be reversed in a generation or two.

A Qatari Poet on the Challenge of Change

"My generation is the confused generation," said Maryam al-Subaiey, a Qatari poet in her early twenties who has traveled around the world reading her poems and representing Qatari youth. She published some of her poems in *Gathering the Tide: An Anthology of Contemporary Arabian Gulf Poetry*.[29]

We met up at Salam Mall in Doha. I had walked through halls of brightly polished stone floors, passing shops like Givenchy and Versace, went up the escalator, and sat down in a newly opened cafe on the upper floor of the mall to meet al-Subaiey. She was wearing her abaya, rings on her fingers, and dangling delicate pearl and diamond bracelets on her wrists. She had just returned from a literary exchange in Derry, Ireland, where she read her poetry.

I wanted to talk to her about how Qataris are adapting to the changes sweeping their country and about changing social norms in a conservative country blown wide open to expatriates.

"In the last decade, Qatar's population has tripled. Qataris have become a minority in their own country. There is a large influx of foreigners. The workplace has changed. The economy has changed. Social life has changed. How do people deal with that?" I asked her.

"There are two streams of thought," al-Subaiey said. "There is a conservative stream that is reinforcing traditions and ideologies and an accepting stream that embraces the change." Her generation's identity is pulled in different directions. It was with her generation that coeducation of men and women at universities in Education City started. She described a disturbing recent social controversy. Young Qatari women had traveled to the Brazilian Amazon to volunteer to build houses in the jungle for needy people and appeared in photos without their headscarves. "Part of society went ballistic," she said, as it set off a frenzy of insulting commentary on Twitter. "People feel fed up with the openness that Qatar is going toward." But an opposing camp on Twitter defended the women as "Qatar's heroes in the Amazon." While she understood that change is difficult, she was exasperated: "People forgot the essence of our religion, doing good things and helping people; it's not about a cloth you put on your head."

I observed that social media and communications technology were making these kinds of societal debates possible, in a way that would not have been possible even a decade ago. As Nadia Oweidat in Jordan had observed about Jordanians, Qataris were online and different from their parents.

Al-Subaiey thought that people were clinging to dress as identity. "This is all because of the changes that are happening and people don't know how to react." One of Maryam's poems, called "Vortex of Change," describes this confusion:[30]

Behind me are the roots I left
In front of me, the fog of unknown future
And in between a black Abaya
Above me, a reflection of an incomplete moon
Below me, engravings of forgotten words
I step towards a light
Hiding behind the fog
Towards something I remembered
Towards a forgotten dream

"I represent a certain category of Qatari society, and a lot of people would disagree with what I said. Some people will say that there is no confusion, no struggle. They hold on to their lifestyle, not integrating. For them, nothing has changed. Others say that there is no identity crisis; we are opening up to the world and want to be an international hub. Our roots are deeply embedded into our culture. We are not afraid of change. Our minds are international but our feet are grounded in the culture."

"What does it mean then to be Qatari amid all of this change?" I asked. "What is your identity now?"

"There are people who manage to get the best from both modernity and traditional life," said al-Subaiey. She received her bachelor's and master's degrees from universities in the UK and has traveled around the world. At the same time, she emphasized the importance of knowing her heritage and culture. "To speak the Qatari way, to have our nice traditions that I enjoy, the way we serve guests, the family obligations that we have, our beautiful traditional clothes on celebrations, colorful dresses and henna for Ramadan." She was worried that some young people do not know traditions, how to speak properly, how to hunt with falcons, or how to fish the traditional way with a sling. "I go hunting. I know how to use a shotgun. But if I don't want something, don't impose it on me and judge me."

Al-Subaiey's family is from the original urban tribes of Qatar. She illustrated the fast pace of change by narrating the history of the generations of her family. She is proud that her great-grandfather established the first official schools in Qatar. He also promoted girls' education, and the first girls' school was in one of his houses. (In the 1950s, there were only an estimated 630 literate people in Qatar out of 25,000 to 50,000 people.)[31] Her grandfather was a merchant who traded with Dubai and India; he was the first to bring a car to Qatar, a blue Volkswagen. At that time, there was no running water. Now, her father asks her to accompany him on errands to help with English, because shop attendants in Qatar often do not speak Arabic. Like some others in her generation, al-Subaiey is bilingual, travels around the world, and has a graduate degree.

"Expatriates are now the majority in Qatar. Do you think that there are tensions in Qatar with all of the different people who live here?" I asked.

"Everyone lives their lives separately. We are a minority in our own country," she said. She felt that many expatriates resented the wealth and generous benefits in education and health that the Qataris received from the country's energy industry while not paying taxes. "But it is our country. The price that the country pays for not being democratic is that we don't pay for these services. This is a completely different social and governmental structure than the rest of the world."

Her comments reminded me of Marwan Muasher's comments in Jordan about the social contract between people and monarchies in the Gulf because of oil and gas wealth. Wealth was distributed within society, but citizens did not have Western-style constitutional democratic accountability—no taxation and no representation.

"Are there particular challenges that you face as a Qatari woman?" I asked.

"In terms of opportunities, everything is available. In terms of laws and opportunities, everything is out there. What Qatari women face are worldwide women's issues." She mentioned lower pay and stereotypes of being too emotional. "But if you are thirty and not married—poor you, you are a spinster."

She gets exasperated with how expatriates view her as a Qatari woman. She finds the situation exaggerated among expatriates who try to use gender issues to blame her culture. Many of these people, she points out, do not take the time to even learn how to say hello in Arabic. "They come with this arrogance, the same arrogance of the colonial mindset—we are here to teach you, to help you build your country. They say, 'Poor you, you have to wear the *shayla* and the abaya. You are oppressed.' There is a stereotype of the Arab world in general. They think it is only about bombing and oppressing women."

But al-Subaiey thinks that her Islamic heritage is full of admirable women and gets annoyed when Arab women are so often presented as victims in Western media. She pointed out that Khadija, the first wife of the Prophet Mohammed, was a trader running her own business. "I admired her entrepreneurial spirit, a strong independent woman regardless of her situation." A later wife of Mohammed, Aisha, rode into battle and was effective in preserving the prophecies of the early Muslim community. One of her heroes is Maryam al-Astrolabi, an Arab woman in tenth-century Aleppo, Syria who was instrumental in refining technology of the astrolabe, a navigation tool that was important for early Arab seafarers and traders.

Part of another poem by al-Subaiey, called "A Stranger in My Country," reads:

Who should I run to?
To the stranger who sees me as backward?
Or the people who see me as a rebel?

"How does your family feel about you writing and traveling?" I asked. Al-Subaiey is unusual among Qatari women in terms of how much she travels alone. When I first moved to Qatar, tradition dictated that if a woman needed to go on a business trip, a male escort (such as a husband, father, or brother) had to travel with her and many organizations paid for the escort's travel as well.

Her family is conflicted. On the one hand, they are proud of her achievements, but they are also under constant pressure from society. Her family is sometimes concerned that people will say that she is too open-minded or too Western. "I travel alone, work with men, and drive a car. It is a deadly combination," she said. When she travels, she does not cover her hair. However, she wears the abaya and *shayla* while in Qatar. "When in Qatar, I live the Qatari way, to be respected and accepted," she said. "For us, the abaya is considered prestige."

Al-Subaiey writes poems about controversial issues. "I need others to know that there are people who think about these things. I write about double standards. Things that should exist because of Islamic rights but don't because of tradition or culture. My writing started as a way for me to let go of my questions or frustrations that I don't have answers for." She writes about daily life, observations on changes in Qatari society, life from the perspective of a young Qatari woman, and labor practices.

An excerpt from her poem about the laborers in Qatar, "The Invisible Army" reads:

They have no expressions
They were wiped out
By the sun, by the dust, by the law, and by us . . .
We choose not to see them
We choose to forget about them
This invisible army that builds our country

Near the Dream Hypermarket

In West Bay, skyscrapers are going up, thirty-five, forty, fifty stories. They start as massive square multistory pits in the sand and then become concrete skeletons. You can see their guts—lines and grids of concrete and steel. Many are beautiful, glass and steel, some modern and sleek, some with Islamic geometric shapes, some garish, some quite elegant. A main noise of the downtown area of West Bay is the clanging of loud pile drivers in the construction sites, as if they are trying to build an entire country from scratch in the span of a few years. Nearby, roads are under construction too. They are being built new or ripped up and built again. While work has been fast for the past decade, the pace quickened after Qatar won the bid to host the 2022 World Cup and began the massive undertaking of building more infrastructure, including stadiums and hotels, to prepare Doha for the future event.

I could see little blue men swarming through the concrete skeletons. They look blue from a distance because of their laborer uniforms. They look like ants. Qatar has been criticized widely for its treatment of laborers. While there is recognition that Qatar is making slow changes to improve these conditions, labor rights violations are shocking and egregious.

Current estimates are that there are over eleven million migrant laborers in the Gulf countries of Qatar, Bahrain, Kuwait, Oman, Saudi Arabia, and the United Arab Emirates.[32] Most of the workers come from Nepal, India, Indonesia, Sri Lanka, Bangladesh, Pakistan, the Philippines, and other South Asian and East Asian countries. A smaller number come from other Arab countries and Africa, as they may not work for wages as low as the others, and because the government of Qatar may fear the demographic implications of bringing in large numbers of men from culturally similar countries, who would expect greater rights.

Friday is the day off in Qatar, the Muslim holy day, the equivalent of Sunday in the United States. I drove through the outskirts of Doha, heralded by car dealerships like Volvo and Peugeot, and then to where the workers live in the Industrial Area—streets of buckled asphalt, concrete tenements, warehouses, abandoned wrecked cars, piles of tires, sewage trucks, garbage and dust, concrete blocks, crates, pickup trucks, and markets. Laundry hung from clotheslines and out the windows. There were clusters of satellite dishes and a few vines hanging over walls. There were balconies with beat-up furniture. Men came out on the balconies, toweling their hair after taking showers. In the streets, men walked around wearing regular clothes, pants and shirts, not the uniforms of the laborers on workdays.

I parked, got out of the car, and wandered around the market. It felt like many a street in India, with shops doing bustling business catering to the needs of the workers, selling items like suitcases, blankets, and food. It smelled of Indian food and sewage.

The Industrial Area is a world of men without women. In Qatar, in the age bracket of fifteen to sixty-four, there are over four males per female.[33] The workers who come to Qatar are mostly male, and they arrive without their families. These men without women are mainly invisible in Qatar's social fabric. There are even rules at the malls on weekends that certain days are "family days." That means that malls will not admit men unaccompanied by a woman. On its face, the law purports to promote respect for women, protecting women, children, and families from hordes of single men ogling them. But in reality what this law does is to prevent men without women—in other words, the migrant workers—from taking part in public life.

There is another kind of vulnerable worker in Qatar—housemaids. They are imported from the Philippines, Indonesia, and elsewhere. When I ask Qataris about wages, they say the going rate for house servants is about $150 per month, with food and accommodation provided. Labor laws that protect the laborers do not apply to the housemaids; the explanation is that the housemaids are part of the family and therefore do not need public regulation. Rights groups are calling for labor laws to extend to this group of workers as well.[34]

One survey of low-income migrant workers found that they come to Qatar for an average of 5.5 years, send remittances home to their families, and then return to their home countries. The average monthly salary of workers in the survey was $291, of which they sent an average of $209 home per month.[35]

Two big problems for these workers are debt and the sponsorship system.

In order to come to Qatar, 70 percent of the workers pay recruitment companies, using their own money or borrowing from family or a bank.

The average amount of debt accrued for visa fees and recruitment costs is $1,031—in other words, the equivalent of almost all of the first four months' income must be used to pay back these costs.[36]

Once in Qatar, the workers submit to the sponsorship, or "*kafala*," system. In this system, the worker cannot quit a job, move to another employer, or leave Qatar without the employer's permission. There are reports of some sponsors denying workers this permission. In the survey, 90 percent of the workers had their passports confiscated by their employers, to prevent them from leaving Qatar without their employer's consent. While passport confiscation was made illegal in 2009, the prohibition is not enforced. A fifth of the workers in the survey reported that their employers regularly did not pay their salary on time or at all. While companies provide accommodation, such as dorm rooms in the labor camps, this means that workers typically share a single room with six other people. There are reports of squalid living conditions in the labor camps as well, with filthy bathrooms, lack of sanitation in kitchens, and overcrowding. Because of the sponsorship system and the restrictions on a worker's movement, many workers are left without recourse when they face problems.

The UK *Guardian* described conditions as "modern day slavery."[37] In 2013, Nepal's ambassador to Qatar, Maya Kumari Sharma, compared Qatar to an "open jail" for the Nepali workers there. When this was reported in the *Guardian,* Qatar complained to the government of Nepal, and Nepal withdrew Sharma.[38]

In the past decade, this system has come under scathing criticism from the international human rights community. The Human Rights Watch's World Report 2013 describes Qatar as having "some of the most restrictive sponsorship laws in the Gulf region, and forced labor and human trafficking are serious problems. The government has failed to address shortcomings in the legal and regulatory framework despite the initiation of many large-scale projects in preparation for Qatar hosting the World Cup in 2022." Human Rights Watch notes that Qatar employs only 150 labor inspectors and that inspections do not include worker interviews.[39] Amnesty International stated, "Urgent action is needed to ensure we do not end up with a World Cup tournament that is built on forced labor and exploitation."[40] The U.S. Department of State's Trafficking in Person's Report labels Qatar as a country not in full compliance with minimum standards, but making efforts to meet those standards.[41]

Qatar acknowledged a thousand deaths of workers from Nepal, India, and Bangladesh in 2012–2013.[42] At current rates, the International Trade Union Confederation estimates that four thousand workers will die in accidents during World Cup construction.[43]

Qatar has put significant effort into branding itself as a modern, progressive, innovative country that invests in education and research and that is becoming a hub for hosting sporting events. The award of the 2022 World Cup was a double-edged sword for Qatar. It gave it attention and prestige, but it also shines a spotlight on its human rights abuses. Qatar's "Spring" has been built on the backs of these people. At the same time, the silver lining is that the World Cup is forcing Qatar to confront labor human rights abuses earlier than elsewhere in the Gulf.

I recalled the experiences of Selemon, a worker from Ethiopia, who described his time working in Qatar to researchers.[44] Promised a job that paid $1,100 per month, he paid $2,440 to a broker for his position in Qatar. When he arrived in Doha, there was no job waiting for him (as his sponsor had lost a hoped-for construction contract), but Selemon still had to pay back his debts. He survived as a day laborer, working ten or eleven hours for $19 per day for a few days a month, and often employers simply did not pay him. He explained, "I cannot tell my family that things are not working out for me because I would make them worried about me. So I tell them that everything is good here." Finally, he found a job painting for $769 per month, with overtime and bonuses. After twenty months, he paid off his debt.

With additional attention to labor practices in Qatar, there have been some efforts to improve the conditions of the workers. Qatar Foundation published standards for treatment of workers, intended to provide a model for the country.[45] There are plans for new national laws as well to improve worker rights and conditions.[46] However, the laws as planned would fall short of recommendations by human rights and trade groups.

I finished my walk around the market in the Industrial Area. These were not happy faces here. It was 120 degrees in the shade. There was no green space, no park. The dusty market was the only social place. These were men on their day off, sitting on tires as a place of recreation. Around me were piles of rubble, stacks of pipes, scrap metal, dusty rocks, asphalt, cars, and trucks. Scrub brush, cranes, tractors, and trucks decorated the flat landscape, barren except for elements of industry. No Qataris were here. This was the land of the workers.

As I drove away, I drove past stores, including the ironically named Dream Hypermarket and the Venus Hypermarket, in a place with broken dreams and few women.

A Ladies-Only Wedding Party

Women in black floated into the banquet hall. Their abayas covered them to their wrists and ankles, and *shaylas* (the Gulf Arabic word for the head-scarf) covered their hair. Some wore black gloves to cover their fingers and black niqabs over their faces to cover all but their eyes.

Designer stiletto shoes peeked out.

As they crossed the threshold, the hall transformed from black to multi-colored as if by a stroke of magic. The women peeled off their covers, and the room filled with glamorous women. Shimmering red, green, gold, and blue gowns materialized. Some dresses were short. Some were long. Dresses were low cut in the back and low cut in the front. Enormous jewels sparkled—emeralds and rubies and lots of pavé diamonds. They wore long, full hair and artful makeup. These Gulf women were stunning divas, à la Hollywood.

The room was filled exclusively with women. Qatari men and women do not celebrate weddings together. And this wedding was no exception.

Like the other women, I entered wearing an evening gown, covered by a black abaya (which I only wear to weddings). Once inside, I joined the other women in the ritual of removing my abaya.

These are not frumpy, timid women. These are bling-bling, in-your-face, look-at-my-flashy-glamour women. But this part of their personality is reserved only for other women or for their own men.

Abayas changed a lot in the years I lived in Doha. When I arrived, they were black and modest. Now, some abayas have become sensual robes—still black, but with colored trim. They can have colored sparkles at the wrist or embroidery up the arms, on the hem, or on the *shayla*. The *shaylas* have changed too. A few years ago, not a strand of hair was in sight, producing a modest, plain effect. But gradually, the shaylas have been creeping back to reveal styled hair underneath. Women in abayas often wear heavy makeup. *Mutahajiba* means a woman who wears a headscarf. There is a play on words about attractive covered women—"*Mutahaja*-babes"–babes in headscarves.

I recalled many conversations with other Americans who said things like: "I think that the headscarf is an instrument of oppression. Muslim women will never be free in the Middle East until they don't have to wear it."

I think that's an exaggeration that places undue emphasis on an article of clothing. Is the problem that it restricts movement? How is that worse than a man's necktie? Is the problem that women cover their hair and men don't? How is that different from American beaches, where men go topless while women don't, or American professional office culture, where women can expose their arms in sleeveless shirts while men do not?

The headscarf's meaning has changed from generation to generation, and varies from country to country. It can be a symbol of many different things: piety, identity, social conservatism, rebellion against secular autocratic governments, or of reduced rights. At one extreme, in Afghanistan, such dress is a symbol of hiding women away, restricting their movement, and reducing their rights. An earlier generation of Arab women around the Middle East threw off the headscarf as a form of liberation. But many Qatari women in this generation see the abaya and *shayla* as markers of identity and status, a form of national dress that makes a cultural statement, separating them from the expatriates who have flooded the country.

Leila Ahmed, an Egyptian scholar of gender and Islam at Harvard University, argues that the headscarf has complex meaning not only regarding women and rights, but with respect to class, culture, and the "interconnected conflict between the culture of the colonizers and that of the colonized." She makes the case that the West seized on the issue of the headscarf as a symbol of the otherness and inferiority of Arab culture and that the West's obsession with this visible symbolic piece of clothing has as much to do with cultural conflicts as it does with women's rights. She writes, "What was created was the fusion between the issues of women, their oppression, and the cultures of Other men. The idea that Other men, men in colonized societies or societies beyond the borders of the civilized West, oppressed women was to be used, in the rhetoric of colonialism, to render morally justifiable its project of undermining or eradicating the cultures of colonized peoples." The headscarf became the symbol of the oppression of women and the backwardness of Islam and a tool with which to assault Muslim societies, she argues.[47]

But I still struggle with its meaning. The clothing itself doesn't bother me. It is the assumptions behind the clothing that bother me. It is the assumption that men are not responsible for their behavior. That a woman's beauty is stronger than a man's self-control. Therefore she has to cover her beauty, to protect the man from himself.

One woman once explained to me that she felt protected by the headscarf.

Protected from what? Men? Why should women need to be protected from men? What's wrong with men that women need protection from them?

Many women in the Middle East believe that dressing modestly and wearing the headscarf is sending a message. A woman is making a statement to all around her that she is pious and loyal to her husband.

Western clothing is designed to send signals also. There are times to accentuate appearance and times not to, times to wear form-fitting clothing and times to wear looser clothing. A business suit is different from a bikini which is different from a cocktail dress which is different from a nun's habit.

When you think about it this way, both Western and Islamic cultures sexualize women through dress. The Islamic world *covers* women more than men, defining them as so sexual that they need to be covered. The West *uncovers* women more than the men, flaunting their sexuality.

Regardless of the assumptions behind the headscarf, it still gets more attention than it deserves. It is often one of the first things that comes to mind, or comes up in conversation, about Islam, perhaps because it is such a visible symbol of cultural differences. Why isn't the same amount of effort spent discussing more important issues, such as women and family custom and law, women and education, women and leadership, or women and employment? The headscarf is not incompatible with improving rights for women in these areas.

There are many professional women in Qatar who wear abayas. Some abaya-wearing Qatari women are in positions of significant leadership— ministers, professors, deans, CEOs of companies, and managers. Admittedly, this is a small layer of elite women.

Wearing the abaya is a woman's way of keeping her identity amid all of the change occurring in society. The Qatari women that I knew embraced the abaya as a symbol. They might not wear it outside of Qatar, but they choose to wear it inside Qatar. At the beginning of airplane flights originating in Qatar, there are many abayas, but they disappear as many women change out of them before landing in another country.

Where does the headscarf come from? There is a verse in the Quran that instructs women to cover their bosom with their *khumur*.[48] There is debate over whether *khumur* means scarf or headscarf. If *khumur* meant headscarf, then the verse would assume that the head is already covered. As I read that verse, to me it seems more about bosoms than hair. If God thought this issue was so important, wouldn't he have said something more direct? Early Muslim women did not cover their heads, although the wives of the Prophet Mohammed were instructed to, as there were many men coming into the compound where they lived and it was viewed as inappropriate for them to attract attention.[49]

In the Gulf, there is reciprocity in dress between men and women. Both genders display bodily modesty, and both genders more or less dress alike in most circumstances, both in long sleeves, long robes to the floor, with a covering for the hair, and covered up to the neck. The women wear black and the men wear white. Of course, there are differences—the men can wear swim trunks in public while women cannot.

A singer on stage finished her song, and everyone clapped, jolting me out of my reverie. It was time for the bride to enter. The bride wore a white wedding gown in the Western tradition. A Muslim wedding is not a public ceremony like a Christian wedding in front of a community in a church. A contract is signed between husband and wife well before the wedding party. The bride reached a stage and sat, and then the guests got up one by one to congratulate her and kiss her on her cheeks.

And then the dancing started. Women at other tables were getting up, going onto the dance floor, and dancing together. They were having a great time, laughing at each other's seductive moves.

Almost no one was sitting now. Everyone was up dancing. But this was no modest dancing. This was a proud celebration of female sexuality. All dancing here is belly dancing. It's about moving the hips and the shoulders, the belly and spine. All were beautiful.

The music was getting louder, and it was becoming harder to hear each other in conversation at the table. Candles flickered and more tables were abandoned as women went to dance on the stage. Another waitress came around with a tray and offered sweets presented on cut crystal dishes. Then came a tray of *fatayer*, little spinach-stuffed pastries. Then, a tray of za'atar spice tea. I enjoyed the constant little offerings of food and drink.

And then it was time for the groom and his father to enter and see the bride. All of the women collected their abayas and covered once more. The room went from women dressed in color to women dressed in black. All covered, except for the bride, so her husband could see her in her uncovered beauty. The groom entered and walked slowly to his bride, and all looked on with thoughts of blessings for the new couple.

Freedom and Shariah

Mohammed el-Moctar believes that there is a constitutional crisis of Islamic civilization. "In Islam, there is the lack of basic consensus on basic core values, which is necessary for any healthy society," he said. El-Moctar is professor of Islam and Political Ethics at the Qatar Faculty of Islamic Studies (QFIS) where he is also associate director of its Center for Islamic Legislation and Ethics. He has written several books on Islamic political thought and contributes essays regularly to Al Jazeera.

Alongside the Western university branch campuses in Education City, QFIS has a unique mandate—to bridge Islamic political theory, jurisprudence, finance, and theology with Western public policy. Unlike Salafist streams of Islamic thinking that advocate facing the challenges of the world by adhering strictly to the early days of Islam, QFIS aims to synthesize Islamic thinking and contemporary social science. Unlike historic centers of Islamic learning that have dwindled over time like the Uqba and Zaytuna in Tunisia, or even like the influential Al-Azhar in Egypt, QFIS is very well funded and able to attract and support some leading Islamic academics.

I met with el-Moctar because I had a number of questions about scholarly trends in thinking about Islam and government. In particular, I wanted to ask him about a concept called "*ijtihad*," independent reasoning or critical thinking within Islam.

Ijtihad played an important role in the early development of Islamic societies and is an important concept now. In the first few centuries of expansion of Islam after the death of the Prophet Mohammed, there was rich activity in political thinking about how Islam, governance, and jurisprudence fit together. The Quran laid out ethical principles, and Muslim scholars for several centuries worked to create laws drawing on those principles as the foundation for Islamic society. This scholarly activity was based on several sources and approaches: the Quran, the words and practices of the Prophet Mohammed (the sunna and hadith), analogy, tradition, consensus, and *ijtihad*.[50] When existing sources had little to say about new situations, scholars used *ijtihad* to develop a solution. But by the tenth century, Islamic scholars came to a consensus that the major questions of Islam and governance had been answered already. The "gates of *ijtihad* were closed," except in very particular circumstances by people with certain qualifications. Some Islamic scholars disagree that the gates of *ijtihad* were closed. However, there is enough consensus that scholars write papers disputing, and conferences are held to discuss reviving the practice of *ijtihad*.[51]

A different trend happened in Europe during the Renaissance of the fourteenth through seventeenth centuries, when ideas of "humanism" spread. Humanism is a school of thought that attaches more importance to human reason than to divine revelation. This new way of thinking and emphasis on human reason served as precursor to Europe's later scientific and economic development. In addition, separation of religion and state evolved as the answer to medieval Europe's problems with sectarian fighting between Catholics and Protestants and between the papacy and local kings.[52] Islam had no such history of separation of religion and state, and political leaders, religious clerics, and the people had for centuries viewed Islam as a complete way of life that encompassed the state, society, and the individual all at once. Many believed that Islam of necessity called for an Islamic empire or state to protect it. The Ottoman sultan was also caliph, serving both temporal and spiritual roles. He was spiritual head of all Islam as well as the leader of the Ottoman Empire.

And then the Middle East declined from the greatness of the Golden Age and the peak of the Ottoman Empire. The Islamic world struggled with the onset of European political and military domination. France and Britain took control of Tunisia and Egypt in the 1880s; 1924 saw the collapse of the Ottoman Empire and end of the caliphate. There was a crisis of identity within Islam. How could modern life and changing world power relations be reconciled with the teachings of the Quran? Thinkers and political activists alike tried to come to terms with what this meant for the universality of Islam, how the Islamic *umma* should organize itself politically (as a caliphate or not), and how Islamic thought should reconcile itself with or resist the encroachment of European culture, in particular the Western idea of the separation of state and religion. The questions of the day were how Muslim countries could meet the challenge of the danger posed by Europe and what the political structure of the Islamic world should be. Arab thinkers began to look to the West with a big question: Why was Western civilization flourishing now, while Middle Eastern civilization was not?

Several answers emerged. One approach (that of the Salafists and the more moderate Muslim Brotherhood) attributed problems as coming from not adhering closely enough to Islamic roots and original values; their solution was cleaving closer to early Islamic practices along with cultural isolation from the West. Thinkers in another movement, called Islamic liberalism or modernism, did not agree with the religious necessity of a caliph or of a particular political system for the Islamic world.[53] They argued that Islam should be a private faith rather than the basis for society (somewhat like the separation of church and state in the West). Some tried to reconcile Islam with Western political thinking and science, arguing that the two were compatible and that Western political structures could be adopted without being detrimental to Islamic faith. Leading Arab Islamic thinkers such as Jamal al-Din al-Afghani, Mohammed Abduh, and Rashid Rida in Egypt argued for internal reform of Islamic political thinking through *ijtihad*, with reinterpretation of historic practices as well as adaptation of Western ideas. They attributed the stagnation of Islamic society to *taqlid*, or adherence to tradition and blind imitation of the past.

I wanted to understand where the debate stood and sought an overview from el-Moctar.

"Are the gates of *ijtihad* closed or open? What do you think the role of *ijtihad* is today in contemporary Islamic political thinking?" I asked el-Moctar.

"*Ijtihad* ended in the fourth century of Islam. Exceptions were isolated and didn't have impact," said el-Moctar. But he thought that *ijtihad* was necessary now in solving some of the problems of our age.

The key to get out of the constitutional crisis of Islamic civilization is "self-confidence," said el-Moctar. "This generation of Muslims needs to have confidence in their abilities and to give less credence to the experience and interpretations of the past," he said. He thought that after colonialism and military defeats in the Arab-Israeli conflict, Muslims felt threatened and rejected anything Western, while they needed to exhibit more confident intellectual leadership. "But that is not possible as long as Muslim societies are weak. Only weak people have this overprotection mode. Because Islamic culture is on the defensive, it is not open to enrich itself. You cannot have self-confidence if you are weak. That is the real issue." He added, "That mode of rejection hurts Islam."

He believed that the Islamic world needed new ideas, rooted in Islam but adapted to the times, as a new basis for society. "I say—guys, let us correct shariah ourselves and then work on what others have done to us," he said. "All of this is not possible without *ijtihad*. A thousand years ago, early Islamic leaders were also human beings interpreting within their own social and political and cultural system."

"The past has a big impact on Islam." El-Moctar paused. "We are suffering from the past. We put too much weight on the interpretation and experience of people who came before us, to the authority of our ancestors."

I asked him about the divisions of Islamic political thinking, between those who argue for adhering to Islam's roots and those who argue that Islam and Western models of governance are compatible.

"We are facing a dilemma here because we have a group of people who see shariah as a threat to freedom and a group of people who see freedom as a threat to shariah. We have a strong secular bloc and a strong Islamist-Salifist bloc. This deprives these societies from a consensus on the basic core values."

"What are the differences in core values between the secularists and the Islamists?" I asked.

"Ninety percent of the debate is really abstract. They really agree with each other. Islamists say they want law to be Islamic—but what does that mean? They want all laws to be taken from the Quran and sunna? But there are not enough laws there. People have to use *ijtihad,* tradition, etcetera, to develop those laws. Or do they mean laws that don't contradict the Quran or sunna? Well, if you look at U.S., Swiss, or German laws, they mostly don't contradict shariah. So we are fighting about something that is more abstract than concrete."

"What are the political values of Islam, or of shariah?" I asked, as I had asked Sayed Ferjani of Ennahda and Yasin Aktay of the AK Party, and heard a similar answer.

El-Moctar said, "Islamic values are not different from other human values," ticking off justice, peace, family. "But because of this unhealthy relationship between weak and strong, the West and the Islamic world, they can see very clearly what is different but not what is in common."

He added that the primary political values are *shura,* or consensus, as the basis for political legitimacy of the state (as Yasin Aktay of the AK Party had told me in Turkey), and *imana,* the idea that public office is a trust given under certain conditions and not to be used for private gain. "All of these are from the Quran. Those values were lost a long time ago."

El-Moctar believes that much of Islamic political theory was based on adaptation to empire, what he calls "imperial jurisprudence." He thinks that Islam needs a new political theory now, adapted to the nation-state and not the empire. "We need jurisprudence for a state. The problem for us is that most Muslims live in a state, but they want to go back to the memory of an empire. Like ISIS," he said referring to ISIS's desire to establish an empire and caliphate. "People are obsessed with empires, in a world in which empires don't exist."

"The world changed for the Middle East after World War I," I observed. "How has Islamic political thinking adapted, as nation-states began in the Middle East, splitting up the idea of a politically unified Islamic community, the *umma?*" I asked.

"Muslims are still fighting World War I today. The old order died. The new order hasn't taken its place. It is a transition. The new order is nation-states. But the states today are not seen as legitimate by their people, because of dictatorship. People want loyalty to a larger entity, like the Islamic *umma,*" he said. Loyalty to the new states could come with minimum success in providing for basic needs, he thought, but many states were not succeeding in providing for the needs of their people.

He admired Ataturk for severing Turkey from outdated laws, while basing society on Islamic values. "What the Arabs need to learn from them is that you need to be harsh with the past sometimes to save the future. The Arabs are soft with the past."

"Does there need to be an Islamic Renaissance? Does Islam need something like the Protestant Reformation that happened in Europe?" I asked.

"It does, but it is the opposite of Christianity. Excesses of the Catholic Church in medieval times led to Protestant reform movements. We have the opposite in Islam, with the excesses of the state against the mosque. In Christianity, it was about freeing the political realm from religion. In Islam, we need to free religion from the state. We need to free the mosque from the state versus the state from the church. Don't let dictators use religion to support dictatorship," he said, referring to Arab governments' tendency to have an official mufti or control Islamic colleges as had happened in Tunisia and Egypt.

He described an article that he had written for Al Jazeera, arguing that some ideas and ideals in the Middle East have become exhausted, like in Europe at the end of the Middle Ages before the Renaissance.[54] "That is exactly what we are suffering from in the Islamic world. Ideas that were inspiring in other times have become a burden."

I pondered how the Arab Spring or the wider awakening that is taking place in the Arab world was about just that—about shedding old ideas of government, society, religion, and finding new ideas as the basis of society. We are in a period of experimentation with ideas. Some of that experimentation is happening at universities like this one. Elsewhere it is happening at the ballot box or on the battlefield—or in the media.

Al Jazeera: the Opinion and the Other Opinion

Al Jazeera is located at an intersection in Doha unofficially called "TV Roundabout." Al Jazeera is on one corner, a shop with a faded sign saying "Panasonic" is on the opposite corner, and takeout shops selling Arabic sweets, kebabs, and *fatayer* are across the road. I drove in through a crowded parking lot, surrounded by extensive construction. Al Jazeera's entrance was small and surprisingly modest for such a controversial and influential news station. The Al Jazeera compound was not impressive, grand, or monumental. Instead, it was a series of small buildings with a dusty parking lot. Inside, I sat in a waiting room with plants, fake laminate wood floors, a TV screen, and awards and plaques. As I waited, a man in a white *thobe* brought in bakhoor incense, and I inhaled the musky scent that wafted around the room. Behind me, the newsroom was open, filled with people in an open space working on computers and with news screens above. Because of ongoing construction, plastic sheets were hung as room dividers near renovations.

Al Jazeera, which means "the island," is one of the most widely broadcast, yet controversial news organizations in the world. It broadcasts to 220 million households in 100 countries.[55] A 2010 University of Maryland and Zogby International Poll found that Al Jazeera was the most watched television network in the Middle East.[56] It has brought a maelstrom of change and openness to a region where traditional media served as the anodyne mouthpiece of autocratic governments. It challenges authoritarian Arab regimes as well as U.S. policy. Well before the Arab Spring protests, Al Jazeera was instrumental in opening up free debate in the Arab world, fomenting demand for more democratic accountability. Hillary Clinton said that Al Jazeera is "changing peoples' minds and attitudes. And like it or hate it, it is really effective."[57] Donald Rumsfeld called their coverage "vicious, inaccurate, and inexcusable."[58]

Al Jazeera was particularly important during the Arab Spring. People around the Middle East watched its coverage of protests in rapt attention. Marc Lynch, a professor of Middle Eastern Studies and Al Jazeera expert at George Washington University, described its role in the Arab Spring: "The notion that there is a common struggle across the Arab world is something Al Jazeera helped create . . . They did not cause these events, but it's almost impossible to imagine all this happening without Al Jazeera."[59] Yet, after the Arab Spring, Al Jazeera's credibility wavered because of a widespread impression in other Arab countries that Al Jazeera took on a new role as an arm of Qatari foreign policy.[60] After the revolutions, there was an impression that coverage aimed to interfere with political decisions, favoring Islamist groups, not only reporting on the news, but trying to shape the news.

I wanted to learn more about Al Jazeera's journalistic philosophy, its role in pioneering free media in the Middle East, its role in the Arab Spring, and how it fits into the changing dynamics of the Middle East now.

I met with Ibrahim Helal, the director of news at Al Jazeera Arabic. Helal manages over six hundred Aljazeera journalists globally. In 2004, he was chosen by the World Economic Forum in Davos as one of the C-100, a council of one hundred of civilization's leaders, and one of the Young Global Leaders of 2004–2006. One of Al Jazeera's original producers during its launch in 1996, he served as director of news in some of the most difficult times, such as during the Palestinian Intifada, the war in Afghanistan, and the war in Iraq. He had also twice left Al Jazeera for stints at the BBC and Abu Dhabi TV. He is Egyptian, with steel-gray hair and a gray suit. His office was littered with papers, with a box of dates for guests sitting on the table in front of his desk.

"How did Al Jazeera start, and what is its philosophy and strategy in journalism?" I asked.

"The vision is daring but simple," he said. From the beginning, the motto of Al Jazeera was "the opinion and the other opinion." Al Jazeera aimed to show multiple perspectives about controversial issues. "Government opinion and the opposition opinion. Those in power and those under that power. We are giving a voice to the voiceless," he said.

When Al Jazeera started, covering both sides of an issue was uncommon for Middle Eastern media. Al Jazeera started when Qatar's amir, Sheikh Hamad, wanted to create news-oriented television with freedom of speech, Helal explained. "Instead of seeing the truth from London, why not from the Arab world?" Helal described how the amir told the startup team to work as if they were at the BBC. And then the amir noted that even at the BBC there were restrictions. "Work with the BBC spirit, but as if you were on Mars," Helal related the amir saying. "Forget you are in Qatar. If someone tries to interfere in your objective Western-standard work, call me. I will defend you as long as it is accurate and it is the 'other opinion.'" Over time, the government of Qatar took significant heat for Al Jazeera's coverage, both from other governments in the region and from the United States.

"Al Jazeera became even bigger than the dream," Helal said, with wonder in his voice.

"Then we thought that we could represent the global south," he said, referring to international development terminology in which developed countries are referred to as the "north" while developing countries, emerging markets, or the "third world" are referred to as the "south." Indeed, until Al Jazeera, the day-to-day history of the world, the interpretation of our times, was the purview of the media of the great powers. World opinion about international affairs was shaped by large Western media conglomerates such as CNN and the BBC. Al Jazeera represented a different voice from an underrepresented part of the world.

Helal described Al Jazeera's early successes and an ability to set the news agenda in some of the hotspots of the world. When Al Jazeera was the only operating international channel in Kandahar and Baghdad during wars there, CNN purchased Al Jazeera footage and broadcast it with the Al Jazeera logo. "That was the first time the world really knew about us. We were setting the agenda, from the south to the north."

"Al Jazeera has been very controversial," I observed. Other Arab governments condemn it for its critical reporting and perceived support for Islamist groups. Islamic movements accuse it of being pro-American, while the U.S. government has at points accused it of giving voice to terrorists. Al Jazeera has been accused of being both anti-American and part of a CIA plot, of being anti-Israeli and pro-Zionist.[61] Yet it is the only Arab media outlet that routinely invites Israeli politicians to participate in debates.[62] It covered dissidents and brought people of opposing views to present those views. "What do you think of these controversies?" I asked.

"Then we are doing something right," he said. "When I teach, a definition of news is that it is something that someone in power wants to not be known." He continued, "We make both sides angry. This costs a political price and is expensive and daring. Of course you make someone angry. We ask tough questions of the regimes."

Al Jazeera's coverage of the Palestinian Intifada and the wars in Afghanistan and Iraq put it on the map of world media as a fearless watchdog, the voice of the Arab street. It could get coverage and news footage that other media channels could not. Disapproval came for many things— for giving voice to controversial issues and figures, for articulating points of view not in line with the interests of great powers, and for its own journalistic ethics. Was it neutral? Was it accurately representing the issues? Was it inflammatory? In the early days, Al Jazeera came across as inexperienced, but vocal. It was one of the only trusted voices in the Middle East during turbulent times.

"Al Jazeera was viewed as an important part of the Arab Spring, as it created a narrative of common causes against governments across the region. What was Al Jazeera's role in the Arab Spring?" I asked.

"There was an illusion that we created the Arab Spring, but we *reported* on it. We represented everyone. We were a fly on the wall. Without us, people would have gone to the streets anyway. Without us, maybe more would be killed. Maybe authorities in Egypt or Tunisia would have killed more people without live coverage." He added, "Al Jazeera became so strong after the Arab Spring."

"Do you think that Al Jazeera lost some of the respect it earned during the Arab Spring? Al Jazeera was once viewed as an edgy rebellious news station that was taking on the great powers and the governments of the Middle East, but now it is associated with the government of Qatar. As Qatar is taking a more visible and controversial role in Middle Eastern politics, has Al Jazeera turned into a tool of Qatari foreign policy? Has Al Jazeera lost street credibility?" I asked.

I knew that when Al Jazeera started, Qatar was not a major player in the affairs of the region, and so Al Jazeera could credibly claim to be bringing unbiased freedom of speech in its coverage and open criticism of Arab leaders. This won Al Jazeera significant trust in its early years.[63] Al Jazeera was an important public diplomacy tool for Qatar, magnifying its influence. Yet over time as Qatar has taken a more interventionist approach in the Middle East, Al Jazeera's reporting is perceived as taking the same political bent as Qatar's foreign ministry.[64] A relatively unknown member of Qatar's royal family with no experience in journalism took over as director general in late 2011, which led to speculation that this would rein the influential channel in, to support desired directions by the amir.[65] Al Jazeera was a particular source of conflict between Qatar and Egypt; after the military overthrow of Egypt's Muslim Brotherhood government, Al Jazeera was the only major network to give significant airtime to the Muslim Brotherhood, with sympathetic, uncritical portrayal of its leaders.[66] In a particularly well-publicized and internationally condemned case, the Egyptian government imprisoned three Al Jazeera journalists on trumped-up charges of supporting terrorists and spreading false news. While the Egyptian government may have aimed to send a message about the channel's alleged role as part of Qatar's foreign policy, the three jour-

nalists appeared to have no such connections, and one had even participated in protests against the Muslim Brotherhood. Egypt, Bahrain, and
Saudi Arabia withdrew their ambassadors to Qatar because of Qatar's support for Islamist groups, including Al Jazeera's role, in 2014. In 2013,
twenty-two of Al Jazeera's staff in Cairo resigned en masse with allegations
that the news channel was biased toward the Muslim Brotherhood.[67]

Others note a double-standard in Al Jazeera's enthusiastic coverage of
Arab Spring uprisings, with significant coverage of events in Tunisia,
Egypt, Libya, and Syria, but light coverage of the violent government
crackdown on Arab Spring protests in Bahrain, in Qatar's backyard. They
also note that Al Jazeera rarely covers events inside Qatar.

Helal acknowledged, "There were mistakes. When you do a lot of
work, you make mistakes." He disagreed, though, that Al Jazeera has lost
its street credibility or that it is influenced by the government of Qatar.
"Once you use the impact of Al Jazeera for Qatar, no one will believe you.
It is important only if it is impartial. Qatar is wise enough to understand
that. Qataris are not angels or sinless, and Qataris blame us for not helping them more," he said. He disagreed that the station followed the lead
of Qatar's foreign policy. "When you do that you lose the edge."

Helal related that he cannot enter Egypt. He would be arrested on
espionage charges for publishing damning documents about Mahmoud
Hegazy, Egypt's head of military intelligence, who argued that to secure
the Sinai, Egypt's relationship with Hamas should be strengthened—
a position that is officially denied by Egypt's president Abdel Fattah
el-Sisi.

Helal emphasized that the diversity of Al Jazeera's team kept it airing
multiple points of view and striving for its goal of "the opinion and the
other opinion." "I drink with those who drink, and I pray with those who
pray. This is the environment I live in. Under our umbrella, we have everyone. In editorial meetings, you will find multiple opinions. This mixture
of nationalities and cultures—it is a crazy mixture. We have gays and athe-
ists. We have Muslim Brotherhood people and people who like Sisi," he
said. Helal said he tells his staff, "I don't care about your behavior. You can
drink. You can pray. You can do whatever you like in your personal life.
But don't let these things impact your judgment."

From Qatar to Egypt

Qatar is a country of contradictions. It is developing a version of Islamic modernity, investing in education and research and opening up to other world cultures and peoples. Qatar is a society of tradition while simultaneously breaking many of those traditions. Women are wearing traditional dress while taking on nontraditional roles. Its Arab Spring was not about protests, but can be viewed as a decade or more of opening up opportunities for its citizens, at the cost of abusive labor practices. It also interfered in other countries' Arab Springs. At the same time as it is investing in cultural openness domestically, it is supporting conservative or violent factions elsewhere in the Middle East. Al Jazeera opened up an era of accountability of regional governments through public discourse and criticism, but is now viewed as supporting a particular Qatari foreign policy political agenda.

As I left, I wondered if Qatar's evolutionary Arab Spring path can endure given the internal contradictions and the repercussions from the more turbulent Arab Springs elsewhere.

From Qatar, I went to Egypt to understand the upheavals in the Arab world's largest country, as what happens in Egypt matters deeply to the rest of the world.

Egypt

Lonely Pyramids

The desert around the pyramids was empty.

I rode a horse from the village of Giza into the desert with Mahmoud, a man I had hired as a guide. From the top of my horse, I could see no other visitors. The pathway along which we rode had no other riders.

My horse was underfed and skinny, with geometric tattoos on its haunches. His hipbones stuck out, with the fur rubbed off on top of the bones. The animals in stables in Giza were all like that.

This was a lonely day for the sole remaining member of the Seven Wonders of the Ancient World. I felt like an explorer with just the vast beige sand of the desert, the tattooed skinny horses, a few fluffy clouds skittering across the sky, and the nine pyramids on the horizon in front of me. The three largest pyramids loomed ahead—Khufu (the Great Pyramid), Khafre, and Menkaure. Six smaller ones sat in their shadows. The Great Pyramid was the tallest man-made structure in the world for nearly four thousand years, until the Eiffel Tower was built in 1889.

Imagine this view. There were the pyramids in front of me, with no other visor-clad camera-toting tourists marring the landscape.

Tourism had fallen precipitously in Egypt since its Arab Spring revolution.[1] Before Egypt's revolution, tourism had accounted for a tenth of GDP.[2] By late 2014, revenues from Egypt's monuments, like the pyramids, were down by 95 percent from pre-2011 levels.[3]

We rode up next to the Great Pyramid, and still there was no one. I got off the horse to stand next to the stone blocks, massive honed chunks of rock as tall as I am.

It was awe inspiring to see this feat of human engineering and advanced social organization. Mahmoud had led tourists here on horses daily from the time he was a boy. And yet pride still shone on his face as he encountered what his ancestors had built.

Ancient Egypt was the longest-lasting political and religious system in world history, enduring for three millennia. Rome only lasted one millennium. Much descended to us from ancient Egyptian ideas and achievements, such as written language, paper, great feats of engineering, spiritual concepts like the Day of Judgment, and temples of surpassing beauty. Toby Wilkinson, a scholar of ancient Egypt, argues that ancient Egyptian society was the first to develop the concept of the nation-state, with the Egyptian political entity based on people with a common identity. Ancient Egypt created the strongman form of governance, with pomp and ceremony to set the ruler apart from the people, patriotic fervor, political propaganda, surveillance of the population, and repression of dissent.[4] Egypt's nation-state, a sense of Egyptian-ness, began with the pharaohs and lasts to this day. It makes Egypt's identity distinct from other Arab countries.[5]

Ancient Egyptian philosophy posited that the created order of the universe and political order were interdependent. The pharaoh, an all-powerful strongman, brought order from chaos. While political forms clearly have changed since then, the metaphor of the all-powerful pharaoh remains potent in political dialogue in Egypt. Egypt's authoritarian military presidents have presented themselves to the Egyptian people as the best alternative to chaos. Protesters in Tahrir Square held signs calling for the downfall of President Hosni Mubarak: "Egypt Better Without Pharaoh."

As we rode our horses through the desert, Mahmoud wanted to show off his skills in American culture. He was an aficionado of American slang. "Smile for the camera" was "whiskey makes us frisky" or "liquor makes us quicker." He liked to say "hunky dorey," "okey dokey," "peachy keen," and "gotcha." He studiously practiced these expressions as part of his tour guide skills to make Americans laugh.

Mahmoud was also eager to talk about the revolution.

"Why did Egypt have a revolution?" I asked, while riding my horse next to his.

"Egyptians revolted because they didn't want military rule. And now they have military rule again," he said, expressing profound disappointment. "There were the same faces before the revolution. There are the same faces after the revolution." But he thought that at least the police were nicer after the revolution. Before the revolution, police often rudely stopped him, demanded his ID, and questioned him. If he objected, the police brought him into the station. After the revolution, that stopped. "Now they say, 'Can I *please* see your ID,'" Mahmoud said. While I was glad that this improvement in police behavior was Mahmoud's experience, I also knew that Egypt's police were cracking down on dissenters with an even heavier hand after the tumult of recent years.

At the same time, Mahmoud observed greater hesitation to express dissent. "Now you can't talk. People are afraid," he said. Indeed, many of the society's leaders, both secularists and Islamists, are now in jail, living outside Egypt because of fears for their safety, or afraid to speak openly about political or societal issues that are viewed as commonplace conversation in other countries.

I asked many people in Egypt what the revolution was about and heard a range of answers, including poverty, corruption, police brutality and lack of respect, the desire for another form of government, lack of economic opportunity for youth, and demands for a government accountable to the people. "Egypt's 2011 revolution put an end to the political order that had dominated the country for over half a century and which managed to combine social stability with steady decline,"[6] wrote Egypt scholar Tarek Osman in *Egypt on the Brink*.

Egypt once was the soul and intellect of the Middle East. It is home to universities, Islamic thinkers, filmmakers, artists, intellectuals, and businesspeople. Egypt, with ninety-two million people, is the largest country in the Arab world and holds a quarter of the Arab world's population. During the last few decades under Mubarak, it became one of the most dysfunctional countries on earth. Is it any wonder that Egyptians sought another solution? Are waves of Arab Spring protests any surprise?

Egypt's narrative, with two governments overthrown in two years, is a complex one. After three decades of rule by President Hosni Mubarak, Egyptians toppled him in their 2011 Arab Spring revolution. As civil society had been weak from decades of authoritarianism, the main organized political force was the Muslim Brotherhood. In parliamentary elections that followed, Islamists (both Muslim Brotherhood and Salafist parties) swept the elections, gaining 75 percent of the seats. Muslim Brotherhood leader Mohammed Morsi was elected president. But after a series of power grabs by Morsi and the Muslim Brotherhood, millions of Egyptians poured into the streets in protest yet again in 2013, fearing that they had overthrown a military dictator only to bring in an Islamist dictator, even one who had come to power through democracy. What incited Egyptians to take to the streets again was Morsi's decree pronouncing all of his actions and decisions immune from judicial review and his assertion that he had the right to take any measure that he deemed necessary to protect the country. He had proclaimed himself above the law.

Unlike Tunisia's Islamists, Egyptian Islamists grabbed so much power so quickly that they outraged a large segment of the population. Unlike Turkey's Islamists, they were incompetent at the business of government. Unlike Iraq's Islamists, they were a moderate group, not a terrorist organization that refused to work within the confines of the nation-state and dispensed with norms of human decency. But the Muslim Brotherhood bungled the opportunity they had to create a stable, inclusive government to heal their polarized society.

After the mass popular protests, Egypt's military overthrew Morsi. Many Egyptians called it Egypt's second revolution; others called it a military coup. Morsi's supporters took to the streets in counter-protests, and the military cracked down on protesters at Rabaa Square in one of history's bloodiest police assaults on civilians. General Abdel Fatah el-Sisi (who led the military overthrow of Morsi) was elected president. Now Egypt is back where it started, with an authoritarian government that promises democracy while suppressing a big segment of society. These events set off riots, growth of an ISIS-affiliated insurgency in the Sinai, sporadic terrorist attacks in cities, and yet another government crackdown on dissent, with arrests of up to forty thousand people under the Sisi regime. Full circle. Is Egypt's new pharaoh, Sisi, fending off chaos or is he making it worse?

Now many Egyptians look to the military government for stability over plurality, making the same pact that their forebearers did. What is Egypt's future? Another long-term military dictatorship? More government overthrows? It is certainly not pluralistic democratic participation, stability, and prosperity. Not in the near term.

External media has reported on Egypt after the revolution through a lens of profound disappointment. *The Washington Post* wrote that Sisi is more brutal than Chile's Augusto Pinochet and less competent.[7] *The Economist* concluded that Sisi is worse than Mubarak.[8] CNN pronounced Egypt's revolution dead.[9] They pointed to killings, mass arrests, and the overthrow of Egypt's first democratically elected government.

While acknowledging the horrific crackdowns under Sisi's counterrevolution, I think it is much more complex than that. A country as big and important as Egypt cannot have a revolution that massive in scale and not have anything profound change. In the short term, not much is better, and many things are worse, in particular in human rights. But Egypt has been irrevocably changed by its revolution and that will manifest itself over time. While the news from Egypt is disturbing, there is still reason to look for deeper long-term changes. The main reason is the fundamental transformation of how the Egyptian people view their own capabilities and their right to accountability from leadership. That will take time to translate into institutions. In my conversations in Egypt, I heard this theme over and over.

I heard about support for Sisi's regime for stabilizing Egypt, preventing it from turning into a theocracy, and making efforts to stimulate the economy, as well as significant criticism of the Sisi government's violent crackdowns, which crippled democracy, divided society over the role of religion, set off an Islamic insurgency, and will take a generation to heal.

Journeying through Egypt, I wanted to explore this complexity. Why did Egyptians have the first revolution in 2011? Why did they have a second revolution/coup in 2013? What did Egyptians gain from these revolutions? What were the mistakes? What is now needed to create a foundation for future prosperity, stability, and a socially healthy society?

Mahmoud and I rode our horses away from the pyramids, past the Sphinx with its missing nose and out of the desert, through Giza and back to the stables. We rode past the Kentucky Fried Chicken and Pizza Hut not far from the pyramids. Business was down in Giza. Mahmoud pointed to closed shops that sold Egyptian souvenirs to tourists, like painted papyrus and perfumes pressed from local plants. Shop owners could not pay rent, electricity, and salaries if there were no tourists.

Mahmoud was frustrated that when he complained about the lack of work, others told him to find another job or to get some more training. "But I have worked all my life in tourism. We all have worked our lives in tourism. They say get another job. But what am I gonna do?" he said. He had to support his wife, two kids, and his mother. And his main skillset is guiding people around the pyramids on horses and camels while throwing American slang at them to make them laugh.

As we said goodbye, he said. "People say that we are not third world—look at our heritage. I say look around, the rest of the world is different from this."

I took a cab back into the center of Cairo. We passed squalid unfinished buildings covered with soot and grime and ramshackle neighborhoods. The buildings were unfinished because Egypt's tax code raised taxes once a building was finished, so the city looked like a perpetual construction zone of intentionally, eternally unfinished buildings. Clogged traffic moved slowly; I could walk faster. There was a constant stream of pedestrians and drivers, like water flowing through the path of least resistance. Donkey carts shared the road with derelict cars with broken headlights. A dead yellow dog lay by the side of the road. An old minivan next to my waiting cab drove with the hood open to cool the engine. Small trucks were piled high with roped-on mounds of bananas or cauliflowers. Women walked through the streets in long headscarves and overcoats. One yellow light blinked at a major intersection; otherwise, there were no streetlights. Garbage trucks too small for the garbage that they must haul away left the overflow by the side of the road, not in garbage cans. Outside a large stately mosque, men were disassembling a thirty-year-old car.

These dirty streets of traffic jams open to the pyramids, the only remaining ancient wonder of the world.

Walking Tahrir Square

Today, Tahrir Square was calm, clogged with traffic, and mainly empty of pedestrians. There was plenty of security. Machine-gun toting soldiers wearing helmets and black masks stood guard near camouflaged tanks, police vehicles, and police dogs. Concrete blockades were positioned in front of the Nile Ritz Carlton.

I walked around Tahrir Square the day before the fourth anniversary of Mubarak's overthrow. The anniversary came and went, with not much marking it apart from a few extra tanks.

I looked around and marveled. A great revolution took place here.

During Egypt's 2011 Arab Spring revolution, images of Tahrir Square were broadcast around the world, with millions of people packed into an immense city square in a mass bucking off military autocratic rule characterized by repression and economic stagnation and rejecting in particular the three-decade rule of Mubarak. Crowds radiated the inspirational energy of youth in their courage and idealism. Here was a sea of united people who had transcended differences, from all walks of life, men and women, youth and families, Muslims and Christians, Islamists and secularists, rich and poor, and people from many political persuasions. Turning on the television and watching scenes from the uprising brought tears of inspiration to my eyes. It was uplifting.

The story of Egypt's revolution unfolded over eighteen vivid days of people camping in tents, performing music, chanting slogans, dancing, making rousing speeches, waving banners, and singing. There were dramatic moments. There was the day that Egyptians call "the battle of the camel," when the regime sent in *baltagiya*, hired thugs riding camels into the crowds to beat people with sticks and knives. The battle of the camel was ironically named after a battle in early Islamic history. There was the day that the army decided to not obey orders of the regime, refusing to fire on the people and sending a signal that they backed, or at least did not oppose, the protesters. There were the times that Muslims formed circles around Christians to protect them while they were praying, and the times that Christians formed circles around Muslims to protect them at prayer. The Mubarak regime felt so under threat that it shut off Egypt's Internet access and mobile networks for six whole days.

Tahrir took on the atmosphere of defiant and celebratory community building, as citizens contributed whatever they had. Doctors and nurses volunteered and set up impromptu clinics. Art teachers donated supplies and helped people make banners. Poets, puppeteers, musicians, and comedians performed for audiences to raise morale. Others organized the logistics of daily life, supplying food stations and portable toilets.[10] When Mubarak finally stepped down, civic pride emerged, and citizen volunteers descended upon Tahrir to clean it up, sweeping it with brooms, washing off graffiti, and removing mounds of trash. They were cleansing their city.

Tahrir Square became the symbol of citizens challenging the entire power structure of Egypt, and indeed of the Arab world. Tahrir Square showcased the best of Egypt and the worst of Egypt, and the best of human nature and the worst of human nature.

But it all went so terribly wrong. Egypt was now what other countries aspired to avoid.[11] A walk around Tahrir Square, a symbolic microcosm of Egypt, illustrated what led to the revolution.

Tahrir ("Liberation") Square was built to be a great center of a great city where great things would happen. Conceived by Ismail Pasha, khedive of Egypt in the late nineteenth century, this quarter of Cairo was meant to be a European-style cosmopolitan "Paris on the Nile," with grand, elegant buildings that would not look out of place in stylish districts of European capitals. Tahrir Square featured a large grassy center for public gatherings.

But decades of neglect had changed that. Cairo was once a city of grandeur and color, with flowers and trees, gracious architecture, and mosques designed with the harmony of Islamic aesthetics. But the greatness of yesterday was buried under the squalor of today. Cairo was now a city the color of dirt. In many places, advertisement posters were the only color.

Now, Tahrir Square was polluted, dilapidated, and clogged with traffic that lacked order. Near the Nile side of the square were once beautiful promenades and trees, but now families slept there on mats or on ripped-up couches under bridges. Once stately buildings built during Egypt's hopeful belle époque a century ago were grimy and in disrepair. Streets were oily asphalt, bordered with blackened, cracked sidewalks piled with trash. Almost everything was run down and decaying, coated with grime from the polluted air. Cars drove three to a lane where there should have been two, without traffic lights, as the traffic lights were broken, wires dangling from poles. Indeed, traffic in Cairo was so badly managed that it annually cost Egypt 4 percent of its GDP.[12] Where the traffic was slow, small children wove in and out of the cars, holding on to car windows trying to entice occupants to roll down the windows and give them a handout. One small girl begging in the traffic wore dirty pink terry-cloth bunny pajamas, with a little hood and bunny ears.

Tahrir's metro stations were closed, their artfully designed red "M" signs broken and hanging crookedly. Mud coated the steps down to the stations, and graffiti on one bolted iron metro door read "freedom."

On one corner of the square was an empty, burned out, multistory concrete skeleton of a building with charred, blackened walls. This was what remained of the headquarters of the ironically named National Democratic Party—Mubarak's political party—that had ruled Egypt effectively as a single-party state. Protesters burned it during Egypt's revolution; it represented decades of Mubarak. Making matters worse, Mubarak had seemed to be grooming his son Gamal to follow in his footsteps as president, giving him increasing levels of responsibility, including as secretary general of the National Democratic Party. But the Egyptian people would tolerate none of that. In 2004 and 2005, the apparent rise to power of Mubarak's son led to a protest movement called Kefaya, which means "enough."

Across the street, past guards with guns and tanks and a fenced-in area with hoops of razor wire, is the Egyptian Museum. I entered the museum through its garden, which is overrun with feral cats. The museum cafe was closed. An empty ice cream stand appeared to have been unused for many weeks, with a cat sleeping on top of the case, ice cream containers still inside.

I walked through the museum's exhibits. Here were housed King Tutankhamen's burial mask of gold and lapis lazuli, mummies, stone statues of the Pharaoh Akhenaton, papyrus, and articles of ancient Egyptian daily life. But King Tut's magnificent gold burial mask was hung sloppily, pinned on sagging, faded blue felt inside dirty, cheap glass cases that no one had bothered cleaning. Stains covered the walls. Paint peeled off the ceilings and dripped down on signs. Priceless statues were piled up as if in a warehouse rather than in a museum of world heritage. The problem was not poverty, but lack of caring. Where was the excellence of the pharaohs? Of a great province of the Roman Empire? Of a capital of a majestic Islamic empire? Of Egypt's belle époque? Of Egypt leading the Arab world under Nasser? Of an inspiring revolution led by youth wanting something better? Egypt could do better than this.

The Egyptian Museum witnessed both moments of beauty and moments of ugliness during the revolution. When the armed forces vacated it, leaving it prey to looters, people linked arms to form a human chain around it to protect the treasures inside.[13] But during the protests, security forces used its leafy gardens for arrests and torture of those whom it had arrested, using electric shocks and beating idealistic youthful protesters with wires, whips, and pipes.

I walked out of the museum and its garden, past the tanks and feral cats, past the Nile Ritz Carlton to the large civil service building called the Mogamaa, fronted by electrical wires hanging sloppily, strung between windows.

The imposing Mogamma embodied the stifling bureaucracy that smothered Egypt and the corruption that marred daily life, from big financial deals to the small bribes that had to be paid in daily life to police and petty officials. Egyptian comedian Adel Imam starred in a film called *Al-Irhab wal Kebab*, a title that rhymes in Arabic and translates to "The Terrorist and the Kebab." In the movie, a man gets so frustrated with bureaucracy at the Mogamma that he ends up in a scuffle with guards, accidentally takes over their weapons, and then unintentionally takes hostages, whom he befriends over their shared bureaucratic plight. But he needs food and so orders kebab as his first demand as a terrorist—but what he really wanted was to be treated with humanity.[14]

From here, I looked at the spaces in the center of the square. Despite the hope and harmony of the protests on the square, there were significant problems with sexual harassment and assault. A number of women protesters were arrested and subjected to virginity tests by Egyptian security forces.[15] Women filed lawsuits against the government about the tests.[16] A famous photo circulated of security forces in Tahrir Square ripping off the black abaya of a woman protester and dragging her away with only a turquoise blue bra covering her torso. The photo became emblematic of security forces' disrespect for women. To protest the treatment of the "blue bra girl," there was a women's march in Tahrir Square. But it was not just the security forces; there were problems with the crowds. For example, on one day of protests in 2013, there were eighty reported cases of mob sexual assault, harassment, and rape.[17] But both women and men fought back. During the protests, Egyptian women started an organization called OPANTISH, Operation Anti-Sexual Harassment, to stop assaults as they were happening. Groups of men formed to protect women from the mobs, such as Tahrir Bodyguards and Welad al-Balad.[18]

I crossed the street and walked around to the American University of

Cairo (AUC), where I had studied Arabic when I was a student. This was where the Arab elites had been educated for the past hundred years, so that by the time they became government, business, or societal leaders, they knew each other from their student days. AUC had built a beautiful new campus in New Cairo, outside of the crowded center. There was now a barricade along AUC, with fences and big blocks of graffiti-covered stone, reminiscent of the stones of the pyramids, protecting AUC's entrance.

Buildings flowed off Tahrir Square into Cairo's downtown. Streets leading off the square were filled with once-elegant buildings, sided with marble and graceful carved arabesques, but most were now in major disrepair. People seemed to have become used to this neglect and squalor.

I felt anger at the dilapidation. There was so much heritage here in this city that was millennia old, with its quarters built in different periods—pharaonic Memphis with the pyramids, Coptic and Roman Cairo with churches and fortresses, old medieval Islamic Cairo with winding alleyways, belle époque Cairo with its European-style buildings, and newer neighborhoods built recently. Parts of Cairo displayed yesteryear's harmony, refined taste, tranquility, and loveliness. But I did not see that in much of Egypt now; it has not taken care of its heritage and assets over the past six decades. Now the new buildings that go up are just thrown up with cinder blocks, appearing structurally unsound and often not even with straight lines. Egypt is a country of squandered wealth, sophistication, and heritage. Arab Spring was about seeking something different.

Three a.m. at the Yacoubian Building

"I will never forget many things. I was about to get killed many times during the revolution," said Alaa al-Aswany, the author of the novel *The Yacoubian Building* and a prominent leader in a leaderless revolution. "I carried people who were killed, and I carried people who were wounded. There were snipers and they were killing people." He described how a sniper looks through the sight of a gun, scans it over a crowd, with the target of the gun seen through an orange or green circle, and then pulls the trigger to kill the person viewed. "Every time a circle stops moving, it is the end of a human life. And you don't know who is next. This happened to me. I was talking to a young guy who got killed two meters away." He shook his head in sadness. "But people were not scared, and they did not run away," he said, perplexed. "I tried to understand this phenomenon, because usually when there are snipers, people run away. That is normal human behavior. But they did not. They carried the dead, and they kept going. During war or revolution, the 'I' becomes 'we.' You don't feel yourself as an individual anymore."

Al-Aswany's novel *The Yacoubian Building* is the bestselling novel of all time of the Arab world and was made into a movie.[19] Published in 2002, it tells the story of the lives of residents of an apartment building not far from Tahrir Square. Al-Aswany is one of a handful of Arab authors who have become mainstream in the West as well, along with Naguib Mahfouz, Egypt's Nobel Prize–winning novelist. *The Yacoubian Building* has been translated into thirty-one languages in one hundred countries.[20] The book deals with sensitive subjects, including poverty, lack of social mobility, prison, torture, terrorism, prostitution, sexual harassment, corruption, and decay of society. *The Wall Street Journal* called al-Aswany "the face of Egypt's uprising."[21]

Al-Aswany has many roles. A working dentist by day (with a dentistry degree from the University of Illinois at Chicago), he was a founding member of the 2004 political movement Kefaya, the precursor movement to the protests at Tahrir Square. He has written articles for Egyptian and international papers for years. I met with al-Aswany at his dental office in Cairo's desert suburb of 6th of October City. It was a three-story villa surrounded by sand in a development under construction. His dental clinic was in the basement. His writing office was on the ground floor. And he lived with his family on the top floor.

In his late fifties, wearing a blue sports jacket, with curly black hair and the scratchy voice of a smoker, he dragged on a cigarette as he spoke, relating his views and stories from the revolution.

"When did you realize that this was a revolution, and not just a protest?" I asked. I knew that he had participated in other protests in other circumstances. He told the story.

"I found myself at three a.m. very close to the Yacoubian Building," he said, "surrounded by thirty young people who knew me. They asked me what to do. I said, 'Guys, we did a good job, and we can go home now, and tomorrow we can make another protest.' They all objected. I said, 'Do you think we are going to arrest Mubarak tonight?' "Al-Aswany related how one young man began to cry because at age thirty and unemployed with a university degree, his future felt hopeless. The young man contended that either they would make Mubarak step down, or Mubarak could kill him. That young man's despair about his prospects was like many others'. Youth joblessness was 60 percent in Egypt, youth unemployment was about 30 percent, and overall unemployment was 13.3 percent in 2014.[22]

"That was the turning pointing in my understanding," said al-Aswany. "When he cried, I said to myself, 'Wait, wait, wait, there is something happening that you don't understand.' I asked them, 'What do you want me to do now?' They said, 'We get back to the square.' I went back to the square with them. I lived in the square eighteen days."

Al-Aswany's schedule in the square was the following. He spent every night there giving speeches when asked by a committee of youth that organized speeches. At six a.m., he returned to his home in the Garden City neighborhood, which was very close to Tahrir Square, to tell his family that he was still alive. He slept a few hours. Every day at one p.m., he gave a press conference for the foreign press at his dental clinic. And then by late afternoon, he went back to Tahrir Square. "Sometimes, I was not sure that what I was living was really real," he said, describing the courage and generosity of spirit surrounding him and the other protesters. "You eat and you drink for days and you never know who brought the food." Even poor people were donating food that they could scarce afford. "We were calling for freedom, bread, social justice, and dignity. These four things," he said, relating a list similar to the list that Lina Ben Mhenni had related about Tunisians' protest demands. "Many people died for that. Many people lost their eyes," he said, due to tear gas.

"The controversial portrayal of Egyptian society in *The Yacoubian Building* sparked public debates about Egypt's problems. What role do you think your book played? What about it resonated?" I asked. "Even my taxi driver coming here got very excited when he saw the name of your dental clinic. He said that your book expressed Egyptian life."

"If I ever played some role in this I am very proud. But the whole country was waking up. I had seventeen literary awards all over the world—of course never in Egypt. The most precious award was in Tahrir. I heard many times, we are here because of what you wrote. I believe this is the most precious literary award I had," he said. He leaned forward.

"Literature is a mirror. You see what you don't want to see in your daily life in a novel. If we are ugly—and we were ugly before the revolution, we were ugly morally—then I should show you how ugly we are. This is literature as I see it."

"Is Egypt ugly or beautiful now?" I asked.

"We were ugly, but the revolution was absolutely beautiful."

"What do you think the revolution has accomplished? Now, reading the English language media, Tunisia is held up as a great success, and Egypt is held up as a great failure. And yet I don't think that is entirely the story. Do you think that the revolution is a disappointment? What has it achieved that is good for Egypt?"

"Practically nothing," he said about short-term achievements, squashing out his cigarette in a glass ashtray. "Because the old regime is back. Because the idea of the revolution in Egypt is more unpopular now than any time before." He sat back in his chair.

But he thought that more had been accomplished in the long term. "The revolution is not a political change. It is a *human* change. Egyptians who were really scared of even *talking* with the police overcame the barrier of fear. This is a basic change, but it is a great achievement. It is irreversible. Of course I am disappointed, like anybody who believed in this revolution, but I am still optimistic." He emphasized, "Egyptians who are living now are no longer the Egyptians who used to live under Mubarak."

He put it in the perspective of other revolutions, like the French revolution, with the pattern of revolution and counterrevolution, taking several decades to achieve its goals, reminding me of the same comparison made by Rula al-Hroub in Jordan.

He thought that the main concept to emerge from the revolution was that of the citizen. "We wanted to be a democratic state like any other democracy, where the most important factor is the citizen, not the president, not the regime, not the police. The simplest citizen."

To explain, he related a history-making debate that he had on television with Ahmed Shafiq, the interim prime minister appointed by Mubarak as a transition when Mubarak stepped down. "I was trying to apply this concept," he said, about the idea that a leader must be accountable to citizen questioning. "Shafiq couldn't stand it. I said, 'I ask you about the people who were killed, and you *must* answer.' I said, 'I am an Egyptian citizen. From now on the simplest citizen has the right to ask you, and you *must* answer.'" Shafiq lost his temper on television and looked inarticulate and insensitive in his response.

"And he was forced to resign his position as interim prime minister the next day," I finished his story. Shafiq only held the position of interim prime minister for two months because of that interaction with al-Aswany.

"You were an important figure in the 2011 revolution, but then you controversially supported the overthrow of Morsi, who was both Islamist and democratically elected. After the revolution, why did you support the military ouster of Morsi?" I asked.

"I didn't vote for Mr. Morsi," he said, although he emphasized that he had encouraged Egyptians to give Morsi a chance when he was elected. "It is the taste of democracy. You must accept a person you cannot tolerate, if he was chosen by the people. But what happened was that he canceled democracy. He made a decree, he canceled the law, and he put himself above the law," he said, referring to Morsi's declaration that his actions were above judicial review. Al-Aswany compared the situation to Peru in 1992, when Peru's President Fujimori dissolved parliament and sent tanks into the streets, leading to suspended international aid and condemnation for putting himself above the law.[23] "That is exactly what I thought. This guy should go. 'We the people' had a right to make an impeachment. At some point, Egypt was very close to a civil war," he observed about the risks from the polarization between the Muslim Brotherhood and the rest of society.

But al-Aswany clarified that while he supported the military intervention to remove Morsi, he never supported Sisi. Democracy was not looking good in Egypt now, he observed, pointing to pressure on the press. Newspapers in Egypt, afraid, would no longer publish al-Aswany's contributions. "Our democracy is what? Torturing people? This is our democracy?"

Al-Aswany reflected that Sisi is trying the same failed policies of his predecessors (Nasser, Sadat, and Mubarak) and is somehow expecting different results. "This formula of a one-man show, the great leader," he called it. "Now, we are repeating the same thing. We have not learned that you will never be able to feed these ninety million people without a real democracy. If you do any achievement, it will be fragile."

"We are not on the right track," he said, shaking his head.

A Four-Finger Symbol of Solidarity

Four fingers spread in the air, with the thumb across the palm, is the symbol of solidarity with the people who were killed or injured by security forces in Rabaa Square on August 14, 2013, in one of the worst government massacres of civilians in history.

I got out of the cab in Rabaa Square and looked around. It now looked like any other busy intersection in Cairo. There were no signs of the violence that occurred here.

Rabaa is a middle-class neighborhood in eastern Cairo, not far from the parade ground where Egypt's president Anwar Sadat was assassinated in 1981. A geometric statue that looks like robotic claws sits in the middle of the intersection. Large billboards advertise Japanese cars and family beach vacations with a smiling mom and dad. On one side of the square is an army base with barbed wire fencing. Surrounding the square are apartment buildings, in need of a paint job, with air-conditioners and satellite dishes hanging out, windows strung with electrical wire and laundry, and trash strewn on the grass. Here, on the grass in front of one building, protesters had set up tents and places for ablutions, ritual cleansing before prayer.

And in one corner was a brand-new mosque with a minaret stretching up to the sky, painted a cream color with mauve trim. This was Rabaa Al-Adawiya Mosque, newly rebuilt by Egypt's army after they burned down the original mosque to clear the square of the protest camp. Armed soldiers now guarded the mosque, which was fronted by orange plastic cones and metal barriers.

For six weeks in July and August 2013, after the overthrow of Morsi, Morsi's supporters staged a sit in here. Rabaa Square was a huge protest tent camp, with kitchens, pharmacies, places to sleep and eat, and a media center. Aerial photos of the protests show a square packed with people, thousands of tiny dots filling the space.[24] At night, there was chanting of slogans, music, lights and banners, people waving the Egyptian flag, and giant posters of a smiling Morsi above the heads of the protesters. Families and kids mingled in striped tents.

On August 14, 2013, Egyptian security violently cleared the camp. Videos and photos showed the carnage: tanks surrounding the square, fires, clouds of black smoke, riot police with helmets and sticks, bodies in blood-soaked shirts lying on the ground, lines of the dead in body bags on the striped carpet of a mosque, wreckage, bloody asphalt and mud, blood dripping down a staircase, faces of grief, a child in a gas mask, crying children, and bandaged people. Videos afterward of the mosque showed a charred, blackened shell of carbon-coated columns.

Human Rights Watch estimated that on that day, at least 817 people were killed and more likely a thousand. Based on interviews with witnesses, they described how government forces opened fire on large crowds of civilians. Security forces blocked the five main entrances to the square. They started with tear gas and within minutes escalated to live fire, without allowing safe exit for those trying to flee the violence. Snipers in government buildings and helicopters shot protesters. Security forces fired directly on the hospital and ordered people to leave their injured behind as they would burn the hospital. There were reports of summary executions and beatings. Human Rights Watch estimated that eighty-five thousand people were in the square during the assault.

The government's justification for this use of deadly force was that the square was a camp of armed terrorists. But in searches afterward, the Ministry of Interior found only fifteen guns.[25]

In the year following the Rabaa Square massacre, at least twenty-two thousand Muslim Brotherhood supporters were arrested, with torture, deprivation of due process, long-term jail terms, and death sentences. By 2015 at least forty thousand people (including secular dissidents) had been imprisoned.[26] In one particularly notable case, a judge sentenced 529 Brotherhood supporters to death for the killing of a single police officer.[27]

How did an inspirational revolution followed by Egypt's first democratically elected government come to this?

Egypt has a long and volatile relationship with the Muslim Brotherhood and other Islamist parties. The Muslim Brotherhood was founded by Hassan al-Banna in 1928, in resistance to British colonial rule and European cultural dominance. Al-Banna called for a return to Islamic piety, viewing Islam as the blueprint for a modern society. The Brotherhood combined Islamic and socialist principles, promoting Islam as an alternative to Western-style liberalism. It appealed to parts of society that had not benefited from the changes sweeping the country. Hassan al-Banna was assassinated by Egyptian police in 1949. When Gamal Abdel Nasser came to power, he banned the Muslim Brotherhood to counter its growing influence, forcing it to go underground. For eighty years, the Muslim Brotherhood remained in opposition, not part of government.

Sayyid Qutb was one of the most influential thinkers to arise from the Muslim Brotherhood, as a leading member in the 1950s and 1960s. He has since served as inspiration for violent movements around the Middle East.

As a university student, Qutb studied in the United States at what is now the University of Northern Colorado. He returned home to Egypt disgusted with American life—in particular with what he saw as its materialism, individualism, racism, superficiality, mixing of the sexes, support for Israel, and the waywardness of American women. At home in Egypt, he joined and became a leader in the Muslim Brotherhood.

Charged with plotting the assassination of Nasser, Qutb was severely tortured while in prison. Afterward, his writing became increasingly violent. He wrote his most influential book, *Milestones on the Road,* while in prison. The book argued that Islam is a complete system of life and a solution to modern troubles. He called for living in an Islamic society without a government, the opposite of the dictatorship that he felt he lived under. In this utopian Islamic society, there would be no servitude of men and no rulers. Qutb rejected the idea of nation-states as a form of government that had been imposed on Muslims by the West. He favored viewing Muslims around the world as part of a single community, or *umma*, not divided into states. Sovereignty of the people, a foundation of Western democracy, he argued, is against Islam's premises of equality in which no one rules over people except for God. In the society he envisioned, there would be no authority except for God; violence should be used to achieve that. Advancing this vision of Islam required both preaching and violent jihadi resistance to overthrow governments and institutions. He was hanged in 1966, on charges of plotting to overthrow the state. Execution silenced him, but it also made him a martyr.

Fertile ground for Islamist approaches, both peaceful and violent, was created in Egypt by unrelenting poverty and Egypt's defeat by Israel in the 1967 war. The 1967 war brought a nationwide sense of humiliation and waves of social anger that led the people to believe the government was not serving their needs. In addition to being an opposition movement, the

Muslim Brotherhood created social services and infrastructure. It positioned itself as the provider, when the government did not. They provided services for the poor, affordable healthcare, food distribution, help to youth in finding jobs, transport, welfare, student accommodation, study groups, and humanitarian activities. By contrast, the government appeared inept and corrupt. People looked to the Brotherhood as an alternative.[28]

A number of signs indicated the increasing role of Islam in public life in Egypt during that time. In 1986, there was one mosque for every 6,031 Egyptians. By 2005, there was one mosque for every 745 Egyptians.[29] From the 1970s to the 1990s, the percentage of women wearing the headscarf increased from 30 percent to over 65 percent.

This societal struggle between political Islam and a repressive military government in Egypt led to decades of armed struggle. The Muslim Brotherhood renounced violence in the 1970s. But from the 1970s to 1990s, other militant Islamic groups conducted seven hundred attacks in Egypt. Between 1982 and 2000, over two thousand Egyptians died in terrorist attacks.[30] Ayman al-Zawahiri, a leader of Al-Qaeda, started as a member of the Muslim Brotherhood.

The struggle for power prevented (or was used as an excuse to preclude) societal negotiations among Islamists, the military, and liberals. Islam became a key route of resistance to the repressive state. At the same time, the Mubarak government dealt with violent Islamic movements as purely a security issue, with arrests, confiscation of financial resources, weapons, and taking control of thousands of mosques.

Trying to prove that the repression was unjustified, in the 1990s and 2000s, the Muslim Brotherhood democratized their internal organization structures, cooperated with secular parties, and moderated policies toward shariah, democracy, political pluralism, minority rights, women's rights, and alternation of power.[31]

During Egypt's 2011 revolution, the Brotherhood intentionally did not take a visible role, in order to not give Egyptians or the world the impression that this was an Islamic revolution. But after the youth overthrew the government, the Muslim Brotherhood was the only organized political entity that was ready to move into governance.

But it was not clear what the Muslim Brotherhood's policies were, what they stood for, or what they were trying to achieve. They did not have a well-thought-out framework or intellectual basis for government. Their experience was being the opposition, not governing. Brookings's Shadi Hamid wrote, "They had survived. They had gained power. Now the question dogging them for years remained: What did they hope to do with that power? Islamists were Islamists for a reason. They weren't liberals in disguise."[32]

When the Muslim Brotherhood was elected to power, they made a number of fatal mistakes. The first was drafting the constitution without consensus from others, introducing a large number of references to Islam. Women, Christians, and liberals walked out of the constitution drafting process. Second, after a series of power struggles with both military leadership and the judiciary, Morsi issued a decree requiring the early retirement of thousands of judges, giving the impression that he planned to stack the judiciary with Islamists. Finally, Morsi's announcement that his instructions had full immunity from the courts was the decree that broke the camel's back.

People went back to protesting in Tahrir Square again in June 2013. Egypt was polarized. Morsi could have used that opportunity to cut a deal, roll back the policies that others found threatening, or step aside for a technocratic government like Ennahda later did in Tunisia in similar circumstances. But he did not.

After Morsi's overthrow by the military, the massacre at Rabaa Square, the subsequent arrests of Morsi's supporters, and Sisi's election, the Sisi government took action to control political Islam, shutting down twenty-seven thousand unregulated mosques and requiring preachers to get a license in affiliation with Al-Azhar, Egypt's state-controlled historic center of Sunni learning.[33] Sisi called for a "revolution in Islam" to combat violent extremism. He was an "improbable reformer" of Islam and acknowledged that a revolution in religious discourse would take decades.[34]

There are different views of the Brotherhood. Were they trying to establish an Islamic dictatorship in Egypt, throwing aside tenets of the rule of law after elections brought them to power? Were they a peaceful democratically elected moderate Muslim group that provided social services to the poor and had the potential to set another example of Islam and democracy, like Turkey and Tunisia? Were they a group that had spawned radical violence over the years, and whose ideology set the stage for violent conflict? The answer depends upon who you talk to.

In jail or exiled, there were no Muslim Brotherhood members for me to interview for this book. The Muslim Brotherhood headquarters moved to London, where the British government keeps a close eye on them.

But two things are clear.

First, the Muslim Brotherhood's disregard for the rule of law and the pluralism and rights of Egyptians had led to their ouster. Second, the crackdown upon them afterward by the military has been far more brutal than anything the Muslim Brotherhood itself had done. This repression and violence was certainly not in line with the ideals for which the Egyptian people revolted against their previously autocratic government.

In May 2015, Morsi was sentenced to death for escaping jail when he was imprisoned under Mubarak. The trial was a sham. The sentence, if carried out, would potentially make Morsi a martyr around the Middle East, with his death easily turned into a simplified narrative of how the first democratically elected president of Egypt was killed for being a pious Muslim. His execution could destabilize Egypt. Indeed, since then, there have been several attacks on security and tourist sites in Cairo and Alexandria, and a battle is raging between the army and ISIS affiliates in the Sinai. There are also rumblings among Muslim Brotherhood youth that peaceful approaches may not be an effective strategy for them.

Why couldn't the Egyptian judiciary try Morsi for the reasons that ignited the protests against him—the abuses of power and the attempts to create another presidency that was above the law? That would create a conversation in society about the limits of power and demonstrate legitimacy in sentencing. But a discussion about abusing power and the proper limits of presidential authority would potentially pose too many risks for the Sisi regime. After all, they are using the same techniques.

Media in the Margin

"The day of the dispersal, I was there. I covered it. It was one of the most challenging and painful experiences," Lina Attalah said about her decision to cover the Rabaa Square massacre at the independent newspaper that she founded, *Mada Masr*. "We told the story of how we were almost going to be killed ourselves, with the same bullets that were killing the Brothers. We went there, when we thought it would be a death camp.

There was something moving about the sympathizers muttering prayers as they were expecting a deathly attack. Not because I sympathize," she said, emphasizing that she did not support the Muslim Brotherhood and viewed them as "disgustingly aggressive." She continued, "In Rabaa, we were telling them—they are killing people, there is excessive use of force, but no one wanted to believe that."

The Egyptian government tightly controlled media coverage of those events, casting their actions as clearing a terrorist camp. Many Egyptians were so fed up with the Muslim Brotherhood that they were ready to believe that.

Attalah was widely criticized for writing the story. "It is important for Egyptians to keep that record, which would be easily erased by power. Our role is to try to mediate the truth." *Mada Masr* means the "range" or "span" of Egypt. Attalah made a conscious decision to not be for or against, but to stay to the margin. She had founded the paper in 2013, right before Morsi's overthrow.[35] "It came out of a sense of desperation—there was nothing else to do," she said about her decision to start a paper that could report independently.

At age thirty-one, Atallah was listed as one of the one hundred most powerful Arab women of 2015.[36] With curly black hair in a ponytail, black-rimmed glasses, baggy red pants, and a black T-shirt, she is petite, not much taller than five feet. She looked tired. I met her at the *Mada Masr* office in Garden City, in an old Art Deco building on the Nile. The office had tall ceilings, beat-up fixtures and doors, and brightly painted plywood tables of red, blue, yellow, and white. Someone had written "democracy" in blue and yellow chalk on a giant chalkboard. Car seats served as benches in the reception area. On the wall was a provocative picture of a man and woman standing peacefully under an umbrella, behind barbed wire with tens of armed security officers staring them down.

Attalah had supported the first revolution in 2011, but not the second in 2013.

In 2011, she was both covering the protests and participating in them. "I was actively savoring the moment of being part of that history, even being beaten up, carrying it on my body somehow and being happy with this organic tie to this piece of history," she said.

But she felt conflicted about the 2013 revolution. She opposed the direction that the Muslim Brotherhood was taking Egypt, but she also saw the protesters as violent. A turning point was when a group of protesters attacked her car, pasting a protest sign on it against her will. She took a bucket with soap and water and washed the sign off her car. And then she decided to report on Rabaa Square.

She thinks that the margin that she inhabits is a tighter place to be, with those who chose the margin physically incarcerated, threatened, out of the country, or grappling with deep depression and despair. *Mada Masr* gave her a purpose that kept her out of the despair that others faced and also kept her from falling into inaction. "If *Mada Masr* didn't exist, I would probably leave the country."

About media crackdowns by the Sisi regime since Morsi's overthrow, Amnesty International concluded, "In Egypt today anyone who challenges the authorities' official narrative, criticizes the government, or exposes human rights violations is at risk of being tossed into a jail cell, often to be held indefinitely without charge or trial or face prosecution on trumped-up charges."[37] As of May 2015, eighteen journalists were jailed in Egypt, with dozens more facing criminal investigations. Imprisonment and sentencing of the three Al Jazeera journalists for "spreading lies" had received particular international attention.

"How independent can you be as an independent newspaper in Egypt?" I asked.

The government had two ways of pressuring media, she explained—direct and indirect. The direct pressure came from government officials calling editors to ask them to ratchet down their coverage of an issue. "No one calls us. You have to remember that we are kids. I don't think that the government thinks it is up to its standards to call a thirty-one-year-old woman editor."

I thought that the government was sorely underestimating her.

The second means of pressure—seeing how others are treated—had a big effect on her paper. A number of her media friends and colleagues were in prison or had been killed. "That is where self-censorship is from. We do not self-censor. But we think about our headlines before doing them." She and her colleagues and friends supported each other through the fear. "Our fear gets diffused by the sense of bravery that people have on the team. That tips the balance on the freedom side of things."

"Was it better before the revolution or after the last revolution, in terms of freedom of speech for media?" I asked.

"Under Mubarak, there was a better balance between sticks and car-rots, and now there are more sticks," she concluded. She was not encouraged by the general direction of Egypt. Her outlook for the future was that Egypt would muddle along for the next decade as a continuously failing state, with waves of dissent popping up from time to time, as part of the revolution-counterrevolution cycle.

But the revolution had left important residues in Egypt, even if these were not felt right away, she thought. "People's relationship with authority has changed. People feel that they can be critical of the state, the regime, and the relationship mediating the government and people. And they can change it." That two government overthrows happened close together showed a newfound sense of agency among the Egyptian people. While Attalah neither viewed the government as on the right track now nor anticipated another mobilization anytime soon, she thought that there was now a cognizance under the surface of government account-ability to the people.

But even with those challenges, she was encouraged that *Mada Masr* had overcome the initial hurdles of finding funding and navigating the postrevolution media environment. "I could be shut down tomorrow. It is a business of risk. But it looks like we can survive somehow."

She thought that the paper was also a management experiment on behalf of the revolution's ideals of making changes through action. She wanted *Mada Masr* to be a political laboratory, not just in what it covers but in how it communicates and engages with fellow citizens. For example, one story about corruption included Excel spreadsheets about government budgets; readers were checking online and interacting with information themselves. "If people managed to organize their plans beyond the eruption in the square, chances are the revolution would have been in a better place today."

How Three Governments Messed Up

"There was a grave mistake to think that the revolution was only about electing a new leadership, rather than changing the rules of the game. We did not risk our lives simply to have new players," said Khaled Fahmy, when I asked him why the Morsi government was overthrown. Fahmy is a professor of Middle Eastern Studies at the American University of Cairo, and he has also taught at New York University, Columbia University, and Harvard University. "We wanted new rules." His described Egypt's government as a "ballotocracy" rather than a democracy, meaning it was authoritarianism by election.

His comments reminded me of democracy categories framed by others. In *Foreign Affairs*, international affairs columnist Fareed Zakaria differentiated "liberal democracy" from "illiberal democracy," noting that in the West, we assumed the word "democracy" to mean liberal democracy, which included not only elections but also constitutional liberalism, which is characterized by rule of law, separation of powers, basic liberties and rights, and peaceful rotation of power.[38] But elections and constitutional liberalism do not always go together; Zakaria argued that constitutional liberalism is more important than elections. Both the Muslim Brotherhood government, and the Sisi government that followed it, could be categorized as illiberal democracies. Robin Wright, a joint fellow at the United States Institute of Peace and the Wilson Center, termed Egypt's government "majoritarianism," or autocratic rule by the largest party.[39]

"When the Muslim Brotherhood government came in, they were democratically elected, chosen by the people. What happened? What were their biggest problems? How did they mess up?" I asked.

Fahmy thought that the Muslim Brotherhood's biggest mistake was thinking that they had more support and legitimacy than they did. Morsi had won 51.7 percent of the vote with only half of Egypt's electorate voting. That meant that only a quarter of Egypt had voted for him. Given that the opposing candidate in the presidential elections, Ahmed Shafiq (who al-Aswany had so famously debated on television), had previously been a member of the Mubarak regime, some of Morsi's voters might have been voting *against* Shafiq instead of *for* Morsi.[40] The Muslim Brotherhood had won, Fahmy thought, because they had remained organized during the time of Mubarak, while other political parties were weak—not because they had a sweeping political mandate. "It has an electoral machine that is capable of turning out the vote," he said. "But Morsi won the elections by a sliver of a margin. This means that the country was divided. His main task was to broaden his coalition and his base and reach out through compromise to the opposition, especially to the secular opposition. They didn't do that."

"Why didn't they do that?" I asked.

The failure of the Muslim Brotherhood that led to their downfall was a failure of mindset and of ideas, he thought. "To put it bluntly, the Muslim Brotherhood's main fatal mistake was not to realize that they are at the helm. This required them to get rid psychologically of the victim mentality in which they have wrapped themselves for eighty years. Now they needed to take another psychological mindset and assume the leadership role, which meant compromise, taking risks, and positioning themselves as a politically responsible organization and not a faction."

Over the years, the Muslim Brotherhood had invested in survival, not new ideas about how to solve Egypt's problems, he thought. "They have not produced a single intellectual figure since Sayed Qutb," he said, noting that new Islamist ideas, either violent or nonviolent, now came from elsewhere. "They were a conservative, inward-looking, cautious group. So when the time came to take the reins of power, they were not ready."

Fahmy added that the Muslim Brotherhood lacked basic technical know-how about politics and economics and had proved incompetent at administration. (Similar to what I had heard about Ennahda in Tunisia.) "No one expected Egypt's problems to be solved overnight. But we expected leadership to have a vision, ideas, a blueprint for how to solve Egypt's problems. But they didn't."

"Some people have said that while the Muslim Brotherhood may have lacked competence, they were also actively undermined by the secularists and the previous military regime. Is that the case?" I asked.

"This is nonsense. There were many individuals and groups who were willing to sit with the Muslim Brotherhood and try to find common ground, including myself and many of my friends. They made our task nearly impossible." He described poorly managed meetings about public issues that degenerated into arguments.

"Is Sisi doing a better job? Under Sisi, what foundations are being put in place for Egypt?" I asked.

"The current regime also has no concrete vision. No new ideas. It goes back economically and politically to ideas formed in the sixties—the economic megaprojects, a police state, cracking down on the religious opposition," he said referring to Nasser-style approaches. "It is not experimenting with anything new."

He was concerned that Sisi's policies would corrode Egypt's institutions. "Egypt has robust institutions," he said, listing the police, the army, the judiciary, the ministries, universities and schools. "They may be corrupt or inefficient, but they are solid. Egypt started its nation-building a hundred years before its neighbors. We still have a state in Egypt," he said, contrasting it with the Arab Spring failed states of Syria and Libya. "The problem with the state is that it is deeply dysfunctional and suffers from two crises: first, of achievement and delivery, and second, of legitimacy. The revolution erupted to bring to the fore these two questions, that something drastic needs to be done." He criticized pressures on state institutions under Sisi, such as draconian death and prison sentences, pressure on the judiciary, firings of faculty at universities for political views, and imprisonment of students. "The question is basically—what kind of institutions will we be left with five years from now. Yes, we will have an army and judiciary, but what kind?"

"Sisi thinks big," he continued, "but maybe Egypt does not need big projects and ideas, but small things and initiatives here and there, another mindset to jumpstart the economy and society. A new mindset was what the revolution was all about. That the *people* are capable of coming up with solutions."

All of this was further polarizing society, he thought. "Civil wars do not erupt suddenly. They erupt out of years of polarization and unbridgeable differences within society. What I am fearful of regarding policies of the present regime is that it is undertaking many measures that on the surface seem to be pacifying the country, but in fact may be undermining the stability of society. It increases the possibility of a civil war in five or ten years if there is no mechanism to resolve the serious tensions in Egyptian society. If Islamists are continuously viewed as non-Egyptians, excommunicated from the community and the Egyptian polity, stripped of any legal or constitutional rights, and can be killed with impunity, that is not only a recipe for increased radicalization, it is a recipe for a civil war. These are Egyptians. We have to learn to live with each other.

"We have to find a way to deal with our different agendas and different hopes for the country. That is what I wish to see, a formula that starts from this pretense that we are a large country, a complex society, and we will not excommunicate each other. We have to find a political system that starts here."

"Even with all of these challenges, with some saying things are worse now than under Mubarak, do you see any reason for optimism in the longer term?" I asked.

He did. "The Egyptian people proved that we exist. The Egyptian government had been behaving for sixty years as if we didn't exist," he said referring to the succession of regimes from Nasser to Sadat to Mubarak. "In the revolution, we said no, we do have a voice, we can express it, and you better listen to us," Fahmy said. "Ultimately despite everything, the current regime derives its legitimacy from us. For us, it is of profound significance. It is the end of a phase. It is a huge turning point.

"When people think that this is final, it is over, or it is a mess, they don't realize that what we are seeing in the Middle East is something of profound significance. We are seeing the modern Arab state system collapse, the way the Ottoman state collapsed after World War I. What was born a century ago was this bizarre map of states that don't reflect the wills of the people. The new map will have to accommodate the people," he said. He believed that in most cases, the borders of states would not change, but the basis of the state and its relationship with the people is undergoing transformation.

"Welcome to Safe Egypt and Its Secure Canal"

The road from Cairo to Ismailiya passed through desert, flanked by groves of mango and orange trees and new mosques. My car passed fields of cows and parks with playgrounds and pink jungle gyms. The landscape became greener before entering Ismailiya, a city on the Suez Canal.

Ismailiya was situated on a stream branching off the Nile, with languid waters, lush greenery growing on its banks, tall grasses, flowering bushes, and birds. But garbage was strewn everywhere and apartment blocks were left unfinished to avoid taxes.

Closer to the canal were lines of cars waiting to cross by ferry. Posted by the lines of cars were soldiers with guns, in beige uniforms and beige helmets with the red, white, and black stripes of the Egyptian flag. Much of Ismailiya, a city on the Suez Canal, was a military zone.

I went to the Beach Club, established in the 1960s for the employees of the Suez Canal. It is the only place in Ismailiya where visitors can get close to the canal. An aspirational sign advertised, "Welcome to safe Egypt and its secure canal." I sat in a grassy park with little tables shaded by umbrellas. Nearby was a yellow sand beach where people could wade just a little bit into the canal. Palm trees and bushes of pink, yellow, and orange flowers offered shade. A hundred yards across was the other side of the canal—the Sinai Peninsula, parts of which the Egyptian government had lost control of to ISIS-affiliates. Ferries shuttled across. People sat flipping through newspapers and watching the ships pass by. There was the rumbling of engines, the tweeting and cawing of birds, chatting of people, and the rustling of palm fronds in the breeze. I ordered a fresh guava juice and sat to watch the ships pass through the canal. A convoy of ships came up through the south: a green and white barge, a red container ship, a blue ship with liquefied natural gas, a ship carrying grain, and a white cruise ship for tourists.

A lot of history happened here. As oil had been of importance to Iraq, this strategic water route had been both Egypt's resource and a temptation for conquering colonial powers. On one side of the canal, I was standing in Africa. A hundred yards across the canal was Asia. It made Egypt a key spot in world transport, logistics, and trade.

When the canal opened in 1869, it changed global shipping and transport by shortening the distance from Europe to Asia by six thousand miles. It was an engineering marvel, requiring twenty thousand men to dig in nonstop shifts for ten years. It also bankrupted Egypt.

At the time the Suez Canal was built, Egypt was a semiautonomous province of the weakening Ottoman Empire. After the canal was built, Britain believed that controlling it was vital to protect the transportation link to their colonial empire in India. To gain control of the canal, the British invaded in 1882, claiming Egypt as their "protectorate." The British occupied Egypt until 1952.

On the way to the Beach Club, I had driven through neighborhoods built by and for the British when they were running the canal. Large Tudor-inspired houses and bungalows of apartments, surrounded by high walls and lush greenery, were close to the water, near parks and a grove of trees, rosebushes, and rhododendrons.

In 1919, at the end of World I and with the fall of the Ottoman Empire, Egyptians revolted, demanding independence from the British. In 1922, Britain recognized Egypt's independence under Egyptian monarch King Fuad, but refused to withdraw its forces from the Suez Canal, similar to how the French initially refused to withdraw from the port at

Bizerte in Tunisia after Tunisian independence. British presence in the Suez kept tensions high.

In 1952, the Free Officers led by Gamal Abdel Nasser plotted a coup that overthrew the British-backed king.[41] In 1956, Nasser nationalized the Suez Canal and British forces withdrew from the canal zone, marking the end of seventy years of British occupation of Egypt. The coup and British withdrawal led to a period of euphoric Egyptian pride in their victory.

But Britain, France, and Israel all worried about the growing power of Nasser. His moves threatened their strategic interests. They plotted to take over the Suez Canal and remove Nasser from power. With agreement among the three countries beforehand, Israel invaded the Sinai, and then France and Britain dropped paratroopers to the canal, ostensibly to "protect" it from conflict between Egypt and Israel, as an excuse to reoccupy it. The United States and the Soviet Union separately intervened, backing Nasser, forcing Britain, France, and Israel to withdraw. The invading countries were humiliated.[42]

Nasser emerged as hero.

One of the greatest political figures in modern Arab history, he became a symbol of dignity, pride, freedom, and Arab aspirations. Yet the institutions that he set up and the leadership style that he embodied paved the way for repression and autocracy. It set a course for Egypt, of nationalist military autocracy, social stability, and steady decline, that lasted until the Arab Spring.[43] In the 1950s, Egypt therefore embarked upon the same path of secular military autocracy as Tunisia and Turkey.

Nasser had personal authority, charisma, and capability—a combination resonant of Turkey's Ataturk and Tunisia's Bourguiba. He was handsome, determined, and strong. Photos show him with a square jaw and hair gray at the temple, in military uniform or in a suit, looking regal in a chair or authoritative at a desk. A passionate orator, photos show him with hands raised in the air in victory in front of a cheering crowd of thousands, backed by strings of lights, banners, and waving flags. Rapture and enthusiasm greeted his speeches, which were broadcast throughout the Arab world. Other photos show him saluting, raising his finger in the air while giving a speech, looking thoughtful with his hand at his temple, puffing a cigarette, or concentrating over a game of chess. Film footage shows a tall man, taller than most who stood around him, with a commanding presence and glamour that attracted all eyes in a room. He gave the impression of integrity, with the force of character and competence needed to build a new country. He was a hero for an age that needed a hero, a people's pharaoh, someone to stand up to the West, and a symbol of the Arab world's defiance after decades of colonial, military, and cultural domination. Thirty-four years old when he came to power, he reawakened Egyptian pride, self-respect, and identity.[44]

Nasser became the symbol of pan-Arab nationalism. Many Arabs hoped that there could be a single Arab country, a unified Arab world that would overcome the boundaries put in place by the British and the French—essentially, the Ottoman Empire without the Ottomans, what Sharif Hussein of Mecca had hoped to achieve during the Arab Revolt. But with borders and a political elite in place in the new countries, there was little political will to make that happen. For a brief period, there was an attempt to make a single country called the United Arab Republic, a union of Egypt with Syria, but that quickly failed.

Nasser brought economic restructuring to Egypt that entailed state-ownership of large industries, redistribution of income, and mega-projects.[45] Nasser took over major banks, requisitioned foreign-owned property, built the Aswan Dam, and reformed agriculture, with the army prominent in administration of those industries. He confronted political Islam, made the Muslim Brotherhood illegal, and absorbed Al-Azhar under the control of the government, as Bourguiba had absorbed the Zaytuna in Tunis. To silence critics of economic and other policies, he resorted to police repression, with torture, coercion, and control of the media, obstructing democratic development. With these changes, the economy stagnated, the bureaucracy became bloated, and the army came to control large parts of the economy, managing disparate projects like housing and factories. Corruption and inefficiency became endemic. And a powerful Islamist opposition emerged.

Nasser did not convert his anticolonial revolution into a well-functioning state.

Nasser's brinkmanship also set Egypt and the Arab world up for a momentous failure in the 1967 Six-Day War, shaping problems in the Middle East to this day.

It started in 1967, when Nasser received false reports from the Soviet Union that Israel was sending troops to the Syrian border. In response, Nasser sent troops to Israel's border, expelled UN peacekeeping forces from the Sinai, closed the Straits of Tiran to Israeli shipping, and signed a defense pact with Jordan. Iraq then deployed troops to Jordan.

Israel struck first.[46] Historians debate whether the war was a preemptive strike by Israel for self-defense or an unjustified attack by Israel on the Arabs. Regardless, it was provoked by Nasser's saber rattling. Within a few days, Israel destroyed the Egyptian and Syrian air forces and conducted a ground offensive to take Sinai from Egypt; Gaza, East Jerusalem, and the West Bank from Jordan; and the Golan Heights from Syria. A thousand Israelis were killed, but 20,000 Arabs were killed. Another wave of 285,000 to 325,000 Palestinian refugees fled Israel; 80,000 to 110,000 Syrians fled as refugees from the Golan Heights.

What did the 1967 war mean? It was a turning point. The military defeat of the Arab states, and of Egypt in particular, was of such magnitude and so precipitous that it was a blow to Arab self-image. It demonstrated that the Israeli military was stronger than the military might of a combination of Arab states and that Israel was politically more skillful than the Arab states. Even though they were the victors, the Israelis also received world sympathy as they had viewed their very existence as being at stake. The world recalled the horrors of annihilation inflicted upon the Jews in World War II. It made the conflict a global one, affecting anyone who identified as an Arab or as a Jew. It also made more Palestinians refugees; the Palestinians, who had not instigated the crisis, became its victims. It meant Israeli occupation of more Arab lands.[47] Muslim and Christian holy places were now under Israeli control. Egypt and Jordan implemented emergency laws to quell the unrest among their own people; in Egypt, emergency laws were used to justify some of the continual repression against which, nearly fifty years later, Arab youth revolted in the Arab Spring.

Nasser offered his resignation, but popular sentiment prevented it. A defeated man, never again the same, Nasser died of a heart attack at age fifty-two in 1970. More than five million Egyptians poured into the streets the day of Nasser's funeral. The nation went into mourning.

As I sat at the Beach Club, someone pointed to the opposite bank of the Suez Canal, paved in stone, with a big sign that said "Welcome to Egypt," where the ferries were shuttling. That side of the canal had been occupied by the Israelis from 1967 until 1973 when Sadat initiated a war to take the Sinai back.

When Nasser died, his less charismatic vice president, Anwar Sadat, inherited the presidency. Originally seen as a yes-man who had ruffled few feathers, Sadat made bold moves when he took the reins of power. He undid some of Nasser's economic policies and curbed Nasser's secret police. In 1973, Sadat launched a surprise attack on Israel to retake the Sinai. Egyptian forces crossed the Suez Canal and advanced into the Sinai, with initial military victories over Israeli forces. Over a period of several weeks, the Israelis launched counterstrikes, regaining some of the territories. The United States and Soviet Union separately intervened to broker a cease-fire. But the early defeat of the Israelis was a boon to Arab pride and morale—they took back some of their lost land, and they showed that they could gain a military victory. This salve to their wounded pride smoothed the way for the 1978 Camp David Accords, in which Egypt and Israel signed a peace treaty and Egypt fully regained the Sinai. But Israel kept the West Bank, Gaza, East Jerusalem, and the Golan Heights. Sadat's visit to Israel and the peace treaty led to his assassination by an Islamist group in 1981, at the parade ground not far from Rabaa Square.

Hosni Mubarak, Sadat's vice president, took over from there. And then what? Not much, really. Tarek Osman, in *Egypt on the Brink*, argues that for decades under Mubarak, Egypt lacked a national project.[48] It was not Nasser's Egyptian nationalism and pan-Arab nationalism. It was not Sadat's peace in the Middle East. It was stagnation. There was no vision that could mobilize the people of Egypt to work together for a common cause or give a compelling explanation for how their lives would be improved. Egypt became a wasteland, with social emptiness, brain drain, despair, drift, and historical defeats. But Egyptians could see inspiration in other parts of the Arab world. There was wealth creation in the Gulf. There was creativity and hipness in Lebanon. There was entrepreneurialism in Jordan. What defined Egypt?

Now the Suez Canal zone is held up as economical hope for Egypt. The Suez Canal Corridor Development Project aims to make the Suez Canal area an industrial and logistics hub. New projects are underway to deepen the canal so that the world's largest tankers can pass through and to dredge a parallel canal for additional lanes.[49] Hope rests on the project to boost Egypt's economy through providing construction and support jobs and through increased revenue from shipping through the passage. Egypt anticipates that the newly dredged canal will increase revenues from $5 billion per year to $13.5 billion per year by 2023.

These plans were funded through public bonds, called "crowd funding," in which the Egyptian public purchased bonds to fund the canal zone development. The bonds sold out in a few days, which has been viewed as a ringing endorsement of Sisi's economic plans.

But critics view the plans as being in the same vein as Egypt's previous, failed grandiose plans, with reliance on large public projects of questionable feasibility and benefit that do not generate the needed jobs, with public regulation stifling growth while enabling corruption.[50] They maintain that the goals are overblown and cannot possibly deliver the desired results.

Are the canal zone plans something new or a repeat of a failed past?

New Rules of the Game

Egypt had a new constitution. Unlike Tunisia's constitution, which was upheld as a model of societal consensus building, Egypt's constitution had been greeted with relative indifference. Its 2014 constitution was the second new constitution after the 2011 revolution. In 2012, upon election, the Islamist-majority parliament wrote a new constitution without consensus from wider society. When Sisi came in, he threw out the 2012 constitution and appointed a new committee to draft a new constitution, adopted in 2014. While there was significant continuity between the 1971, 2012, and 2014 constitutions, the new 2014 constitution does several things. It limits the president to two four-year terms. Islam is the state religion, but there is explicit freedom of belief. There is stated equality between women and men. It outlaws political parties based on religion, race, gender, and geography. But it still leaves significant political power with the military, judiciary, and police.[51] Like the 2012 constitution, the 2014 constitution was also criticized for not being inclusive. The U.S. State Department expressed concern that it was a product of a polarized environment and a lack of free debate.[52]

Amr El-Shobaki served on the Committee of Fifty, respected people selected from leadership of civil society and tasked with redrafting the constitution in 2014. He chaired the committee on Egypt's system of governance. A former member of parliament, he has written a number of books on political systems and political Islam in the Middle East and contributes opinion pieces to Egyptian newspapers.

I met Shobaki in his office in the Cairo neighborhood of Dokki, in an old Art Deco building that had not been maintained. I passed through an entryway of stained marble walls and old chandeliers and rode the creaking elevator up. In his office, Shobaki sat, in a blue shirt and tie, in front of a desk with a computer and a high pile of papers.

"In the 2012 constitution that was thrown out, I understand that the biggest points of debate were about the role of religion," I said, "What were the problems with Egypt's 2012 constitution?"

Egypt's biggest mistake after the 2011 revolution, thought Shobaki, was not agreeing on the constitution before having the elections that brought the Muslim Brotherhood to power in both the parliament and the presidency. "The right way would have been to establish the rules of the game and the political competition. The rules are the constitution." Because the constitution was drafted by the Islamists with an attitude of exclusion, "There was the risk of becoming a religious state and that led to the overthrow of the Muslim Brotherhood."

I observed that after the revolution, there was a big debate in Egyptian society: Should there be a constitution first or elections first? It echoed Fareed Zakaria's ideas about liberal democracy—which should come first, the "liberal" or the "democracy"? After a referendum, the Egyptian people chose the elections first, ending up with democracy without liberalism, which led those who did not want to live in a religious state feeling very threatened about their rights.

That was a key to Tunisia's success, I thought, having presidential elections only after the drafting of the constitution in which all sides agreed to the definition of the president's power. Egypt's constitution did not place limits on presidential power prior to electing Morsi, leaving the door open to misuse of power.

"When you were creating the 2014 constitution, how was the Committee of Fifty trying to solve some of the problems that had led to the revolution? What were the biggest points of debate or creativity in the 2014 constitution?" I asked.

Shobaki described the debate about the form of government and power of the president as a main point of controversy in the 2014 constitution.

The question was whether Egypt would have a presidential system or a parliamentary system. A presidential system would create a strong president who was directly elected by the people, as in the United States. In a parliamentary system, people elect the parliament, which chooses the prime minister; the prime minister is accountable to parliament. In the end, the choice was a presidential system.

Shobaki had been in the middle—on the side of the presidential system, but with limits on the power of the president. He said he wanted a democratic presidential system like the United States', not a "pharaonic presidential system, like Mubarak." Others had advocated for a stronger presidency. "People *wanted* an authoritarian regime," Shobaki explained, in particular the extreme right. "Now people say that with the chaos, we need a strong president." Those who advocated a parliamentary system argued for it because Egypt's former presidential system, with extensive powers given to the president, had enabled a regime like Mubarak's. Shobaki did not endorse a parliamentary system since he thought that a parliamentary system would push Egypt to chaos. Egypt did not have a strong civil society. Decades of political repression had weakened the organization of political parties other than Mubarak's ruling National Democratic Party and the Muslim Brotherhood.

But to prevent another authoritarian regime within the presidential system, the constitution placed term limits on the president—a big change from the time of Nasser, Sadat, and Mubarak, when being president meant being president for life.

"To me, it looks like there is a significant risk that term limits will not be heeded. Egypt does not have a history of peaceful rotation of power. Do you think that the term limits in the constitution will actually be applied?" I asked Shobaki.

"Inshallah," he said, a phrase that means "God-willing," but with the underlying implication that the outcome is not certain.

"We protected this article," he said about term limits, explaining that there is a provision in the constitution (Article 226) that states that two items in the constitution cannot be amended: first, the term limits and reelection of the president, and second, provisions concerning freedom and human rights. "I don't think that Sisi can change this. But who will follow him? Another military person?" Shobaki hoped for peaceful transition of power to a civilian or someone from a political party.

Articles in the 2014 constitution concerning political life were also an accomplishment, he thought. "It is now easier to make new political parties. This was harder before. We encouraged society to take initiative and develop political parties."

"Given the new 'rules of the game,' as you put it, with the constitution, as well as the other political realities, what will Egypt look like in ten years?" I asked him.

"Egypt is at an intersection. We can hope that we become a democratic country. But we have to work, move, and fight. Another option is to be a failed state. Egypt will not be like Somalia or Libya, but we could have partial chaos, major problems," he said.

And then he observed that what is needed are gradual constructive changes, reforms, and implementation of the constitution, as opposed to another revolution that aims to overthrow the system. "For me, I don't want to destroy the state to create a new one, like the Communist Revolution, or what happened in the American intervention in Iraq," he said.

He cautioned that while the youth had an idealistic vision of rapid positive change, many people in Egyptian society did not want such fast change, and in fact, Egypt's weak civil society was not capable of producing such fast change. "The youth need to respect the Egyptian people and understand why people voted for Sisi. They are really afraid from what happened in the region. Look what happened in Libya, Yemen, Syria, and Iraq. Conservative people don't like the revolution. For them, Sisi presented himself as a protector of the nation and the people. The majority of youth didn't want Sisi, but now they understand the culture of fear of chaos," he said. "But my point of view is that we will go to chaos if we don't start a reform of the state, with changes in institutions, administration, security, and services."

Having a good constitution was not the main problem, he thought. "The problem in Egypt is that we don't *apply* the constitution and the law." Several scholars I had interviewed also commented that Egypt is not a country with rule of law, which diminished the importance of the constitution. "Life is not rosy in Egypt," he added. His words were cynical, but he somehow had a jovial air about him as he said it.

"To change this cycle, we have to try to build a civil society that is stronger and more courageous." The failure of civil society had begun with Nasser's military intervention and was worsened by Mubarak.

"Can Egypt build a strong civil society, given all of the turbulence?" I asked.

"I am optimistic because we have a new generation that now understands that we need to construct something, not to be protesters all the time. That is the problem of the youth who protested. They know how to protest against everything. But to deliver something for the people? What is your program? What will you change and deliver?"

I thought Lina Attalah and her colleagues were a prime example of just that—building the ideals of the revolution into the daily grind of creating civil society.

Shobaki emphasized that he understood the need to protest and the desire for change. "I spent eighteen days in Tahrir," Shobaki said. He was happy that he had been alive to see that moment, as he had lived thirty years under Mubarak. He ticked off on his fingers. When he was at university, there was Mubarak. When he went to Paris to get his Ph.D., there was Mubarak. When he got married and had children, there was Mubarak.

But now was the time for reform, not revolution. "That was phase one. Phase two is more important: to deliver something and create an alternative."

Al-Azhar Waking Up

At 8:30 in the morning, old medieval Cairo was just waking up, quiet and tranquil. I entered Al-Azhar, a thirteen-hundred-year-old mosque that was the foremost center of learning and authority in Sunni Islam. Per their requirements, I covered my hair and removed my shoes to walk barefoot on cool ancient marble. Nearby, someone was mopping the marble in the center of the wide-open courtyard and someone else was vacuuming the carpet on the floor of the mosque. Like at the Mosque of Uqba in Tunisia, columns in the mosque and around the colonnade did not match; they had been taken from Roman and other sites, creating a mix of colored marbles and styles that symbolically reflected the heritage that Islam was integrating and building upon. Under a covered colonnade hung with green glass lanterns, men wearing *galabeyas* sat talking quietly, contemplated, or prayed. Nearby were carved wooden screens of calligraphy and geometric shapes. Minarets were coated in the grime of a thousand years, but I could see red and white bricks as well as blue tile peeking through the beige. Feral cats ran through the mosque. Honking cars of a city waking up broke through the cool tranquility.

Al-Azhar was founded in 970 AD in Cairo. Like Uqba and Zaytuna in Tunisia, Al-Azhar is one of the oldest universities in the world, offering studies in Islamic law, jurisprudence, grammar, astronomy, and logic. The Jewish philosopher Maimonides, whose writings were important for developing Christian theology, lectured there. Scholars at Al-Azhar preserved the works of the Greek philosophers, whose works are foundational to Western culture as well, when these works were lost to the West during the European dark ages.

Egypt's intellectual history in the past century has been heavily influenced by several thinkers associated with Al-Azhar. The late nineteenth and early twentieth centuries were a period of intellectual ferment and experimentation. Ways to guide Egypt out of the Ottoman era and colonial dominance by Europeans were sought, as was a conceptual framework for the nation to structure society, government, spirituality, and development.

Two prominent thinkers affiliated with Al-Azhar, described as "Islamic modernists" or "Islamic liberals," are Mohammed Abduh and Jamal al-Din al-Afghani (whose views about *ijtihad* were described earlier). They have also been described as "neo-Mu'tazilites," after the school of Islamic thinking that flourished in the eighth- to tenth centuries, a school of thought similar to European humanism that held that reason and critical thinking were the final arbiters in knowledge, more important than religious doctrine and text. In mainstream Sunni Islam, the Mu'tazilites lost the debate, and prophecy and the traditions of the Prophet Mohammed were concluded to be of greater weight than human reason.

Al-Afghani wrote about the need to restore Islamic societies to their former prominence. Condemning the inner decay of Islamic civilization, he called for revival. He thought that Islam was compatible with a modern life based on science and rationality. Abduh built on al-Afghani's writing, arguing that Islam needed to be reformulated. The essential should be separated from the nonessential, preserving the fundamentals of the faith while ridding it of historical traditions that were preventing Islamic societies from developing. He argued for *ijtihad*, viewing Islam as a set of general moral, spiritual, and societal guidelines that needed to be reinterpreted anew for each age. Each new generation had an obligation to apply principles of Islam to their generation with new results to prevent stagnation.[53] Blind imitation (*taqlid*) and slavish acceptance of historical precedent would not serve Islamic societies; the social arrangements of bygone eras were not necessary for all eras. Admiring the social progress that he saw in Europe, compared to the stagnation in some places in the Arab world, Abduh famously quipped, "I went to the West and saw Islam, but no Muslims; I got back to the East and saw Muslims, but not Islam."[54]

When Egyptians were trying to work out their post-Ottoman, anticolonial identity, blind intellectual Taha Hussein, educated both at Al-Azhar and in France, proposed Pharaonism, looking to Egypt's pre-Islamic past for identity and viewing Egypt as part of a larger Mediterranean civilization. Egypt was no longer Ottoman. Was it Egyptian? Arab? Muslim and Christian? European? Or something uniquely Egyptian, or pharaonic? Hussein advocated identity based on Egyptian-ness.

But in 1961, Nasser nationalized Al-Azhar (as Bourguiba did with the Zaytuna and Uqba), taking it under government control, appointing its faculty (instead of having them elected by Islamic scholars), and adding secular subjects such as business, medicine, engineering, and more. Colonialism and then nationalization of Al-Azhar led to a decline in quality and its religious authority. It was defunded, with its curriculum defined by faculty appointed by the state, lowering educational standards so that it no longer attracted the best and brightest. "This process left a vacuum in religious authority in modern Islam. The disintegration of the traditional institutions of Islamic learning and authority meant a descent into a condition of virtual anarchy in regard to the mechanisms of defining Islamic authenticity," wrote Khaled Abou el Fadl. This vacuum in quality of religious thinking and religious authority of Islam's historic institutions was filled by popular movements and self-appointed religious scholars who did not have rigorous training or education. "Islamic intellectual culture witnessed an unprecedented level of deterioration," wrote Abou el Fadl.

As a result of state control, Al-Azhar became less respected and was viewed as part of the regime. It had been coopted. The real momentum of the Islamic movement was now outside of Al-Azhar.[55] Much of the intellectual momentum in Islam transferred to extremist groups.

Al-Azhar in recent decades has been viewed as a centrist institution, distancing itself from both the Muslim Brotherhood and the Salafists. It is historically Sufi in character, with a pacifist orientation and veneration of saints. Both the sheikh and the grand mufti of Al-Azhar are Sufis.[56]

After Sisi's coup against the Muslim Brotherhood, both the grand mufti of Al-Azhar and the Christian Coptic pope stood by Sisi's side at the announcement, indicating their support.

Sisi turned to Al-Azhar to support his proposed "revolution in Islam." Al-Azhar responded with a plan to correct the image of Islam through social media, foreign visits, publications, interfaith conferences to fight extremism, and fatwas to suit the modern age.[57] "We should closely examine the situation we are in. It does not make sense that the thought we sanctify pushes this entire nation to become a source of apprehension, danger, murder, and destruction in the entire world," said Sisi in a speech at Al-Azhar, about his proposed revolution in Islam.[58] The sheikh of Al-Azhar blamed extremism on "bad interpretations" of both the Quran and the life of Mohammed and called for reforms in education to combat this.[59] To combat extremist fatwas, Al-Azhar created a Monitor of Infedilizing Fatwas Department, whose job it is to refute fatwas that it views as not-Islamic.[60] The grand mufti described ISIS as enemies of God and Mohammed, but refused to go as far as calling them "apostate."[61]

There is now controversy over what Al-Azhar's role is. Should it be a state-controlled beacon of moderate Islam? Should it take a more activist role?[62]

I left Al-Azhar and wandered the thousand-year-old streets behind it, with derelict buildings and mounds of garbage piled against ancient stone walls. A dog slept on top of the garbage. I walked past a woman and a baby at a corner bookseller; she was shouting for all to hear about the misdeeds of her husband. Garbage cans were painted in the red, white, and black stripes of Egypt. But the cats were cleaning themselves, even in this environment.

Students were arriving at Al-Azhar on motorbikes. These winding cobblestone streets must once have been lovely, with a harmony of good taste, white stone, trees in alleyways, carved wood doors, windows and latticework on balconies. I sat on a stone bench to contemplate a pleasant square, with its palm trees and beaten copper lanterns. The buildings were graceful old stone on the bottom, and then piled carelessly with additional stories of brick or concrete block. The stories were crooked with mortar sloppily spilling out of the joints. The square was filled with the trash of a dysfunctional state.

A young man walked by through the alleyways, balancing on his head a wooden platform about six feet by three feet, piled with hundreds of pieces of freshly baked Egyptian flatbread. A loaf of bread fell in the dirt; a man picked it up and put it back with the rest of the bread. Severed cow heads rested in bloody baskets on the street in front of shops. Outside the entrance to Al-Azhar mosque, four men were butchering a cow in the bed of a black Toyota pickup trick.

Neither the mosque itself nor its neighborhood has been maintained as it should. How can ideas, pride, and order be sustained within a religion when its central symbols of it are not preserved? What does it say when the world's foremost historic center of Islamic learning is situated in piles of trash and surrounded by homeless people sleeping in the streets? Isn't it time to renovate Al-Azhar's facilities and renew the ideas coming from it?

"As Far as My Eyes Could See, There Were Only Women"

"The big accomplishment of the revolution, and now I am thinking of women, is that the people can do something. They can take part in shaping their future. Every woman was using her voice to say no or yes and to participate in the debate. This kind of collective responsibility in envisaging the country's policies was a great achievement. After the revolution, everybody became very politically minded. Especially women. They became concerned with public issues, not only marriage, divorce, and family law or women's issues per se, but the security of the country, the right of the people to express their opinion, and terrorism," said Mervat Talawy.

Talawy, the head of Egypt's National Council for Women, sat at her desk in her office in Heliopolis, a district of Cairo built in 1905. Talawy was one of five women on Egypt's Committee of Fifty tasked with drafting the 2014 constitution after Morsi's overthrow. She served as Egypt's minister of insurance and social affairs from 1997 to 1999 under Mubarak, as well as Egyptian ambassador to both Japan and Austria. A petite woman who described herself as "an old civil servant," she wore a pink tweed suit.

I asked her what she thought the challenges were for women in Egypt, not specifying any particular government—and then she narrated her struggle for women's rights under the Muslim Brotherhood government.

Women's participation increased by necessity under Morsi's Muslim Brotherhood government, she thought. "They tried to alienate women, to remove them from their posts, and to change what the curriculum in schools said about women. I am saying so, because every day I was sending a letter to the minister of education and other ministers. Why did you remove page X because it has a picture of a woman unveiled in the photos? Why did you remove the picture of Hoda Shaarawi?" she asked, referring to one of Egypt's first feminists, who threw off the veil in public in 1919. "Why did you remove the page where President Nasser was giving the right to vote to women? They deleted that page and they put the opinion of Hassan al-Banna, the leader of the Muslim Brotherhood." She was exasperated.

In her role heading the National Council for Women during the Muslim Brotherhood government, Talawy had a file of complaints on her desk, where senior women had been demoted from positions of authority in government because they were women.

For the five months that the Islamists had the majority in parliament, "They wanted to change all the laws concerning women," she said. She listed measure after measure. First, there was an attempt to change the legal age of marriage, reducing it from eighteen to twelve, as some Islamist parliamentarians wanted to emulate early marriage in the Quran. Second, under current Egyptian law, divorced women maintain custody of children until the child is fifteen; the Islamist majority in parliament wanted to reduce it to age seven. Third, they attempted to remove the penalty on the doctors or medical workers who performed female circumcision, or female genital mutilation. Fourth, they tried to abolish women's right to initiate divorce.

The interpretation of Islam that they were using to justify these legal changes was far more conservative than Egypt's traditional religious interpretations, which had been developed over time at Al-Azhar. Talawy viewed Al-Azhar as an ally against the Muslim Brotherhood. "We stood very firm on the National Council for Women. Al-Azhar also was supporting us. We defeated them on all those four measures."

Talawy was puzzled and angry about the interpretations of Islam that had recently become prevalent in Egypt. "A hundred years ago, forget even about a thousand years ago, in Egypt, it was not like that." She noted Egypt's liberal Islamic thinkers who had been affiliated with Al-Azhar and who had promoted freedoms and equality for women. She blamed religious television shows for expounding an extremist interpretation and lauded Sisi's call for a revolution in Islam.

Other challenges for women under the Muslim Brotherhood were cultural, she thought. Islamists viewed themselves as enforcers of women's dress and movement on the streets. She dealt with many complaints of harassment of unveiled women. "They cannot walk in the street safely, because you have these groups of men with long beards. They give themselves the right to criticize you or touch you and tell you bad words because you are not covered. They threaten." Talawy described how one such man threatened to throw acid on the face of one of her household staff if the staff member did not wear the headscarf. "They were imposing themselves as the ruler on the streets, what to wear, how to walk.

"That is why, for us, we were so astonished," she said, about Western media's framing the overthrow of Morsi as a coup ousting a democratically elected leader. "How come the West was not understanding and was supporting people like this, particularly in the women's case? For me, it is very surprising."

Because of these problems, women were a driving force in the 2013 overthrow of Morsi, she said. "That is why their voice was louder than men's. I went to Tahrir Square. I stood on a platform addressing the women and, to my surprise, when I looked down, as far as my eyes could see, there were only women."

Talawy's comments about the problems of women with political Islam were far more troublesome than the comments I had heard from women in Tunisia, Turkey, and Qatar. This was something different.

Proud of her work on gender in the new 2014 constitution, she introduced Article 11, which describes equality of women in five areas: economic, social, cultural, civil, and judicial. "For the first time, we have woman as a citizen in the constitution, because in the constitution of Morsi, they did not use the word 'woman,' but 'motherhood' and 'childhood.'" In other words, women were referred to by their roles, but not as people on their own. This issue reminded me of Tunisia's debate and protests against describing women as "complementary" to men in their constitution.

Article 11 also said that the government has responsibility for protecting women against violence and that women should be in the judiciary. "Egypt has only forty-one women judges, out of thousands of men." Talawy fought hard to get thirty more female judges appointed. Indeed, Egypt has a low proportion of women in the judiciary, with only .4 percent in 2012.

Egypt ranked 129 out of 142 countries on the World Economic Forum's 2014 Gender Gap Report.[63] Egyptian women have 33 percent illiteracy compared to 18 percent illiteracy for men. While women have nearly equal rates of higher education as men, women's labor force participation in Egypt, according to the World Bank, is 24 percent.[64] There is low political participation, with only 2 percent of parliamentary members being women in the 2012 elections. Talawy pressed for a quota system for women's political representation in parliament during the drafting of the constitution and succeeded. But for some educated professional women things are different. For example, nearly a quarter of Egypt's ambassadors are women, and the percentage of women in senior management in media was 44 percent in 2012.[65]

During the drafting of the constitution, Talawy worked to get women from multiple social strata to testify before the Committee of Fifty: educated women, poor women from slums, women who were providers for their families, handicapped women, elderly women who were reliant on the government for survival, and women who were against early marriage. The women spoke about their problems and concerns to the committee.

"We got good results in the constitution, but I have to tell you that the implementation is not as rosy because of the social culture. We need a lot of work to change the social culture," she said, tapping her forehead, "because the extremism of the religious messages left a very bad impact on the people. For the past thirty or forty years, these religious groups were allowed to spread wrong interpretations of Islam. They were changing the culture of the people, the personality of the Egyptians, let alone the essence of the religion."

"What do you think are the policy priorities for women?" I asked.

The first, Talawy thought, was implementing the new constitution and its newly expressed rights for women. That would require either revising existing legislation or drafting new legislation, such as in the field of family law. Next, she called for economic policies that enabled financial independence for women, such as access to credit, changes in pension policies, and equal treatment under the tax code for women who were the providers for their families, pointing to data from the National Council for Women that women were primary providers for 30 percent of Egyptian families. Third, she said, "we have to change the social culture. Women are not for reproductive health only. To give birth and that's it. No. They are valuable human resources, they are citizens, and they should take care of the social well-being of the whole country."

She was encouraged by signs that Egyptian women are taking matters into their own hands, describing women's groups that have organized against violence, female circumcision, and early marriage, and young women who are pressing for the right to enter the army. "The women themselves recognized that they can do something. So there is this new spirit coming up."

Overall, Talawy was optimistic about the direction of the country and Sisi's leadership. "This gentleman's mind is focused on improving the status of Egypt politically, economically, and socially. It will take time. We don't expect results tomorrow. Because after thirty or forty years of mishaps, you cannot solve problems immediately. I think we are on the right track."

Mary and Jesus Slept Here

At the entrance to the narrow lanes of Coptic Cairo, soldiers in camouflage carrying guns ushered me through a metal detector. I walked through it with my bag, jacket, and belt, setting off its alarms, but no one checked me.

I descended to the level of the old city and its churches, wandering through winding medieval alleyways, neatly swept clean, through a cemetery, near ruins of a Roman fortress, and past vendors of trinkets depicting St. George the Dragon Slayer. Over time, Cairo grew up layer by layer, and the streets outside of the Christian quarter are a good fifteen feet higher than the winding stone streets inside, built from the seventh to ninth centuries.

I arrived at the Church of the Sacred Family. It is said that Mary and Jesus slept here. When they fled Herod, they came to Egypt. For more than three years, they stayed in a cave by the Nile. This church was built over the cave, guarding it as a holy sanctuary.

The Church of the Sacred Family was under renovation with workers chipping off old plaster to replace it. Under plastic sheeting and curtains of canvas, I stood on the stone floor by the entrance to the cave, not permitted to enter, only to look. Nearby were wooden doors inlaid with ivory crosses. Chandeliers of brass hung from the ceiling. A well, said to have been used by Mary and Jesus, still held water. There was a painting of Mary and Jesus, whose birth story echoes Egyptian mythology of virgin births and whose mother and son relationship mimics that of ancient Egyptian gods Isis and Horus. Ancient Egyptian society always had female deities, and Mary took over from Isis, filling a gap in the male-dominated Christian Trinity.

The Copts have a long history in Egypt. Liturgical Coptic is a language descended from the language spoken by the ancient Egyptians. Ancient Egyptian hieroglyphics were deciphered by comparing them with liturgical Coptic. Today, Copts speak Egyptian Arabic. They remain one of the oldest and largest Christian communities in the Middle East, though their numbers are declining. They are estimated to be about 5 to 10 percent of Egypt's population.[66]

According to tradition, Christianity was introduced in Egypt in 42 AD and spread. Important to the establishment of early Christian theology, the Church of Alexandria was second only to the Church in Rome, as one of the four Apostolic Sees. Egypt was largely Coptic Christian from the days of early Christianity until Arab Muslims conquered it in 641 AD. Conversion to Islam and introduction of the Arabic language was a slow and uneven process that took place over centuries.[67] Muslims became a majority around the ninth century through conversions of the Christians and immigration of Muslim soldiers from the Gulf and Syria.

Identity is a complex issue in Egypt. Both Arab nationalism and Islamism conflict with Coptic pre-Arab identity. For example, Sadat made shariah the principal source of law for Egypt's constitution, and a statement to that effect remains in the 2014 Egyptian constitution. Islam's status as the basis of the state excludes Christians (most Jews left Egypt after the 1948 and 1967 wars with Israel). A state based on Arab nationalism also excludes those who do not identify as Arab, like the Copts in Egypt, Kurds in the Kurdish regions, Amazighs in North Africa, and others.[68]

Egypt's Copts have experienced increasing marginalization since Nasser's coup.[69] Sadat even imprisoned the Coptic pope. Copts have been barred from many positions of public leadership and face job discrimination. It can be difficult to build or repair a church, as it requires a presidential decree. There has been a rise of hate crimes against the Copts, such as attacks on churches.[70] Copts complain of minimal protection from law enforcement.[71] For example, on New Year's Day in 2011, weeks before the revolution, a car bomb at a church in Alexandria killed twenty-three parishioners and injured dozens more.[72]

The violent razing of the camp at Rabaa Square inflamed sectarian tensions. Copts were somehow viewed as responsible. In August 2013, there were attacks on Coptic schools, shops, homes, and churches, with forty churches looted and torched and at least twenty-three others damaged. Security forces reportedly did not intervene.[73] The military promised to rebuild the churches, but it has been slow in keeping the promise.

During the drafting of the constitution in 2012, the Copts withdrew, along with women and liberals, after realizing that the constitution would not reflect the multiple identities of Egypt and protesting the Islamist monopolization of the document. The draft constitution inserted the church as intermediaries between the Coptic people and the state, rather than giving all citizens equal rights and processes before the law.[74]

When Sisi took over and announced a new interim government, he included three Copts in the cabinet, notably in the important trade ministry. In an unprecedented gesture, Sisi visited a Coptic church during a Christmas service; none of his predecessors had attended a church service. He made remarks about national unity and about how they were all Egyptians.[75]

ISIS beheaded twenty-one Egyptian Coptic Christians in Libya in February 2014.[76] That day I was browsing in the tourist shop of Arsany, a Copt in his late forties with thinning hair, a prominent nose, and a tattoo of the cross on his wrist. His multistory shop sold all the trinkets of Egypt: silver jewelry, alabaster vases, painted papyrus, turquoise beaded necklaces, stone carvings, and leather bean bags imprinted with graceful Queen Nefertiti's face. Pictures of the bearded, robed Coptic pope adorned the walls.

Arsany wore his salesman face and tried to do a pitch about the paintings that I was looking at. Then his eyes teared up, and he walked away to compose himself. This happened two more times.

"Did you hear?" he asked finally. He related that, with his wife and sons, he had watched the video of the beheadings, filmed on a beach in front of the Mediterranean, which turned red with blood. The images would not leave him for months. Then he turned on his shopkeeper's smile again to mask his tearing eyes. "Are you having a good time?" he asked suavely. "Yes, it is a good day," he pronounced, and then took a long inhale.

It meant a lot to him that Sisi had paid a visit to express his condolences to the Coptic pope. Copts had been scared for their safety under the Muslim Brotherhood government.

Many Muslim friends called Arsany to express their condolences. "I know that is not what your religion is about," he had told them. Christians and Muslims got along for a thousand years in Egypt, he knew. "There are good Christians and bad Christians, good Muslims and bad Muslims, and good Jews and bad Jews."

Life in Cemeteries and Garbage Dumps

A sandstorm blew over the City of the Dead. The air was a dirty beige, obscuring visibility, and making the world look like a gritty smear. A tree grew inside a garbage barrel, a speck of green amid the living, the dead, and the haze of sand in the air.

The City of the Dead was the burial ground of Cairo's noble families for several hundred years, starting in 640 AD. Streets of tombs were built as neighborhoods with burial structures one or two stories high, on top of underground tombs, so that the living could visit their dead, picnic, and even sleep there during the visit.

The four-mile-long cemeteries have been occupied as slums since Nasser's presidency in the 1960s, due to rapid population growth and urbanization that the city was not equipped to handle. As time passed, family tombs filled with destitute people who moved here seeking a home. The poor living in the tombs displaced the picnics of remembrance of the wealthy deceased.

While there are no accurate numbers of the population of the City of the Dead, estimates range from 500,000 to up to 1 million.[77] There is limited electricity, water, and sanitation, although recent government initiatives have aimed to improve infrastructure. Mausoleums serve as bedrooms. Cemetery gardens serve as family areas.

As I stood on a hill above the City of the Dead, the tombs looked tidily swept out inside their walls, with exposed courtyards of brick. Then my taxi took me through its dirt roads, passing herds of goats, a man selling potato chips, another selling oranges, and a barber cutting hair in a corner tomb with a chair in front of a mirror. Garbage was strewn in the streets. There was neglected but once beautiful ironwork and stonework with inscriptions in Arabic, crafted for the dead in more affluent times.

Egypt has one of the largest slum populations in the world.[78] An estimated 12 to 16 million Egyptians live in slums—about 20 percent of Egypt's total population and 40 percent of Cairo's population.[79] Slums are called the "Ashwa'iyyat," meaning "randoms" because they grow up haphazardly, without proper planning for public services and city infrastructure. Slums developed in dilapidated areas of the old historic urban core, urban pockets elsewhere in the city, and settlements in agricultural and desert lands on the fringes of Cairo.

Egypt is a lower-middle-income country, with GDP per capita of $3,140.[80] There are significant problems with poverty, worse since the revolution. The World Food Program has some startling statistics.[81] Nearly a third of Egypt's children have stunted growth because of poor nutrition and half of the children are anemic; 17 percent live with food insecurity. A quarter of the population lives below the poverty line, and another quarter hover just above it, classified as "near poor." In 2008, 15 percent of the population was living on $2 per day or less.[82]

My Egyptian friend Hussein attributed Egypt's revolution to hunger. "It is a very dangerous thing to not have your biological needs met," he said.

Egypt's experiments with a progression of ideologies have failed its poor, whether the liberalism and leaning toward Europe before World War II, the pan-Arab nationalism led by Nasser, or the military dictatorships of Sadat and Mubarak. These frameworks for society did not improve economic and social conditions or provide dignity. As Egyptians saw that these secular models did not help them, many increasingly became supportive of other solutions. The Muslim Brotherhood was a key force in the slums providing food, education, and healthcare, and helping with other social services.

The Sisi government announced a campaign to develop the slums, with promises of trash removal, paved roads, and lighting. It announced plans to build a million housing units for low-income Egyptians. But as efforts are made to remove people from unsafe housing, many fear evictions will split up communities, distance people from their livelihoods, and provide smaller dwellings, forcing them to leave family members behind.[83]

My taxi left the City of the Dead and drove to Garbage City, a slum at the foot of the Mokattam hills, near a Mercedes dealership, where twenty to thirty thousand people live amid the garbage that they sort for a living. On the road approaching it, the wind carried the sweet, rotten smell of garbage into the car. We drove through the neighborhood's narrow lanes of mudbrick and cement buildings, with piles of open garbage, stacks of car parts, and mounds of garbage wrapped in plastic canvas sheeting. Flies hovered in the air. A woman in a purple robe stood amid bales of garbage while holding an infant, having a conversation with another woman, and laughing. A child's handprints in paint marked the wall of a home. A donkey cart pulled a pile of fresh melons to sell. Residents sat in a corner cafe and smoked waterpipes next to heaps of garbage.

Abandoning the Troubles of Old Cairo

"You will see a big difference between Old Cairo and New Cairo. It is like America," observed my taxi driver, Omar, as we drove to New Cairo.

Cairo had become so polluted and congested that two new cities had been built from scratch in the desert to relieve some of the pressure on the city center. They are still under construction—6th of October City (where I met Alaa al-Aswany) and New Cairo. Most of the residents are affluent Egyptians, although initial plans for the cities intended them to provide significant lower income housing.

The rich abandoned the troubles of Cairo to make their own new cities nearby.

The drive out of the center of Cairo leads into a district of wide streets, shopping malls with international chains, and compounds of garden villas with names like Mountain View (although there are no mountains in sight). Rows of palm trees front wide streets. The air is clean. We passed office parks of companies with recognizable international names, and unfinished apartment buildings' brick and concrete skeletons, with signs proclaiming "middle-class housing."

It is another world. We just left Egypt and entered America or Europe, or maybe Dubai or Qatar.

Omar dropped me off at Cairo Festival City. It could have been a mall in California—except that as we entered the mostly empty parking lot, guards conducted bomb checks with a mirror under the body of the car. Police opened the trunk for a bomb-sniffing dog on a leash to sniff it out.

The mall was luxurious in comparison with the rest of Cairo, operating on a separate economic scale, one of Western prosperity. Its prices were out reach of for most Egyptians. Perhaps it was because of this that it felt empty, with few shoppers. I walked past American and European chains like IKEA, Starbucks, Marks & Spencer, H&M, and Toys"R"Us— the middle-class shops of the West that are affordable only to the wealthy in Egypt. There was a grand opening sign for Victoria's Secret, with pictures of lingerie-clad models engulfed in fluffy white feathers.

This was a thousand years from the medieval Cairo neighborhood of Al-Azhar.

Some have wondered whether the stark differences between old and new and between rich and poor here will serve to stoke further social tensions.

The satellite cities of Cairo are now becoming part of Cairo's overall sprawl. Each was planned to house 5 million people in the coming decades, as Cairo creaks under the weight of its 20 million residents. It is the biggest city in the Middle East and Africa. But after a decade and a half of building New Cairo, it only houses a few hundred thousand.[84] New developments, planned initially under Mubarak, have come under legal action for corruption and criticism for impressions of unfairness between social classes.[85] New Cairo has not grown as much as expected, failing to attract enough residents, because there is not affordable public transport to areas with jobs, and not enough jobs here to attract more of Cairo's poor.[86]

In 2015, the Sisi government announced a project to build a new yet-to-be-named Egyptian capital in the desert in the next five to seven years, with 5 million people, 600 hospitals, 1,250 mosques and churches, 2,000 schools and colleges, and 1.1 million homes. It will be the largest purpose-built capital city in history and will be funded and developed by Emirati Mohamed Alabbar, the builder of the world's tallest skyscraper, the Burj Khalifa in Dubai—the same investor in the project to create downtown Erbil.[87] It would capitalize on UAE experience in creating new cities in the desert in the span of a few years.

Like the plans for the Suez Canal zone and for New Cairo, many are questioning the chances of success of the new unnamed capital. Egypt has a history of failed projects in the desert: cities, farms, industrial zones, tourism resorts, and development corridors have not met their desired goals.[88] Attempts to solve Egypt's woes with mega-projects have rarely lived up to expectations.

On the drive back, Omar said that he was cautiously optimistic about Egypt's new direction. "Give Sisi a chance. Maybe it takes five years." But he acknowledged that there were many problems to be solved.

He told me that he had lived in Abu Dhabi for a year before coming back to Egypt during the revolution to protect his family. "There, I feel like I am human. There, they treat you with respect," he said. "Here, no. Before the revolution they treated us like animals." He kept repeating that phrase—humans, not animals.

As I spent more time traveling in Egypt, the difference between humans and animals came up in three different conversations with taxi drivers and tour guides. Did this mean that Egyptian society was struggling so much with basic decency that the people felt a need to assert their humanity and propose humanity as a standard for others? Basic norms of dignity were missing—Egypt's was a revolution about dignity.

Self-Correcting Institutions

The answer lies in Egypt's institutions, thought Nabil Fahmy. An Egyptian career diplomat, Fahmy was Egypt's foreign minister from June 2013 to July 2014, in the interim period between the overthrow of Morsi and the election of Sisi. Born in New York, he also served as Egypt's ambassador to the United States. He is now the founding dean of the School of Public Affairs at the American University of Cairo. His office was at their new campus in New Cairo, in a beautiful, walkable complex of stone university buildings, far from the old campus's busy, barricaded setting of Tahrir Square.

I interviewed him to understand what, if anything, would set Egypt up for the hopeful future envisioned by the revolution. "What do you think that the revolution accomplished? Has it all gone backward? To the outside world, it looks pretty dark. Or, are there some changes that will set Egypt up in the future to be a healthy, prosperous, and stable society?" I asked.

Fahmy acknowledged the disappointments. "We all fell into the enthusiasm and emotion of the moment and felt that this could be resolved quickly," he said. But after sixty years of a particular political system and set of institutions, merely removing the president would not fix Egypt in a matter of months. "These societal changes take time."

Four things bode well for Egypt's institutions going into the future, he thought.

First, through the 2011 and 2013 revolutions, the Egyptian people discovered their voice. "It has not been translated yet into the level of Egyptian institutional practices. But politicians know and feel that they are accountable." As evidence, he described how politicians now make a point to explain things publicly, which they did not do in the past. (Later in 2015, Egypt's cabinet was forced to resign because of a corruption scandal, although about half of the ministers were reappointed to different ministerial positions in the new cabinet.)

Second, the term limits on the president, in both the 2012 and 2014 constitutions, gave society protection. "I'll live with anything else if you give me term limits. Because that gives me government accountability. Then we could work on the rest. If leaders know they are in there because they have been chosen for a reason, it is going to end, and they are held accountable, they will act in a much better fashion and govern rather than rule."

Third, he saw signs that Egypt's institutions were beginning to self-correct.

He made a comparison to U.S. institutions and how they self-correct their problems. "I lived in America during 9/11 and also when the U.S. went into Iraq. There is a laundry list of when U.S. institutions went overboard. But the strength of your system is that you came out yourselves and said that this is unacceptable—we need to change this," he said. He pointed to signs that Egypt was beginning this also, giving the example of the security crackdowns. He acknowledged the unacceptable use of force by Egyptian security. But security repression had led to public debate in the media, court cases, and a defensive posture by security forces. In the face of public scrutiny, security forces first denied that these events happened. Then, they rescinded their denial, acknowledging that excesses were committed by individuals, while claiming that it was not policy. In other words, they were responding to public pressure in some way.

"As long as Egyptians are saying, 'You are right, here,' and 'You are wrong there,' like every other country in the world, we will gain the confidence and practice of correcting ourselves," he said.

Fourth, there is a readiness to deal with Egypt's problems in a way that has not been evident for decades. He pointed to two areas now under public debate that were previously untouchable, such as Sisi's "revolution in Islam" effort and reducing government subsidies for food and energy, which were significant expenditures. Sisi started with cutting fuel subsidies, reducing the government deficit, and making investment easier for large businesses and foreign investors (although that has yet to translate to an improved business climate for small enterprises).[89] "There is a readiness to deal with the challenges that exist. And there is a desire to get things done."

A remaining challenge was for Egypt to develop pluralistic ethics—institutional and cultural.

"The strong suit in your system," he said, referring to American liberal democracy, "is that one party may win elections. It gains influence. It doesn't gain more rights. The losing party does not lose its rights. It just loses its influence." Not having a set of rights in place with a consensus-based constitution before elections had let the Muslim Brotherhood begin ruling without constraints on their behavior or constraints on removing rights of others. His point was similar to Amr Shobaki's observation that Egypt's mistake was not establishing rules of the game before elections, not agreeing on a set of rights and restrictions that all could live with.

Fahmy said that sometimes people asked him why instead of removing Morsi militarily Egypt couldn't just wait for a few years until the next election, when presumably the Muslim Brotherhood would be voted out because of poor performance. Fahmy was adamantly opposed to this approach. He pointed out that the Islamists had drafted a constitution that was fundamentally changing Egyptian identity and removing rights, moving away from pluralistic respect for important parts of Egyptian society. "That leaves me out. Egyptians like me are worried about having our identities taken from us. That is why we couldn't wait four years.

"You need also to cultivate a political ethic where people of a different point of view not only express their opinion but also accept the role of other opinions. We are a pluralistic society. But we are still searching for pluralistic ethics. You have to change the culture, not just the institutions, but people in society."

But I wondered now if Egypt's Islamists were left out, with their identity taken from them. A sustainable system, in which people (both secularists and Islamists) thought that they could make their voice heard without resorting to violence, would depend on including both.

The Google Guy

When questioned by his staff about Egypt's protests, President Obama reportedly said, "What I want is for the kids on the street to win and for the Google guy to become president."[90] But he acknowledged that it would not be so easy. "What I think is that this is going to be long and hard."

Wael Ghonim was "the Google guy." Like Alaa al-Aswany, he was an important leader in a leaderless revolution.

In 2010, Ghonim, a Google executive in his early thirties, anonymously started the Facebook page "We Are All Khaled Said."[91] Said was a young Egyptian man who was brutally beaten to death by police forces in Alexandria. Ghonim did not know Khaled Said, but he was horrified when he saw leaked photos of Said, with a broken nose and fractured skull, lying in a pool of blood. Ghonim decided to do something about it. The "We Are All Khaled Said" Facebook page that Ghonim started garnered 3 million "friends"; Egyptians were outraged that security forces could act in this way with impunity.

Through the Facebook page, Ghonim and others organized demonstrations on National Police Day, January 25, 2011. Other Facebook pages joined in and mobilized people as well. The stated purpose of the protests was fourfold: ending poverty, placing a two-term limit on the presidency, firing the autocratic interior minister, and annulling Egypt's emergency law, which had been in place nearly continuously since 1967, that gave the government the right to imprison and interrogate Egyptians for up to six months without a warrant or attorney. While the Tunisian protesters had overthrown Ben Ali just weeks before, Ghonim and others did not expect that this would turn into full revolution in Egypt.

After the protests started, Ghonim's identity slipped. Egyptian security took him into custody for eleven days in blindfolded solitary confinement. When Google publicized that he was missing, the international attention afforded a level of protection to him. Ghonim did not undergo the torture that other activists did. On the day of his release, he went on Egyptian national television to talk about the protests. He broke down in tears when reading a list of the protest's dead. His emotional response on television mobilized Egypt further, and the following day, there was an even larger turnout at Tahrir Square. At the square, Ghonim supported other protesters' calls for an end of the Mubarak regime and became a symbol of the revolution in Egypt. Some wanted him to take a political leadership role, but he neither wanted nor was prepared for that kind of role.

After the revolution, he wrote an impassioned book called *Revolution 2.0* narrating the story of how he became an accidental activist and highlighting the role of technology in keeping governments accountable. He donated the book's $2.5 million proceeds to charity.

Ghonim represents a new generation of Egyptians, not accepting of the repression that came before them, the deal of trading silence for stability. He used his skills to organize others. But he would not have been able to organize them had there not been so many youth who were eager to respond to such calls.

I spoke with him in order to understand how he viewed the purpose of the revolution and how events had transpired since the revolution.

"In your view, what was the revolution about in Egypt?" I asked.

"I like the question about *your view*," Ghonim said, noting that the revolution was about different things to different people. "Many people went to the street wanting something that was different. I was shoulder-to-shoulder, head-to-head with someone. Their definition of freedom is my oppression, and my definition of freedom is threatening to their values," he said. Overall, he thought that the revolution was about democratic change, making government officials accountable, embarking on the right path toward the freedom of speech, freedom of press, personal freedoms, protecting minorities, and removing Mubarak who had been in power for thirty years. "All these values. That was the revolution."

"Did it achieve those goals? What did it achieve?" I asked.

"It is too early to answer. The people who are pessimistic now are equally immature about their opinion as the people who were super optimistic at the beginning. This thing was so massive that you would definitely expect change. There are good moments; there are huge struggles. This struggle is probably going to continue for a while," he said.

But a key factor to watch over time to understand the impact of the revolutions was citizen engagement, he thought. "Dictators do not want people engaged. They see running a country as their personal business. There is an exclusive group of people who are allowed to engage. My activism goal was to encourage more people to be engaged, to join the movement. There are more people engaged in activism now, invested in political ambitions, and actively involved. Hopefully they are going to put things on the right track on the long term."

"You were very optimistic at the time of the revolution, but now the pendulum in Egypt has swung the other way with counterrevolution. What did the optimists overlook?" I asked.

"For me, it was the lack of political savvyness. I was hardly politically active throughout my life, with very little background and almost no knowledge of history. Everything was new, not just to me, but also to the nonpoliticized masses who did not understand power structures or how elections could be won. In my view, it was the lack of experience that we overlooked," he said. "But that was also a blessing in the very short term during the early days of the revolution. Lack of experience motivated people to action. If you talked to experienced people back in January 2011, they would say you could never bring down Mubarak.

"Next, the wave of people who became politically interested after the revolution lacked the ability to organize and work in teams. I also think that there was a lot of overlooking of what it was about the regime that people were trying to change. Thinking that the problem was just Mubarak and a bunch of businessmen was overlooking the bigger crisis. The old regime involved many stakeholders. They were not an orchestrated group, but many organizations, not synced, but with each protecting their interests, like the judiciary, police, army, businessmen, the National Democratic Party leadership—all these are different stakeholders behind a regime. Summing things up, thinking that as soon as Mubarak goes, everything is fine, was naive." His comments reminded me of what Aykan

Erdemir in Turkey had said about removing the strongman on top. Just removing that shallow layer is not enough to create change. Societal change is a generational project.

"There was beautiful solidarity in Tahrir Square during the revolution, but that dissolved quickly afterward. Why did that happen?" I asked.

"Because it was solidarity against, and not solidarity for. At the time, no one discussed what we were going to do after Mubarak was gone. We didn't sit down and say that we are going to have a roadmap, a constitution, etcetera. At that time, everybody needed one another. What happened was a call on Facebook to protest and bring down Mubarak after Tunisia. There wasn't much dialogue about what should happen next. As soon as the big enemy Mubarak went away, the person that everyone was opposing went away, everybody wanted their interests to kick in. There wasn't political experience in Egypt, and people didn't know how to make concessions to each other, seeing concessions as defeat," he said. He also thought that the Muslim Brotherhood, as the most organized entity at that time, lost its opportunity to play a constructive role. "They were short-sighted. This led them to where they are now," he said.

After hearing similar comments from others, it made me wonder specifically what the Muslim brotherhood could have done to have created solidarity among the hopeful Egyptians. It made me sad that Sisi was not learning from its mistakes and acting as a uniter of the country.

"What happens next? How can solidarity in Egypt be rebuilt?" I asked.

"Unfortunately, I don't think this will happen soon."

His outlook was understandably bleak given the mass arrests of both liberal revolution figures as well as Muslim Brotherhood members. This is a long-term process.

Ghonim is trying to do his part to promote citizen engagement. He started a new media company based in California called Parlio, funded by Yahoo!'s Marissa Mayer and Fadi Ghandour of Aramex.

"Why is that needed?" I asked.

Ghonim started Parlio because he thought that Facebook was not set up to handle necessary debates about important issues in the world. "It gets people with confirmation biases, and creates echo chambers. We thought of a different experience. We want to make sure that the nature of conversations was thoughtful, civil, and diverse. A safe haven for conversation, soliciting ideas, understanding perspectives of people on the ground.

We are trying to be a place for informed conversations between people," he said, saying that it aspired to be the "Facebook for serious discussions."

His engaging in the daily work of civil society was similar to what Lina Attalah was doing with Mada Masr. Egypt's youth protesters were applying themselves toward building the future.

"In Egypt throughout the revolution, we didn't have enough discussions among ourselves," he concluded. "It was all broadcasting opinions rather than discussing perspectives. Few people were thinking of implications; they were dragged into action without enough thinking," he said.

He continued, "I am concerned about how we can fix things. The situation is polarized. For me, all that needs to be put aside. What we need to focus on is how can we minimize damage and how can we move forward."

As Ghonim noted, now is the time for reflection, and much reflection is taking place in the Arab world about what comes next.

From Egypt Onward

Egypt is undergoing profound change. The news coming from the country is dire, with government suppression of dissidents and a growing insurgency in the Sinai. But Egypt is beginning a process of societal evolution. There is a fundamental cultural change that occurred with Egypt's revolution—a growing sense of agency among the Egyptian people and demands for accountability from the government. That change has not yet developed into government institutions. That will take time.

What needs to happen in Egypt is a societal process of negotiating, whether through a constitution or other means, to determine how Egypt's diverse population—of whatever religion, gender, piety, age, and political persuasion—will create a place for everyone in society at the table. That was what the revolution was trying to achieve.

It has not achieved it yet, but a process of transformation has started. The process is delicate and can be fractured with the wrong moves by the Sisi government, as well as by the growing Salafist-Jihadist insurgency. But it is not too late.

CONCLUSION

I made my way through the entrance to Cairo's messy and chaotic airport, passing through crowded security lines and into the tranquility of the gates. After living out of a suitcase for about a year of travel, reading history, and conducting conversations with fascinating people, I was heading back home. Now it was time to try to make sense of what I had learned for this book.

I completed my post-Arab Spring journey through six countries of the Middle East, touring pivotal historic sites and meeting people instrumental in shaping their societies. After a journey through a region on fire and talking with revolutionaries and Islamists, youth and titans of industry, intellectuals and doers, government leaders and media watchdogs, I came away with admiration for these men and women who are forming the futures of their countries. I was humbled by the opportunity to talk with them and inspired by their courage, integrity, resourcefulness, and aspirations. They have dedicated their efforts, put their education and ideas to work, and in some cases risked their personal safety to make societal changes.

As my plane took off to return to the United States, I looked over the dusty sprawl of Cairo, with its miles of vibrant apartment blocks that hug the Nile. From this height, both physically and metaphorically, I concluded that the transformations initiated by the Arab Spring are not fully predictable, but are more actively underway than they appear when look-ing only at the daily events in the news.

With the Arab Spring, the Middle East is undergoing profound change. The Arab Spring is reshaping the order set up a century ago when the Ottoman Empire split into modern, autocratic nation-states. Mass so-cietal rejection of a government model that combined poor economic op-portunities, police disrespect for citizens, and few routes for democratic participation set the stage for the Arab Spring. The Arab Spring was an indictment of the Middle East state system and a demand for something new and constructive.

The Arab Spring was not only about revolutions, nor should the sole focus be on the protest movements between 2011 and 2013. The Arab Spring included a range of experiences over multiple years all with the goal of developing new models for societies that were not realizing their potential. The Arab Spring had multiple storylines, lessons learned, and approaches. In some countries, this meant years of increased peaceful investment in development activity. In other countries, civil protests resulted in negotiations between government and society and gradual changes. In yet other countries, governments were violently overthrown, or put down threats to their existence. And after the revolutions, some countries are mired in destructive civil wars, facing down threats to their stability, with tragic refugee crises that promise to reshape the region much as did the population movements after World War I and the end of the Ottoman Empire.

Therefore, "Arab Spring" is not the right term. The word "spring" is too simplistically merry a word for the complex changes that are under-way. And many people in the region are not Arabs. It is easy to be stuck in the baggage of the metaphor. But this is still the phrase that we have for it.

Some declare the Arab Spring over and its revolutions a failure, with counterrevolutions ranging from political to violent. The news from the Middle East after the Arab Spring is often dismal. But the reality is much more complex. It is too short a time frame to fully understand it. Pessimis-tically declaring the Arab Spring a failure in 2016 would be as naive as optimistically declaring it a success in 2011. Something comes next—but what? It will take a generation or more to fully realize its effects. Mehran Kamrava at Georgetown comes to a similar conclusion; he argues that the "ruling bargain" in the Middle East is changing with the Arab Spring, although the outcome is not yet set.[1] It is not clear yet what will emerge.

In many countries, in the wake of the protests, small, quiet, and incremental changes are taking place (even in Egypt). At the root of these changes are both a newfound sense of agency among the people of the Middle East and a wariness of the too fast change that created chaos in some countries. There are new or revised constitutions, with calls for new social contracts with pluralistic inclusion in society, accountability, and participation. Relationships between peoples with varying religious, ethnic, or national identities are being redefined. How Islam fits into governance of society is being both peacefully debated and violently fought over. Women are remodeling their roles, rights, and responsibilities. Youth are rejecting the social order of stagnation and stability to which their parents acquiesced. Business and government leaders are recognizing the need for new educational and economic models that offer merit-based opportunities.

But in other countries, borders are being challenged, and there are mass migrations of people displaced by violent conflict, inflicting untold human suffering. In some places, the Arab Spring has unleashed conflict and deepened religious, social, class-based, political, and ethnic cleavages in society. Some parts of the Middle East are unlikely to enjoy stability and prosperity for a decade or more, with civilians suffering damage to their bodies, minds, and communities that will take generations to heal.

In the six countries I chose to look at for this book, there are changes underway and challenges to the ruling bargains. Tunisia has a new constitution created through negotiation among secular and Islamist actors in society that forges consensus between liberal and Islamic values and that constrains government power. Tunisia created a new social contract for society, a potential model for other countries in the region. Its civil society leaders won the 2015 Nobel Peace Prize for these very developments. But Tunisia faces risks to its stability (with sixty tourists killed in terrorist attacks in 2015 and as the largest contributor of foreign fighters to ISIS). Turkey is a major power in the region, with a dynamic economy and a robust, albeit imperfect, democracy. Turkish citizens rejected movements toward authoritarianism through their 2013 protests and later by denying the AK Party the majority in 2015 parliamentary elections. While the AK Party later regained the parliamentary majority, the message had been sent that the government is accountable to the people. Iraq is a failed state with centrifugal forces pulling it apart, with its regions undergoing radically different experiences. With ISIS on their doorstep, the Kurdistan Region's investment in development is on pause now. ISIS has taken over big swaths of Iraq and Syria to create yet another post–Arab Spring model of governance—a violent quasi-state that is displacing people and ruling through terror. Jordan made incremental constitutional and economic changes to meet the demands of protesters, but the protesters also put on the brakes after seeing chaos in their neighbors. Qatar has been investing in Middle Eastern knowledge creation and higher education, but has done so at the expense of political participation of its people and the exploitation of its laborers. It has also funded violent factions in Arab Spring civil wars in Syria and Libya. Egyptians overthrew a military dictator, elected an incompetent president whose actions threatened to create an Islamist dictatorship, overthrew him, and elected another military authoritarian who has arrested people en masse, all the while taking steps to stimulate the economy.

What do all of these changes mean? Judgment about what the Arab Spring accomplished could perhaps best be made on the basis of the aims of the Arab Spring. Calls of the revolution were often more about economic rights, social justice, and behavior of security forces than about the freedoms of Western liberal democracy. In interviews around the region, I asked, What were you trying to achieve? I heard a range of responses. Common answers were reducing poverty, corruption, nepotism, police brutality and lack of respect, injustice, economic marginalization, and lack of economic opportunities for youth. People talked about the desire for another form of government, greater economic opportunities, and simply "a decent life." The four stated, chanted goals of protesters in Tunisia were employment, freedom, social justice, and dignity. In Egypt, they were similar—freedom, bread, social justice, and dignity. In Jordan, protest demands were mainly economic, with some demand for constitutional changes.

There is a compelling case to be made that countries across the Middle East, as a group, are not looking very democratic several years after the 2011 events. Tarek Masoud at Harvard concludes, "Arab democracy seems further away today than it has at any point in the last twenty-five years."[2]

I would propose that liberal democracy is not the only measure of the aftermath of the Arab Spring—it is one of a number of goals (political, economic, social, and legal) that could be summed up as creating a good society. We conflate the term "democracy" with a package of elements that make up a good society, and electoral democracy is but one (albeit very important) piece. There are other changes underway in Middle East countries not mired in civil wars that give cause for measured optimism in the long run: removing stagnant governments, newfound official or tacit accountability, experimentation with government models, seeking to create new social contracts through constitutions, economic stimuli, increased investment in public services, reining in the behavior of the police (or at least having public debates about their behavior), popular sentiments that freedom of speech is an irreversible right, and more.

What can we learn from other great waves of revolutions in modern history? The American Revolution, French Revolution, the "Springtime of Nations" of 1848, the Russian Revolution, and the 1989 revolutions that swept Eastern Europe and the Soviet Bloc (also named after a season, the "Autumn of Nations," or labeled various "color" and "flower" revolutions). While they unfolded in different ways, their implications often took several decades to be understood. While we can learn from history, perhaps every revolution is unique to itself.

No one can predict the future. Few would have predicted that stable autocratic governments around the region would have been toppled in a matter of months in 2011. Five years ago, few would have imagined that a medieval Islamist group would declare a caliphate, inflict brutal violence on a region's population, and take over parts of Iraq and Syria. After Egypt's 2011 revolution, few would have predicted a second revolution in 2013. What will the Middle East look like in the next few decades? We have all been surprised so far.

Out of the upheaval that was the Arab Spring, a pessimistic scenario looking forward could see continued violence and warfare, ISIS as a country, and a repressive Egypt that undergoes another revolution in a decade. But another scenario could see the Arab Spring movements over time translating ideals into institutions, building prosperous societies, with economic opportunities, quality education, pluralistic participation, and equal rights before the law regardless of identity, with citizens empowered to shape their future.

This generation will likely not witness the full results of its revolutions.

But what will happen in two decades when the generation of youth who overthrew governments because of shared ideals will have more presence in leadership roles in society? While youth protesters toppled governments or forced change, that same generation of youth will now need to determine how it will develop the gradual changes needed to support the ideals of the Arab Spring.

NOTES

Introduction

1 Kareem Fahim, "Slap to a Man's Pride Set Off Tumult in Tunisia," *The New York Times*, January 21, 2011.

2 Harvey Morris, "A Kurdish Spring on Many Fronts," *The New York Times*, March 21, 2013; David L. Phillips, *The Kurdish Spring: A New Map of the Middle East* (Transaction Publishers, 2015).

3 Doaa (al-Ahram) Khalifa, "Egypt's Slum Crisis Persists Amid Housing Abundance," *Ahram Online*, January 12, 2013.

4 World Bank, "GDP Per Capita, PPP (Current International $)," http://data.worldbank.org/indicator/NY.GDP.PCAP.PP.CD.

5 "The Economist Intelligence Unit's Quality-of-Life Index," *The Economist*, November 21, 2004, www.economist.com/media/pdf/QUALITY_OF_LIFE.pdf.

6 This section is based on William L. Cleveland and Martin Bunton, *A History of the Modern Middle East*, 5th ed. (Westview Press, 2012); David Fromkin, *A Peace to End All Peace: The Fall of the Ottoman Empire and the Creation of the Modern Middle East* (Holt Paperbacks, 2010); Albert Hourani and Malise Ruthven, *A History of the Arab Peoples* (Belknap Press, 2010); Ira M. Lapidus, *A History of Islamic Societies*, 3rd ed. (Cambridge University Press, 2014).

7 Stephen Howe, *Empire: A Very Short Introduction* (Oxford University Press, 2002), Chapter 2.

8 Valery A. Tishkov, "Forget the 'Nation': Post-Nationalist Understanding of Nationalism," *Ethnic and Racial Studies* 23, no. 4 (2000).

9 Khaled Abou el Fadl, *The Great Theft: Wrestling Islam from the Extremists* (Harper San Francisco, 2005), p. 18.

10 World Bank, "Opening Doors: Gender Equality and Development in the Middle East and North Africa," The World Bank: MENA Development Report, 2013; Sanja Kelly and Julian Breslin, eds., *Women's Rights in the Middle East and North Africa: Progress Amid Resistance* (Freedom House, 2010).

11 Trading Economics, "Employment to Population Ratio—15+-Female (percent) in Middle East and North Africa," www.tradingeconomics.com/middle-east-and-north-africa/employment-to-population-ratio-15-plus—female-percent-wb-data.html.

12 World Health Organization, "Prevalence of Female Genital Cutting among Egyptian Girls," *Bulletin of the World Health Organization* 86, no. 4 (2008).

13   Ina V. S. Mullis et al., "PIRLS 2011 International Results in Reading," TIMSS & PIRLS International Study Center, 2012.

14   Hassan M. Fattah, "Kuwait Grants Political Rights to Its Women," *The New York Times*, May 17, 2005.

15   Jules Cretois, "Muslim Women Redefine Feminism," *Al-Monitor*, April 4, 2013.

16   Ragui Assaad and Farzaneh Roudi-Fahimi, "Youth in the Middle East and North Africa: Demographic Opportunity or Challenge?," Population Reference Bureau, 2007.

17   Justin Yifu Lin, "Youth Bulge: A Demographic Dividend or a Demographic Bomb in Developing Countries?," The World Bank, http://blogs.worldbank.org/developmenttalk/youth-bulge-a-demographic-dividend-or-a-demographic-bomb-in-developing-countries.

18   World Economic Forum, "Global Agenda Councils—Youth Unemployment Visualization 2013," www.weforum.org/community/global-agenda-councils/youth-unemployment-visualization-2013.

19   World Bank, "The Road Not Traveled: Education Reform in the Middle East and North Africa," The World Bank: MENA Development Report, https://openknowledge.worldbank.org/handle/10986/6303.

20   Shanghai Ranking, "Academic Ranking of World Universities 2014," www.shanghairanking.com/ARWU2014.html.

Tunisia

1   "Tunisia's Ben Ali Appears in First Photos since His Overthrow," *Al Arabiya News*, August 28, 2013.

2   "Hope Springs," *The Economist*, December 20, 2014.

3   "Tunisia Wins Again," *The New York Times*, December 25, 2014.

4   Michael J. Willis, *Politics and Power in the Maghreb: Algeria, Tunisia and Morocco from Independence to the Arab Spring* (Columbia University Press, 2012); Kenneth J. Perkins, *A History of Modern Tunisia*, 2nd ed. (Cambridge University Press, 2013).

5   Brian Klaas, "The Long Shadow of Ben Ali: How a Decades-Old Fake Coup Attempt Is Taking Its Toll on Tunisia," *Foreign Policy*, December 17, 2013; "Amnesty Urges Justice for Tunisians Tortured under Ben Ali," www.globalpost.com/dispatch/news/afp/131008/amnesty-urges-justice-tunisians-tortured-under-ben-ali.

6   Sudarsan Raghavan, "In Tunisia, Luxurious Lifestyles of a Corrupt Government," *The Washington Post*, January 28, 2011.

7   World Bank, "New World Bank Study Details Manipulation of Regulations by Former Tunisian Regime Officials," www.worldbank.org/en/news/press-release/2014/03/27/world-bank-manipulation-former-tunisian-officials.

8   Elizabeth Dickinson, "The First Wikileaks Revolution?," *Foreign Policy*, January 13, 2011.

9   Marc Fisher, "In Tunisia, Act of One Fruit Vendor Sparks Wave of Revolution through Arab World," *The Washington Post*, March 26, 2011.

10   Rachid Khechana, "Tunisia's Democratic Revolution and Its Uncertain Future," Aspenia Online, December 2, 2013.

11   Bouazza Ben Bouazza and Paul Schemm, "Second Tunisia Assassination Could Spell End to Islamist Government," *The Washington Post*, July 26, 2013.

12   Rick Gladstone, "Anti-American Protests Flare Beyond the Mideast," *The New York Times*, September 14, 2012.

13   David D. Kirkpatrick, "New Freedoms in Tunisia Drive Support for ISIS," *The New York Times*, October 21, 2014.

14   "President Essebsi, a Lifetime in Tunisia Politics," *euronews*, December 22, 2014.

15   Ines Oueslati, "How Nidaa Tunis Won the Elections," *Al-Monitor*, October 29, 2014.

16   Lina Ben Mhenni, "A Tunisian Girl," http://atunisiangirl.blogspot.com/.

17   "Protesters Killed in Tunisia Riots," Al Jazeera, January 9, 2011.

18 "Lina Ben Mhenni," *The Guardian,* 2015.

19 "Revolution," *CNN,* January 22, 2014; "Tunisian Elections: Beware, Beware, My Hunger and My Anger," *The Guardian,* October 22, 2011.

20 Rania Said, "Djerba, Tunisia: Garbage Disposal, the Environmental Crisis, and the Awakening of Ecoconsciousness," *Jadaliyya,* September 1, 2014.

21 Tunisia Live, "Salma Rekik: Leader Party of Nahdtha," www.tunisia-live.net/whoswho /salma-rekik/.

22 Carlotta Gall, "Secularist Win Is Confirmed in Tunisia," *The New York Times,* October 30, 2014.

23 "Tunisia: High Rate of Unemployment among Youth and Women," *Tunis Times,* May 25, 2014.

24 World Bank, "The Unfinished Revolution: Bringing Opportunity, Good Jobs and Greater Wealth to All Tunisians," www.worldbank.org/en/country/tunisia/publication/unfinished -revolution.

25 "Tunisian President Says Country 'in a State of War,'" Al Jazeera, July 5, 2015.

26 Virgil, *The Aeneid* (Penguin Classics, 2008), 14.

27 Discussion of Carthage's history is based upon explanations in the Carthage National Museum and Bardo National Museum, as well as in Richard Miles, *Carthage Must Be Destroyed: The Rise and Fall of an Ancient Civilization* (Penguin Books, 2011) and A&E Television Networks, "History—Engineering an Empire: Carthage" (2008).

28 Lonely Planet, "Best Value Destinations for 2015," www.lonelyplanet.com/travel-tips-and -articles/best-value-destinations-for-2015.

29 "Tunisia Finmin Says Next Govt Needs to Revive Privatisation," *Reuters,* October 18, 2011.

30 Observatory of Economic Complexity, "Learn More About Trade in Tunisia," http://atlas .media.mit.edu/profile/country/tun/.

31 Roland Oliver, J. D. Fage, and G. N. Sanderson, *The Cambridge History of Africa,* vol. 6 (Cambridge University Press, 1985), 180.

32 Discussion of colonialism in Tunisia is based upon: Willis, *Politics and Power in the Maghreb,* and Perkins, *A History of Modern Tunisia.*

33 Ali Ben Mabrouk, "Reflecting on Bourguiba, 13 Years after His Death," *Tunisia Live,* April 9, 2013; "In the Shade of Bourguiba," *The Economist,* November 4, 2014.

34 "Habib Bourguiba: Father of Tunisia," BBC News, April 6, 2000.

35 Albert Memmi, *The Colonizer and the Colonized* (Beacon Press, 1991), 23.

36 Leaders, "Kamal Samari," www.leaders.com.tn/article/kamal-samari?id=6264.

37 Anthony Shadid, "Islamists' Ideas on Democracy and Faith Face Test in Tunisia," *The New York Times,* February 17, 2012.

38 Ibid.

39 Lally Weymouth, "An Interview with Tunisia's Rachid Ghannouchi, Three Years after the Revolution," *The Washington Post,* December 12, 2013.

40 Willis, *Politics and Power in the Maghreb*; Perkins, *A History of Modern Tunisia.*

41 Abby Ohlheiser, "The Associated Press's New Definition of 'Islamist,'" *Slate,* www.slate.com /blogs/the_slatest/2013/04/05/_islamist_definition_changed_in_the_ap_stylebook_two _days_after_illegal.html.

42 Nazanine Moshiri, "Interview with Rachid Ghannouchi," Al Jazeera, February 7, 2011.

43 Bobby Ghosh, "Time 100: The List: Rached Ghannouchi, Politician," *Time,* April 18, 2012.

44 Mary Beth Sheridan, "In Birthplace of Arab Spring, Tunisia's Islamists Get Sobering Lesson in Governing," *The Washington Post,* November 21, 2014.

45 Barbara Slavin, "Tunisians Lose Faith in Ennahda, Revolution," *Al-Monitor,* September 30, 2013.

46 Ira M. Lapidus, *A History of Islamic Societies,* 2nd ed. (Cambridge University Press, 2002), p. 290; Hourani and Ruthven, *A History of the Arab Peoples,* 1–10.

47 Willis, *Politics and Power in the Maghreb,* 74–75; Perkins, *A History of Modern Tunisia,* 140–145.

48   Willis, *Politics and Power in the Maghreb.*

49   Joseph Croitoru, "The Ambivalent Revival of Islamic Traditions," *Qantara,* 2012, http://en.qantara.de/content/controversy-surrounding-the-al-zaytuna-mosque-in-tunis -the-ambivalent-revival-of-islamic.

50   Amina al-Zayani, "Zaytuna Mosque Maintains Its Social, Political Role in Tunisia," *Al-Monitor,* February 25, 2014.

51   Tom Heneghan, "Ambiguous Religion Policy Backfires on Tunisia's Ruling Islamists," *Reuters,* September 3, 2013.

52   Draft of the Constitution of the Republic of Tunisia, 2012, www.constitutionnet.org/files /2012.08.14_-_draft_constitution_english.pdf.

53   Monica Marks, "'Complementary' Status for Tunisian Women," *Foreign Policy,* August 20, 2012; "Tunisian Women Protest to Demand Equality," BBC News, August 14, 2012; S. T. McNeil, "Wording on Women Sparks Protest in Tunisia," Al Jazeera, August 19, 2012.

54   Mounira M. Charrad and Amina Zarrugh, "The Arab Spring and Women's Rights in Tu-nisia," E-International Relations, www.e-ir.info/2013/09/04/the-arab-spring-and-womens -rights-in-tunisia/; Mounira M. Charrad, "Family Law Reforms in the Arab World: Tunisia and Morocco," 2012, www.un.org/esa/socdev/family/docs/egm12/PAPER-CHARRAD .pdf.

55   Borzou Daragahi, "Term Used for Women in Tunisia's Draft Constitution Ignites Debate, Protests," *The Washington Post,* August 16, 2012.

56   UNICEF, "Tunisia: MENA Gender Equality Profile: Status of Girls and Women in the Middle East and North Africa," 2011, www.unicef.org/gender/files/Tunisia-Gender-Eqaulity -Profile-2011.pdf.

57   Lamia Ben Youssef Zayzafoon, *The Production of the Muslim Woman: Negotiating Text, His-tory, and Ideology* (Lexington Books, 2005); Erik Churchill, "Tahar Haddad: A Towering Figure for Women's Rights in Tunisia," The World Bank, 2013.

58   Richard H. Curtiss, "Women's Rights an Affair of State for Tunisia," Washington Report on Middle East Affairs, 1993.

59   Kelly and Breslin, *Women's Rights in the Middle East and North Africa.*

60   UNICEF, "Tunisia: MENA Gender Equality Profile: Status of Girls and Women in the Middle East and North Africa."

61   World Bank, "Proportion of Seats Held by Women in National Parliaments (%)," http:// data.worldbank.org/indicator/SG.GEN.PARL.ZS.

62   Naveena Kottoor, "Tunisia's Ennahda and Ettakattol Women Mps Celebrate," BBC News, January 28, 2014.

63   Eileen Byrne, "The Women MPs Tipped to Play Leading Roles in Tunisia's New Assem-bly," *The Guardian,* October 28, 2011.

64   Isobel Coleman, *Paradise beneath Her Feet: How Women Are Transforming the Middle East* (Random House, 2013), p. xxxii.

65   Mounira M. Charrad and Amina Zarrugh, "Equal or Complementary? Women in the New Tunisian Constitution after the Arab Spring," *The Journal of North African Studies* 19, no. 2 (2014).

66   Constitution of the Tunisian Republic, 2014, www.jasmine-foundation.org/doc/unofficial _english_translation_of_tunisian_constitution_final_ed.pdf.

67   Asma Smadhi and Robert Joyce, "We Are a Model, We Are an Example,' Assembly Mem bers React to Constitution Vote," *Tunisia Live,* January 28, 2014.

68   Albert Hourani, *Arabic Thought in the Liberal Age, 1798–1939* (Cambridge University Press, 1983), Chapter 4.

69   Michael Snyder, "Tunisia's New Constitution: An Eleventh-Hour Victory for Press Free-dom" (Freedom House, 2014), https://freedomhouse.org/blog/tunisia-new-constitution -eleventh-hour-victory-press-freedom#.Vcf3QK2Yog4.

70   "The Best and Worst of Tunisia's New Constitution," *Al-Monitor,* January 29, 2014.

71   "Tunisian Politician Mohamed Brahmi Assassinated," BBC News, July 25, 2013.

72   Constitution of the Tunisian Republic.

73   Charles J. Adams, "Mawdudi and the Islamic State," in *Voices of Islamic Resurgence*, ed. John
      Esposito (1983), Oxford University Press; Abou el Fadl, *The Great Theft : Wrestling Islam
      from the Extremists* (Harper San Francisco, 2005), 82.

74   Zaid al-Ali and Donia Ben Romdhane, "Tunisia's New Consititution: Progress and Chal-
      lenges to Come," openDemocracy, https://www.opendemocracy.net/arab-awakening
      /zaid-al-ali-donia-ben-romdhane/tunisia%E2%80%99s-new-constitution-progress-and
      -challenges-to-.

75   Mehdi Hasan, "Mehdi Hasan Talks to Tunisian Politician Mehrezia Labidi on Gender, De-
      mocracy and the Arab Spring," *New Statesman*, April 18, 2012.

76   Yetkin Yildirim, "Peace and Conflict Resolution in the Medina Charter," *Peace Review* 18,
      no. 1 (2006).

Turkey

1   WorldAtlas, "Largest Cities of the World (by Metro Population)," WorldAtlas, www
      .worldatlas.com/citypops.htm.

2   Judith Herrin, *Byzantium: The Surprising Life of a Medieval Empire* (Penguin UK, 2008),
      9–15.

3   For additional interviews with Korhan Gümüş, see "How Mosques and Other New Build-
      ings May Damage One of Europe's Finest Cities," *The Economist*, December 1, 2012; Bar-
      çin Yinanç, "Taksim Is a Site of Struggle for Ideological Predominance," *Hurriyet Daily
      News*, June 3, 2013; Constanze Letsch, "Istanbul Sees History Razed in the Name of
      Regeneration," *The Guardian*, March 1, 2012.

4   "The Media in Crisis," Freedom House, www.freedomhouse.org/report/democracy-crisis
      -corruption-media-and-power-turkey/media-crisis#.U-9Orkjq9QY.

5   Daniel Steinvorth and Bernhard Zand, "A Country Divided: Where Is Turkey Headed?,"
      June 24, 2013, www.spiegel.de/international/world/protests-reveal-the-deep-divisions
      -in-turkish-society-a-907498.html.

6   Discussion of Turkey's politics in recent decades is based on: Soner Cagaptay, *The Rise of
      Turkey: The Twenty-First Century's First Muslim Power* (Potomac Books, 2014); Stephen
      Kinzer, *Crescent and Star: Turkey Between Two Worlds* (Macmillan, 2008).

7   David A. Graham, "Turkish President Erdogan's Triple Defeat," *The Atlantic*, June 7, 2015.

8   Max Fisher, "The Photo That Encapsulates Turkey's Protests and the Severe Police Crack-
      down," *The Washington Post*, June 3, 2013.

9   AFP, "'Chapulling': Turkish Protesters Spread the Edgy Word," *The Express Tribune*, June
      8, 2013.

10   See Brandon Jourdan, "Taksim Commune: Gezi Park and the Uprising in Turkey," You-
      Tube, August 8, 2013; Özcan Tekdemir, "Taksim Gezi Parkı Belgeseli (Documentary),"
      YouTube, June 4, 2013.

11   "Gezi Park Protests: Brutal Denial of the Right to Peaceful Assembly in Turkey," Amnesty
      International, 2013, www.amnesty.org/en/library/asset/EUR44/022/2013/en/0ba8c4cc
      -b059-4b88-9c52-8fbd652c6766/eur440222013en.pdf.

12   Stratfor (Strategic Forecasting), "No Arab Spring: Turkey's Violent Protests in Context,"
      Forbes, June 3, 2013.

13   Constanze Letsch, "A Year after the Protests, Gezi Park Nurtures the Seeds of a New Tur-
      key," *The Guardian*, May 29, 2014.

14   Discussion of the history of the Ottoman Empire is based on Caroline Finkel, *Osman's
      Dream: The History of the Ottoman Empire* (Basic Books, 2007); Jason Goodwin, *Lords of
      the Horizons: A History of the Ottoman Empire* (Random House, 2011); Patrick Balfour
      Kinross, *The Ottoman Centuries: The Rise and Fall of the Turkish Empire* (Cape, 1977);
      Philip Mansel, *Constantinople, City of the World's Desire, 1453–1924* (John Murray, 2006).

15   Herrin, *Byzantium,* 16–18.

16   Ibid.; Mansel, *Constantinople,* Chapter 1.

17   Jim Bradbury, *The Routledge Companion to Medieval Warfare* (Routledge, 2004)., 68; Mansel, *Constantinople,* Chapter 1.

18   G. F. Haddad, "Conquest of Constantinople," Sunnah, www.sunnah.org/msaec/articles /Constantinople.htm.

19   Chase F. Robinson, "The Caliph Has No Clothes," *The New York Times,* July 16, 2014.

20   Walter Cronkite, "The Incredible Turk," (PublicResourceOrg, 1958); Can Dündar, *Mustafa* (Warner Bros., 2008).

21   Mike Dash, "The Ottoman Empire's Life-or-Death Race," *Smithsonian,* March 22, 2012.

22   Peter Hart, *The Great War: A Combat History of the First World War* (Oxford University Press, 2013), 77; Niamh Foster, "Islam and the Great War," undated, http://islamandthegreatwar .umwblogs.org/british-documentary-the-ottoman-empire-in-world-war-i/.

23   Orhan Pamuk, *Istanbul* (Random House, 2006), 109.

24   Cagaptay, *The Rise of Turkey,* 15.

25   "Buildings in Levent," Emporis www.emporis.com/zone/levent-istanbul.

26   World Bank, "GDP (Current US$)," http://data.worldbank.org/indicator/NY.GDP.MKTP .CD.

27   "Women in the United States Congress, 1917–2014: Biographical and Committee Assignment Information, and Listings by State and Congress," Washington, DC: Congressional Research Service, 2014; "GDP Growth (Annual %)," http://data.worldbank.org /indicator/NY.GDP.MKTP.KD.ZG.

28   "Country and Lending Groups," http://data.worldbank.org/about/country-and-lending -groups.; "GDP Per Capita (Current US$): 1999–2003," http://data.worldbank.org /indicator/NY.GDP.PCAP.CD?page=2&order=wbapi_data_value_2009%20wbapi_ data_value%20wbapi_data_value-first&sort=asc.

29   Claire Obusan, "Cost of Living Large," *Forbes,* March 11, 2010.

30   Yilmaz Akyüz and Korkut Boratav, "The Making of the Turkish Financial Crisis," United Nations Conference on Trade and Development (UNCTAD), 2002.

31   Daniel Dombey, "Six Markets to Watch: Turkey: How Erdogan Did It—and Could Blow It," *Foreign Affairs,* January/February 2014.

32   Jesse Colombo, "Why the Worst Is Still Ahead for Turkey's Bubble Economy," *Forbes,* March 5, 2014.

33   Tim Arango, "Corruption Scandal Is Edging Near Turkish Premier," *The New York Times,* December 25, 2013.

34   OECD, "PISA 2012 Results in Focus," 2014, www.oecd.org/pisa/keyfindings/pisa-2012 -results-overview.pdf.

35   "Part 2: Country Profiles: The Global Gender Gap Report," (World Economic Forum, 2013).

36   Elana Beiser, "Second Worst Year on Record for Jailed Journalists," New York: Committee to Protect Journalists, 2013.

37   Susan Corke et al., "Democracy in Crisis: Corruption, Media, and Power in Turkey," Freedom House, 2014, www.freedomhouse.org/sites/default/files/Turkey%20Report%20 -%202-3-14.pdf.

38   Reporters Without Borders, "2015 World Press Freedom Index," https://index.rsf.org/#!/.

39   "Turkey's Biggest Media Group Gets a Colossal Tax Fine," *The Economist,* September 10, 2009.

40   Benjamin Harvey, "Dogan Rises as Erdogan Photo Op Signals Better Relations," *Bloomberg Businessweek,* April 20, 2012.

41   Yeginsu, Ceylan, "Opposition Journalists under Assault in Turkey," *The New York Times,* September 17, 2015. www.nytimes.com/2015/09/18/world/europe/opposition-journalists -in-turkey-increasingly-face-violent-attacks.html.

42   Documentaries about the battle of Gallipoli include: Kurt Ulus, "Çanakkale (Gallipoli)

1915," YouTube, December 8, 2013; news2youmedia, "The Gallipoli Catastrophe Documentary," YouTube, August 16, 2013; "Gallipoli: The Untold Stories (WWI Documentary)," YouTube, April 1, 2014. For descriptions of the strategy and battle see: David Fromkin, *A Peace to End All Peace: The Fall of the Ottoman Empire and the Creation of the Modern Middle East* (Holt, 2009); John Keegan, *The First World War* (Knopf, 1999); Barbara W. Tuchman, *The Guns of August* (Macmillan, 1962).

43   Department of Veterans Affairs, "The Gallipoli Campaign," Australian Government, http://web.archive.org/web/20130313050857/www.dva.gov.au/news_archive/Documents/The%20Gallipoli%20Campaign.pdf.

44   Discussion of battle strategy relied on Muharebe Alanlari and Gezi Rehberi, *Gallipoli Battlefield Guide* (MB books, 2005).

45   Henry Kissinger, *Diplomacy* (Simon & Schuster, 1995); G. John Ikenberry, *After Victory: Institutions, Strategic Restraint, and the Rebuilding of Order after Major Wars* (Princeton University Press, 2000), Chapter 1.

46   Fromkin, *A Peace to End All Peace,* Chapter 1.

47   Kemal H. Karpat, *Studies on Ottoman Social and Political History: Selected Articles and Essays,* vol. 81 (Brill, 2002), 766; "Demographics of the Ottoman Empire," Wikipedia, http://en.wikipedia.org/wiki/Demographics_of_the_Ottoman_Empire; Stanford Jay Shaw, *History of the Ottoman Empire and Modern Turkey* (Cambridge University Press), 241.

48   Justin McCarthy, *The Ottoman Peoples and the End of Empire* (Bloomsbury Academic, 2001), 86.

49   Matthew J. Gibney and Randall Hansen, *Immigration and Asylum: From 1900 to the Present,* vol. 3 (ABC-CLIO, 2005); Renée Hirschon, *Crossing the Aegean: An Appraisal of the 1923 Compulsory Population Exchange between Greece and Turkey* (Berghahn Books, 2003), 85.

50   G. W. Prothero, *Anatolia* (H.M. Stationery Office, 1920), 62–63.

51   "Bill Clinton's Statement Concerning Ataturk: Address to the International Trade Organization," Helenic Resources Net, www.hri.org/news/turkey/trkpr/2000/00-01-05.trkpr.html.

52   John F. Kennedy, "Message to the Turkish People on the Occasion of 25th Anniversary of the Death of Mustafa Kemal Ataturk," http://upload.wikimedia.org/wikipedia/commons/c/ce/JFKennedy_on_Ataturk_1963.pdf.

53   "World Leaders and Press Pay Tribute to Ataturk," Ataturk Today, www.ataturktoday.com/AtaturkWorldPressLeadersTribute.htm.

54   Background in this section is based on Patrick Balfour Kinross, Baron, *Atatürk: The Rebirth of a Nation* (Weidenfeld and Nicolson, 1964); Andrew Mango, *Ataturk: The Biography of the Founder of Modern Turkey* (Overlook TP, 2002); Dündar, "Mustafa" (Warner Bros, 2008); Walter Cronkite, "The Incredible Turk." (PublicResourceOrg, 1958); Tolga Levent, "Mustafa Kemal Ataturk Documentary English," (Turkey, 2013).

55   Soner Cagaptay, "After Erdogan, Turkey's Future Will Be Liberal," *The New York Times,* August 14, 2014; Kinzer, *Crescent and Star*; Peter Kenyon, "Turkey's AK Party Still Defies Easy Categorization," NPR, January 3, 2013.

56   "Profile: Recep Tayyip Erdogan," BBC News Europe, August 11, 2014; Steven A. Cook, "Keep Calm, Erdogan," *Foreign Affairs,* June 3, 2013; "Recep Tayyip Erdoğan: Prime Minister of the Republic of Turkey," Columbia University, www.worldleaders.columbia.edu/participants/recep-tayyip-erdoğ.

57   "Erdogan Goes to Prison," *Hürriyet Daily News,* March 27, 1999.

58   Kinzer, *Crescent and Star,* Chapter 1.

59   Cagaptay, "After Erdogan, Turkey's Future Will Be Liberal."

60   "Turkish Journalist Sues Police over Protest Arrest," *The Washington Times,* November 11, 2014.

61   Mustafa Akyol, "Will Turkey's CHP Reconcile with Islam?," *Al-Monitor,* September 7, 2014.

62 "Recep Tayyip Erdoğan: 'Women Not Equal to Men,'" *The Guardian,* November 24, 2014.

63 Christiane Gruber, "The Visual Emergence of the Occupy Gezi Movement, Part Three: Democracy's Workshop," *Jadaliyya,* July 8, 2013.

64 Manning and Brudnick, "Women in the United States Congress, 1917–2014: Biographical and Committee Assignment Information, and Listings by State and Congress," (Congressional Research Service, 2014).

65 Soner Cagaptay and Rüya Perincek, "No Women, No Europe," *Hürriyet Daily News,* January 20, 2010.

66 "12 Percent of Turkish CEOs Are Women: World Bank," *Hürriyet Daily News,* February 11, 2012; Kelly Wallace, "No Movement for Women at the Top in Corporate America," CNN, http://edition.cnn.com/2013/12/11/living/no-change-on-women-board-seats-parents/.

67 Janine Zacharia, "Turkey Hopes to Grow Economic Ties and Influence within Middle East," *The Washington Post,* April 8, 2010; Dan Bilefsky, "Syrians' New Ardor for a Turkey Looking Eastward," *The New York Times,* July 24, 2010.

68 "Population Censuses," Turkish Statistical Institute, www.turkstat.gov.tr/PreTablo.do?alt_id=1047; Gaziantep Chamber of Industry, "Statistics," www.gso.org.tr/english/default.asp?syf=industry.

69 Roy Gutman, "Syrian Opposition Plan to Oust Islamist Extremists Awaits U.S. Hearing," *Miami Herald,* July 12, 2014.

70 David McDowall, *A Modern History of the Kurds,* 3rd ed. (I. B. Tauris, 2004), Chapters 6–7; Ali A. Allawi, *Faisal I of Iraq* (Yale University Press, 2014), 415–461.

71 David W. Lesch, "A Path to Peace in Syria," *Foreign Policy,* July 2, 2014.

72 Liz Sly, "New U.S. Help Arrives for Syrian Rebels as Government, Extremists Gain," *The Washington Post,* July 27, 2014.

73 Nick Cumming-Bruce, "Syrian Refugees Surpass 3 Million, U.N. Says," *The New York Times,* August 29, 2014.

74 OCHA, "Syria Crisis: Situation Overview," http://syria.unocha.org/.

75 "Syria Regional Refugee Response: Turkey," United Nations High Commissioner for Refugees (UNHCR), http://data.unhcr.org/syrianrefugees/country.php?id=224; "Syrian Refugees Get to Work in Turkey," *Al-Monitor,* July 22, 2014.

76 Semih Idiz, "Turkey's Syrian Refugee Problem Spirals out of Control," *Al-Monitor,* July 20, 2014, www.al-monitor.com/pulse/originals/2014/07/idiz-turkey-syrian-refugees-local-tension-adana-istanbul.html#; "Gaziantep City," Ministry of Tourism, http://gaziantepcity.info/en/home; "One out of 10 People in Gaziantep Is Syrian," *Today's Zaman,* February 16, 2014.

77 "Turkey's Syrian Refugee Problem Spirals Out of Control."

78 Mac McClelland, "How to Build a Perfect Refugee Camp," *The New York Times,* February 13, 2014.

79 Aaron Stein, "Turkey's Evolving Syria Strategy," *Foreign Affairs,* February 9, 2015.

80 Rebecca Collard, "Why Turkey Has Finally Declared War on ISIS," *Time,* July 24, 2015.

81 Martin Chulov, "Ascendant Kurds Emerge from Syrian Civil War as Major Power Player," *The Guardian,* August 1, 2015.

82 Ian Bremmer, "These 5 Stats Explain Turkey's War on ISIS—and the Kurds," *Time,* July 31, 2015.

Iraq

1 Georges Vernez, Shelly Culbertson, and Louay Constant, *Strategic Priorities for Improving Access to Quality Education in the Kurdistan Region—Iraq* (RAND Corporation, 2014); Louay Constant et al., *Improving Technical Vocational Education and Training in the Kurdistan Region—Iraq* (RAND Corporation, 2014).

2   "Erbil International Airport Growing by 50% in 2012; Mahan Air, Qatar Airways and Transavia.Com New This Year," *Anna.Aero,* June 13, 2012, www.anna.aero/2012/06/13 /erbil-international-airport-growing-by-50pc-in-2012/.

3   Jon Harper, "Obama Doubling US Troop Levels in Iraq," *Stars and Stripes,* November 7, 2014.

4   Kenneth T. Walsh, "Obama Fulfills Campaign Promise in Declaring Iraq War Over," *U.S. News & World Report,* October 21, 2011.

5   Steve Hopkins, "Full Horror of the Yazidis Who Didn't Escape Mount Sinjar," *Daily Mail,* October 14, 2014.

6   Renad Mansour, "How the Kurds Helped Draw the United States Back into Iraq," Carnegie Middle East Center, 2015, http://carnegie-mec.org/2015/06/29/how-kurds-helped-draw -united-states-back-to-iraq/ib65.

7   Harper, "Obama Doubling US Troop Levels in Iraq."

8   Erbil Tourism, "History of Erbil," www.erbiltourism2014.com/en/erbil/history.

9   Thomas L. Friedman, "Iraq's Best Hope," *The New York Times,* June 3, 2014.

10   "Timeline: Invasion, Surge, Withdrawal; U.S. Forces in Iraq," *Reuters,* December 15, 2011; Tim Arango and Michael S. Schmidt, "Last Convoy of American Troops Leaves Iraq," *The New York Times,* December 18, 2011.

11   "Iraq Body Count," Iraq Body Count Project, https://www.iraqbodycount.org/.

12   Catherine Lutz, "US and Coalition Casualties in Iraq and Afghanistan," Watson Institute for International Studies, Brown University, 2013, http://watson.brown.edu/costsofwar/files /cow/imce/papers/2013/USandCoalition.pdf.

13   Amy Belasco, "The Cost of Iraq, Afghanistan, and Other Global War on Terror Operations since 9/11" (Congressional Research Service, 2014).

14   Terri Tanielian et al., *Invisible Wounds of War: Psychological and Cognitive Injuries, Their Consequences, and Services to Assist Recovery* (RAND Corporation, 2008).

15   David S. Cloud and Brian Bennett, "U.S., Allies Rush Heavy Weapons to Kurds to Fight Militants in Iraq," *Los Angeles Times,* August 11, 2014.

16   "Iraq IDP Figures Analysis," Internal Displacement Monitoring Centre (IDMC), www .internal-displacement.org/middle-east-and-north-africa/iraq/figures-analysis.

17   UNHCR, "2015 Unhcr Country Operations Profile-Iraq," United Nations High Commissioner for Refugees (UNHCR), www.unhcr.org/pages/49e486426.html.

18   Sarah El-Rashidi, "Iraq's 2 Million IDPs Struggling," *Iraq Pulse,* December 30, 2014.

19   Ed Butler, "Iraqi Kurdistan's Battle with Baghdad over Oil Revenues," BBC News, April 10, 2015.

20   World Bank, "The Kurdistan Region of Iraq Needs an Estimated US$1.4 Billion This Year to Stabilize the Economy," www.worldbank.org/en/news/press-release/2015/02/12 /kurdistan-region-iraq-stabilize-economy.

21   Butler, "Iraqi Kurdistan's Battle with Baghdad over Oil Revenues."

22   "Oil Prices Volatile after Opec Maintains Output Level," BBC News, June 5, 2015.

23   Nicky Woolf, "Is Kurdistan the Next Dubai?," *The Guardian,* May 5, 2010; "Kurdistan— the Other Iraq," www.theotheriraq.com.

24   Armando Cordoba, "Premier Barzani: 'Downtown Erbil' a 'Milestone' for Kurdistan," *Rudaw,* October 28, 2013.

25   "Kurdistan Region of Iraq 2020: A Vision for the Future," Ministry of Planning, Kurdistan Regional Government, 2013.

26   "ISIS Claims Deadly Erbil Car Bomb Attack," *Al Arabiya News,* April 17, 2015.

27   UNESCO Office for Iraq, "Revitalization Project of Erbil Citadel," www.unesco.org/new /en/iraq-office/culture/erbil-citadel/.

28   Erbil Tourism, "History of Erbil."

29   UNESCO, "Erbil Citadel," http://whc.unesco.org/en/list/1437.

30   Kathryn Slanski, "A City That Goes Way, Way Back," *NPR,* February 4, 2007.

31   Matthew E. Falagas, Effie A. Zarkadoulia, and George Samonis, "Arab Science in the
      Golden Age (750–1258 CE) and Today," *Journal of the Federation of American Societies for
      Experimental Biology* 20, no. 10 (2006).

32   Charles Tripp, *A History of Iraq*, 3rd ed. (Cambridge University Press, 2007); Phebe Marr,
      The Modern History of Iraq, 3rd ed. (Westview Press, 2011).

33   *Authorization for Use of Military Force against Iraq Resolution of 2002*, Public Law 107–243,
      107th Congress.

34   Tripp, *A History of Iraq*; Marr, *The Modern History of Iraq*; Ned Parker, "The Iraq We Left
      Behind," *Foreign Affairs,* March/April 2012; Norma Percy, "Part One: The Iraq War, Epi-
      sode 1 of 3," BBC World Service, September 18, 2013; *Frontline*, "Losing Iraq," July 29,
      2014.

35   McDowall, *A Modern History of the Kurds,* xi; Phillips, *The Kurdish Spring,* Chapter 1.

36   Phillips, *The Kurdish Spring,* Chapter 1.

37   Ceylan Yeginsu, "Turkey Attacks Kurdish Militant Camps in Northern Iraq," *The New York
      Times,* July 25, 2015.

38   Susan F. Kinsley, "Whatever Happened to the Iraqi Kurds?," *News from Middle East Watch,*
      March 11, 1991; "Introduction : Genocide in Iraq: The Anfal Campaign against the
      Kurds," Human Rights Watch, www.hrw.org/reports/1993/iraqanfal/ANFALINT.htm;
      Marr, *The Modern History of Iraq*; George Black, *Genocide in Iraq: The Anfal Campaign
      against the Kurds (Middle East Watch Report),* Human Rights Watch, 1993; McDowall, *A
      Modern History of the Kurds,* 366, 428; Human Rights Watch/Middle East, *Iraq's Crime of
      Genocide: The Anfal Campaign against the Kurds,* Human Rights Watch, 1994.

39   Yaroslav Trofimov, "The State of the Kurds," *The Wall Street Journal,* June 19, 2015.

40   "Iraqi Kurds Mark 25 Years since Halabja Gas Attack," BBC News, March 16, 2013;
      "1988: Thousands Die in Halabja Gas Attack," BBC News, March 16, 2008; Tripp, *A His-
      tory of Iraq.*

41   MEMRI-TV, "Iraqi MP Breaks Down in Tears Pleading Parliament to Save Yazidis from
      Genocide," August 5, 2014.

42   Robert Mackey, "Iraqi Who Made Emotional Plea to Help Yazidis Is Injured in Crash of
      Relief Flight," *The New York Times,* August 12, 2014.

43   "Who, What, Why: Who Are the Yazidis?," BBC News, August 8, 2014.

44   "Iraq: ISIS Escapees Describe Systematic Rape," *Human Rights Watch,* 2015.

45   "Response to the IDP Crisis in Iraq-2015," International Organization for Migration
      (IOM), 2015.

46   Abigail Haworth, "Vian Dakhil: Iraq's Only Female Yazidi MP on the Battle to Save Her
      People," *The Guardian,* February 8, 2015.

47   Jon Hilsenrath and Janet Hook, "Defense Secretary Opens Possibility to Strategy Shift
      on Iraq," *The Wall Street Journal,* May 24, 2015.

48   Audrey Kurth Cronin, "ISIS Is Not a Terrorist Group," *Foreign Affairs,* March/April 2015.

49   Hilsenrath and Hook, "Defense Secretary Opens Possibility to Strategy Shift on Iraq" *The
      Wall Street Journal,* May 24, 2015; Graeme Wood, "What ISIS Really Wants," *The Atlantic,*
      March 2015.

50   Charles Lister, "Profiling the Islamic State," Brookings Institution, 2014.

51   Ibid.

52   Howard J. Shatz, "To Defeat the Islamic State, Follow the Money," *Politico Magazine,*
      September 10, 2014; Cronin, "ISIS Is Not a Terrorist Group."

53   Howard J. Shatz, "How ISIS Funds Its Reign of Terror," RAND, September 8, 2014, www
      .rand.org/blog/2014/09/how-isis-funds-its-reign-of-terror.html.

54   Dexter Filkins, "The Fight of Their Lives," *The New Yorker,* September 29, 2014.

55   Cronin, "ISIS Is Not a Terrorist Group"; "Turkey Agrees to Assist U.S. with Airstrike
      against ISIS," *The New York Times,* July 27, 2015.

56   "ISIS Is Not a Terrorist Group"; Nick Robins-Early, "Where Does ISIS Stand a Year after
      It Declared Its Caliphate?," *The Huffington Post,* July 1, 2015.

57   Douglas A. Ollivant, "Iraq after the Islamic State: Politics Rule," War on the Rocks, http://warontherocks.com/2015/02/iraq-after-the-islamic-state-politics-rule/.

58   "Iraq," Internal Displacement Monitoring Centre, www.internal-displacement.org/middle-east-and-north-africa/iraq/.

59   Medyan Dairieh, "The Islamic State," VICE News 2014, https://www.youtube.com/watch?v=AUjHb4C7b94.

60   Lister, "Profiling the Islamic State."

61   Wood, "What ISIS Really Wants."

62   Cole Bunzel, "From Paper State to Caliphate: The Ideology of the Islamic State," The Brookings Institution, 2015.

63   Shadi Hamid, "The Roots of the Islamic State's Appeal," The Atlantic, October 31, 2014.

64   Lister, "Profiling the Islamic State."

65   Robin Wright, "The Clash of Civilizations That Isn't," The New Yorker, February 25, 2015.

66   Wood, "What ISIS Really Wants."

67   Abou el Fadl, The Great Theft: Wrestling Islam from the Extremists, Chapters 5, 7.

68   Jack Jenkins, "What the Atlantic Left out About ISIS According to Their Own Expert," Think Progress, February 20, 2015.

69   Ibid.; Sarah el Sirgany and Ian Lee, "A Battle for the Soul of Islam," CNN, February 6, 2015.

70   "Open Letter to Dr. Ibrahim Awwad al-Badri, Alias 'Abu Bakr al-Baghdadi', to the Fighters and Followers of the Self-Declared 'Islamic State,'" September 19, 2014, http://lettertobaghdadi.com/14/english-v14.pdf.

71   "The Failed Crusade," Dabiq, September 2014.

72   Lister, "Profiling the Islamic State"; Wood, "What ISIS Really Wants."

73   Tim Arango, "ISIS Transforming into Functioning State That Uses Terror as Tool," The New York Times, July 21, 2015; Stephen M. Walt, "What Should We Do if the Islamic State Wins," Foreign Policy, June 10, 2015.

74   Howard J. Shatz, "To Defeat the Islamic State, Follow the Money," Politico Magazine, September 10, 2014.

75   "Iraqi Prime Minister 'Retires' Army Chief of Staff," France 24, June 20, 2015; Jack Moore, "Iraq Death Toll Surges to 10-Month High," Newsweek, July 2, 2015.

76   Greg Jaffe and Loveday Morris, "Defense Secretary Carter: Iraqis Lack 'Will to Fight' to Defeat Islamic State," The Washington Post, May 24, 2015.

77   Paul McLeary, "Why Are the Islamic State's Commanders So Much Better Than the Iraqi Army's?," Foreign Policy, May 26, 2015.

78   See the Iraqi Constitution, 2005, www.iraqinationality.gov.iq/attach/iraqi_constitution.pdf.

79   Guy Taylor, "Baghdad Eyes Formation of National Guard to Fight Islamic State," The Washington Times, June 8, 2015.

80   Ali A. Allawi, The Crisis of Islamic Civilization (Yale University Press, 2010).

81   Ali A. Allawi, The Occupation of Iraq: Winning the War, Losing the Peace (Yale University Press, 2008).

82   "Reflections on the Revolutions in the Arab World," Middle East Institute, 2013.

83   "Dr. Ali Allawi-Biography," www.aliallawi.com/biography.php; "Biography-Ali Abdul Amir Allawi," BBC News, March 13, 2007.

84   Ali A. Allawi, Faisal I of Iraq (Yale University Press, 2014), 415–461.

85   "Fanar Haddad," Middle East Institute, www.mei.edu/profile/fanar-haddad.

86   Fanar Haddad, Sectarianism in Iraq: Antagonistic Visions of Unity (Oxford University Press, 2011).

87   "The End of Sykes Picot," 2014, https://www.youtube.com/watch?v=i357G1HuFcI.

88   Sara Pursley, "'Lines Drawn on an Empty Map': Iraq's Borders and the Legend of the Artificial State (Part 1)," Jadaliyya, June 2, 2015.

89   Fanar Haddad, "Getting Rid of Maliki Won't Solve Iraq's Crisis," The Washington Post, June 17, 2014.

90   James F. Jeffrey and Dennis Ross, "Making Sense of Chaos in the Middle East," The Wash-
      ington Institute, www.washingtoninstitute.org/policy-analysis/view/making-sense-of
      -chaos-in-the-middle-east-multiple-wars-multiple-alliances.

91   Samuel R. Berger et al., "Key Elements of a Strategy for the United States in the Middle
      East," The Washington Institute, www.washingtoninstitute.org/policy-analysis/view/key
      -elements-of-a-strategy-for-the-united-states-in-the-middle-east.

92   "The Iraq Opportunity," Northern Gulf Partners, www.northerngp.com/cgi-bin
      /opportunity.

93   "International: Total Petroleum and Other Liquids Production-2014," US Energy Informa-
      tion Administration (EIA), www.eia.gov/beta/international/index.cfm.

94   World Bank, "GDP Per Capita Growth (Annual %)," http://data.worldbank.org
      /indicator/NY.GDP.PCAP.KD.ZG.

95   Martin Woollacott, "One in Six Iraqis Are in Exile, and They Want This War," The Guard-
      ian, August 15, 2002.

96   World Bank, "GDP Per Capita (Current US$)," http://data.worldbank.org/indicator/NY
      .GDP.PCAP.CD.

97   Akin Oyedele, "This Week's Collapse in Oil Prices Has Been Months in the Making," Busi-
      ness Insider, July 7, 2015; E.L., "Why the Oil Price Is Falling," The Economist, December 8,
      2014.

98   World Bank, "Internet Users (Per 100 People)," http://data.worldbank.org/indicator/IT
      .NET.USER.P2.

99   "Erbil Rotana Hotel," World Travel Awards, www.worldtravelawards.com/profile-30441
      -erbil-rotana-hotel.

Jordan

1   Sharmila Devi, "King Abdullah Makes Plea for Peace on American Comedy Show," The
     National-World, September 25, 2010.

2   Frank Jacobs, "Winston's Hiccup," The New York Times, March 6, 2012.

3   Jan Lahmeyer, "Jordan: Historical Demographical Data of the Whole Country," Population
     Statistics, www.populstat.info/Asia/jordanc.htm.

4   Rula Samain, "Keeping the Ancestors' Tongue Alive," The Jordan Times, October 14, 2008;
     Charles P. Wallace, "Circassians' Special Niche in Jordan: 'Cossacks' Seem Out of Place in
     Arab Palace," Los Angeles Times, May 17, 1987.

5   Sarah A. Tobin, "Jordan's Arab Spring: The Middle Class and Anti-Revolution," Middle
     East Policy Council 19, no. 1 (Spring 2012).

6   Philip Robins, A History of Jordan (Cambridge University Press, 2004); Kamal S. Salibi, The
     Modern History of Jordan (I. B. Tauris, 1998). Albert Hourani and Malise Ruthven, A His-
     tory of the Arab Peoples (Belknap Press, 2010).

7   Tobin, "Jordan's Arab Spring."

8   "Selected Indicators," Department of Statistics, Jordan, 2014.

9   Osama Al Sharif, "Is Jordan's 'Arab Spring' Over?" Al-Monitor, September 15, 2013.

10   "Arab Uprising: Country by Country—Jordan," BBC News, December 16, 2013.

11   David Rohde, "In Jordan, the Arab Spring Isn't Over," The Atlantic, July 19, 2013.

12   Jamal Halaby, "Hundreds of Jordanians Set up Protest in Capital," The Washington Post,
     March 24, 2011; "Protest Camp Set up in Jordan Capital," Al Jazeera, March 24, 2011.

13   Tobin, "Jordan's Arab Spring."

14   Nicholas Seeley, "Violent Protests in Syria, Bahrain, Yemen-and Now Jordan," The Chris-
     tian Science Monitor, March 25, 2011.

15   "Jordan Mulls Constitutional Reform to Weaken King, Boost Protections," CNN,
     August 19, 2011; Marwan Muasher, "Jordan's Proposed Constitutional Amendments—a
     First Step in the Right Direction" Carnegie Endowment for International Peace, 2011,

http://carnegieendowment.org/2011/08/17/jordan-s-proposed-constitutional-amend ments-first-step-in-right-direction.

16 World Bank, "Labor Force Participation Rate, Female (% of Female Population Ages 15+) (Modeled ILO Estimate)," http://data.worldbank.org/indicator/SL.TLF.CACT.FE.ZS ?order=wbapi_data_value_2013+wbapi_data_value+wbapi_data_value-last&sort=asc.

17 The Constitution of the Hashemite Kingdom of Jordan, 1952, www.constitutionnet.org /files/2011_constitution_-_jordan_english_final.pdf.

18 Robins, *A History of Jordan,* 187; Curtis Ryan, "Reform Retreats Amid Jordan's Political Storms," Middle East Research and Information Project, 2005.

19 "Marwan Muasher," Carnegie Endowment for International Peace, http://carnegieen dowment.org/experts/?fa=563.

20 Marwan Muasher, *The Arab Center: The Promise of Moderation* (Yale University Press, 2008); Marwan Muasher, *The Second Arab Awakening: And the Battle for Pluralism* (Yale University Press, 2014).

21 "About Aramex," Aramex Delivery Unlimited, www.aramex.com/about-us/default.aspx; Fadi Ghandour, "How I Did It: The CEO of Aramex on Turning a Failed Sale into a Huge Opportunity," *Harvard Business Review* (March 2011).

22 Christopher M. Schroeder, *Startup Rising: The Entrepreneurial Revolution Remaking the Middle East* (St. Martin's Press, 2013), 12–15.

23 Rory Jones, "IFC, Aramex Founder to Launch VC Fund for MENA Tech Startups," *The Wall Street Journal,* January 8, 2014.

24 United Nations Development Program, "Arab Development Challenges Report 2011," Cairo, 2011.

25 Rina Bhattacharya and Hirut Wolde, "Constraints on Growth in the Mena Region," International Monetary Fund, February 2010.

26 "Surfing the Shabaka," *The Economist,* April 10, 2014.

27 Stephanie Baker, "The Arab World's Silicon Valley: Jordan Emerges as an Internet Hub," *The Washington Post,* October 17, 2012.

28 T. E. Lawrence, *Seven Pillars of Wisdom* (CreateSpace Independent Publishing Platform, 2014).

29 Salibi, *The Modern History of Jordan,* 32–33.

30 Scott Anderson, "The True Story of Lawrence of Arabia," *Smithsonian,* July 2014.

31 Lawrence, *Seven Pillars of Wisdom.*

32 Salibi, *The Modern History of Jordan*; Hourani and Ruthven, *A History of the Arab Peoples.*

33 Ghazi bin Muhammad, *The Tribes of Jordan at the Beginning of the Twenty-First Century* (Turab, 1999), 18.

34 "City of Karak," www.alkarak.net.

35 Karen Armstrong, *Holy War: The Crusades and Their Impact on Today's World* (Anchor Books, 2001), 65, 272; "The Crusades, Even Now," *The New York Times,* 1999.

36 Stephen Tomkins, "Crusaders Capture Jerusalem" (Christian History Institute, 2009).

37 Jay Rubenstein, "Crusade Vs. Jihad: Which Is Worse?," *Huffington Post,* December 19, 2011.

38 "Remarks by the President Upon Arrival," http://georgewbush-whitehouse.archives.gov /news/releases/2001/09/20010916-2.html; Peter Ford, "Europe Cringes at Bush 'Crusade' against Terrorists," *The Christian Science Monitor,* September 19, 2001.

39 Jethro Mullen and Brian Todd, "Battling 'Crusaders': ISIS Turns to Glossy Magazine for Propaganda," CNN, September 17, 2014.

40 Marc A. Thiessen, "To the Terrorists, Obama Is 'Crusader in Chief,'" *The Washington Post,* February 9, 2015.

41 Oliver Miles, "We Must Beware—ISIS Wants the West to Conduct a Crusade," *The Guardian,* September 26, 2014.

42 Suha Ma'ayeh, "How Jordan Got Pulled into the Fight against ISIS," *Time,* February 26, 2015.

43 Vanessa O'Brien, "A Last Ditch Effort to Rescue the River Jordan," Deutsche Welle, 2012,

www.dw.com/en/a-last-ditch-effort-to-rescue-the-river-jordan/a-16179528; Peter Schwartz-stein, "Biblical Waters: Can the Jordan River Be Saved?," *National Geographic,* February 22, 2014.

44   Herbert Samuel, "An Interim Report on the Civil Administration of Palestine, During the Period 1st July, 1920–30th June, 1921" (UNISPAL, 1921).

45   Bernard Lewis, "Studies in the Ottoman Archives-I," *Bulletin of the School of Oriental and African Studies* 16, no. 3 (1954).

46   "United Nations Special Committee on Palestine Report," United Nations, http://en.wikisource.org/wiki/United_Nations_Special_Committee_on_Palestine_Report.

47   "General Progress Report and Supplementary Report of the United Nations Conciliation Commission for Palestine, Covering the Period from 11 December 1949 to 23 October 1950," United Nations Conciliation Commission for Palestine, 1950; "Final Report of the United Nations Economic Survey Mission for the Middle East," United Nations Economic Survey Mission for the Middle East, 1949.

48   Robert P. G. Bowker, *Palestinian Refugees: Mythology, Identity, and the Search for Peace* (Lynne Rienner Publishers, 2003).

49   "Libya's 'Revolutionary Jew' Returns to Restore Tripoli Synagogue," *The Guardian,* October 3, 2011.

50   Ada4567, "The Forgotten Refugees—Full Documentary Movie," YouTube, August 23, 2012.

51   Jewish Virtual Library, "Fact Sheet: Jewish Refugees from Arab Countries," American-Israeli Cooperative Enterprise, www.jewishvirtuallibrary.org/jsource/talking/jew_refugees.html.

52   UNHCR, "Facts and Figures About Refugees," www.unhcr.org.uk/about-us/key-facts-and-figures.html; "General Progress Report and Supplementary Report of the United Nations Conciliation Commission for Palestine, Covering the Period from 11 December 1949 to 23 October 1950", http://unispal.un.org/unispal.nsf/b792301807650d6685256cef0073cb80/93037e3b939746de8525610200567883?OpenDocument.

53   Olga Khazan, "Why Demographics Are Still a Concern for Some Israeli Jews," *The Washington Post,* January 1, 2013.

54   World Bank, "Data: population, total," http://data.worldbank.org/indicator/SP.POP.TOTL.

55   Central Intelligence Agency, "The World Factbook: Israel," https://www.cia.gov/library/publications/the-world-factbook/geos/is.html

56   Jody Rudoren and Jeremy Ashkenas, "Netanyahu and the Settlements," *The New York Times,* March 12, 2015. www.nytimes.com/interactive/2015/03/12/world/middleeast/netanyahu-west-bank-settlements-israel-election.html

57   UNRWA, "Where We Work: Jordan Camp Profiles," United Nations Relief and Works Agency, www.unrwa.org/where-we-work/jordan/camp-profiles?field=13.

58   "UNRWA," United Nations Relief and Works Agency for Palestine Refugees in the Near East, www.unrwa.org/?id=86.

59   "Where We Work: Jordan," United Nations Relief and Works Agency, www.unrwa.org/where-we-work/jordan.

60   "Regional Study: Palestinian Refugee Students Attending UN Schools Achieve Above-Average Results on International Assessments," United Nations Relief and Works Agency, 2014.

61   Rublis, *A History of Jordan,* 133–141; Hourani and Ruthven, *A History of the Arab Peoples,* Chapter 25; Salibi, *The Modern History of Jordan,* 197–243.

62   "Child Marriages Double among Syrian Refugees in Jordan," *I24 News,* December 13, 2014; "2014 Syria Regional Response Plan, Strategic Overview: Mid-Year Update," UN High Commissioner for Refugees, 2014.

63   "Zaatari Refugee Camp: Rebuilding Lives in the Desert," BBC News Middle East, September 3, 2013.

64   UNHCR, "Syria Regional Refugee Response: Zaatari Refugee Camp." http://data.unhcr.org/syrianrefugees/settlement.php?id=176&region=77&country=107.

65 "Regional: RRP6 Monthly Update—August 2014 (Education)," http://data.unhcr.org/syrianrefugees/download.php?id=7289.

66 3RP, "Regional Refugee & Resilience Plan 2015–2016 in Response to the Syria Crisis: Regional Strategic Overview," 2015.

67 UNHCR, "Syria Regional Refugee Response: Regional Overview," UN High Commissioner for Refugees, http://data.unhcr.org/syrianrefugees/regional.php.

68 "Jordan Response Plan for the Syria Crisis: Executive Summary 2015," Jordan Response Platform for the Syria Crisis, 2015.

69 Ian Black, "Patience Running Out in Jordan after Influx of Syrian Refugees," *The Guardian,* December 1, 2014; Shteiwi Musa, Jonathan Walsh, and Christina Klassen, "A Review of the Response to Syrian Refugees in Jordan," Center for Strategic Studies, 2014.

70 Gil Loescher and James Milner, "Protracted Displacement: Understanding the Challenge," *Forced Migration Review* 33 (2009).

71 Brian Michael Jenkins, *The Dynamics of Syria's Civil War* (RAND Corporation, 2014).

Qatar

1 Qatar National Bank (QNB), "Qatar Economic Insight," www.qnb.com/cs/Satellite?blobcol=urldata&blobheader=application%2Fpdf&blobkey=id&blobtable=MungoBlobs&blobwhere=1355498217480&ssbinary=true.

2 World Bank, "GDP Per Capita, Ppp (Current International $)."

3 Trade Arabia, "Qatar Infrastructure Contracts to Hit $30bn in 2014," Al Hilal Publishing & Marketing Group, www.tradearabia.com/news/CONS_267212.html; Qatar Projects Magazine, "Nearly $60bn Worth of Infrastructure Projects Will Now Go Ahead in Qatar Following Its Successful Bid to Host the 2022 World Cup," Michael Tully Planet Group, http://qatar.tpg-media.com/2011/nearly-60bn-worth-of-infrastructure-projects-will-now-go-ahead-in-qatar-following-its-successful-bid-to-host-the-2022-world-cup/.

4 Ministry of Development Planning and Statistics, "Qatar Statistics Authority Population Structure," www.qsa.gov.qa/eng/populationstructure.htm.

5 Qatar National Bank (QNB), "Qatar Economic Insight."

6 Thomas L. Friedman, "Did Dubai Do It?," *The New York Times,* November 18, 2014.

7 Habib Toumi, "Public Sector in Qatar to Get 60 Per Cent Pay Rise," *Gulf News,* http://gulfnews.com/news/gulf/qatar/public-sector-in-qatar-to-get-60-per-cent-pay-rise-1.862595.

8 Courtney Trenwith, "Alcohol Ban Lifted for New Hotel on the Pearl-Qatar," *Arabian Business,* November 5, 2014, www.arabianbusiness.com/alcohol-ban-lifted-for-new-hotel-on-pearl-qatar-570594.html; Doha News Team, "Restaurants: Still No Alcohol at the Pearl," *Doha News,* December 25, 2011, http://dohanews.co/restaurants-still-no-alcohol-at-the-pearl/.

9 Max Fisher, "The Middle East, Explained in One (Sort of Terrifying) Chart," *The Washington Post,* August 26, 2013, www.washingtonpost.com/blogs/worldviews/wp/2013/08/26/the-middle-east-explained-in-one-sort-of-terrifying-chart/.

10 U.S. Department of State, "U.S. Relations with Qatar, Fact Sheet," U.S. Department of State, 2014.

11 Hugh Miles, *Al-Jazeera: The Inside Story of the Arab News Channel that Is Challenging the West,* (Grove Press, 2006), 6.

12 David Blair and Richard Spencer, "How Qatar Is Funding the Rise of Islamist Extremists," *The Telegraph,* 2014, www.telegraph.co.uk/news/worldnews/middleeast/qatar/11110931/How-Qatar-is-funding-the-rise-of-Islamist-extremists.html.

13 Roula Khalaf and Abigail Fielding Smith, "Qatar Bankrolls Syrian Revolt with Cash and Arms," *Financial Times,* May 16, 2013; Elizabeth Dickinson, "The Case against Qatar," *Foreign Policy,* September 30, 2014.

14   David D. Kirkpatrick, "Muslim Brotherhood Says Qatar Ousted Its Members," *The New York Times,* September 13, 2014.

15   David Cohen, "Remarks of under Secretary for Terrorism and Financial Intelligence David Cohen before the Center for a New American Security on 'Confronting New Threats in Terrorist Financing,'" news release, 2014, www.treasury.gov/press-center/press-releases /pages/jl2308.aspx.

16   Robert Tuttle, "Qatar Regulates Charities as U.S. Urges Stop to Terror Funding," *Bloomburg Business,* September 15, 2014.

17   Dickinson, "The Case against Qatar."

18   Rajiv Chandrasekaran, "Qatar's Friends-with-Everyone Policy Rankles Gulf Neighbors and Leads to Charges of Double-Dealing," *The Washington Post,* October 4, 2014, www .washingtonpost.com/world/national-security/qatars-friends-with-everyone-approach -rankles-some-of-its-persian-gulf-neighbors/2014/10/04/b89977f8-4a7b-11e4-b72e -d60a9229cc10_story.html.; Lina Khatib, "Qatar's Foreign Policy: The Limits of Pragmatism," *International Affairs* 89, no. 2 (2013).; David Roberts, "Qatar's Foreign Policy Adventurism: The Emir's Plan to Win over Uncle Sam," *Foreign Affairs,* June 25, 2013, www .foreignaffairs.com/articles/139533/david-roberts/qatars-foreign-policy-adventurism.; Sigurd Neubauer, "Qatar's Changing Foreign Policy," *Sada,* April 8, 2014.

19   Kristian Coates Ulrichsen, "Qatar and the Arab Spring: Policy Drivers and Regional Implications," Carnegie Endowment for International Peace, 2014.

20   Danna Harman, "Backstory: Rein of the Robo-Jockey," *The Christian Science Monitor,* February 20, 2007.

21   Peter Kovessy, "Study: More Qatar Deaths Caused by Road Accidents Than Common Diseases," *Doha News,* 2014, http://dohanews.co/study-qatar-deaths-caused-road-accidents -common-diseases/.

22   Joy S. Moini et al., *The Reform of Qatar University* (RAND Corporation, 2009).

23   Shanghai Ranking, Academic Ranking of World Universities-2013, www.shanghai ranking.com/ARWU2013.html; Best Global Universities, 2015, www.usnews.com/education /best-global-universities.

24   Shelly Culbertson et al., *Launching the Qatar National Research Fund* (RAND Corporation, 2012).

25   "Masdar Institute," https://www.masdar.ac.ae/; "Premium Business Park," Dubai World Central, www.dwc.ae/business-park/.

26   "Oasis in the Desert," *Times Higher Education,* 2009, www.timeshighereducation.co.uk /features/oasis-in-the-desert/408895.article.

27   Catriona Davies, "Mideast Women Beat Men in Education, Lose Out at Work," CNN International, 2012.

28   World Bank, "Middle East and North Africa: Women in the Workforce," http://web .worldbank.org/WBSITE/EXTERNAL/COUNTRIES/MENAEXT/EXTMNAREG TOPPOVRED/0,contentMDK:22497617~pagePK:34004173~piPK:34003707~theSiteP K:497110,00.html.

29   Patty Paine, Jeff Lodge, and Samia Touati, eds., *Gathering the Tide: An Anthology of Contemporary Arabian Gulf Poetry* (Ithaca Press, 2011).

30   Poems quoted here are with permission of Maryam al-Subaiey.

31   Jill Crystal, *Oil and Politics in the Gulf: Rulers and Merchants in Kuwait and Qatar,* Cambridge Middle East Library (Book 24) (Cambridge University Press, 1990), 141; "2015 Revision of World Population Prospects," United Nations, http://esa.un.org/unpd/wpp /unpp/p2k0data.asp.

32   Andrew Gardner et al., "A Portrait of Low-Income Migrants in Contemporary Qatar," *Journal of Arabian Studies* 3, no. 1 (2013).

33   Ibid.

34   Daniel Dombey, "Six Markets to Watch: Turkey: How Erdogan Did It—and Could Blow

It", *Foreign Affairs*, (January/February 2014), www.foreignaffairs.com/articles/140338/daniel-dombey/six-markets-to-watch-turkey.

35   Andrew Gardner et al., "A Portrait of Low-Income Migrants in Contemporary Qatar", *Journal of Arabian Studies* 3, no. 1 (2013).

36   Ibid.

37   Pete Pattisson, "At 16, Ganesh Got a Job in Qatar. Two Months Later He Was Dead," *The Guardian,* September 25, 2013.

38   "Qatar Examining Allegations of Labour Abuses," *Gulf Times,* 2013, www.gulf-times.com/qatar/178/details/366945/qatar-examining-allegations-of-labour-abuses.

39   "World Report 2013: Qatar," *Human Rights Watch,* 2013.

40   "Six Markets to Watch: Turkey: How Erdogan Did It—and Could Blow It."

41   US Department of State, "Trafficking in Persons Report 2013," US Department of State, www.state.gov/j/tip/rls/tiprpt/2013/index.htm.

42   Owen Gibson, "Qatar Government Admits Almost 1,000 Fatalities among Migrants," *The Guardian,* May 14, 2014.

43   Ira Boudway, "The 2022 Fifa World Cup Could Be Deadly for Qatar's Migrant Workers," *Bloomberg Businessweek,* May 14, 2014.

44   Silvia Pessoa, Laura Harkness, and Andrew Gardner, "Ethiopian Labor Migrants and the "Free Visa" System in Qatar," *Human Organization* 73, no. 3 (2014).

45   "QF Mandatory Standards of Migrant Workers' Welfare for Contractors & Sub-Contractors," Qatar Foundation, 2013.

46   James M. Dorsey, "Qatar in Quandary over Labor Laws Ahead of 2022 World Cup," *Hürriyet Daily News,* 2014.

47   Leila Ahmed, *Women and Gender in Islam: Historical Roots of a Modern Debate* (Yale University Press, 1992), Chapter 8.

48   "The Qur'an and Hijab," Ahlul Bayt Digital Islamic Library Project (DILP), www.al-islam.org/hijab-muslim-womens-dress-islamic-or-cultural-sayyid-muhammad-rizvi/quran-and-hijab.

49   *Women and Gender in Islam: Historical Roots of a Modern Debate,* Chapter 3; Amina Wadud, *Qur'an and Woman: Rereading the Sacred Text from a Woman's Perspective* (Oxford University Press, 1999), Chapters 2, 4.

50   John L. Esposito, *Islam: The Straight Path,* 4th ed. (Oxford University Press, 2010), Chapters 3, 6; Hourani and Ruthven, *A History of the Arab Peoples,* Chapter 4.

51   "Ijtihad: Reinterpreting Islamic Principles for the Twenty-First Century," in *Special Report 125,* United States Institute of Peace, 2004; Wael B. Hallaq, "Was the Gate of Ijtihad Closed?," *International Journal of Middle East Studies* 16, no. 1 (1984).

52   Ahmet Davutoglu, "Philosophical and Institutional Dimensions of Secularism: A Comparative Analysis," in *Islam and Secularism in the Middle East,* ed. Azzam Tamimi and John L. Esposito (Hurst & Company, 2000); John L. Esposito, "Islam and Secularism in the Twenty-First Century," in *Islam and Secularism in the Middle East.*

53   Hourani, *Arabic Thought in the Liberal Age, 1798–1939;* Abou el Fadl, *The Great Theft: Wrestling Islam from the Extremists* (Harper San Francisco, 2005).

54   Mohamed el-Moctar el-Shinqiti, "Pursuing an Islamic Metamorphosis," Al Jazeera, October 17, 2010.

55   "About Us," Al Jazeera Media Network, www.aljazeera.com/aboutus/default.html.

56   Shibley Telhami, "2010 Annual Arab Public Opinion Survey," University of Maryland with Zogby International Poll, 2010.

57   "Hillary Clinton Calls Al Jazeera 'Real News,' Criticizes U.S. Media," *Huffington Post,* 2011; David Folkenflik, "Clinton Lauds Virtues of Al Jazeera: 'It's Real News,'" NPR, 2011.

58   Alice Fordham, "Up next on al-Jazeera: Donald Rumsfeld," *The Washington Post,* 2011.

59   Katherine Schulten, Sarah Kavanagh, and Holly Epstein Ojalvo, "Ways to Teach About the Unrest in Egypt," *The New York Times,* January 31, 2011.

60 Alexander Kühn, Christoph Reuter, and Gregor Peter Schmitz, "After the Arab Spring: Al-Jazeera Losing Battle for Independence," *Spiegel Online International,* February 15, 2013; Marc Lynch, *The Arab Uprising: The Unfinished Revolutions of the New Middle East* (Public Affairs, 2012), 126.

61 Hugh Miles, *Al-Jazeera: The Inside Story of the Arab News Channel that Is Challenging the West* (Grove Press, 2005), 195, 341.

62 Kühn, Reuter, and Schmitz, "After the Arab Spring."

63 Khatib, "Qatar's Foreign Policy."

64 Kühn, Reuter, and Schmitz, "After the Arab Spring"; Neubauer, "Qatar's Changing Foreign Policy."

65 Hugh Miles, "Al-Jazeera Boss Steps Down: Strains with Qatar Royals?," BBC News, October 1, 2011.

66 Gregg Carlstrom, "Why Egypt Hates Al Jazeera," *Foreign Policy,* February 19, 2014.

67 Mohamed Hassan Shaban, "22 Resign from Al-Jazeera Egypt in Protest over Bias," *Asharq Al-Awsat,* July 10, 2013; Jessica Chasmar, " 'We Aired Lies': Al-Jazeera Staff Quit over Biased Egypt Coverage," *The Washington Times,* July 9, 2013.

Egypt

1 Adla Ragab, "Recent Development of TSA in Egypt," 2014, http://dtxtq4w60xqpw.cloudfront.net/sites/all/files/pdf/14th_meeting_egypt.pdf.

2 Dalia Farouk, "Egypt Tourist Numbers Decline 20.5 Pct in June Year-on-Year," *Ahram Online,* July 16, 2014, http://english.ahram.org.eg/NewsContent/3/12/106415/Business/Economy/Egypt-tourist-numbers-decline—pct-in-June-yearony.aspx; Matt Smith, "Egypt Tourist Numbers to Rise 5–10 Pct in 2014-Minister," *Reuters,* September 11, 2014.

3 Patrick Kingsley, "Egypt's Tourism Revenues Fall after Political Upheavals," *The Guardian,* August 29, 2014.

4 Toby Wilkinson, *The Rise and Fall of Ancient Egypt* (Random House, 2013), Chapter 2.

5 Lapidus, *A History of Islamic Societies,* 564, 650, 830.

6 Tarek Osman, *Egypt on the Brink: From Nasser to the Muslim Brotherhood, Revised and Updated* (Yale University Press, 2013), 1.

7 Elliott Abrams, "Sissi Is No Pinochet," *The Washington Post,* April 24, 2015, www.washingtonpost.com/opinions/hes-no-pinochet/2015/04/24/8c8d642e-e212-11e4-905f-cc896d379a32_story.html.

8 "Worse Than Mubarak," *The Economist,* May 2, 2015, www.economist.com/news/middle-east-and-africa/21650160-abdel-fattah-al-sisi-has-restored-order-egypt-great-cost-worse?frsc=dg|c.

9 Ian Lee, "Mubarak Cleared: Drama Not Over Yet, but Egypt's Revolution Is Dead," CNN International, November 29, 2014, http://edition.cnn.com/2014/11/29/world/africa/egypt-mubarak-analysis/.

10 Mohamed Elshahed, "Tahrir Square: Social Media, Public Space," *Places Journal,* February 2011, https://placesjournal.org/article/tahrir-square-social-media-public-space/.

11 "Egypt Profile—Timeline," *BBC News Magazine,* May 18, 2015, www.bbc.com/news/world-africa-13315719.,

12 Barbara Speed, "Cairo's Traffic Problems Are Costing Egypt around 4 Per Cent of Its GDP," *CityMetric,* October 8, 2014.

13 Ali Abdel Mohsen, "Egypt's Museums: From Egyptian Museum to 'Torture Chamber' " *Egypt Independent,* April 20, 2011; "Egypt: End Torture, Military Trials of Civilians," *Human Rights Watch,* March 11, 2011; Liam Stack, "Complaints of Abuse in Army Custody," *The New York Times,* March 17, 2011.

14 Wahid Hamid, "Terrorism and Kebab," 1993, https://www.youtube.com/watch?v=_1tSL8UEPZo.

15 Habiba Mohsen, "What Made Her Go There? Samira Ibrahim and Egypt's Virginity Test Trial," Al Jazeera, March 16, 2012.

16 Isobel Coleman, " 'Blue Bra Girl' Rallies Egypt's Women Vs. Oppression," *CNN*, December 22, 2011.

17 Patrick Kingsley, "80 Sexual Assaults in One Day—the Other Story of Tahrir Square" *The Guardian*, July 5, 2013.

18 Sarah el-Sirgany, "In Egypt, Women Lead Fight against Mob Sexual Assaults," *Al-Monitor*, December 7, 2012; Engy Abdelkader, "99.3% of Egyptian Women, Girls Have Been Sexually Harassed," *Huffington Post*, June 4, 2013.

19 Claudia Roth Pierpont, "Found in Translation," *The New Yorker, January 18*, 2010.

20 Alaa al-Aswany, "Facebook Page: Alaa al-Aswany," https://www.facebook.com/Alaa AlAswanyAuthor?sk=info&tab=page_info.

21 Matthew Kaminski, "The Face of Egypt's Uprising," *The Wall Street Journal*, April 13, 2011.

22 "Egypt UPR Briefing: The Right to Work," Center for Economic and Social Rights, 2014; Population Council, "Survey of Young People in Egypt (SYPE) Final Report," Population Council. West Asia and North Africa Office, 2011.

23 William R. Long, "Peru's President Rules by Decree: South America: Fujimori Holds Congressional Leaders Prisoner, Censors News. The U.S. Calls the Move a 'Regrettable Step Backwards' and Suspends Aid Program," *Los Angeles Times*, April 7, 1992.

24 SOS-EGYPTE, "Massacre De Rabia Al Adawiya" 2013, https://www.youtube.com/watch ?v=h7qg-W0FMnU; Shahzad Mansoory, "Cairo Crises: Rabaa Al Adaweya Mosque on Fire," 2013, https://www.youtube.com/watch?v=_bpI2vQzQZk.

25 "Egypt: Rab'a Killings Likely Crimes against Humanity," *Human Rights Watch*, August 12, 2014.

26 Ibid.

27 Mada Masr, "529 Brotherhood Supporters Sentenced to Death in Minya," *The Morning Digest*, March 24, 2014.

28 Osman, *Egypt on the Brink*, Chapter 3.

29 Michael Slackman, "Stifled, Egypt's Young Turn to Islamic Fervor," *The New York Times*, February 17, 2008.

30 Osman, *Egypt on the Brink*, 106.

31 Hamid, "The Roots of the Islamic State's Appeal."

32 Ibid.

33 Rami Galal, "Egypt Closes 27,000 Places of Worship," *Al-Monitor*, March 3, 2015; "Egyptian Authorities Close 55,000 Mosques," *Middle East Monitor (MEMO)*, September 11, 2013.

34 Bret Stephens, "Islam's Improbable Reformer," *The Wall Street Journal*, March 20, 2015; Nada Nader, "Al-Sisi Reasserts Needs to Revolutionise Religious Discourse," *Daily News Egypt*, March 23, 2015.

35 Leslie T. Chang, "The News Website That's Keeping Press Freedom Alive in Egypt," *The Guardian*, January 27, 2015.

36 "The 100 Most Powerful Arab Women 2015: Lina Attalah," *ArabianBusiness.com*, March 1, 2015.

37 "World Press Freedom Day: Journalists under Attack in Egypt," *Amnesty International*, May 3, 2015.

38 Fareed Zakaria, "The Rise of Illiberal Democracy," *Foreign Affairs*, November/December 1997.

39 Robin Wright, "With This Redo, Egypt Can Do Better," *The New York Times*, June 13, 2014.

40 "Mohamed Morsi Fast Facts," CNN, June 7, 2015.

41 "A Riche History," *The Economist*, December 17, 2011; Karim el-Sayed and Dina Waked, "Café Riche: In Pursuit of a Nonquantitative Business Model," American University of Cairo, 2007.

42 BBC, "The Other Side of the Suez," July 22, 2012; Hourani and Ruthven, *A History of the Arab Peoples*, Chapter 21.

43 Osman, *Egypt on the Brink,* Chapter 2; Hourani and Ruthven, *A History of the Arab Peoples,* Chapter 21; Lapidus, *A History of Islamic Societies,* 568–570.

44 Chronos Media, "Nasser-People's Pharaoh," (1979), https://www.youtube.com/watch ?v=NaJogPC9ACI

45 Osman, *Egypt on the Brink,* Chapter 2; Hourani and Ruthven, *A History of the Arab Peoples,* Chapter 21; Lapidus, *A History of Islamic Societies,* 568–570.

46 Stephen Phizicky, Ilan Ziv, and Yair Raveh, "Six Days in June," 2007, www.imdb.com/title /tt1033631/.

47 Hourani and Ruthven, *A History of the Arab Peoples,* Chapter 21.

48 Osman, *Egypt on the Brink,* 18, 113.

49 Maria Golia, "The New Suez Canal Project and Egypt's Economic Future," Middle East Institute, 2014; Waad Ahmed et al., "Energy Deals Dominate Egyptian Economic Development Conference on Saturday," *Ahram Online,* March 15, 2015.

50 Allison Corkery and Heba Khalil, "Nothing New on the Nile," *Foreign Policy,* March 12, 2015; "Thinking Big: Another Egyptian Leader Falls for the False Promise of Grand Projects," *The Economist,* March 19, 2015.

51 "Egypt Referendum: '98% Back New Constitution,'" BBC News, January 19, 2014.

52 Bassem Sabry, "Problems Ahead for Egypt Constitution Debate," *Al-Monitor* September 30, 2013; David D. Kirkpatrick, "Overwhelming Vote for Egypt's Constitution Raises Concern," *The New York Times,* January 18, 2014; "Constitution of the Arab Republic of Egypt 2014 (Unofficial Translation)," 2014.

53 The history in this section is based on: Hourani, *Arabic Thought in the Liberal Age, 1798– 1939*; Lapidus, *A History of Islamic Societies*; Hourani and Ruthven, *A History of the Arab Peoples*; Osman, *Egypt on the Brink.*

54 Hourani, *Arabic Thought in the Liberal Age, 1798–1939,* Chapter VI.

55 Osman, *Egypt on the Brink,* Chapters 2, 3.

56 Jonathan Brown, "Salafis and Sufis in Egypt," in *The Carnegie Papers*, Carnegie Endowment for International Peace, 2011.

57 Lucy Westcott, "Senior Muslim Cleric Calls for Islamic Teaching Overhaul to Curb Extremism," *Newsweek,* February 23, 2015.

58 "Al-Azhar Top Cleric Calls for Religious Teaching Reform," BBC News, February 23, 2015.

59 Ibid.

60 Hanan Fayed, "Al-Azhar Responds to Sisi's Call for 'Religious Revolution,'" *The Cairo Post,* January 2, 2015.

61 Ahmed Fouad, "Al-Azhar Refuses to Consider the Islamic State an Apostate," *Al-Monitor,* February 12, 2015.

62 Ahmed Morsy and Nathan J. Brown, "Egypt's Al-Azhar Steps Forward," Carnegie Endowment for International Peace, 2013.

63 "The Global Gender Gap Report 2014," World Economic Forum, http://reports .weforum.org/global-gender-gap-report-2014/.

64 World Bank, "Labor Force, Female (% of Total Labor Force)" http://data.worldbank.org /indicator/SL.TLF.TOTL.FE.ZS.

65 Data provided to the author by Egypt's National Council for Women.

66 Conrad Hackett, "How Many Christians Are There in Egypt?," Pew Research Center, 2011.

67 Lapidus, *A History of Islamic Societies,* 59–63.

68 Hourani, *Arabic Thought in the Liberal Age, 1798–1939,* Chapter XI.

69 Khairi Abaza and Mark Nakhla, "The Copts and Their Political Implications in Egypt," The Washington Insttitue, 2005.

70 Jason Brownlee, "Violence against Copts in Egypt," Carnegie Endowment for International Peace, 2013.

71 Moheb Zaki, "Egypt's Persecuted Christians," *The Wall Street Journal,* May 18, 2010.

72 "Egypt Church Blast Death Toll Rises to 23," *Reuters,* January 4, 2011.

73 Betsy Hiel, "Egypt's Churches Charred to Shells," *Tribune-Review,* January 17, 2015;

"Egypt: Mass Attacks on Churches," *Human Rights Watch,* August 21, 2013; "Egypt: Freedom in the World 2014," Freedom House, https://freedomhouse.org/report/freedom-world/2014/egypt#.VSt0xWaq62w.

74   "Egypt's Churches Withdraw from Constituent Assembly," *Ahram Online,* November 17, 2012; Nariman Youssef, "Egypt's Draft Constitution Translated," *Egypt Independent,* February 12, 2012.

75   "Sisi Makes Surprise Coptic Christmas Visit," *Al Arabiya News,* January 7, 2015.

76   Jared Malsin, "Libya and Egypt Launch Airstrikes against Isis after Militants Post Beheadings Video," *The Guardian,* February 15, 2015.

77   Harrison Jacobs, "Meet the Egyptian Families Who Live among the Tombs in Cairo's Massive Cemetery," *Business Insider,* November 19, 2014.

78   Sarah Sabry, "Could Urban Poverty in Egypt Be Grossly Underestimated?," Centre for Development Policy and Research, 2010.

79   Amina Kheiri, "Egypt's Slums: A Ticking Time Bomb," *Al-Monitor,* November 7, 2013.

80   World Bank, "Egypt, Arab Rep.," http://data.worldbank.org/country/egypt-arab-republic.

81   "The Status of Poverty and Food Security in Egypt: Analysis and Policy Recommendations, Preliminary Summary Report," World Food Progamme, 2013.

82   "Literacy Rate, Adult Total (% of People Ages 15 and above)" http://data.worldbank.org/indicator/SE.ADT.LITR.ZS/countries/1W-EG?display=graph.

83   "Amnesty International Finds Forced Evictions, Discrimination against Women in New Report on Egyptian Housing Crisis," Amnesty International, www.amnestyusa.org/news/press-releases/amnesty-international-finds-forced-evictions-discrimination-against-women-in-new-report-on-egyptian.

84   Patrick Kingsley, "A New New Cairo: Egypt Plans £30bn Purpose-Built Capital in Desert," *The Guardian,* March 16, 2015.

85   Jack Shenker, "Desert Storm," *The Guardian,* June 10, 2011.

86   Thanassis Cambanis, "To Catch Cairo Overflow, 2 Megacities Rise in Sand," *The New York Times,* August 24, 2010.

87   Kingsley, "A New New Cairo"; "Egypt Unveils Plans to Build New Capital East of Cairo," BBC News, March 13, 2015.

88   Khaled Fahmy, "Chasing Mirages in the Desert," *Cairobserver,* March 14, 2015.

89   "Another Egyptian Leader Falls for the False Promise of Grand Projects," *The Economist,* March 19, 2015.

90   Mark Landler, "Obama Seeks Reset in Arab World," *The New York Times,* May 11, 2011.

91   Wael Ghonim, *Revolution 2.0: The Power of the People Is Greater Than the People in Power: A Memoir* (Houghton Mifflin Harcourt, 2012); Fouad Ajami, "Egypt's 'Heroes with No Names,'" *The Wall Street Journal,* February 12, 2011; Jose Antonio Vargas, "Spring Awakening: How an Egyptian Revolution Began on Facebook," *The New York Times,* February 17, 2012.

Conclusion

1   Mehran Kamrava, ed. *Beyond the Arab Spring: The Evolving Ruling Bargain in the Middle East,* 1st ed. (Oxford University Press, 2014), 2–81.

2   Tarek Masoud, "Has the Door Closed on Arab Democracy?," *Journal of Democracy* 26, no. 1 (2015).

BIBLIOGRAPHY

A&E Television Networks. "History—Engineering an Empire: Carthage." 2008.

Abaza, Khairi, and Mark Nakhla. "The Copts and Their Political Implications in Egypt." The Washington Insttitue, 2005.

Abdelkader, Engy. "99.3% of Egyptian Women, Girls Have Been Sexually Harassed." *Huffington Post,* June 4,2013.

Abou el Fadl, Khaled. *The Great Theft : Wrestling Islam from the Extremists.* Harper San Francisco, 2005.

"About Aramex." Aramex Delivery Unlimited. www.aramex.com/about-us/default.aspx.

"About Us." Al Jazeera Media Network. www.aljazeera.com/aboutus/default.html.

Abrams, Elliott. "Sissi Is No Pinochet." *The Washington Post*, April 24, 2015. www.washing tonpost.com/opinions/hes-no-pinochet/2015/04/24/8c8d642e-e212-11e4-905f-cc896d 379a32_story.html.

Ada4567. "The Forgotten Refugees—Full Documentary Movie." YouTube, August 23, 2012. https://www.youtube.com/watch?v=KH8RL2XRr48.

Adams, Charles J. "Mawdudi and the Islamic State." In Esposito, *Voices of Islamic Resurgence*, 99–132. Oxford University Press.

AFP. " 'Chapulling': Turkish Protesters Spread the Edgy Word." *The Express Tribune,* June 8, 2013.

Ahmed, Leila. *Women and Gender in Islam: Historical Roots of a Modern Debate.* Yale University Press, 1992.

Ahmed, Waad, Randa Ali, Deya Abaza, Mariam Rizk, and Marwa Hussein. "Energy Deals Dominate Egyptian Economic Development Conference on Saturday." *Ahram Online*, March 15, 2015.

Ajami, Fouad. "Egypt's 'Heroes with No Names.' " *The Wall Street Journal*, February 12, 2011.

Akyol, Mustafa. "Will Turkey's CHP Reconcile with Islam?" *Al-Monitor*, September 7, 2014.

Akyüz, Yilmaz, and Korkut Boratav. "The Making of the Turkish Financial Crisis." Geneva: United Nations Conference on Trade and Development (UNCTAD), 2002.

Al-Ali, Zaid, and Donia Ben Romdhane. "Tunisia's New Consitition: Progress and Challenges to Come." OpenDemocracy. https://www.opendemocracy.net/arab-awakening/zaid-al-ali -donia-ben-romdhane/tunisia%E2%80%99s-new-constitution-progress-and-challenges-to-.

"Al-Azhar Top Cleric Calls for Religious Teaching Reform." BBC News, February 23, 2015. www .bbc.com/news/world-middle-east-31580130.

al-Zayani, Amina. "Zaytuna Mosque Maintains Its Social, Political Role in Tunisia." *Al-Monitor*, February 25, 2014.

al-Aswany, Alaa. "Facebook Page: Alaa al-Aswany." https://www.facebook.com/AlaaAlAswany Author?sk=info&tab=page_info.

al Sharif, Osama. "Is Jordan's 'Arab Spring' Over?" *Al-Monitor*, September 15, 2013.

Alanlari, Muharebe, and Gezi Rehberi. *Gallipoli Battlefield Guide*. MB books, 2005.

Alexandria and Amman. "Salafism: Politics and the Puritanical." *The Economist*, June 27, 2015. www.economist.com/news/middle-east-and-africa/21656189-islams-most-conservative -adherents-are-finding-politics-hard-it-beats.

Allawi, Ali A. *The Crisis of Islamic Civilization*. Yale University Press, 2010.

———. "Dr. Ali Allawi-Biography." www.aliallawi.com/biography.php.

———. *Faisal I of Iraq*. Yale University Press, 2014.

———. *The Occupation of Iraq: Winning the War, Losing the Peace*. Yale University Press, 2008.

———. "Reflections on the Revolutions in the Arab World." Middle East Institute, 2013.

"Amnesty International Finds Forced Evictions, Discrimination against Women in New Report on Egyptian Housing Crisis." Amnesty International. www.amnestyusa.org/news/press -releases/amnesty-international-finds-forced-evictions-discrimination-against-women-in -new-report-on-egyptian.

"Amnesty Urges Justice for Tunisians Tortured under Ben Ali." www.globalpost.com/dispatch /news/afp/131008/amnesty-urges-justice-tunisians-tortured-under-ben-ali.

Anderson, Scott. "The True Story of Lawrence of Arabia." *Smithsonian*, July 2014.

"Another Egyptian Leader Falls for the False Promise of Grand Projects." *The Economist*, March 19, 2015. www.economist.com/news/middle-east-and-africa/21646806-another-egyptian-leader -falls-false-promise-grand-projects-thinking-big?zid=304&ah=e5690753dc78ce919090830 42ad12e30.

"Arab Uprising: Country by Country—Jordan." BBC News, December 16, 2013. www.bbc.com /news/world-12482679.

Arango, Tim. "Corruption Scandal Is Edging Near Turkish Premier." *The New York Times*, December 25, 2013.

———. "ISIS Transforming into Functioning State That Uses Terror as Tool." *The New York Times*, July 21, 2015.

Arango, Tim, and Michael S. Schmidt. "Last Convoy of American Troops Leaves Iraq." *The New York Times*, December 18, 2011.

Armstrong, Karen. "The Crusades, Even Now." *The New York Times Magazine*, September 19, 1999.

———. *Holy War: The Crusades and Their Impact on Today's World*. Anchor Books, 2001.

Assaad, Ragui, and Farzaneh Roudi-Fahimi. "Youth in the Middle East and North Africa: Demographic Opportunity or Challenge?" Population Reference Bureau, 2007.

Authorization for Use of Military Force against Iraq Resolution of 2002. Public Law 107–243. 107th Congress.

Baker, Stephanie. "The Arab World's Silicon Valley: Jordan Emerges as an Internet Hub." *The Washington Post*, October 17, 2012.

BBC. "The Other Side of the Suez." 2012.

Beiser, Elana. "Second Worst Year on Record for Jailed Journalists." Committee to Protect Journalists, 2013.

Belasco, Amy. "The Cost of Iraq, Afghanistan, and Other Global War on Terror Operations since 9/11." Congressional Research Service, 2014.

Ben Bouazza, Bouazza, and Paul Schemm. "Second Tunisia Assassination Could Spell End to Islamist Government." *The Washington Post*, July 26, 2013.

Ben Mabrouk, Ali. "Reflecting on Bourguiba, 13 Years after His Death." *Tunisia Live*, April 9, 2013.

Ben Mhenni, Lina. "Revolution." CNN, January 22, 2014.

———. "Tunisian Elections: Beware, Beware, My Hunger and My Anger." *The Guardian*, October 22, 2011.

————. "A Tunisian Girl." http://atunisiangirl.blogspot.com/.

Berger, Samuel R., Stephen Hadley, James F. Jeffrey, Dennis Ross, and Robert Satloff. "Key Elements of a Strategy for the United States in the Middle East." The Washington Institute. www.washingtoninstitute.org/policy-analysis/view/key-elements-of-a-strategy-for-the -united-states-in-the-middle-east.

"The Best and Worst of Tunisia's New Constitution." Al-Monitor, January 29, 2014.

"Best Global Universities." 2015. www.usnews.com/education/best-global-universities.

Bhattacharya, Rina, and Hirut Wolde. "Constraints on Growth in the Mena Region." International Monetary Fund, February 2010.

Bilefsky, Dan. "Syrians' New Ardor for a Turkey Looking Eastward." The New York Times, July 24, 2010.

"Bill Clinton's Statement Concerning Ataturk: Address to the International Trade Organization." Helenic Resources Net. www.hri.org/news/turkey/trkpr/2000/00-01-05.trkpr.html.

bin Muhammad, Ghazi. The Tribes of Jordan at the Beginning of the Twenty-First Century. Turab, 1999.

"Biography—Ali Abdul-Amir Allawi." BBC News, March 13, 2007.

Black, George. Genocide in Iraq: The Anfal Campaign against the Kurds (Middle East Watch Report). Human Rights Watch, 1993.

Black, Ian. "Patience Running Out in Jordan after Influx of Syrian Refugees." The Guardian, December 1, 2014.

Blair, David, and Richard Spencer. "How Qatar Is Funding the Rise of Islamist Extremists." The Telegraph, September 20, 2014. www.telegraph.co.uk/news/worldnews/middleeast/qatar /11110931/How-Qatar-is-funding-the-rise-of-Islamist-extremists.html.

Boudway, Ira. "The 2022 Fifa World Cup Could Be Deadly for Qatar's Migrant Workers." Bloomberg Businessweek, May 14, 2014.

Bowker, Robert P. G. Palestinian Refugees: Mythology, Identity, and the Search for Peace. Lynne Rienner Publishers, 2003.

Bradbury, Jim. The Routledge Companion to Medieval Warfare. Routledge, 2004.

Bremmer, Ian. "These 5 Stats Explain Turkey's War on ISIS—and the Kurds." Time, July 31, 2015.

Brown, Jonathan. "Salafis and Sufis in Egypt." In The Carnegie Papers. Washington, DC: Carnegie Endowment for International Peace, 2011.

Brownlee, Jason. "Violence against Copts in Egypt." Carnegie Endowment for International Peace, 2013.

"Buildings in Levent." Emporis. www.emporis.com/zone/levent-istanbul.

Bunzel, Cole. "From Paper State to Caliphate: The Ideology of the Islamic State." The Brookings Institution, 2015.

Butler, Ed. "Iraqi Kurdistan's Battle with Baghdad over Oil Revenues." BBC News, April 10, 2015.

Byrne, Eileen. "The Women MPs Tipped to Play Leading Roles in Tunisia's New Assembly." The Guardian, October 28, 2011.

Cagaptay, Soner. "After Erdogan, Turkey's Future Will Be Liberal." The New York Times, August 14, 2014.

————. The Rise of Turkey: The Twenty-First Century's First Muslim Power. Potomac Books, 2014.

————. "12 Percent of Turkish CEOs Are Women: World Bank." Hürriyet Daily News, February 11, 2012.

Cagaptay, Soner, and Rüya Perincek. "No Women, No Europe." Hürriyet Daily News, January 20,2010.

Cambanis, Thanassis. "To Catch Cairo Overflow, 2 Megacities Rise in Sand." The New York Times, August 24, 2010.

Carlstrom, Gregg. "Why Egypt Hates Al Jazeera." Foreign Policy, February 19, 2014.

Chandrasekaran, Rajiv. "Qatar's Friends-with-Everyone Policy Rankles Gulf Neighbors and Leads to Charges of Double-Dealing." The Washington Post, October 4, 2014. www.washingtonpost

.com/world/national-security/qatars-friends-with-everyone-approach-rankles-some-of-its
-persian-gulf-neighbors/2014/10/04/b89977f8-4a7b-11e4-b72e-d60a9229cc10_story.html.

Chang, Leslie T. "The News Website That's Keeping Press Freedom Alive in Egypt." *The Guardian,* January 27, 2015.

Charrad, Mounira M. "Family Law Reforms in the Arab World: Tunisia and Morocco." 2012. www.un.org/esa/socdev/family/docs/egm12/PAPER-CHARRAD.pdf.

Charrad, Mounira M., and Amina Zarrugh. "The Arab Spring and Women's Rights in Tunisia." E-International Relations. www.e-ir.info/2013/09/04/the-arab-spring-and-womens-rights -in-tunisia/.

———. "Equal or Complementary? Women in the New Tunisian Constitution after the Arab Spring." *The Journal of North African Studies* 19, no. 2 (2014): 230–43.

Chasmar, Jessica. " 'We Aired Lies': Al-Jazeera Staff Quit over Biased Egypt Coverage." *The Washington Times,* July 9, 2013.

"Child Marriages Double among Syrian Refugees in Jordan." *I24 News,* December 13, 2014. www.i24news.tv/en/news/international/middle-east/54326-141213-child-marriages -double-among-syria-refugees-in-jordan.

Chronos Media. "Nasser-People's Pharaoh," (1979). https://www.youtube.com/watch?v=NaJog PC9ACI.

Chulov, Martin. "Ascendant Kurds Emerge from Syrian Civil War as Major Power Player." *The Guardian,* August 1, 2015.

Churchill, Erik. "Tahar Haddad: A Towering Figure for Women's Rights in Tunisia." The World Bank, 2013.

"City of Karak." www.alkarak.net/.

Cleveland, William L., and Martin Bunton. *A History of the Modern Middle East* 5th ed. Westview Press, 2012.

Cloud, David S., and Brian Bennett. "U.S., Allies Rush Heavy Weapons to Kurds to Fight Militants in Iraq." *Los Angeles Times,* August 11, 2014.

Cohen, David. "Remarks of under Secretary for Terrorism and Financial Intelligence David Cohen before the Center for a New American Security on 'Confronting New Threats in Terrorist Financing.' " News release, 2014. www.treasury.gov/press-center/press-releases/pages/jl2308 .aspx.

Coleman, Isobel. " 'Blue Bra Girl' Rallies Egypt's Women Vs. Oppression." CNN, December 22, 2011.

———. *Paradise beneath Her Feet: How Women Are Transforming the Middle East.* Random House, 2013.

Collard, Rebecca. "Why Turkey Has Finally Declared War on ISIS." *Time,* July 24, 2015.

Colombo, Jesse. "Why the Worst Is Still Ahead for Turkey's Bubble Economy." *Forbes,* March 5, 2014.

Constant, Louay, Shelly Culbertson, Cathleen Stasz, and Georges Vernez. *Improving Technical Vocational Education and Training in the Kurdistan Region—Iraq.* RAND Corporation, 2014.

Constitution of the Arab Republic of Egypt 2014 (Unofficial Translation). 2014. www.sis.gov.eg /Newvr/Dustor-en001.pdf.

The Constitution of the Hashemite Kingdom of Jordan. 1952. www.constitutionnet.org/files /2011_constitution_-_jordan_english_final.pdf.

Cook, Steven A. "Keep Calm, Erdogan." *Foreign Affairs,* June 3, 2013.

Cordoba, Armando. "Premier Barzani: 'Downtown Erbil' a 'Milestone' for Kurdistan." *Rudaw,* October 28, 2013.

Corke, Susan, Andrew Finkel, David J. Kramer, Carla Anne Robbins, and Nate Schenkkan. "Democracy in Crisis: Corruption, Media, and Power in Turkey." Freedom House, 2014. www .freedomhouse.org/sites/default/files/Turkey%20Report%20-%202-3-14.pdf.

Corkery, Allison, and Heba Khalil. "Nothing New on the Nile." *Foreign Policy,* March 12, 2015.

Cretois, Jules. "Muslim Women Redefine Feminism." *Al-Monitor,* April 4, 2013.

Croitoru, Joseph. "The Ambivalent Revival of Islamic Traditions." *Qantara,* August 22, 2012.

http://en.qantara.de/content/controversy-surrounding-the-al-zaytuna-mosque-in-tunis-the
-ambivalent-revival-of-islamic.

Cronin, Audrey Kurth. "ISIS Is Not a Terrorist Group." *Foreign Affairs*, March/April 2015.

Cronkite, Walter. "The Incredible Turk." PublicResourceOrg, 1958. https://www.youtube.com
/watch?v=q9EkewZea3k.

Crystal, Jill. *Oil and Politics in the Gulf: Rulers and Merchants in Kuwait and Qatar*. Cambridge
Middle East Library (Book 24). Cambridge University Press, 1990.

Culbertson, Shelly, Michael G. Mattock, Bruce R. Nardulli, Abdulrazaq al-Kuwari, Gary Cec-
chine, Margaret C. Harrell, John A. Frield, and Richard E. Darilek. *Launching the Qatar
National Research Fund*. Tr-722-QF. RAND Corporation, 2012.

Cumming-Bruce, Nick. "Syrian Refugees Surpass 3 Million, U.N. Says." *The New York Times*,
August 29, 2014.

Curtiss, Richard H. "Women's Rights an Affair of State for Tunisia." Washington Report on
Middle East Affairs, 1993.

Dairieh, Medyan. "The Islamic State." VICE News, 2014. https://www.youtube.com/watch
?v=AUjHb4C7b94.

Daragahi, Borzou. "Term Used for Women in Tunisia's Draft Constitution Ignites Debate, Protests." *The Washington Post*, August 16, 2012.

Dash, Mike. "The Ottoman Empire's Life-or-Death Race." *Smithsonian*, March 22, 2012.

Davies, Catriona. "Mideast Women Beat Men in Education, Lose out at Work." CNN International, June 6, 2012.

Davutoglu, Ahmet. "Philosophical and Institutional Dimensions of Secularism: A Comparative
Analysis." In Azzam Tamimi and John L. Esposito, eds. *Islam and Secularism in the Middle
East*, 170–208.

"Demographics of the Ottoman Empire." Wikipedia. http://en.wikipedia.org/wiki/Demographics
_of_the_Ottoman_Empire.

Department of Veterans Affairs. "The Gallipoli Campaign." Australian Government. http://
web.archive.org/web/20130313050857/www.dva.gov.au/news_archive/Documents/The%20
Gallipoli%20Campaign.pdf.

Devi, Sharmila. "King Abdullah Makes Plea for Peace on American Comedy Show." *The National-
World*, September 25, 2010.

Dickinson, Elizabeth. "The Case against Qatar." *Foreign Policy*, September 30, 2014.

———. "The First Wikileaks Revolution?" *Foreign Policy*, January 13, 2011.

Doha News Team. "Restaurants: Still No Alcohol at the Pearl." *Doha News*, December 25, 2011.
http://dohanews.co/restaurants-still-no-alcohol-at-the-pearl/.

Dombey, Daniel. "Six Markets to Watch: Turkey: How Erdogan Did It—and Could Blow It."
Foreign Affairs, January/February, 2014.

Dorsey, James M. "Qatar in Quandary over Labor Laws Ahead of 2022 World Cup." *Hürriyet
Daily News*, November 17, 2014.

Draft of the Constitution of the Republic of Tunisia. 2012. www.constitutionnet.org/files/2012
.08.14_-_draft_constitution_english.pdf.

Dündar, Can. *Mustafa*. Warner Bros., 2008.

E.L. "Why the Oil Price Is Falling." *The Economist*, December 8, 2014.

"The Economist Intelligence Unit's Quality-of-Life Index." *The Economist*, November 21, 2004.
www.economist.com/media/pdf/QUALITY_OF_LIFE.pdf.

"Egypt's Churches Withdraw from Constituent Assembly." *Ahram Online*, November 17, 2012.
http://english.ahram.org.eg/NewsContent/1/64/58411/Egypt/Politics-/Egypts-churches
-withdraw-from-Constituent-Assembly.aspx.

"Egypt Church Blast Death Toll Rises to 23." *Reuters*, January 4, 2011.

"Egypt: End Torture, Military Trials of Civilians." *Human Rights Watch*, March 11, 2011. www
.hrw.org/news/2011/03/11/egypt-end-torture-military-trials-civilians.

"Egypt: Freedom in the World 2014." Freedom House. https://freedomhouse.org/report/freedom
-world/2014/egypt#.VSt0xWaq62w.

"Egypt: Mass Attacks on Churches." *Human Rights Watch*, August 21, 2013. www.hrw.org/news
   /2013/08/21/egypt-mass-attacks-churches.
"Egypt Profile-Timeline." *BBC News Magazine,* May 18, 2015. www.bbc.com/news/world-africa
   -13315719.
"Egypt: Rab'a Killings Likely Crimes against Humanity." *Human Rights Watch*, August 12, 2014.
   www.hrw.org/news/2014/08/12/egypt-rab-killings-likely-crimes-against-humanity.
"Egypt Referendum: '98% Back New Constitution.'" BBC News, January 19, 2014.
"Egypt Unveils Plans to Build New Capital East of Cairo." BBC News, March 13, 2015.
"Egypt UPR Briefing: The Right to Work." Center for Economic and Social Rights, 2014. www
   .cesr.org/downloads/egypt-UPR2014-right-to-work.pdf.
"Egyptian Authorities Close 55,000 Mosques." *Middle East Monitor (MEMO)*, September 11,
   2013. https://www.middleeastmonitor.com/news/africa/7328-egyptian-authorities-close-55000
   -mosques.
el-Moctar el-Shinqiti, Mohamed. "Pursuing an Islamic Metamorphosis." Al Jazeera, October 17,
   2010.
el-Rashidi, Sarah. "Iraq's 2 Million IDPs Struggling." *Iraq Pulse*, December 30, 2014.
el-Sayed, Karim, and Dina Waked. "Café Riche: In Pursuit of a Nonquantitative Business Model."
   American University of Cairo, (2007).
el-Sirgany, Sarah. "In Egypt, Women Lead Fight against Mob Sexual Assaults." *Al-Monitor*,
   December 7, 2012.
el-Sirgany, Sarah, and Ian Lee. "A Battle for the Soul of Islam." CNN, February 6, 2015.
Elshahed, Mohamed. "Tahrir Square: Social Media, Public Space." *Places Journal,* February 2011.
   https://placesjournal.org/article/tahrir-square-social-media-public-space/.
"The End of Sykes Picot." 2014. https://www.youtube.com/watch?v=i357G1HuFcI.
"Erbil International Airport Growing by 50% in 2012; Mahan Air, Qatar Airways and Transa-
   via.Com New This Year." *Anna.Aero*, June 13, 2012. www.anna.aero/2012/06/13/erbil
   -international-airport-growing-by-50pc-in-2012/.
"Erbil Rotana Hotel." World Travel Awards. www.worldtravelawards.com/profile-30441-erbil
   -rotana-hotel.
Erbil Tourism. "History of Erbil." www.erbiltourism2014.com/en/erbil/history.
"Erdogan Goes to Prison." *Hürriyet Daily News,* March 27, 1999.
Esposito, John L. "Islam and Secularism in the Twenty-First Century." In Azzam Tamimi and
   John L. Esposito, eds. *Islam and Secularism in the Middle East*, 1–12.
———. *Islam: The Straight Path*, 4th ed.: Oxford University Press, 2010.
Fahim, Kareem. "Slap to a Man's Pride Set Off Tumult in Tunisia." *The New York Times*, Janu-
   ary 21, 2011.
Fahmy, Khaled. "Chasing Mirages in the Desert." *Cairobserver*, March 14, 2015.
"The Failed Crusade." *Dabiq*, September 2014. http://media.clarionproject.org/files/islamic-state
   /islamic-state-isis-magazine-Issue-4-the-failed-crusade.pdf.
Falagas, Matthew E., Effie A. Zarkadoulia, and George Samonis. "Arab Science in the Golden
   Age (750–1258 C.E.) and Today." *Journal of the Federation of American Societies for Experi-
   mental Biology* 20, no. 10 (2006): 1581–86.
"Fanar Haddad." Middle East Institute. www.mei.edu/profile/fanar-haddad.
Farouk, Dalia. "Egypt Tourist Numbers Decline 20.5 Pct in June Year-on-Year." *Ahram Online*,
   July 16, 2014. http://english.ahram.org.eg/NewsContent/3/12/106415/Business/Economy/Egypt
   -tourist-numbers-decline—pct-in-June-yearony.aspx.
Fattah, Hassan M. "Kuwait Grants Political Rights to Its Women." *The New York Times*, May 17,
   2005.
Fayed, Hanan. "Al-Azhar Responds to Sisi's Call for 'Religious Revolution.'" *The Cairo Post*,
   January 2, 2015.
Filkins, Dexter. "The Fight of Their Lives." *The New Yorker*, September 29, 2014.
"Final Report of the United Nations Economic Survey Mission for the Middle East." United
   Nations Economic Survey Mission for the Middle East, 1949. http://unispal.un.org/UNISPAL
   .NSF/0/C2A078FC4065D30285256DF30068D278.

Finkel, Caroline. *Osman's Dream: The History of the Ottoman Empire*. Basic Books, 2007.

Fisher, Marc. "In Tunisia, Act of One Fruit Vendor Sparks Wave of Revolution through Arab World." *The Washington Post*, March 26, 2011.

Fisher, Max. "The Middle East, Explained in One (Sort of Terrifying) Chart." *The Washington Post*, August 26, 2013. www.washingtonpost.com/blogs/worldviews/wp/2013/08/26/the-middle-east-explained-in-one-sort-of-terrifying-chart/.

———. "The Photo That Encapsulates Turkey's Protests and the Severe Police Crackdown." *The Washington Post*, June 3, 2013.

Folkenflik, David. "Clinton Lauds Virtues of Al Jazeera: 'It's Real News.'" NPR, March 3, 2011.

Ford, Peter. "Europe Cringes at Bush 'Crusade' against Terrorists." *The Christian Science Monitor*, September 19, 2001.

Fordham, Alice. "Up Next on Al-Jazeera: Donald Rumsfeld." *The Washington Post*, September 30, 2011.

Foster, Niamh. "British Documentary: The Ottoman Empire in World War I." Undated. http://islamandthegreatwar.umwblogs.org/british-documentary-the-ottoman-empire-in-world-war-i/.

Fouad, Ahmed. "Al-Azhar Refuses to Consider the Islamic State an Apostate." *Al-Monitor*, February 12, 2015.

Friedman, Thomas L. "Did Dubai Do It?" *The New York Times*, November 18, 2014.

———. "Iraq's Best Hope." *The New York Times*, June 3, 2014.

Fromkin, David. *A Peace to End All Peace: The Fall of the Ottoman Empire and the Creation of the Modern Middle East*. Holt Paperbacks, 2010.

Frontline. "Losing Iraq." July 29, 2014. www.pbs.org/wgbh/pages/frontline/losing-iraq/.

Galal, Rami. "Egypt Closes 27,000 Places of Worship." *Al-Monitor*, March 3, 2015.

Gall, Carlotta. "Secularist Win Is Confirmed in Tunisia." *The New York Times*, October 30, 2014.

"Gallipoli: The Untold Stories (WWI Documentary)." YouTube, April 1, 2014. https://www.youtube.com/watch?v=erKCg74_14U.

Gardner, Andrew, Silvia Pessoa, Abdoulaye Diop, Kaltham al-Ghanim, Kien Le Trung, and Laura Harkness. "A Portrait of Low-Income Migrants in Contemporary Qatar." *Journal of Arabian Studies* 3, no. 1 (2013): 1–17.

Gaziantep Chamber of Industry. "Statistics." www.gso.org.tr/english/default.asp?syf=industry.

"Gaziantep City." Ministry of Tourism. http://gaziantepcity.info/en/home.

"General Progress Report and Supplementary Report of the United Nations Conciliation Commission for Palestine, Covering the Period from 11 December 1949 to 23 October 1950." United Nations Conciliation Commission for Palestine, 1951. http://unispal.un.org/unispal.nsf/b792301807650d6685256cef0073cb80/93037e3b939746de8525610200567883?OpenDocument.

"Gezi Park Protests: Brutal Denial of the Right to Peaceful Assembly in Turkey." Amnesty International, 2013. www.amnesty.org/en/library/asset/EUR44/022/2013/en/0ba8c4cc-b059-4b88-9c52-8fbd652c6766/eur440222013en.pdf.

Ghandour, Fadi. "How I Did It: The CEO of Aramex on Turning a Failed Sale into a Huge Opportunity." *Harvard Business Review*, March 2011.

Ghonim, Wael. *Revolution 2.0: The Power of the People Is Greater than the People in Power: A Memoir*. Houghton Mifflin Harcourt, 2012.

Ghosh, Bobby. "Time 100: The List: Rached Ghannouchi, Politician." *Time*, April 18, 2012.

Gibney, Matthew J., and Randall Hansen. *Immigration and Asylum: From 1900 to the Present*. Vol. 3. ABC-CLIO, 2005.

Gibson, Owen. "Qatar Government Admits Almost 1,000 Fatalities among Migrants." *The Guardian*, May 14, 2014.

Gladstone, Rick. "Anti-American Protests Flare Beyond the Mideast." *The New York Times*, September 14, 2012.

"The Global Gender Gap Report 2014." World Economic Forum. http://reports.weforum.org/global-gender-gap-report-2014/.

Golia, Maria. "The New Suez Canal Project and Egypt's Economic Future." Middle East Institute, 2014.

Goodwin, Jason. *Lords of the Horizons: A History of the Ottoman Empire.* Random House, 2011.

Graham, David A. "Turkish President Erdogan's Triple Defeat." *The Atlantic*, June 7, 2015.

Gruber, Christiane. "The Visual Emergence of the Occupy Gezi Movement, Part Three: Democracy's Workshop." *Jadaliyya*, July 8, 2013.

Gutman, Roy. "Syrian Opposition Plan to Oust Islamist Extremists Awaits U.S. Hearing." *Miami Herald*, July 12, 2014.

"Habib Bourguiba: Father of Tunisia." BBC News, April 6, 2000.

Hackett, Conrad. "How Many Christians Are There in Egypt?" Pew Research Center, 2011.

Haddad, Fanar. "Getting Rid of Maliki Won't Solve Iraq's Crisis." *The Washington Post*, June 17, 2014.

———. *Sectarianism in Iraq: Antagonistic Visions of Unity.* Oxford University Press, 2011.

Haddad, G. F. "Conquest of Constantinople." Sunnah. www.sunnah.org/msaec/articles/Constantinople.htm.

Halaby, Jamal. "Hundreds of Jordanians Set up Protest in Capital." *The Washington Post*, March 24, 2011.

Hallaq, Wael B. "Was the Gate of Ijtihad Closed?". *International Journal of Middle East Studies* 16, no. 01 (1984): 3–41.

Hamid, Shadi. "The Roots of the Islamic State's Appeal." *The Atlantic*, October 31, 2014.

Hamid, Wahid. "Terrorism and Kebab." 1993. https://www.youtube.com/watch?v=_1t SL8UEPZo.

Harman, Danna. "Backstory: Rein of the Robo-Jockey." *The Christian Science Monitor*, February 20,2007.

Harper, Jon. "Obama Doubling US Troop Levels in Iraq." *Stars and Stripes*, November 7, 2014.

Hart, Peter. *The Great War: A Combat History of the First World War.* Oxford University Press, 2013.

Harvey, Benjamin. "Dogan Rises as Erdogan Photo Op Signals Better Relations." *Bloomberg Businessweek,* April 20, 2012.

Hasan, Mehdi. "Mehdi Hasan Talks to Tunisian Politician Mehrezia Labidi on Gender, Democracy and the Arab Spring." *New Statesman*, April 18, 2012.

Haworth, Abigail. "Vian Dakhil: Iraq's Only Female Yazidi MP on the Battle to Save Her People." *The Guardian*, February 8, 2015.

Heneghan, Tom. "Ambiguous Religion Policy Backfires on Tunisia's Ruling Islamists." *Reuters*, September 3, 2013.

Herrin, Judith. *Byzantium: The Surprising Life of a Medieval Empire.* Penguin UK, 2008.

Hiel, Betsy. "Egypt's Churches Charred to Shells." *Tribune-Review*, January 17, 2015.

"Hillary Clinton Calls Al Jazeera 'Real News,' Criticizes U.S. Media." *Huffington Post,* March 3, 2011.

Hilsenrath, Jon, and Janet Hook. "Defense Secretary Opens Possibility to Strategy Shift on Iraq." *The Wall Street Journal*, May 24, 2015.

Hirschon, Renée. *Crossing the Aegean: An Appraisal of the 1923 Compulsory Population Exchange between Greece and Turkey.* Berghahn Books, 2003.

"Hope Springs." *The Economist*, December 20, 2014.

Hopkins, Steve. "Full Horror of the Yazidis Who Didn't Escape Mount Sinjar." *Daily Mail*, October 14, 2014.

Hourani, Albert. *Arabic Thought in the Liberal Age, 1798–1939.* Cambridge University Press, 1983.

Hourani, Albert, and Malise Ruthven. *A History of the Arab Peoples.* Belknap Press, 2010.

"How Mosques and Other New Buildings May Damage One of Europe's Finest Cities." *The Economist*, December 1, 2012.

Howe, Stephen. *Empire: A Very Short Introduction.* Oxford University Press, 2002.

Human Rights Watch/Middle East. *Iraq's Crime of Genocide: The Anfal Campaign against the Kurds.* Human Rights Watch, 1994.

Idiz, Semih. "Turkey's Syrian Refugee Problem Spirals Out of Control." *Al-Monitor,* July 20, 2014. www.al-monitor.com/pulse/originals/2014/07/idiz-turkey-syrian-refugees-local-tension -adana-istanbul.html#.

"Ijtihad: Reinterpreting Islamic Principles for the Twenty-First Century-Ijtihad Reinterpreting Islamic Principles for the Twenty First Century." In *Special Report 125.* United States Institute of Peace, 2004. http://dspace.africaportal.org/jspui/bitstream/123456789/15036/1/Ijtihad %20Reinterpreting%20Islamic%20Principles%20for%20the%20Twenty%20first%20 Century.pdf?1.

Ikenberry, G. John. *After Victory: Institutions, Strategic Restraint, and the Rebuilding of Order after Major Wars.* Princeton University Press, 2000.

"In the Shade of Bourguiba." *The Economist,* November 4, 2014.

"International: Total Petroleum and Other Liquids Production-2014." U.S. Energy Information Administration (EIA). www.eia.gov/beta/international/index.cfm.

"Introduction : Genocide in Iraq: The Anfal Campaign against the Kurds." Human Rights Watch. www.hrw.org/reports/1993/iraqanfal/ANFALINT.htm.

"Iraq." Internal Displacement Monitoring Centre. www.internal-displacement.org/middle-east -and-north-africa/iraq/.

"Iraq Body Count." Iraq Body Count Project., https://www.iraqbodycount.org/.

"Iraq IDP Figures Analysis." Internal Displacement Monitoring Centre (IDMC). www.internal -displacement.org/middle-east-and-north-africa/iraq/figures-analysis.

"The Iraq Opportunity." Northern Gulf Partners. www.northerngp.com/cgi-bin/opportunity.

"Iraq: ISIS Escapees Describe Systematic Rape." *Human Rights Watch*, 2015. www.hrw.org/news /2015/04/14/iraq-isis-escapees-describe-systematic-rape.

Iraqi Constitution. 2005. www.iraqinationality.gov.iq/attach/iraqi_constitution.pdf.

"Iraqi Kurds Mark 25 Years since Halabja Gas Attack." BBC News, March 16, 2013.

"Iraqi Prime Minister 'Retires' Army Chief of Staff." *France 24*, June 20, 2015. www.france24 .com/en/20150629-iraqi-pm-retires-army-chief-zebari-al-abadi-islamic-state.

"ISIS Claims Deadly Erbil Car Bomb Attack." *Al Arabiya News,* April 17, 2015.

Jacobs, Frank. "Winston's Hiccup." *The New York Times*, March 6, 2012.

Jacobs, Harrison. "Meet the Egyptian Families Who Live among the Tombs in Cairo's Massive Cemetery." *Business Insider*, November 19, 2014.

Jaffe, Greg, and Loveday Morris. "Defense Secretary Carter: Iraqis Lack 'Will to Fight' to Defeat Islamic State." *The Washington Post*, May 24, 2015.

Jasmine Foundation-Tunisia. "Constitution of the Tunisian Republic." 2014. www.jasmine -foundation.org/doc/unofficial_english_translation_of_tunisian_constitution_final_ed.pdf.

Jeffrey, James F., and Dennis Ross. "Making Sense of Chaos in the Middle East." The Washington Institute. www.washingtoninstitute.org/policy-analysis/view/making-sense-of-chaos-in-the -middle-east-multiple-wars-multiple-alliances.

Jenkins, Brian Michael. *The Dynamics of Syria's Civil War.* RAND Corporation, 2014.

Jenkins, Jack. "What the Atlantic Left Out About ISIS According to Their Own Expert." *Think Progress*, February 20, 2015.

Jewish Virtual Library. "Fact Sheet: Jewish Refugees from Arab Countries." American-Israeli Cooperative Enterprise. www.jewishvirtuallibrary.org/jsource/talking/jew_refugees.html.

Jones, Rory. "IFC, Aramex Founder to Launch VC Fund for MENA Tech Startups." *The Wall Street Journal*, January 8, 2014.

"Jordan Mulls Constitutional Reform to Weaken King, Boost Protections." CNN, August 19, 2011.

"Jordan Response Plan for the Syria Crisis: Executive Summary 2015." Jordan Response Platform for the Syria Crisis, 2015. https://drive.google.com/file/d/0B2ulC5rjYSnceVZvdmJveGpfcVU /view?pli=1.

Jourdan, Brandon. "Taksim Commune: Gezi Park and the Uprising in Turkey." YouTube, August 8, 2013.

Kaminski, Matthew. "The Face of Egypt's Uprising." *The Wall Street Journal*, April 13, 2011.

Kamrava, Mehran, ed. *Beyond the Arab Spring: The Evolving Ruling Bargain in the Middle East*, 1st ed: Oxford University Press, 2014.

Karpat, Kemal H. *Studies on Ottoman Social and Political History: Selected Articles and Essays*. Vol. 81. Brill, 2002.

Keegan, John. *The First World War*. Knopf, 1999.

Kelly, Sanja, and Julian Breslin, eds. *Women's Rights in the Middle East and North Africa: Progress Amid Resistance*, Freedom House, 2010.

Kennedy, John F. "Message to the Turkish People on the Occasion of 25th Anniversary of the Death of Mustafa Kemal Ataturk." http://upload.wikimedia.org/wikipedia/commons/c/ce/JFKennedy_on_Ataturk_1963.pdf.

Kenyon, Peter. "Turkey's AK Party Still Defies Easy Categorization." NPR, January 3, 2013.

Khalaf, Roula , and Abigail Fielding Smith. "Qatar Bankrolls Syrian Revolt with Cash and Arms." *Financial Times,* May 16, 2013.

Khalifa, Doaa (al-Ahram). "Egypt's Slum Crisis Persists Amid Housing Abundance." *Ahram Online*, January 12, 2013.

Khatib, Lina. "Qatar's Foreign Policy: The Limits of Pragmatism." *International Affairs* 89, no. 2 (2013): 417–31.

Khazan, Olga. "Why Demographics Are Still a Concern for Some Israeli Jews." *The Washington Post*, January 1, 2013.

Khechana, Rachid. "Tunisia's Democratic Revolution and Its Uncertain Future." Aspenia Online, December 2, 2013.

Kheiri, Amina. "Egypt's Slums: A Ticking Time Bomb." *Al-Monitor*, November 7, 2013.

Kingsley, Patrick. "80 Sexual Assaults in One Day—the Other Story of Tahrir Square." *The Guardian*, July 5, 2013.

———. "Egypt's Tourism Revenues Fall after Political Upheavals." *The Guardian*, August 29, 2014.

———. "A New New Cairo: Egypt Plans £30bn Purpose-Built Capital in Desert." *The Guardian*, March 16, 2015.

Kinross, Patrick Balfour. *Atatürk: The Rebirth of a Nation*. Weidenfeld and Nicolson, 1964.

———. *The Ottoman Centuries: The Rise and Fall of the Turkish Empire*. Cape, 1977.

Kinsley, Susan F. "Whatever Happened to the Iraqi Kurds?" *News from Middle East Watch*, March 11, 1991.

Kinzer, Stephen. *Crescent and Star: Turkey between Two Worlds*. Macmillan, 2008.

Kirkpatrick, David D. "Muslim Brotherhood Says Qatar Ousted Its Members." *The New York Times*, September 13, 2014.

———. "New Freedoms in Tunisia Drive Support for ISIS." *The New York Times*, October 21, 2014.

———. "Overwhelming Vote for Egypt's Constitution Raises Concern." *The New York Times*, January 18, 2014.

Kissinger, Henry. *Diplomacy*. Simon & Schuster, 1995.

Klaas, Brian. "The Long Shadow of Ben Ali: How a Decades-Old Fake Coup Attempt Is Taking Its Toll on Tunisia." *Foreign Policy*, December 17, 2013.

Kottoor, Naveena. "Tunisia's Ennahda and Ettakattol Women MPs Celebrate." BBC News, January 28, 2014.

Kovessy, Peter. "Study: More Qatar Deaths Caused by Road Accidents Than Common Diseases." *Doha News,* March 6, 2014). http://dohanews.co/study-qatar-deaths-caused-road-accidents-common-diseases/.

Kühn, Alexander, Christoph Reuter, and Gregor Peter Schmitz. "After the Arab Spring: Al-Jazeera Losing Battle for Independence." *Spiegel Online International,* February 15, 2013.

"Kurdistan-the Other Iraq." www.theotheriraq.com/.

"Kurdistan Region of Iraq 2020: A Vision for the Future." Ministry of Planning, Kurdistan Regional Government, 2013. www.ekrg.org/files/pdf/KRG_2020_last_english.pdf.

Lahmeyer, Jan. "Jordan: Historical Demographical Data of the Whole Country." Population Statistics. www.populstat.info/Asia/jordanc.htm.

Landler, Mark. "Obama Seeks Reset in Arab World." *The New York Times*, May 11, 2011.

Lapidus, Ira M. *A History of Islamic Societies*, 3rd ed.: Cambridge University Press, 2014.

———. *A History of Islamic Societies*, 2nd ed.: Cambridge University Press, 2002.

Lawrence, T. E. *Seven Pillars of Wisdom*. CreateSpace Independent Publishing Platform, 2014.

Leaders. "Kamal Samari." www.leaders.com.tn/article/kamal-samari?id=6264.

Lee, Ian. "Mubarak Cleared: Drama Not Over Yet, but Egypt's Revolution Is Dead." CNN International, November 29, 2014. http://edition.cnn.com/2014/11/29/world/africa/egypt-mubarak -analysis/.

Lesch, David W. "A Path to Peace in Syria." *Foreign Policy*, July 2, 2014.

Letsch, Constanze. "Istanbul Sees History Razed in the Name of Regeneration." *The Guardian*, March 1, 2012.

———. "A Year after the Protests, Gezi Park Nurtures the Seeds of a New Turkey." *The Guardian*, May 29, 2014.

Levent, Tolga. "Mustafa Kemal Ataturk." Turkey, 2013. https://www.youtube.com/watch?v=ru MrEIXFev4.

Lewis, Bernard. "Studies in the Ottoman Archives-I." *Bulletin of the School of Oriental and African Studies* 16, no. 3 (1954): 469–501.

"Libya's 'Revolutionary Jew' Returns to Restore Tripoli Synagogue." *The Guardian*, October 3, 2011.

Lin, Justin Yifu. "Youth Bulge: A Demographic Dividend or a Demographic Bomb in Developing Countries?" The World Bank. http://blogs.worldbank.org/developmenttalk/youth-bulge -a-demographic-dividend-or-a-demographic-bomb-in-developing-countries.

"Lina Ben Mhenni." *The Guardian*, 2015. www.theguardian.com/profile/lina-ben-mhenni.

Lister, Charles. "Profiling the Islamic State." Brookings Institution, 2014.

Loescher, Gil, and James Milner. "Protracted Displacement: Understanding the Challenge." *Forced Migration Review* 33 (2009): 9–11.

Lonely Planet. "Best Value Destinations for 2015." www.lonelyplanet.com/travel-tips-and-articles /best-value-destinations-for-2015.

Long, William R. "Peru's President Rules by Decree : South America: Fujimori Holds Congressional Leaders Prisoner, Censors News. The U.S. Calls the Move a 'Regrettable Step Backwards' and Suspends Aid Program." *Los Angeles Times*, April 7, 1992.

Lutz, Catherine. "US and Coalition Casualties in Iraq and Afghanistan." Brown University, Watson Institute for International Studies, 2013.

Lynch, Marc. *The Arab Uprising: The Unfinished Revolutions of the New Middle East*. Public Affairs, 2012.

Ma'ayeh, Suha. "How Jordan Got Pulled into the Fight against ISIS." *Time*, February 26, 2015.

Mackey, Robert. "Iraqi Who Made Emotional Plea to Help Yazidis Is Injured in Crash of Relief Flight." *The New York Times*, August 12, 2014.

Malsin, Jared. "Libya and Egypt Launch Airstrikes against Isis after Militants Post Beheadings Video." *The Guardian*, February 15, 2015.

Mango, Andrew. *Ataturk: The Biography of the Founder of Modern Turkey*. Overlook, 2002.

Manning, Jennifer E., and Ida A. Brudnick. "Women in the United States Congress, 1917–2014: Biographical and Committee Assignment Information, and Listings by State and Congress." Congressional Research Service, 2014.

Mansel, Philip. *Constantinople, City of the World's Desire, 1453–1924*. John Murray, 2006.

Mansoory, Shahzad. "Cairo Crises: Rabaa Al Adaweya Mosque on Fire." 2013. https://www .youtube.com/watch?v=_bpI2vQzQZk.

Mansour, Renad. "How the Kurds Helped Draw the United States Back into Iraq." Carnegie Middle East Center, 2015.

Marks, Monica. "'Complementary' Status for Tunisian Women." *Foreign Policy*, August 20, 2012.

Marr, Phebe. *The Modern History of Iraq*, 3rd ed.: Westview Press, 2011.

"Marwan Muasher." Carnegie Endowment for International Peace. http://carnegieendowment .org/experts/?fa=563.

"Masdar Institute." https://www.masdar.ac.ae/.

Masoud, Tarek. "Has the Door Closed on Arab Democracy?" *Journal of Democracy* 26, no. 1 (2015): 74–87.

Masr, Mada. "529 Brotherhood Supporters Sentenced to Death in Minya." *The Morning Digest*, March 24, 2014.

McCarthy, Justin. *The Ottoman Peoples and the End of Empire*. Historical Endings. Bloomsbury Academic, 2001.

McClelland, Mac. "How to Build a Perfect Refugee Camp." *The New York Times*, February 13, 2014.

McDowall, David. *A Modern History of the Kurds*, 3rd ed. I. B. Tauris, 2004.

McLeary, Paul. "Why Are the Islamic State's Commanders So Much Better Than the Iraqi Army's?" *Foreign Policy*, May 26, 2015.

McNeil, ST. "Wording on Women Sparks Protest in Tunisia." Al Jazeera, August 19, 2012.

"The Media in Crisis." Freedom House. www.freedomhouse.org/report/democracy-crisis-corruption-media-and-power-turkey/media-crisis#.U-9Orkjq9QY.

Memmi, Albert. *The Colonizer and the Colonized*. Beacon Press, 1991.

MEMRI-TV. "Iraqi MP Breaks Down in Tears Pleading Parliament to Save Yazidis from Genocide." August 5, 2014.

Miles, Hugh. "Al-Jazeera Boss Steps Down : Strains with Qatar Royals?" BBC News, October 1, 2011.

———. *Al-Jazeera: The inside Story of the Arab News Channel That Is Challenging the West*. Grove Press, 2005.

Miles, Oliver. "We Must Beware—ISIS Wants the West to Conduct a Crusade." *The Guardian*, September 26, 2014.

Miles, Richard. *Carthage Must Be Destroyed: The Rise and Fall of an Ancient Civilization*. Penguin Books, 2011.

Ministry of Development Planning and Statistics. "Qatar Statistics Authority Population Structure." www.qsa.gov.qa/eng/populationstructure.htm.

"Mohamed Morsi Fast Facts." CNN, June 7, 2015.

Mohsen, Ali Abdel. "Egypt's Museums: From Egyptian Museum to 'Torture Chamber'" *Egypt Independent*, April 20, 2011.

Mohsen, Habiba. "What Made Her Go There? Samira Ibrahim and Egypt's Virginity Test Trial." Al Jazeera, March 16, 2012.

Moini, Joy S., Tora K. Bikson, C. Richard Neu, and Laura DeSisto. *The Reform of Qatar University*. MG-796-Qatar. RAND Corporation, 2009.

Moore, Jack. "Iraq Death Toll Surges to 10-Month High." *Newsweek*, July 2, 2015.

Morris, Harvey. "A Kurdish Spring on Many Fronts." *The New York Times*, March 21, 2013.

Morsy, Ahmed, and Nathan J. Brown. "Egypt's Al-Azhar Steps Forward." Carnegie Endowment for International Peace, 2013.

Moshiri, Nazanine. "Interview with Rachid Ghannouchi." Al Jazeera, February 7, 2011.

Muasher, Marwan. *The Arab Center: The Promise of Moderation*. Yale University Press, 2008.

———. "Jordan's Proposed Constitutional Amendments-a First Step in the Right Direction." Carnegie Endowment for International Peace, 2011.

———. *The Second Arab Awakening: And the Battle for Pluralism*. Yale University Press, 2014.

Mullen, Jethro, and Brian Todd. "Battling 'Crusaders': ISIS Turns to Glossy Magazine for Propaganda." CNN, September 17, 2014.

Mullis, Ina V. S., Michael O. Martin, Pierre Foy, and Kathleen T. Drucker. "PIRLS 2011 International Results in Reading." TIMSS & PIRLS International Study Center, 2012.

Musa, Shteiwi, Jonathan Walsh, and Christina Klassen. "A Review of the Response to Syrian Refugees in Jordan." Center for Strategic Studies, 2014.

Nader, Nada. "Al-Sisi Reasserts Needs to Revolutionise Religious Discourse." *Daily News Egypt*, March 23, 2015.

Neubauer, Sigurd. "Qatar's Changing Foreign Policy." In *Sada*, April 8, 2014.

news2youmedia. "The Gallipoli Catastrophe Documentary." YouTube, August 16, 2013. https://www.youtube.com/watch?v=8dj8mQ6cgR8.

"1988: Thousands Die in Halabja Gas Attack." BBC News, March 16, 2008.

O'Brien, Vanessa. "A Last Ditch Effort to Rescue the River Jordan." Deutsche Welle, August 27, 2012.

"Oasis in the Desert." *Times Higher Education,* November 5, 2009. www.timeshighereducation .co.uk/features/oasis-in-the-desert/408895.article.

Observatory of Economic Complexity. "Learn More About Trade in Tunisia." http://atlas.media .mit.edu/profile/country/tun/.

Obusan, Claire. "Cost of Living Large." *Forbes,* March 11, 2010.

OCHA. "Syria Crisis: Situation Overview." http://syria.unocha.org/.

OECD. "PISA 2012 Results in Focus." 2014. www.oecd.org/pisa/keyfindings/pisa-2012-results -overview.pdf.

Ohlheiser, Abby. "The Associated Press's New Definition of 'Islamist.'" *Slate.* www.slate.com /blogs/the_slatest/2013/04/05/_islamist_definition_changed_in_the_ap_stylebook_two _days_after_illegal.html.

"Oil Prices Volatile after Opec Maintains Output Level." BBC News, June 5, 2015.

Oliver, Roland, J. D. Fage, and G. N. Sanderson. *The Cambridge History of Africa.* Vol. 6, Cambridge University Press, 1985.

Ollivant, Douglas A. "Iraq after the Islamic State: Politics Rule." War on the Rocks. http:// warontherocks.com/2015/02/iraq-after-the-islamic-state-politics-rule/.

"The 100 Most Powerful Arab Women 2015: Lina Attalah." ArabianBusiness.com, March 1, 2015.

"One out of 10 People in Gaziantep Is Syrian." *Today's Zaman,* February 16, 2014.

"Open Letter to Dr. Ibrahim Awwad al-Badri, Alias 'Abu Bakr al-Baghdadi,' to the Fighters and Followers of the Self-Declared 'Islamic State,'" September 19, 2014. http://lettertobaghdadi .com/14/english-v14.pdf.

Osman, Tarek. *Egypt on the Brink: From Nasser to the Muslim Brotherhood, Revised and Updated.* Yale University Press, 2013.

Oueslati, Ines. "How Nidaa Tunis Won the Elections." *Al-Monitor,* October 29, 2014.

Oyedele, Akin. "This Week's Collapse in Oil Prices Has Been Months in the Making." *Business Insider,* July 7, 2015.

Paine, Patty, Jeff Lodge, and Samia Touati, eds. *Gathering the Tide: An Anthology of Contemporary Arabian Gulf Poetry.* Ithaca Press, 2011.

Pamuk, Orhan. *Istanbul.* Random House, 2006.

Parker, Ned. "The Iraq We Left Behind." *Foreign Affairs,* March/April 2012.

"Part 2: Country Profiles: The Global Gender Gap Report." World Economic Forum, 2013. www3.weforum.org/docs/GGGR13/GGGR_CountryProfiles_2013.pdf.

Pattisson, Pete. "At 16, Ganesh Got a Job in Qatar. Two Months Later He Was Dead." *The Guardian,* September 25, 2013.

Percy, Norma. "Part One: The Iraq War, Episode 1 of 3." BBC World Service, September 18, 2013.

Perkins, Kenneth J. *A History of Modern Tunisia.* 2nd ed. Cambridge University Press, 2013.

Pessoa, Silvia, Laura Harkness, and Andrew Gardner. "Ethiopian Labor Migrants and the 'Free Visa' System in Qatar." *Human Organization* 73, no. 3 (2014).

Phillips, David L. *The Kurdish Spring: A New Map of the Middle East.* Transaction Publishers, 2015.

Phizicky, Stephen, Ilan Ziv, and Yair Raveh. "Six Days in June." 2007. www.imdb.com/title /tt1033631/.

Pierpont, Claudia Roth. "Found in Translation." *The New Yorker,* January 18, 2010.

"Population Censuses." Turkish Statistical Institute, www.turkstat.gov.tr/PreTablo.do?alt _id=1047.

Population Council. "Survey of Young People in Egypt (Sype) Final Report." Population Council. West Asia and North Africa Office, 2011.

"Premium Business Park." Dubai World Central. www.dwc.ae/business-park/.

"President Essebsi, a Lifetime in Tunisia Politics." *Euronews,* December 22, 2014.

"Profile: Recep Tayyip Erdogan." BBC News Europe, August 11 2014.

"Protest Camp Set up in Jordan Capital." Al Jazeera, March 24, 2011.

"Protesters Killed in Tunisia Riots." Al Jazeera, January 9, 2011.

Prothero, G. W. *Anatolia*. H.M. Stationery Office, 1920.

Pursley, Sara. "'Lines Drawn on an Empty Map': Iraq's Borders and the Legend of the Artificial State (Part 1)." *Jadaliyya*, June 2, 2015.

"Qatar Examining Allegations of Labour Abuses." *Gulf Times,* September 27, 2013. www.gulf -times.com/qatar/178/details/366945/qatar-examining-allegations-of-labour-abuses.

Qatar National Bank (QNB). "Qatar Economic Insight." www.qnb.com/cs/Satellite?blobcol =urldata&blobheader=application%2Fpdf&blobkey=id&blobtable=MungoBlobs&blobwhe re=1355498217480&ssbinary=true.

Qatar Projects Magazine. "Nearly $60bn Worth of Infrastructure Projects Will Now Go Ahead in Qatar Following Its Successful Bid to Host the 2022 World Cup." Michael Tully Planet Group. http://qatar.tpg-media.com/2011/nearly-60bn-worth-of-infrastructure-projects-will -now-go-ahead-in-qatar-following-its-successful-bid-to-host-the-2022-world-cup/.

"QF Mandatory Standards of Migrant Workers' Welfare for Contractors & Sub-Contractors." Qatar Foundation, April 20, 2013. www.qf.org.qa/app/media/2379.

"The Qur'an and Hijab." Ahlul Bayt Digital Islamic Library Project (DILP). www.al-islam.org /hijab-muslim-womens-dress-islamic-or-cultural-sayyid-muhammad-rizvi/quran-and-hijab.

Ragab, Adla. "Recent Development of TSA in Egypt." January 2014. http://dtxtq4w60xqpw .cloudfront.net/sites/all/files/pdf/14th_meeting_egypt.pdf.

Raghavan, Sudarsan. "In Tunisia, Luxurious Lifestyles of a Corrupt Government." *The Washington Post*, January 28, 2011.

"Recep Tayyip Erdoğan: 'Women Not Equal to Men,'" *The Guardian*, November 24, 2014.

"Recep Tayyip Erdoğan: Prime Minister of the Republic of Turkey." Columbia University. www .worldleaders.columbia.edu/participants/recep-tayyip-erdoğ.

"Remarks by the President Upon Arrival." http://georgewbush-whitehouse.archives.gov/news /releases/2001/09/20010916-2.html.

Reporters Without Borders. "2015 World Press Freedom Index." https://index.rsf.org/#!/.

"Response to the IDP Crisis in Iraq-2015." International Organization for Migration (IOM), February 2015.

"A Riche History." *The Economist*, December 17, 2011.

Roberts, David. "Qatar's Foreign Policy Adventurism: The Emir's Plan to Win over Uncle Sam." *Foreign Affairs,* June 25, 2013. www.foreignaffairs.com/articles/139533/david-roberts/qatars -foreign-policy-adventurism.

Robins-Early, Nick. "Where Does ISIS Stand a Year after It Declared Its Caliphate?" *The Huffington Post*, July 1, 2015.

Robins, Philip. *A History of Jordan*. Cambridge University Press, 2004.

Robinson, Chase F. "The Caliph Has No Clothes." *The New York Times*, July 16, 2014.

Rohde, David. "In Jordan, the Arab Spring Isn't Over." *The Atlantic*, July 19, 2013.

Rubenstein, Jay. "Crusade Vs. Jihad: Which Is Worse?" *Huffington Post*, December 19, 2011.

Ryan, Curtis. "Reform Retreats Amid Jordan's Political Storms." Middle East Research and Information Project, June 10,2005.

Sabry, Bassem. "Problems Ahead for Egypt Constitution Debate." *Al-Monitor*, September 30, 2013,

Sabry, Sarah. "Could Urban Poverty in Egypt Be Grossly Underestimated?" Centre for Development Policy and Research, 2010.

Said, Rania. "Djerba, Tunisia: Garbage Disposal, the Environmental Crisis, and the Awakening of Ecoconsciousness." *Jadaliyya*, September 1, 2014.

Salibi, Kamal S. *The Modern History of Jordan*. I. B. Tauris, 1998.

Samain, Rula. "Keeping the Ancestors' Tongue Alive." *The Jordan Times*, October 14, 2008.

Samuel, Herbert. "An Interim Report on the Civil Administration of Palestine, During the Period 1st July, 1920–30th June, 1921." UNISPAL, 1921.

Schroeder, Christopher M. *Startup Rising: The Entrepreneurial Revolution Remaking the Middle East*. St. Martin's Press, 2013.

Schulten, Katherine, Sarah Kavanagh, and Holly Epstein Ojalvo. "Ways to Teach About the Unrest in Egypt." *The New York Times*, January 31, 2011.

Schwartzstein, Peter. "Biblical Waters: Can the Jordan River Be Saved?" *National Geographic*, February 22, 2014.

Seeley, Nicholas. "Violent Protests in Syria, Bahrain, Yemen-and Now Jordan." *The Christian Science Monitor*, March 25, 2011.

"Selected Indicators." Department of Statistics, Jordan, 2014. www.dos.gov.jo/dos_home_a /jorfig/2013/1.pdf

Shaban, Mohamed Hassan. "22 Resign from Al-Jazeera Egypt in Protest over Bias." *Asharq Al-Awsat*, July 10, 2013.

Shadid, Anthony. "Islamists' Ideas on Democracy and Faith Face Test in Tunisia." *The New York Times*, February 17, 2012.

Shanghai Ranking. "Academic Ranking of World Universities 2014." www.shanghairanking .com/ARWU2014.html.

———. "Academic Ranking of World Universities-2013." www.shanghairanking.com /ARWU2013.html.

Shatz, Howard J. "To Defeat the Islamic State, Follow the Money." *Politico Magazine*, September 10 2014.

———. "How ISIS Funds Its Reign of Terror." RAND Corporation, September 8, 2014.

Shaw, Stanford Jay. *History of the Ottoman Empire and Modern Turkey*. Cambridge University Press, 1976–77.

Shenker, Jack. "Desert Storm." *The Guardian*, June 10, 2011.

Sheridan, Mary Beth. "In Birthplace of Arab Spring, Tunisia's Islamists Get Sobering Lesson in Governing." *The Washington Post*, November 21, 2014.

"Sisi Makes Surprise Coptic Christmas Visit." *Al Arabiya News*, January 7, 2015.

Slackman, Michael. "Stifled, Egypt's Young Turn to Islamic Fervor." *The New York Times*, February 17, 2008.

Slanski, Kathryn. "A City That Goes Way, Way Back." NPR, February 4, 2007.

Slavin, Barbara. "Tunisians Lose Faith in Ennahda, Revolution." *Al-Monitor*, September 30, 2013.

Sly, Liz. "New U.S. Help Arrives for Syrian Rebels as Government, Extremists Gain." *The Washington Post*, July 27, 2014.

Smadhi, Asma, and Robert Joyce. "'We Are a Model, We Are an Example:' Assembly Members React to Constitution Vote." *Tunisia Live*, January 28, 2014.

Smith, Matt. "Egypt Tourist Numbers to Rise 5–10 Pct in 2014—Minister." *Reuters*, September 11, 2014.

Snyder, Michael. "Tunisia's New Constitution: An Eleventh-Hour Victory for Press Freedom." Freedom House, January 30, 2014.

SOS-EGYPTE. "Massacre De Rabia Al Adawiya." 2013. https://www.youtube.com/watch ?v=h7qg-W0FMnU.

Speed, Barbara. "Cairo's Traffic Problems Are Costing Egypt around 4 Per Cent of Its GDP." *CityMetric*, October 8, 2014.

Stack, Liam. "Complaints of Abuse in Army Custody." *The New York Times*, March 17, 2011.

"The Status of Poverty and Food Security in Egypt: Analysis and Policy Recommendations, Preliminary Summary Report." World Food Progamme, 2013. http://documents.wfp.org/stellent /groups/public/documents/ena/wfp257467.pdf.

Stein, Aaron. "Turkey's Evolving Syria Strategy." *Foreign Affairs*, February 9, 2015.

Steinvorth, Daniel, and Bernhard Zand. "A Country Divided: Where Is Turkey Headed?" June 24, 2013. www.spiegel.de/international/world/protests-reveal-the-deep-divisions-in-turkish-society -a-907498.html.

Stephens, Bret. "Islam's Improbable Reformer." *The Wall Street Journal*, March 20, 2015.

Stratfor (Strategic Forecasting). "No Arab Spring: Turkey's Violent Protests in Context." *Forbes*, June 3, 2013.

"Surfing the Shabaka." *The Economist*, April 10, 2014.

"Syrian Refugees Get to Work in Turkey." *Al-Monitor*, July 22, 2014.

Tanielian, Terri, Lisa H. Jaycox, David M. Adamson, M. Audrey Burnam, Rachel M. Burns, Leah B. Caldarone, and Robert A. Cox, et al. *Invisible Wounds of War: Psychological and Cognitive Injuries, Their Consequences, and Services to Assist Recovery*. RAND Corporation, 2008.

Taylor, Guy. "Baghdad Eyes Formation of National Guard to Fight Islamic State." *The Washington Times*, June 8, 2015.

Tekdemir, Özcan. "Taksim Gezi Parkı Belgeseli (Documentary)." YouTube, June 4, 2013.

Telhami, Shibley. "2010 Annual Arab Public Opinion Survey." University of Maryland with Zogby International, 2010.

3RP. "Regional Refugee & Resilience Plan 2015–2016 in Response to the Syria Crisis: Regional Strategic Overview." 2015.

Thiessen, Marc A. "To the Terrorists, Obama Is 'Crusader in Chief.'" *The Washington Post*, February 9, 2015.

"Thinking Big: Another Egyptian Leader Falls for the False Promise of Grand Projects." *The Economist*, March 19, 2015.

"Timeline: Invasion, Surge, Withdrawal; U.S. Forces in Iraq." *Reuters*, December 15, 2011.

Tishkov, Valery A. "Forget the 'Nation': Post-Nationalist Understanding of Nationalism." *Ethnic and Racial Studies* 23, no. 4 (2000): 625–50.

Tobin, Sarah A. "Jordan's Arab Spring: The Middle Class and Anti-Revolution." *Middle East Policy Council* 19, no. 1 (Spring 2012).

Tomkins, Stephen "Crusaders Capture Jerusalem." Christian History Institute. 2009.

Toumi, Habib. "Public Sector in Qatar to Get 60 Per Cent Pay Rise." Gulf News. September 7, 2011. http://gulfnews.com/news/gulf/qatar/public-sector-in-qatar-to-get-60-per-cent-pay-rise -1.862595.

Trade Arabia. "Qatar Infrastructure Contracts to Hit $30bn in 2014." Al Hilal Publishing & Marketing Group. www.tradearabia.com/news/CONS_267212.html.

Trading Economics. "Employment to Population Ratio-15+-Female (%) in Middle East and North Africa." 2013. www.tradingeconomics.com/middle-east-and-north-africa/employment -to-population-ratio-15-plus—female-percent-wb-data.html.

"Trafficking in Persons Report 2013." U.S. Department of State. (2013). www.state.gov/j/tip/rls /tiprpt/2013/index.htm.

Trenwith, Courtney. "Alcohol Ban Lifted for New Hotel on the Pearl-Qatar." *Arabian Business*, November 5, 2014. www.ArabianBusiness.com/alcohol-ban-lifted-for-new-hotel-on-pearl -qatar-570594.html.

Tripp, Charles. *A History of Iraq*. 3rd ed.: Cambridge University Press, 2007.

Trofimov, Yaroslav. "The State of the Kurds." *The Wall Street Journal*, June 19, 2015.

Tuchman, Barbara W. *The Guns of August*. Macmillan, 1962.

"Tunisia Finmin Says Next Govt Needs to Revive Privatisation." *Reuters*, October 18, 2011.

Tunisia Live. "Salma Rekik: Leader Party of Nahdtha." 2014. www.tunisia-live.net/whoswho /salma-rekik/.

"Tunisia Wins Again." *The New York Times*, December 25, 2014.

"Tunisia: High Rate of Unemployment among Youth and Women." *Tunis Times*, May 25, 2014.

"Tunisia's Ben Ali Appears in First Photos since His Overthrow." *Al Arabiya News*, August 28, 2013.

"Tunisian Politician Mohamed Brahmi Assassinated." BBC News, July 25, 2013.

"Tunisian President Says Country 'in a State of War.'" Al Jazeera, July 5, 2015.

"Tunisian Women Protest to Demand Equality." BBC News, August 14, 2012.

"Turkey Agrees to Assist U.S. with Airstrike against ISIS." *The New York Times*, July 27, 2015.

"Turkey's Biggest Media Group Gets a Colossal Tax Fine." *The Economist*, September 10, 2009.

"Turkish Journalist Sues Police over Protest Arrest." *The Washington Times*, November 11, 2014.

Tuttle, Robert. "Qatar Regulates Charities as U.S. Urges Stop to Terror Funding." *Bloomberg Business*, September 15, 2014.

"2015 Revision of World Population Prospects." United Nations. 2015. http://esa.un.org/unpd /wpp/unpp/p2k0data.asp.

Ulrichsen, Kristian Coates. "Qatar and the Arab Spring: Policy Drivers and Regional Implications." Carnegie Endowment for International Peace, 2014.

Ulus, Kurt. "Çanakkale (Gallipoli) 1915." YouTube, December 8, 2013.

UNESCO. "Erbil Citadel." 2015. http://whc.unesco.org/en/list/1437.

UNESCO Office for Iraq. "Revitalization Project of Erbil Citadel." 2015. www.unesco.org/new /en/iraq-office/culture/erbil-citadel/.

UNHCR. "Facts and Figures About Refugees." www.unhcr.org.uk/about-us/key-facts-and -figures.html.

———. "Regional: RRP6 Monthly Update—August 2014 (Education)." http://data.unhcr.org /syrianrefugees/download.php?id=7289.

———. "Syria Regional Refugee Response: Regional Overview." UN High Commissioner for Refugees (UNHCR). January 26, 2015 http://data.unhcr.org/syrianrefugees/regional.php.

———. "Syria Regional Refugee Response: Turkey." United Nations High Commissioner for Refugees (UNHCR). September 14, 2014 http://data.unhcr.org/syrianrefugees/country.php ?id=224.

———. "Syria Regional Refugee Response: Zaatari Refugee Camp." 2015. http://data.unhcr .org/syrianrefugees/settlement.php?id=176&region=77&country=107.

———. "2015 UNHCR Country Operations Profile-Iraq." United Nations High Commissioner for Refugees (UNHCR). 2015. www.unhcr.org/pages/49e486426.html

———. "2014 Syria Regional Response Plan, Strategic Overview: Mid-Year Update." UN High Commissioner for Refugees, 2014. www.unhcr.org/syriarrp6/midyear/docs/syria-rrp6-myu -strategic-overview.pdf.

United Nations Development Program. "Arab Development Challenges Report 2011." Cairo, February 21, 2012.

UNICEF. "Tunisia: MENA Gender Equality Profile: Status of Girls and Women in the Middle East and North Africa." October 2011.

"UNRWA." United Nations Relief and Works Agency for Palestine Refugees in the Near East. www.unrwa.org/?id=86.

———. "Regional Study: Palestinian Refugee Students Attending UN Schools Achieve Above-Average Results on International Assessments." Amman, Jordan: United Nations Relief and Works Agency, November 13, 2014.

———. "Where We Work: Jordan." United Nations Relief and Works Agency. www.unrwa.org /where-we-work/jordan.

———. "Where We Work: Jordan Camp Profiles." United Nations Relief and Works Agency. July 1, 2014. www.unrwa.org/where-we-work/jordan/camp-profiles?field=13.

"United Nations Special Committee on Palestine Report." United Nations. http://en.wikisource .org/wiki/United_Nations_Special_Committee_on_Palestine_Report.

www"U.S. Relations with Qatar, Fact Sheet." U.S. Department of State, August 26, 2014. www .state.gov/r/pa/ei/bgn/5437.htm.

Vargas, Jose Antonio. "Spring Awakening: How an Egyptian Revolution Began on Facebook." *The New York Times*, February 17, 2012

Vernez, Georges, Shelly Culbertson, and Louay Constant. *Strategic Priorities for Improving Access to Quality Education in the Kurdistan Region—Iraq*. RAND Corporation, 2014.

Virgil. *The Aeneid*. Penguin Classics, 2008.

Wadud, Amina. *Qur'an and Woman: Rereading the Sacred Text from a Woman's Perspective*. Oxford University Press, 1999.

Wallace, Charles P. "Circassians' Special Niche in Jordan: 'Cossacks' Seem Out of Place in Arab Palace." *Los Angeles Times*, May 17, 1987.

Wallace, Kelly. "No Movement for Women at the Top in Corporate America." CNN, December 11, 2013. http://edition.cnn.com/2013/12/11/living/no-change-on-women-board-seats -parents/.

Walsh, Kenneth T. "Obama Fulfills Campaign Promise in Declaring Iraq War Over." *U.S. News & World Report*, October 21, 2011.

Walt, Stephen M. "What Should We Do If the Islamic State Wins." *Foreign Policy*, June 10, 2015.

Westcott, Lucy. "Senior Muslim Cleric Calls for Islamic Teaching Overhaul to Curb Extremism." *Newsweek*, February 23, 2015.

Weymouth, Lally. "An Interview with Tunisia's Rachid Ghannouchi, Three Years after the Revolution." *The Washington Post*, December 12, 2013.

"Who, What, Why: Who Are the Yazidis?" BBC News, August 8, 2014.

Wilkinson, Toby. *The Rise and Fall of Ancient Egypt*. Random House, 2013.

Willis, Michael J. *Politics and Power in the Maghreb : Algeria, Tunisia and Morocco from Independence to the Arab Spring*. Columbia University Press, 2012.

Wood, Graeme. "What ISIS Really Wants." *The Atlantic*, March 2015.

Woolf, Nicky. "Is Kurdistan the Next Dubai?" *The Guardian*, May 5, 2010.

Woollacott, Martin. "One in Six Iraqis Are in Exile, and They Want This War." *The Guardian*, August 15, 2002.

World Bank. "Country and Lending Groups." 2014. http://data.worldbank.org/about/country-and-lending-groups.

———. "Egypt, Arab Rep." 2015. http://data.worldbank.org/country/egypt-arab-republic.

———. "GDP (Current US$)." 2014. http://data.worldbank.org/indicator/NY.GDP.MKTP.CD.

———. "GDP Growth (Annual %)." 2014. http://data.worldbank.org/indicator/NY.GDP.MKTP.KD.ZG.

———. "GDP Per Capita (Current US$)." 2014. http://data.worldbank.org/indicator/NY.GDP.PCAP.CD.

———. "GDP Per Capita (Current US$): 1999–2003." 2014. http://data.worldbank.org/indicator/NY.GDP.PCAP.CD?page=2&order=wbapi_data_value_2009%20wbapi_data_value%20wbapi_data_value-first&sort=asc.

———. "GDP Per Capita Growth (Annual %)." 2015. http://data.worldbank.org/indicator/NY.GDP.PCAP.KD.ZG.

———. "GDP Per Capita, PPP (Current International $)." 2015. http://data.worldbank.org/indicator/NY.GDP.PCAP.PP.CD.

———. "Internet Users (Per 100 People)." 2015. http://data.worldbank.org/indicator/IT.NET.USER.P2.

———. "The Kurdistan Region of Iraq Needs an Estimated US $1.4 Billion This Year to Stabilize the Economy." February 12, 2015. www.worldbank.org/en/news/press-release/2015/02/12/kurdistan-region-iraq-stabilize-economy.

———. "Labor Force, Female (% of Total Labor Force)." 2015. http://data.worldbank.org/indicator/SL.TLF.TOTL.FE.ZS.

———. "Labor Force Participation Rate, Female (% of Female Population Ages 15+) (Modeled ILO Estimate)." 2015. Http://data.worldbank.org/indicator/SL.TLF.CACT.FE.ZS?order=wbapi_data_value_2013+wbapi_data_value+wbapi_data_value-last&sort=asc.

———. "Literacy Rate, Adult Total (% of People Ages 15 and above)."2015. http://data.worldbank.org/indicator/SE.ADT.LITR.ZS/countries/1W-EG?display=graph.

———. "Middle East and North Africa: Women in the Workforce." April 2010. http://web.worldbank.org/WBSITE/EXTERNAL/COUNTRIES/MENAEXT/EXTMNAREG TOPPOVRED/0,contentMDK:22497617~pagePK:34004173~piPK:34003707~theSitePK:4 97110,00.html.

———. "New World Bank Study Details Manipulation of Regulations by Former Tunisian Regime Officials." March 27, 2014. www.worldbank.org/en/news/press-release/2014/03/27/world-bank-manipulation-former-tunisian-officials.

———. "Opening Doors: Gender Equality and Development in the Middle East and North Africa." MENA Development Report, June 2, 2013.

———. "Proportion of Seats Held by Women in National Parliaments (%)." 2015. http://data.worldbank.org/indicator/SG.GEN.PARL.ZS.

———. "The Road Not Traveled: Education Reform in the Middle East and North Africa." MENA Development Report. 2008. https://openknowledge.worldbank.org/handle/10986/6303.

————. "The Unfinished Revolution: Bringing Opportunity, Good Jobs and Greater Wealth to All Tunisians." September 17, 2014. www.worldbank.org/en/country/tunisia/publication /unfinished-revolution.

World Economic Forum. "Global Agenda Councils—Youth Unemployment Visualization 2013." www.weforum.org/community/global-agenda-councils/youth-unemployment-visualization -2013.

World Health Organization. "Prevalence of Female Genital Cutting among Egyptian Girls." *Bulletin of the World Health Organization* 86, no. 4 (2008): 241–320.

"World Leaders and Press Pay Tribute to Ataturk." Ataturk Today. www.ataturktoday.com/Ataturk WorldPressLeadersTribute.htm.

"World Press Freedom Day: Journalists under Attack in Egypt." *Amnesty International*, May 3, 2015. https://www.amnesty.org/press-releases/2015/05/world-press-freedom-day-journalists -under-attack-in-egypt/

"World Report 2013: Qatar." *Human Rights Watch*, 2013. www.hrw.org/world-report/2013/country -chapters/qatar.

WorldAtlas. "Largest Cities of the World (by Metro Population)." WorldAtlas. www.worldatlas .com/citypops.htm.

"Worse Than Mubarak." *The Economist* (May 2, 2015). www.economist.com/news/middle-east -and-africa/21650160-abdel-fattah-al-sisi-has-restored-order-egypt-great-cost-worse ?frsc=dg|c.

Wright, Robin. "The Clash of Civilizations That Isn't." *The New Yorker*, February 25, 2015.

————. "With This Redo, Egypt Can Do Better." *The New York Times*, June 13, 2014.

Yeginsu, Ceylan. "Opposition Journalists under Assault in Turkey," *The New York Times*, September 17, 2015. www.nytimes.com/2015/09/18/world/europe/opposition-journalists -in-turkey-increasingly-face-violent-attacks.html

————. "Turkey Attacks Kurdish Militant Camps in Northern Iraq." *The New York Times*, July 25, 2015.

Yildirim, Yetkin. "Peace and Conflict Resolution in the Medina Charter." *Peace Review* 18, no. 1 (2006): 109–17.

Yinanç, Barçin. "Taksim Is a Site of Struggle for Ideological Predominance." *Hürriyet Daily News,* June 3, 2013.

Youssef, Nariman. "Egypt's Draft Constitution Translated." *Egypt Independent*, February 12, 2012.

"Zaatari Refugee Camp: Rebuilding Lives in the Desert." BBC News Middle East, September 3, 2013.

Zacharia, Janine. "Turkey Hopes to Grow Economic Ties and Influence within Middle East." *The Washington Post*, April 8, 2010.

Zakaria, Fareed. "The Rise of Illiberal Democracy." *Foreign Affairs*, November/December 1997.

Zaki, Moheb. "Egypt's Persecuted Christians." *The Wall Street Journal*, May 18, 2010.

Zayzafoon, Lamia Ben Youssef. *The Production of the Muslim Woman: Negotiating Text, History, and Ideology.* Lexington Books, 2005.

INDEX